Conducting
Psychological
Assessment

A Guide for Practitioners

Conducting Psychological Assessment

A Guide for Practitioners

A. JORDAN WRIGHT

WILEY

John Wiley & Sons, Inc.

Library of Congress Cataloging-in-Publication Data

Wright, A. Jordan.
     Conducting psychological assessments : a guide for practitioners / A. Jordan Wright.
        p.   cm.
     ISBN 978-0-470-53675-9 (pbk.); ISBN 978-0-470-921-38-8 (ebk); ISBN 978-0-470-92139-5 (ebk);
     ISBN 978-0-470-92140-1 (ebk)
        1. Psychodiagnostics.   I. Title.
     RC469.W75   2010
     616.89'075—dc22

                                                                    2010023269

10 9 8 7 6 5 4 3 2 1

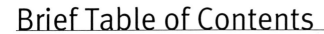

Brief Table of Contents

Contents

Preface

While many texts for students learning how to conduct psychological assessments focus, rightly so, on the use of individual tests, there is more to the process than just testing; testing is only part of the process. Unless the assessor is knowledgeable about psychological tests and knows how to use them, the entire process of assessment is futile. However, while using tests properly is necessary for good assessment, it is not sufficient. This text is meant to inform students and clinicians about the *second* step in learning how to conduct assessments. After clinicians have learned the ins and outs of psychological tests themselves, this text provides a step-by-step methodology for conducting entire individual assessments from beginning to end.

The major objectives of this text are

- To present the process of assessment from beginning to end in logical, clear steps that provide a basic structure for the process.
- To promote a process that necessarily takes into account the imperfection of both clinical intuition and psychological tests themselves.
- To illustrate the process as clearly as possible through case examples.

The approach, organization, and structure of this book are meant to mirror the natural progression of individual assessment. Although many assessments are not as "clean" as the linear steps presented in this text might suggest, organizing them in this way can help make difficult cases easier to manage. Even when input from outside sources, murky and unclear presentation of the client, or any other roadblock complicates cases, the step-by-step method presented in this text can help simplify the process. The *content* of psychological assessments is most often extremely complex and confusing (as humans are prone to being), so the more straightforward the process of assessment can be, the better.

Acknowledgments

I would like to acknowledge a few people without whom this book would never have been possible, each for different reasons. Two teachers, mentors, colleagues, and friends have been especially formative in my work as a psychologist: Drs. Jill Backfield and Barry A. Farber at Columbia University. Dr. Backfield helped me begin my journey with assessment, and Dr. Farber has supported it relentlessly. The early stages of the book-writing process would not have been possible without my supervisee and friend, Emily Bly, who pored over early chapters to help clarify the tone of the book. Reviewers who helped focus my efforts include Dr. Ken Rice from the University of Florida and Dr. Jay Lebow from Northwestern University. The people at Wiley, especially Patricia Rossi, have seen this project through from beginning to end with me. And the endless patience of my doctoral students at Teachers College, Columbia University, and of Matt Frost has truly been invaluable.

A. Jordan Wright, PhD

Conducting
Psychological
Assessment

A Guide for Practitioners

Conducting Psychological Assessment

Introduction to Part I:

THE HYPOTHESIS TESTING MODEL

Psychological assessment has long been a mysterious, intuited process, taught to psychologists in training test by test, with components of conceptualization, integration, and report writing somewhat tacked onto the end of the process. While psychologists seem to unconsciously agree on the purpose of psychological assessment, its utility has been debated in the literature. At its most basic, psychological assessment provides a catalog of an individual's cognitive, emotional, and psychological strengths, weaknesses, deficits, and resources. At its best, it provides dynamic insights into the inner workings of an individual, yielding invaluable information for diagnosis, potential intervention, and prognosis.

Claims for the utility of assessment have ranged significantly, from merely categorizing an individual's strengths and weaknesses, to clarifying diagnosis and prognosis, to describing a person's personality in its entirety. While these all may be effective approaches to assessment, it is most practical and pragmatic to talk about why and how psychological assessment can be useful to the mental health field (and to related fields, such as medicine) in general. This book presents a model of psychological assessment designed to ensure that assessors provide ethical and competent services and make useful contributions to the lives of the individuals they assess.

Psychological assessment should be used to help answer whatever referral questions are present and to make clear and specific recommendations to help the individual being assessed function better in his or her life. While this may include an analysis of strengths and weaknesses, a diagnosis, and a description of personality structure, the central goal of making useful (and realistic) recommendations should never be forgotten. This important concept is revisited throughout this text, as it is easy to lose sight of the importance of this seemingly simple goal: determining what will be most useful to the individual being assessed.

A few examples can illustrate how psychological assessment can be useful to different people. First, consider a high-level executive who is trying to get a promotion at work. While an assessment may include his level of cognitive and intellectual functioning and details of his personality dynamics, the ultimate goal should be to inform what would likely help him grow in such a way that he can successfully get the promotion, if possible. Some possible findings from an assessment with such an individual may relate to his interpersonal style or decision-making skills. These are areas extremely important to executives' growth, and recommendations on how to improve them can be explicitly made.

Next, consider a child presenting disruptive behavior at school (or consider the child's parents, at their wits' end). An assessment can help identify what is likely underlying the disruptive behavior, which could include anything from attention-deficit/hyperactivity disorder (ADHD) to depression to an adjustment disorder. Recommendations for each of these problems would look *very* different. A child with depression would likely not benefit from psychostimulant medication, just as a child with ADHD would not benefit from antidepressant medication. An assessment can help the parents clarify what is likely going on and recommend to other service providers what type of treatment would likely succeed.

This text is a primer for the *process* of psychological assessment and testing, rather than a guide to using any single test. There are six major processes that make up any psychological assessment:

1. Conducting a clinical interview
2. Choosing a battery of tests
3. Administering, scoring, and interpreting tests
4. Integrating and conceptualizing information gathered from test results, the clinical interview, behavioral observations, and other sources
5. Writing a psychological assessment report
6. Providing feedback to the individual assessed and/or the referral source

While most psychological assessment texts focus on test administration, scoring, and interpretation (see Groth-Marnat, 2009; Lezak, Howieson, Loring, Hannay, & Fischer, 2004; Sattler, 2008; Weiner & Greene, 2007), and while there are many works on clinical interviewing (see MacKinnon, Michels, & Buckley, 2006; McConaughy, 2005; J. Sommers-Flanagan & Sommers-Flanagan, 2002; Sullivan, 1970), few have focused specifically on the fourth step, the use of all data collected throughout the assessment to come up with a fully integrated, coherent picture of the individual being tested that will support clear, specific, and useful recommendations. Similarly, sample reports can be extremely useful in formatting the *structure* of a psychological assessment report, but few texts have focused on the conceptual *content* of good reports.

THE HYPOTHESIS TESTING MODEL

The importance of psychological assessment lies in the fundamental assumption that there are aspects of our functioning that we are not entirely aware of or cannot effectively articulate. If every person had a clear and accurate understanding of what was going on for him or her, the only form of assessment necessary would be clinical interviews. An even more efficient method would be to administer surveys that rely on individuals' self-reporting. However, because there is not a single person who is entirely aware of all aspects of his or her functioning, we combine multiple methods of evaluation, including self-report, objective measures, clinical observation, and (perhaps both most controversially and most intriguingly) projective measures, to develop a more accurate impression of current functioning. It is important to note (as most texts on psychological assessment do) that testing and assessment provide a picture of how the individual being assessed is *currently* functioning. While inferences about past functioning and future prognosis can be made, the tests themselves are measuring individuals *at that particular moment in time*, at that particular point in history. Many people not in the mental health field confuse psychologists with psychics, and it should be made clear that assessment results cannot predict the future with 100% accuracy.

There is no perfect measure. No self-report is made without bias and "blind spots," no test has perfect reliability and validity, and no single method of measurement should be taken as gospel. The validity of every single test in existence has been challenged (some specific criticisms are addressed in the chapter on testing). For this reason, a humble approach to using tests is necessary to build a reader's confidence in the assertions made in the final report. The hypothesis testing model uses the strengths of each individual test, as well as clinical acumen, while assuming that each individual measure is flawed. Each individual assessment can be treated as a research study by (a) making hypotheses and testing them to rule out possibilities and incorporate others, and (b) using multiple tests and multiple methods, which provide more solid data and allow the assessor to be much more confident in his or her findings. The basics of the hypothesis testing model follow.

Step 1: Clinical Assessment

The first step of the hypothesis testing model is to conduct a thorough clinical interview. You will then use the results of this interview, together with background information collected from various sources, to *create hypotheses*. Clinical interviews can vary dramatically from assessor to assessor (see MacKinnon, Michels, & Buckley, 2006; McConaughy, 2005; J. Sommers-Flanagan & Sommers-Flanagan, 2002; and Sullivan, 1970 for theories on clinical interviewing). While some scholars advocate the use of structured clinical interviews (these can be especially useful in neuropsychological assessment), others advocate the use of open-ended, unstructured conversations. One model for the process of conducting—and, more importantly, *using*—a clinical interview is discussed in more detail in Chapter 1. The *clinical assessment* is a combination of the information gathered from the clinical interview and other sources of report, such as referral parties, previous records, and collateral interviews. This clinical assessment has two goals: (1) assessing impairment in functioning and (2) generating hypotheses.

The first goal is to assess specifically what, if any, is the impairment in functioning. Most assessments are conducted because there is a suspicion of some sort of impairment in the functioning of the individual being assessed. Individuals usually come for an assessment with a presenting problem, a specific difficulty they are having. These presenting problems may be reported by the individuals themselves, or they may be defined by whoever refers the individual for the assessment, perhaps a treating clinician, a primary care physician, a teacher, or any other person who knows the individual being assessed. For example, social and interpersonal functioning, emotional well-being, or behavioral problems may be affecting how well the individual can function on a day-to-day basis.

While some impairments may be overtly evident, reported openly as the referral question or presenting problem, there are often more subtle impairments in functioning, more covert issues that are impeding the person's ability to be happy, maintain stable relationships or employment, or function optimally in some way. For example, an individual may be referred for testing because he is having subjective difficulty with his parents' divorce. Upon assessment, however, it may turn out that he generally has difficulty with change and ambiguity, which may be affecting him in other areas of his life.

Occasionally, though rarely (depending on the type of practice you have), individuals present for an assessment with no real impairment in functioning, but simply "to learn more about myself" or because they find it interesting (or because they are mental health professionals in training). While there may be no major impairments in functioning, there are almost certainly areas of individuals' lives that could be improved. It is important in both instances, however, to keep in mind that assessments are not entirely about weakness and impairment. While the former situation calls for specific recommendations for improving suboptimal functioning, both situations also entail a clear survey of what's going *right*—that is, where the strengths and aptitudes lie.

The second goal of the clinical assessment, specific to the hypothesis testing model, is to generate hypotheses. For this step, a thorough understanding of psychodiagnosis is necessary. General theories of behavior, *regardless of theoretical orientation*, are also extremely important. Based on the "findings" of the clinical assessment, you should list all possible causes of the functional impairment. This step is, of course, aspirational; it is impossible, given our current understandings of human functioning, to be able to understand and enumerate *all* possible dynamics and underpinnings of a single problem. However, using whatever your individual theory and orientation are as guides can help you cover your bases. This process is extremely important in determining how to approach the assessment, and it is discussed further in Chapter 1.

Step 2: Selecting Tests

Based on the hypotheses generated from Step 1, the assessor selects a testing battery. The specific parameters that inform this process are addressed in Chapter 2, but essentially, tests should be chosen based on an established set of criteria, which should include their own internal psychometric properties, what exactly they assess, and how they assess it. Great care should be taken to include *multiple measures* of the same constructs—multiple tests to assess the same hypothesis. For example, if low self-esteem is a hypothesis, several psychometrically established tests should be chosen to assess self-esteem from multiple angles, such as the MMPI-2, which has a specific scale for self-esteem, and several projective measures, which assess self-esteem in a significantly different way. These can be combined later with the clinical interview data and behavioral observations to make assertions about whether there is evidence for or against this hypothesis.

Step 3: Testing

To repeat, no test is perfect; no measure is without flaws and grounds for criticism. While the testing battery is malleable, able to be altered throughout the process, it is best to err on the side of including too many assessments rather than too few. This of course poses logistical problems, given time and monetary constraints. But the key is to remember that you can be more confident having three separate tests that report the same findings and support the same conclusions than having only one or even two. This does not necessarily mean that having two is inadequate, but when time and other constraints permit, having more data is better, just as in any research project.

After choosing a testing battery, administration and scoring of the chosen tests are the next steps. *There is no way to fake this.* Nothing compensates for poverty of skill in administration and scoring. These are perhaps two of the most important steps in the entire process, which could explain why most texts, and indeed assessment courses, focus on them, and rightly so. Mistakes made in these two steps can invalidate the entire process. Whereas you can find support on all steps after these two, using supervision and consultation to interpret and beyond, you basically have one shot at correct administration of all tests per assessment, without in-the-moment help or support. The strictest discipline should be used in making sure that all tests are administered and scored in their appropriate, standardized way. Even slight adjustments can skew interpretation based on a normative sample that was tested in a different way.

For example, if you are administering a subtest such as Digit Span from a Wechsler intelligence test, which requires you to read numbers aloud at a specific, slow pace and requires the individual being assessed to repeat them back, if you read the numbers more quickly than directed, you are making the task much easier. The client's score on your faster version of this test will be compared to a normative sample that received the test in the slower, standardized way. Your client's score will look higher than it should and not reflect the client's actual ability. Even this seemingly benign and minor variation from the standardized procedure can skew the data and cause misleading results to emerge. As assessment is a stepwise, hierarchical process, all steps after administration and scoring of the tests are predicated on the assumption that administration and scoring are absolutely correct and valid.

Similarly, although it is not addressed at length in this text, the ability to apply correct interpretation of all tests used is absolutely critical to the competence of the assessor, the ethical application of assessment, and the utility of the final product. Again, many texts focus almost exclusively on the correct and appropriate interpretation of results garnered from individual test instruments (see Groth-Marnat, 2009; Lezak, Howieson, Loring, Hannay, & Fischer, 2004; and Weiner & Greene, 2007 for excellent examples). It is vital to know the limitations of each test, so that interpretation does not overstep the bounds of what each individual test is able to do. In the integration process, it is also important to understand the psychometric strengths and weaknesses and conceptual criticisms of each test to judge how best to apply the results in the overall framework of the conceptualization.

Step 4: Integration of All Data

Perhaps the most delicate step of all, and unfortunately the step generally least addressed in both training and psychological assessment literature, is the integration of all data compiled. This constitutes the "mystical" step in which, somehow, all the data collected coalesce into a coherent, concise description of an entire person. This step need not be so mystical;

a major focus of this text is to help assessors understand this process clearly. In the hypothesis testing model, this step is where test results and behavioral observations are combined with clinical assessment data to address each of the hypotheses. Every hypothesis generated should be addressed by the testing process. A detailed explanation of this process is presented in Chapter 4 of this text.

In addition to integrating all of the data collected into themes, the process of fitting the themes together into a coherent narrative is presented. Specifically, a straightforward presentation of themes, of strengths and weaknesses, of issues and dynamics, can easily lack face validity and thus buy-in from the parties receiving the feedback. A more narrative approach, telling a story of how the themes that emerged from the assessment fit and work together to explain the impairment in functioning, will make more sense to the individual being assessed and the individual who made the referral, and they will be more easily remembered by both parties. The end result is that the individuals being assessed and the referral sources will be more likely to take the recommendations made at the end of the report.[1]

Step 5: Writing the Assessment Report

Many texts provide sample reports, which vary in style, length, and even purpose. While templates of previous reports are an excellent source of reference for structuring future reports (and, indeed, an assessment report structure is presented in Chapter 5), the process of writing up individual sections has had little discussion in previous psychological assessment texts. Finding the balance between using professional language while not using too much psychological jargon is perhaps one of the hardest skills to learn. Making sure to give reports professional weight without making them too difficult to understand can at times feel more like an art than a science. While it is extremely comforting to know what sections are necessary for a good assessment report, understanding exactly

---

[1]It is important to note that while no systematic empirical study has been conducted on this theory that a narrative approach will affect how readily patients take recommendations, the theory is based on amassed clinical evidence.

what should go *within* each section and how it should be presented is extremely important and can be a delicate task. Chapter 5 of this text presents strategies for writing up assessment reports so that they are professional and straightforward and fulfill the goal of providing logical, useful recommendations.

Step 6: Providing Feedback

Although it is often given a chapter or at least a mention in texts on psychological assessment, this step perhaps shows the most variation across clinicians and scholars. No consistent model for providing feedback has been developed and adopted widely throughout the field. Although that challenge is beyond the scope of the current text, several models and guiding principles for providing feedback are presented in Chapter 6. In general, feedback should be provided at a level that, as with the write-up, is both professional and understandable. This means that based on the assessment itself and the individual being assessed, feedback sessions must be both specifically tailored and flexible. Clinical skill is perhaps most necessary during this step, as at any moment you may need to change course, empathize, console, support, or explain a concept in a different way.

For example, on hearing that he or she has a specific diagnosis such as a learning disorder, an individual may react in different ways. That individual may be relieved to hear an explanation for the difficulties he or she has been having in school. On the other hand, the individual may be upset by the diagnosis. In the latter case, an assessor must use his or her clinical skill and intuition to determine the course of the feedback session. The assessor may have to shift to a more explicitly supportive stance, empathizing with the difficulty of receiving the news.

Alternatively, the focus of the assessment may need to be more psychoeducational, reflecting the individual's need to more fully understand the diagnosis and its implications (dispelling any misconceptions), as well as outlining what can be done to alleviate the symptoms of the disorder. Although this example is obviously oversimplified, an assessor must be able to be flexible throughout a feedback session, given that individuals' reactions to feedback are as varied as individuals themselves.

One of the most useful advantages of the hypothesis testing model is that it enables you to be both clear and confident in the "story" you are telling, which supports clear recommendations. While clinicians have differing values when it comes to recommendations and referrals, it is ethically essential to make sure that, in the feedback session, the individual being assessed is absolutely clear as to the content of what you are presenting, including both the results and the recommendations. Depending largely on the setting, the referral questions, and your own clinical values, follow-up with the individual being assessed may be necessary to make sure he or she is able to follow through with the recommendations.

Again, remember that the ultimate goal of assessment is to make clear, useful recommendations that have a high likelihood of improving a person's life and functioning. The entire (lengthy) process has been a complete failure if the person is unable for any reason to understand or engage with the recommendations. It is important to note that, of course, some clients may *choose* not to take the recommendations, through their own will, which should not at all be considered a failure on the part of the assessor.

SUMMARY

The hypothesis testing model of psychological assessment treats each individual assessment case as a research study. Using a multimethod approach, every single assessment should include both self-report and other objective measures of functioning. Additionally, every report should include both cognitive and personality/emotional measures. While cognitive and personality/emotional assessments are often presented separately (and indeed are tested quite differently), they are part of the same system that makes up the functioning individual sitting across from you in the assessment room. Integrating the results from multiple varied sources of data can seem daunting. However, by organizing the *process* clearly, the hypothesis testing model takes the mystery out of conceptualizing an individual's dynamics in a comprehensive way.

The hypothesis testing model is built on a traditional model of testing, with clear additions. While almost every theory of assessment includes a clinical interview and collection of background data from multiple sources, each uses these data differently. The hypothesis testing model uses the data from the clinical interview along with background information to generate hypotheses of what is contributing to the impairment in the individual's functioning. These hypotheses drive the selection of a targeted battery of tests, ensuring that all potential dynamics and diagnoses are being addressed by the tests selected. Organizing and presenting the results generates a coherent narrative of what is happening with the individual. This narrative supports clear, specific, and useful recommendations for improving the person's functioning. As with any research study, evidence must be amassed to support any conclusions drawn. As is the goal of any clinical interaction, feedback and recommendations must be presented in a clear, empathic, and supportive manner.

CHAPTER 1

Clinical Interviewing and Hypothesis Building

The first focus of the hypothesis testing model of psychological assessment, not surprisingly, is building hypotheses. While several different sources of information contribute to the process, the primary source is the clinical interview, either with the client or with the client's parents or primary caregivers if the client is a child. The purpose of the psychological assessment is to identify what is likely causing impairment in the individual's functioning (and then to make recommendations to ameliorate this impairment).

The first important step is to figure out in what way the individual's functioning is impaired; this is most often the *presenting problem* or the *referral question*. The issues reported by either (a) the individual himself or herself or (b) whoever referred him or her for the assessment are most often at least part of what is impaired in or is impairing his or her functioning. However, most often, what is reported at first (the "presenting problem") is only part of what is actually disturbing the individual or is merely the result of something else that he or she is not even aware of. Practitioners should be both open to the original presenting complaint and ready to consider the possibility of impediments the individual is not aware of. The nature of the presenting problem most often becomes apparent through the process of the clinical interview, the collection of other background information, and your own clinical observations (including a mental status evaluation and behavioral observations). While many texts can help with the *process* of clinical interviewing, including developing clinical skills like empathizing, asking open-ended questions, and determining how best to make an individual feel more comfortable in sharing information, here we will focus on the *content* of the interview and how it can be used to inform your developing hypotheses.

THE CLINICAL INTERVIEW

For the purposes of a psychological assessment, the clinical interview has three major components: (1) the presenting problem (and its history), (2) a symptomatic evaluation, and (3) a psychosocial evaluation. The summary chart that follows (Table 1.1) may help you make sure you collect all the relevant information you need to form a complete picture of how the individual views himself or herself. This sheet provides a useful framework for collecting essential information, but it does not prescribe a specific method or an order in which to do so. On the contrary, most assessors prefer to be unstructured during the clinical interview process, allowing the individual to speak freely and openly, and hold back from asking specific follow-up questions unless some information remains unclear. The assessor is in charge of setting the tone of the initial session, with the goal of providing as relaxed an environment as possible. Clients will feel better about an assessment session that is relaxed and will be more likely to be open and disclose more information.

Presenting Problem and Its History

The first component of the clinical interview, the presenting problem, is related to the issues that constitute the reason for the assessment, as well as the history of these issues. Clients can come in for many reasons, from specific functional impairment to subjective distress. For example, clients

TABLE 1.1   COMPONENTS OF THE CLINICAL INTERVIEW

Presenting Problem and History of Presenting Problem Includes assessment of dangerousness to self/others	
Symptomatic Evaluation	**Psychosocial Evaluation**
Developmental history	Family history
Psychiatric history	Educational/vocational history
Alcohol/substance abuse history	Criminal/legal history
Medical history	Social history
Family medical and psychiatric history	Psychosexual history
	Multicultural evaluation

may present with problems on the job or in their relationships, which are specific impairments in their functioning. Others may come in because they feel bad in some way, such as depressed or anxious. Many are unclear when discussing their presenting problem, however. For example, clients who are "stuck" in therapy with a referring clinician may be unclear how to move forward in their treatment, but they are often unaware of what is specifically getting in the way of the work. Still, whatever problem emerges in the clinical interview as likely needing attention, regardless of how specific, vague, simple, or complex, constitutes part of the presenting problem.

Presenting Problem

The presenting problem includes whatever complaint the individual identifies as the reason for the assessment. An assessment of danger of harm to self or others, including the possibility of self-harm or suicidality (suicidal tendencies), aggressiveness or homicidality (homicidal tendencies), and any suspicion of child abuse, should *always* be part of the initial meeting.[1] Again, the presenting problem is at times relatively straightforward, but sometimes factors can get in the way of its being clear, including guardedness on the part of the client, a client's lack of psychological mindedness and insight, or simply a diffuse client presentation. At times, the presenting problem needs to be reassessed at the end of the interview, once the client has become more comfortable and more disclosing with the assessor. When the client is somewhat vague with his or her presenting problem, some areas you may consider asking specifically about are presented in Table 1.2.

Not all of these areas will apply to every case, but they are a good way to keep yourself organized and make sure that you do not miss any vital information. The Case of David (p. 18) will illustrate how the clinical interview can unfold.

History of Presenting Problem

The assessor should always work to develop a detailed history of the problem, including when it began (date of onset); if there was a precipitating event; how continuous or intermittent the problem has been (what has been its course), including when and how it got worse or better during

---

[1]For detailed discussions on assessment of dangerousness, see Craig, Browne, Hogue, and Stringer (2004) and J. Sommers-Flanagan and Sommers-Flanagan (2002).

TABLE 1.2   **COMPONENTS OF ASSESSING THE**
                   PRESENTING PROBLEM

Current stressors

Cognitive status complaints
    Attention/concentration
    Memory
    Language problems
    Problem solving
    Decision making
    Hallucinations
    Delusions

Emotional status complaints
    Mood
        Helplessness
        Hopelessness
        Worthlessness
        Crying
        Manic symptoms
    Anxiety
    Appetite
    Sleep
    Energy level
    Hobbies
    Libido

Suicidal ideation
    Ideation
    Intent
    Plan
    Means

Homicidal/aggressive ideation
    Ideation
    Intent
    Plan
    Means

THE CASE OF DAVID: PRESENTING PROBLEM

David is a 23-year-old Hispanic client who comes in because of academic difficulty in college, requesting an evaluation for a learning disorder or possible attention-deficit/hyperactivity disorder. While this is all the information given at the time of referral, during the initial interview (and usually at the very beginning), you will need to find out all the relevant details about his academic functioning. You may begin by asking generally about what it is like for him at school, and depending on the information you receive, you may have to ask specific follow-up questions about certain aspects. These may include what he is studying, whether he is struggling in all of his classes or just particular ones, the specific nature of his difficulty (whether he loses concentration, has difficulty reading, cannot retain information, or simply does poorly on exams, for example), the nature of his ability to concentrate in other contexts, and, perhaps most importantly, information about any mood or anxiety problems. He states that he simply has trouble keeping focused when reading or writing is involved, no matter where he is.

Throughout the initial phase of this first interview, it becomes clear that David truly is struggling in school, though he seems to be struggling in other areas of his life as well. He reports that he has difficulty paying attention to tasks that involve reading and writing. He also reports, however, that he has been struggling with depression for the past three years, when "everything fell apart." Although he was able to report on what was happening three years ago, it is important to understand the presenting problem as it is impacting him now. Thus, you need to understand what he means by struggling with "depression." When asked about the depression itself, he reports that he gets extremely "down" many days, sometimes to the point of not being able to even go to school, which is also impacting his academic functioning. In order to get more specific, you may have to ask about specific aspects of depression, including appetite, sleep, motivation, energy level, and so forth. What emerges is that his appetite is reportedly "okay," that he sometimes has difficulty sleeping because he is worried about failing out of school, and that on his "down days" he is not motivated to do anything. He reports feeling as though school is hopeless and that perhaps he should just quit and "save myself the worry."

At this point, it becomes crucial for you to assess his degree of suicidal ideation (and homicidal, though it seems less likely). For David, this should not be that difficult as it ties directly in to what he is reporting. There are many ways you could ask him if he has ever considered harming or killing himself, but the important thing is to be absolutely clear about what you are asking. Do not leave room for him to misinterpret what you mean by your question. For example, a question like "Does it ever get so bad that it's hard to go on?" is simply too vague and open for him to misinterpret. Your best bet is usually to ask, in as empathic a tone of voice as possible, "Have you ever thought about hurting yourself or killing yourself?" The same is important for assessing aggressiveness and homicidality. For both, David denies ever seriously thinking about them. Because there is minimal ideation (only nonserious thoughts) and seemingly no intent, there is no need to assess for means and a plan for either suicidality or homicidality.

the time since the struggle began; and any previous assessments conducted. Inquiring into previous assessments provides an opportunity to gain a prior clinician's perspective on the history of the problem in addition to that of the individual being assessed. Consulting with the prior clinician not only provides potentially rich data and cross-verification but also provides the individual you are assessing with a sense of continuity and coherence to the his or her ongoing assessment and care.

THE CASE OF DAVID: HISTORY OF PRESENTING PROBLEM

With David, this is the point at which you need to do two things in the interview; because there are basically two major presenting problems (the cognitive/academic problem and the depression), you must inquire about the history of each of these. Because so much came out at the beginning of the interview about the depression, and because he specifically mentioned that the onset was three years ago when "everything fell apart," you may want to start there and ask about what was going on for him three years ago when he first became depressed. With depression (as with many other presenting problems) it is important to assess this current episode, its onset, and its course, along with as any other history of similar problems before the current episode. You might begin by asking David what happened three years ago.

When asked what happened three years ago, David reports that his girlfriend, his "high school sweetheart," broke up with him. He reported that she

(Continued)

had been cheating on him when they went to separate colleges, but he did not find out until she told him while breaking up with him. He was already struggling academically in college, and at about the same time his best friend died in a drunk driving accident (his friend was a passenger in a car that was hit by a drunk driver). At this point, he reports that he had to take some time off from his studies and he had left college for a few years. He only recently returned to school, where he is again struggling academically.

Interestingly, David did not give you much information about the actual nature of the depressive symptoms, so you have to ask more specifically about those. At that time, three years ago, he implied that he became depressed, but you need to figure out exactly what went on with him at that time. When you ask specifically, he reports that he got "pretty depressed" and did not want to leave his dorm room for a few months. He tells you that he cut off ties with most of his friends, did not speak much to his family, lost some weight, and did not sleep much during that time. At the urging of his academic advisor (who had granted him a leave of absence from school because of his friend's death), he entered individual psychotherapy about six months after he became depressed. When asked about the course, whether or not it has been pretty constant or has gotten better or worse at times, he says that it is "definitely better than it was," but that there have not been any periods since then when he was not "down" for a significant period of time.

When you are confident that you have enough information about the current episode, it makes sense to move on to whether or not he has any history of similar problems in the past. When you ask this, however, he simply states that he has never been depressed before, that he was "a happy child."

Because academic difficulty is not as episodic as depression, it does not make as much sense to ask about the current episode of academic difficulty. Instead, you could ask more broadly about his academic functioning in school growing up. When you do, he states that attention and concentration have always been difficult for him, telling you that he was "an average student" throughout school, "probably 'cause I didn't read that much." He tells you that his grades never fluctuated significantly and that they were always passing, though barely so.

Symptomatic Evaluation

The second component (though there is no reason it needs to come in this order during an actual interview) of the clinical interview is a symptomatic evaluation. This component is important in understanding the actual content of the problem, including the symptomatic and medical features of what may be impairing the client's functioning. Assessors should ask specific questions about symptoms related to different psychiatric diagnoses, as well as observe them during the clinical interview and the entire assessment. Similar to medical interviews, in order to fully understand what is going on for a client, an assessor must inquire about family history, medical history, and substance use history.

Developmental History

The assessment of developmental history can be seen as a crossover between the symptomatic evaluation and the psychosocial evaluation, as it has some components that are physiological and some that are environmental and interpersonal. It begins with specific questions about the early developmental environment, including if there were any known problems during the pregnancy of the individual's mother, as well as during labor and delivery. Following these medical questions, you should ask about significant events during infancy and childhood, including developmental milestones (such as lateness in achieving developmental milestones like sitting up, crawling, walking, talking, and toileting). Also included should be any childhood behavioral problems, significant accidents, and traumas. Some basic information it is generally useful to assess during the assessment of developmental history is shown in Table 1.3.

TABLE I.3   **COMPONENTS OF ASSESSING DEVELOPMENTAL HISTORY**

Problems during pregnancy

Problems around birth/delivery

Developmental milestones
　　Sitting up
　　Crawling
　　Walking
　　Speaking
　　Toileting
　　Socialization

THE CASE OF DAVID: DEVELOPMENTAL HISTORY

When you ask about his developmental history, David reports that he does not know of any difficulties with his mother's pregnancy or his birth. Similarly he tells you he thinks he met all of his developmental milestones on time. He does tell you that he has difficulty remembering anything before about the age of 8, and he cites the age of 16 as his "most significant year," as that is when he stopped using drugs. Obviously these are two areas you would need to ask about in further detail (anything that happened around the age of 8 and his drug use prior to age 16).

Discussing what happened at the age of 8, he says "nothing significant that I can think of." He talks briefly about his family history (see the section on family history, which follows), but he cannot identify anything specific that makes it difficult for him to remember his life before then. He does tell you that is when he began using substances, though. At this point, it makes sense to begin doing the alcohol and substance use evaluation in the interview. See the section on substance abuse that follows for the information that David discloses when discussing his drug history.

As with the suicidality assessment discussed previously, an assessment of childhood trauma should be included in this section of the interview. Asking about childhood trauma can be awkward and difficult, but again you must be clear about what you are asking. When you ask him if he ever had any traumas as a child, he simply replies, "No." Specifying further, just to confirm that he was never abused, raped, or neglected, again he responds that he never was.

Psychiatric History

The history of psychiatric symptoms and treatments is extremely important for understanding the actual course of the individual's problems. You should be sure to collect information on any past hospitalizations, past harm or threat of harm to self or others, and any psychotropic medications taken in the past. If there were previous treatments, you should obtain a release of information to get the records of these treatments or, at the very least, to speak with the previous treating clinicians. This is especially important when there have been previous hospitalizations or a history of medication, because these can be markers of a more serious psychiatric condition.

TABLE 1.4   COMPONENTS OF ASSESSING PSYCHIATRIC
HISTORY

Any history of psychiatric diagnosis

Any history of psychiatric treatment, including

    Type of professional seen
    Reason for treatment
    Dates of treatment
    Frequency of visits
    Duration of treatment
    Outcome of treatment

Any history of psychiatric medication

Reviewing these previous records and speaking to previous treating clinicians serves the goal of obtaining as much information and data as possible in order to provide a more comprehensive assessment of the individual. Consider the example of a client referred for an assessment to evaluate her competency to care for her children. She will likely present positively or even be genuinely unaware of her own struggle with psychopathology, but a review of her psychiatric records may uncover important information (e.g., a history of psychosis, aggressiveness toward her children, or poor impulse control). This information will be crucial in deciding whether or not she is fit to parent her children, though obviously her current functioning and the possibility that she has changed must always be considered.

The basic information important to understanding psychiatric history is presented in Table 1.4.

Alcohol/Substance Use History

Both past and present use of alcohol and other drugs should be explored. Even social use of alcohol may affect the individual's functioning and should be discussed. For example, an individual who presents as depressed and reports the social use of alcohol may not understand how alcohol, a depressant, can exacerbate his or her symptoms, even in what he or she considers to be low doses. Included in the assessment of alcohol and other substance

THE CASE OF DAVID: PSYCHIATRIC HISTORY

You already know that David is currently in therapy, so you know he has a history of mental health treatment. When you ask him more specifically if he has ever been diagnosed with anything, he says that he was diagnosed as a child with dyslexia, and he was medicated at that time, but he does not remember with what medication. He cannot even remember when in his childhood this occurred, though it happened before he was 8 years old.

He has been in treatment for the past two-and-a-half years, following the difficult time in his life when he had to take a leave of absence from school. He has been in weekly therapy with the same therapist since then, and he has been prescribed Wellbutrin by the school's psychiatrist, whom he sees once a month for medication management. When you ask more about the treatment, he tells you that it is "something like cognitive-behavior treatment" and that it has been very helpful for him. Although he still struggles with depression, he says he "functions better" than he did before. He says he has never been to another mental health professional before.

use should be the type(s) of substance, the onset of use (both dates and circumstances), the length of time and duration of use, the amount of use, and any previous treatments for use. It is also important to ascertain whether the individual feels that his or her use of substances has caused any type of impact, positive or negative, on his or her life. Additionally, attitudes about using and quitting can be extremely useful later on in the assessment process. For example, an individual who abuses alcohol but denies that this is a problem may be using the substance to cope with stress, restrict emotions, or escape reality, all hypotheses that may be supported elsewhere in the testing. Important aspects of questioning alcohol and other substance use are listed in Table 1.5.

Medical History

Despite the fact that an assessor is not a medical doctor, both present and past medical status should be explored, including any serious medical illnesses, hospitalizations, and any medications taken currently or in the past. Medical history and status can significantly affect current psychological functioning. If any medications are currently being taken, make sure to note for how long they

TABLE 1.5   COMPONENTS OF ASSESSING ALCOHOL/
                   SUBSTANCE USE HISTORY

Alcohol use

Past

  Amount

  Frequency

Present

  Amount

  Frequency

Impact of use on life

Other drug use (including abuse of prescription and over-the-counter drugs)

Past

  Amount

  Frequency

Present

  Amount

  Frequency

Impact of use on life

THE CASE OF DAVID: ALCOHOL/SUBSTANCE ABUSE HISTORY

David reported earlier in the interview that he began using drugs around the age of 8 and quit using them around 16. Because he brought this information up unsolicited, there is reason to believe (a) that it is significant (though use of drugs by any 8-year-old is significant) and (b) that he will likely speak openly about it. When you ask about his history of using drugs and alcohol, he begins to tell his story of rather significant substance abuse.

David began using drugs around the age of 7 or 8, smoking one or two marijuana joints after school. By the time he was 10, he was getting drunk on alcohol "frequently." When words like this arise in this context, it is important to find out more specifically what he means, as the word "frequently" may mean something different to him than it does to you.

(Continued)

Specifying, he said he drank every day and got drunk at least every other day, if not more often. By 10 or 11 he also began experimenting with other drugs, including PCP and cocaine. Arrested for public intoxication and illegal possession of narcotics, he was sent to a juvenile detention center at age 16. It was at this time he began attending Alcoholics Anonymous (AA) meetings, which he says have continually helped him remain sober and substance free since he was 16. He says that he never used any other substances and was never in any form of drug treatment other than AA.

The major question David seems to have left unanswered is why and how he began using drugs at such an early age. When you ask him, he discusses his family situation growing up, but he has no specific, concrete precipitating event other than being offered marijuana by "older kids at school." He says he was naïve, but the feeling of being high on marijuana was "too good to quit, much better than I felt in the rest of my life." At this point, a small red flag may be going up in your mind about possible depression (or anxiety or something else) going on for him at that time. When asked, however, he denies any problems before then, that he can remember. He says that being high was simply "a great feeling."

It is relatively clear that substance use has impacted David's life significantly, though you as the assessor have to make the judgment of whether to press for more details about the impact of the drugs on his life. At this point, though, you may decide simply to move on with the interview, keeping in mind that no matter what information you get, it will be limited.

have been taken, for what they were prescribed, and any changes in dosage or administration that have occurred during their use. It will be important to note any temporal relationships between changes in the medical history and changes in the presenting problem and symptomatology. Consider an individual who loses consciousness and then shortly afterward becomes extremely moody and irritable. This temporal relationship between loss of consciousness and mood change may be a significant warning sign that a medical or neurological problem (e.g., multiple sclerosis) could be the root cause of the psychological presentation. It is also important to note the date and results of the individual's last comprehensive physical examination. Among other things, this serves as an indicator of the individual's investment in self-care as well as his or her level of awareness of health status. The important components to consider when assessing medical history are listed in Table 1.6.

TABLE 1.6   COMPONENTS OF ASSESSING MEDICAL
                   HISTORY

Current medical illnesses
   Date of onset
   Course
   Treatment and medications

Past significant medical illnesses
   Date of onset
   Course
   Treatment and medications

History of loss of consciousness

THE CASE OF DAVID: MEDICAL HISTORY

David denies any major medical problems, currently or in the past. When asked about his last physical exam, however, he states that he does not think he has had one since he was a child, though he is quick to add, "I've always been healthy as a horse—well, except for all the drugs, I guess," and laughs. Although some assessors may feel differently, you may want to, at that moment, recommend to him that he go for a physical exam, just to rule out any medical problems that may be affecting him. However, given the pattern of symptoms, it seems unlikely that his problems have a medical cause.

Family Medical and Psychiatric History

Because of what is known about the heritability of both medical and psychiatric illnesses, not to mention what is known about children being raised by parents with mental illness, it is important to ask about any significant medical and psychiatric illnesses in both the immediate and distant family of the individual being assessed. A significant example of the impact of heredity is the research suggesting that an individual whose parent has bipolar disorder is at much higher risk for developing a mood disorder (Downey & Coyne, 1990; Hammen, Burge, Burney, & Adrian, 1990;

THE CASE OF DAVID: FAMILY MEDICAL HISTORY

David does not know of any significant medical or psychiatric illnesses within his immediate or extended family. When this information is unknown or is denied by a client, there is not much more to be asked, so it likely makes sense just to move on with the interview with David.

Weissman et al., 2006). Knowing this information about someone who has come in for an assessment can alert the assessor to possible symptoms or to view problems—either current or past—in a different light. It may be especially important to point out to the client that psychiatric illnesses are often undiagnosed (e.g., many people, upon reflection, will note that some family members were likely depressed, even though they were never formally diagnosed or treated for depression). The topics to assess related to family medical and psychiatric history are the same as when assessing the client's own medical and psychiatric history, with the addition of discussing possible undiagnosed illnesses in family members.

Psychosocial Evaluation

Whereas the symptomatic evaluation helps to clarify the *content* of the individual's current functioning, including symptomatology, the psychosocial evaluation is designed to examine the *context* of the individual's world, with both its intrapsychic and interpersonal demands. The scope of the presenting problem often reaches beyond individual symptoms. It is essential to consider that symptoms are manifested within a larger context of relating to others and that, as such, they will likely be affecting interpersonal functioning, educational and work functioning, and many other areas of life.

Family History

It is important to note both current and past family structure, such as number of siblings, who served as the primary caregiver of the individual, and number and ages of any children, in addition to any other significant details. As to the individual's current family life, if he or she is married or has a significant partner, you should get a description of the relationship,

TABLE 1.7   COMPONENTS OF ASSESSING FAMILY HISTORY

Family of origin structure
Primary caregiver(s), including quality of relationship
Siblings, including quality of relationship
Significant family events

Current family status/structure
Romantic relationship
Children
Significant family events

THE CASE OF DAVID: FAMILY HISTORY

The information on David's family of origin emerges throughout the initial interview, but not as a discrete line of inquiry. When asked about his developmental history earlier in the interview, he disclosed that he was raised as the only child of his mother and he had never known his father. David was born in New York, though his mother was originally from Chile. She has worked as a home health aide for David's whole life. He said, "It was easier not having a father 'cause I had a lot less structure," a factor he feels contributed to his ability to use drugs at such an early age. He said he thinks his father is in Chile, but he is not sure, and he has never had "the urge" to search for him.

To this point, David has given you quite a bit of factual information about his family of origin. What he has not shared, though, is the quality of his relationship with his mother (his only real immediate family). You may want to ask him to talk about his mother and what kind of person she is, or you may ask specifically about their relationship as he was growing up and now, but either way you must somehow get information on the quality of this relationship. When asked, he describes his mother as "nice," with very little other information. When probed a bit further, he does disclose that she is "a little clueless to have let me do what I did," but he says they have a relatively good relationship now.

including its history and the quality, in the words of the person being assessed. Any significant history within the family, such as traumas or deaths, should also be included in this part of the assessment. The aspects of clients' families of origin and current families are listed in Table 1.7.

Educational/Vocational History

A thorough assessment of educational history should be discussed, including the highest level of school completed, general functioning within school (including grades, in general), and educational aspirations. It should also be noted whether there is a history of any academic difficulties, learning disabilities, and special class placements. Additionally, information on current and past occupational functioning should be acquired, including career path, general level of work functioning and productivity, and career aspirations. Specific components of assessing educational and vocational/occupational history are listed in Table 1.8.

TABLE 1.8   COMPONENTS OF ASSESSING EDUCATIONAL/VOCATIONAL HISTORY

Educational history

   Highest level of education completed

      Years

      Degree

      Subject

School history

      Learning disabilities

      Special education

      Repeating a grade

      Attentional problems in school

      Hyperactivity in school

      Behavioral/emotional problems in school

      General grades

Vocational history

   Current job

      Length of time working in current job

      Quality of job performance

      Satisfaction with current job

   Past jobs

      Length of time working in past jobs

      Quality of job performance

      Satisfaction with past jobs

   Career aspirations

THE CASE OF DAVID: EDUCATIONAL/ VOCATIONAL HISTORY

For David, the educational/vocational history is actually part of the presenting problem and its history, so very little additional information is necessary. He tells you (with a smile) that he is majoring in psychology, though, as stated earlier, he is anxious about being able to finish the program. When asked if he has ever worked, he tells you that he worked at a clothing retail store through high school to help his mother pay the bills and to support his drug habit. He says that he never really enjoyed it, but he found it "easy to do."

Criminal/Legal History

You should note any history of legal problems. It is absolutely necessary to assess past legal involvement, including whether or not the individual is on probation or parole, because this will inform how best to proceed with the assessment. For example, a detailed history of criminal behavior could support a potential hypothesis of antisocial or even psychopathic traits. As such, you would want to make sure to design the testing battery to assess those traits specifically. This portion of the assessment is especially important if the individual indicated during the symptomatic evaluation that he or she has the potential to harm himself or herself or others, in that this risk, in combination with a criminal history, may be magnified. Areas to consider when assessing legal history are listed in Table 1.9.

TABLE 1.9   COMPONENTS OF ASSESSING CRIMINAL/ LEGAL HISTORY

Current criminal/legal involvement
   Probation/parole
   Lawsuits
   Impact of current legal involvement on day-to-day life

Past criminal/legal involvement
   Probation/parole
   Lawsuits
   Impact of past legal involvement on day-to-day life

THE CASE OF DAVID: CRIMINAL/LEGAL HISTORY

David's legal involvement ("thank God," he says) was limited to his drug arrest and time in juvenile detention. He says he is extremely grateful that all of his legal problems happened on his juvenile record and are much less likely to impact him in his adult life in the future. He denies any other involvement with the law.

When it comes to criminal and legal history, it is extremely important to be aware of subtle and slight reactions on your part, including facial expressions. To elicit the most open and honest responses from the client, you have to work hard to appear nonjudgmental and difficult to shock when discussing illegal activity. The more you treat this information like any other background information (like what the client had for breakfast), the better your rapport will be and the more likely you will be to get valid information.

Social History

A history of socialization should be evaluated, including current number of friends and the quality of these friendships. Additionally, the kinds of social networks and social activities that the individual participated in while growing up are of interest, as they may illustrate some of the reasons behind the current difficulties the individual is facing. Whether or not the individual has a best friend may prove important information later in the assessment process, as well. It is also extremely important to note any history of interpersonal difficulties. For example, because a diagnosis on Axis II almost invariably includes interpersonal impairment, a history of difficulty in the interpersonal domain may prove diagnostically important. Any current significant relationships, if not described in the family history section, may be described in detail here, again including their length and quality. The areas to consider when assessing social history are listed in Table 1.10.

Psychosexual History

Perhaps one of the more delicate topics to assess during the clinical interview is the psychosexual history of the individual. Psychosexual functioning refers to all of the psychosocial issues related to sexuality, including history

TABLE 1.10   COMPONENTS OF ASSESSING SOCIAL HISTORY

Current social support system
Best friend(s)
Current romantic relationship

Social history
History of interpersonal difficulties
History of romantic relationships

THE CASE OF DAVID: SOCIAL HISTORY

David says he has always been extremely sociable and friendly, "except when I isolate myself in my dorm room." He says he was "very popular" at the age of 16 when he stopped using drugs, and it was at this point that he met his high school girlfriend, who broke up with him three years ago. He says other people find him to be "happy-go-lucky and positive," so he finds making friends extremely easy. He has several very good friends at college, and several good friends from high school whom he keeps in touch with. His best friend from high school, as reported previously, died three years ago in a car accident, "and I'm still mourning him, I think." He has not been in a romantic relationship since his high school girlfriend broke up with him.

David paints the picture of an extremely sociable, friendly, outgoing, happy person, not exactly what would be expected from someone who has been struggling with depression for the past three years. He seems to have an extremely good support network, though one that struggled to get him out of his dorm room for at least six months. Again, a red flag may be going up, and follow-up questioning may be warranted. You may ask if his social life was different before and after the depression, as well as if it is different now than it was two-and-a-half or three years ago. When asked, he admits that he did cut off ties with most people three years ago when he became depressed, but he has found it extremely easy to reconnect with them and build new relationships in the past year-and-a-half or so, since he has progressively been feeling better, "with the help of therapy."

of romantic and sexual behavior and exploration, sexual adjustment and attitudes, gender identification, and sexual orientation. Although this part of the psychosocial evaluation may be more relevant in some cases than others, it is important to at least rule out the possibility that psychosexual issues may be affecting an individual's current psychological functioning. Included in this evaluation should be a history of sexual development, including whether the individual's pubertal development was on time, early, or late. Additionally, you should ask specifically about any history of sexual violence or molestation, as a victim, witness, or perpetrator. Again, there will be some cases where it is plainly evident that some areas of psychosexual history are not relevant, such as for young children. In such cases, there is no need to make the individual being assessed (or yourself) unnecessarily uncomfortable by probing into areas that clearly have no relevance.

Toward the goal of creating a comfortable environment that will produce the most accurate picture of the client possible, it is important to approach inquiry about psychosexual history in as straightforward and unapologetic a manner as possible. Any anxiety on the part of the assessor will likely engender anxiety in the individual being assessed, so it is most effective to ask questions frankly in a way that shows you are not embarrassed by their content. This will not only increase the person's comfort while being assessed, but will also increase the likelihood that he or she will be open and honest about topics that may be embarrassing to share in another context. Try to approach questions in this domain as if you were asking mundane questions; ask about history of sexual behavior as if you were asking what he or she watches on television. Also, try to avoid judgmental terms and covert meanings—use language that is plain and honest (e.g., when asking a woman about her onset of puberty, ask around what age she got her first period, rather than asking when her "special visitor" first arrived). Some areas that may be relevant in this part of the interview are listed in Table 1.11.

Multicultural Evaluation

It is impossible to understand an individual without understanding the cultural environment in which he or she is functioning.[2] Include in this section of the evaluation specific facts—for example, the individual's primary and

---

[2]For a more in-depth discussion on multicultural evaluation in clinical interviewing, see Suzuki, Ponterotto, and Meller (2008).

TABLE 1.11   COMPONENTS OF ASSESSING PSYCHOSEXUAL
                  HISTORY

Sexual orientation and identity

Current sexual activity
   Frequency
   Partner(s)
   Level of satisfaction

Past sexual activity
   Pubertal onset
   History of sexual activity
   History of sexual abuse, trauma, or violence

THE CASE OF DAVID: PSYCHOSEXUAL HISTORY

For David, you have some of this information already, at least related to romantic relationships. When asked, he says that he is heterosexual and has only ever dated his high school girlfriend. He says they were sexually active until they broke up, "but I haven't been much interested in sex since then." When asked about his sexual development, he says it was "normal, which is a surprise considering the crowd I was hanging out with!" He denies ever questioning his sexuality and ever having witnessed or been a part of sexual violence or misconduct. He does add that he feels he is ready to start dating again, though, and makes a joke about whether the assessor knows of any girls for him.

secondary languages and migration history, if there is one. It is important to evaluate the individual's cultural, racial, and spiritual/religious identity. For example, consider a teenage boy who self-identifies as "bicultural," since he was born into an Indian family but goes to school with mostly Caucasian peers. How he has reconciled his cultural identity, navigating his starkly contrasting worlds at home and at school, as well as how he feels about these differing worlds and himself within them, may impact his current functioning considerably. It is important to note that even individuals who are part of the majority culture (White males, for example) may have less obvious, but just as significant, cultural, racial, or spiritual identity struggles. For individuals who

TABLE 1.12   COMPONENTS OF CONDUCTING A
                MULTICULTURAL EVALUATION

Language

Immigration history

    When immigrated to current country

    Length of time in current community

    Acculturation issues

Cultural, racial, and ethnic identity

Spiritual and religious history and identity

Sexual identity

---

immigrated to their current countries, any history of acculturation issues, even if the individual feels that he or she has fully acculturated at present, should also be evaluated. Information that can be included in this section of the interview, when applicable, is given in Table 1.12.

THE CASE OF DAVID: MULTICULTURAL EVALUATION

David's mother is Chilean, and David was born and raised in New York. They spoke Spanish at home, though he spoke English at school growing up. Already, there is an area of potential impact on his life that you can ask about. Additionally, when thinking about the cultural context in which David was raised, questions of ethnic and cultural identity and spiritual and religious upbringing and current beliefs arise. You should inquire into each of these.

David tells you that he is bilingual and has never had difficulty with either Spanish or English. In fact, he says growing up that was one area that made him feel "special and smart," even as he struggled with school, because he was fluent in two languages. His mother is Catholic, as is her entire family, most of whom are in Chile, and David was raised in the Catholic church. He says that he is no longer religious, though, and has not been to church since he was in juvenile detention. He says that he never really had difficulty with his cultural identity, feeling that "I am just American—New Yorkers are from everywhere." He has never been to Chile and has never met most of his extended family. He describes himself as having "a universalist worldview," and when asked what he means by that, he simply states that he believes in equality throughout the world.

MENTAL STATUS EVALUATION

While the client is a major source of information about what is going on with his or her functioning, because every person's self-awareness is somewhat limited, other sources of data are essential. One of the most important tools for evaluating a person's current functioning is clinical observation. The mental status evaluation (MSE) is a useful way of organizing clinical observation data.[3] The MSE was designed as a method for identifying, in particular, individual characteristics that may seem outside of the normal range of functioning. Although there are several different ways to organize information for the MSE, one basic method is described here and is summarized in Table 1.13. Additionally, a form for recording MSE data is provided in Table 1.14.

Appearance and Behavior

One of the most important indicators of current functioning is how someone appears and behaves. Appearance includes not only clothing and grooming

TABLE 1.13   COMPONENTS OF THE MENTAL STATUS EVALUATION

Mental Status Evaluation

Appearance and behavior	Thought process and content
Grooming	Goal-directed thinking
Motor activity	Hallucinations and delusions
Relatedness	Depressive and anxious ideation
Speech and language	Suicidality and homicidality
Speech patterns	**Cognition**
Receptive language	Attention and concentration
Expressive language	Memory
Mood and affect	**Prefrontal functioning**
Self-reported mood	Judgment
Observed affect	Planning and impulse control
Mood-affect congruence	Insight

_____

[3]For a more in-depth discussion on the mental status evaluation, see J. Sommers-Flanagan and Sommers-Flanagan, 2002.

(i.e., how adequate his or her hygiene is), but also the level of motor activity (e.g., psychomotor retardation or hyperactivity) and coordination (fine and gross motor functioning) displayed. Behavior refers both to any abnormal or repetitive behaviors, such as constant shifting or throat-clearing, and to the individual's relatedness toward you, including cooperativeness, friendliness, guardedness, and eye contact. Appearance and behavior can, even before testing, clue you in to the possibility of some reasons for functional impairment. For example, a client appearing fidgety and agitated may indicate several things, including anxiety, mania, or the effects of a drug.

Consider a man who comes into your office for the clinical interview with his hair disheveled, his shirt tucked in only halfway on one side, his collar askew, and his zipper down. This significantly unexpected and inappropriate appearance can be a major clue that something is not going particularly well for him at the moment (those words, *at the moment* are extremely important, as he may have sick children at home, or something else that may cause situational distress). His appearance may signify something more serious as well, though, such as disorganized thinking and behavior associated with psychosis. Whatever it signifies, it is extremely important to note, because ultimately whatever emerges from the assessment should ideally explain why he came in so disheveled.

Alternatively, consider a woman who comes in wearing inappropriately tight and seductive clothing, showing significant amounts of cleavage. Already you have clinical information, "clues," as to some possibilities of her functioning. When you consider that she is being assessed as part of a custody evaluation for her children, her overly seductive attire may make sense, especially when the assessment reveals her underlying personality and coping structure. She may simply be working hard to be seen favorably by the assessor, which may on the one hand relate to her desperation to get her children back, but on the other hand may reveal some sort of narcissistic or histrionic presentation.

Finally, consider a woman who comes in for the clinical interview, makes very little eye contact, looks down at the floor, fidgets with her hands constantly, and does not seem to answer questions directly. This behavior is likely significant for one of many reasons. She clearly seems to be somewhat anxious, though her anxiety could be related to many different things, including social/stranger anxiety, fear of what her assessment will reveal, or generalized anxiety. Alternatively, she could have interpersonal skills deficits related to some type of pervasive developmental disorder. Whatever the reason for the behavior, it is important to note and to incorporate into the assessment—her behavior is significant clinical data that must be used or explained by the results of the assessment.

Speech and Language

A person's language functioning critically affects your ability to adequately assess him or her in all other domains of functioning. For example, if you observe that the client does not understand what you are saying, you will need to adjust the selection of tests for the battery to make sure he or she will be able to comprehend the test instructions. Similarly, if an individual's vocabulary is so limited that he or she cannot make his or her point known, then much of the information from the clinical interview will need to be interpreted with this barrier in mind.

Language should be evaluated separately for (a) receptive and (b) expressive elements. Receptive language refers to language comprehension; you should note whether the person seems to understand all that you are saying and whether he or she requires you to repeat questions, comments, and instructions. Expressive language refers to the individual's actual use of language to make his or her points known, including the developmental vocabulary level, clarity of expression, and appropriateness of word use. Aspects of speech such as volume, rate, and tone should be evaluated separately from the language itself.

Consider a client who comes in for an assessment and during the clinical interview does not seem to understand clearly the questions you are asking, despite the fact that you are being clear and simple in your language. This same client may have difficulty understanding the directions for some of the testing instruments, especially the more complicated ones (e.g., the figure weights subtest of the WAIS-IV has long and somewhat confusing directions, because the task itself is somewhat conceptually novel and difficult). Not only is this good clinical information—difficulty understanding language would certainly impair interpersonal relationships, educational and occupational functioning, and so forth—but it informs what alterations to your testing battery may need to be made. This person with clear receptive language difficulties may benefit from a cognitive evaluation that utilizes the Test of Nonverbal Intelligence, 3rd Edition (TONI-3), a language-free intelligence measure, for example. Difficulties with receptive language can be related to several things, including an organic or neurological problem, overwhelming anxiety, or even psychosis. As with any aspect of mental status, this information should provide more data to the whole picture of what is going on for him or her, and the ultimate "picture" of the client should make sense in connection with this receptive language difficulty.

Consider also another client who comes in with loud, pressured, cluttered speech. Her expressive language is so pressured that she trips over her words, stutters, and at times gets so overwhelmed by the rate of her words that she cannot get a single one out. Again, there are many possibilities as to why this may be happening for her: She could be overwhelmed by anxiety within the current situation, she could suffer from a more pervasive anxiety disorder, she could have some sort of neuropsychological or cognitive condition, or something else entirely different could be going on. It is important to capture this information here, however, so that you can work it into the assessment results to contribute to the overall picture of the client.

Mood and Affect

An important distinction in the MSE is the difference between mood and affect. Mood refers to the current emotional state of the individual, *as reported by the client himself or herself.* Affect refers to the *observed* emotional state of the individual, such as what his or her facial expression or general body language communicates to you as the assessor. While it is important to evaluate mood and affect separately, it is extremely important to decide whether both are (a) appropriate to the situation and (b) appropriate to each other. This latter concept, whether the individual reports a mood similar to the affect that you observe, is known as mood-affect congruence. Affect can be mood-incongruent for many reasons, and noting this will be important later in the assessment. For example, consider a woman who reports feeling sad and depressed but does not stop laughing or smiling throughout the entire interview. The fact that she does not *seem* depressed to you, contrary to her own report, may prove notable when you are reviewing the results from her testing.

Alternatively, many individuals may report feeling "fine," despite the fact that their affect is notably depressed (e.g., they do not smile or even look at you during the interview, they speak slowly, they sigh often). This mood-incongruent affect may inform you about their levels of insight, the possible stigma of mental illness, or even fears of being diagnosed as depressed. Not only will this incongruence be additional data for the assessment, but it can help inform you to be slightly more gentle and reassuring during the whole process.

Thought Process and Content

Just as it is important to evaluate the emotional state of the individual, evaluating the thought process and content can provide you with extremely useful pieces of data when you create a picture of what may be going on for an individual. Thought process refers to *how* an individual thinks, whether in a goal-directed, logical way, or in a way that suggests some problem in thinking, such as tangential, circumstantial, magical, or concrete thinking. An individual who, when asked questions, consistently goes off topic in a seeming stream-of-consciousness delivery can be labeled as having tangential thought process. A person with tangential thinking may have actual cognitive or thought difficulties, possibly including dementia or psychosis, though it may be attributable to other factors, such as current emotional distress or anxiety. Someone with circumstantial thinking will eventually veer back onto the point and answer the question, though in a roundabout way. Circumstantial thinking, while sometimes difficult to follow, usually does not indicate a serious functional problem, though it may inform some difficulties in communication and interpersonal functioning. Again, when evaluating this domain, it is important that you have evaluated the individual's language abilities, as this is the primary mode by which you can observe his or her thought process.

Consider a client who comes in and seems to be thinking quite slowly and in a concrete way. When you ask him about his difficulties, he can consider only very specific, concrete examples, such as getting fired from his job recently and not understanding why. He may have difficulty even coming up with hypotheses as to why he might have been fired, though he reports that his ex-boss told him that he was making multiple errors in his tasks. All this information comes out slowly, and he seems unable to think abstractly about why his boss may have fired him. This concrete and slow thought process is important to note because it may relate to low cognitive ability, a rigid personality style, or some other possible cognitive deficit. Again, this will likely "fit" into the picture of the client that emerges from the assessment.

Thought content refers to *what* the individual thinks about. Specifically, we are most interested in abnormal thought and perceptual content, such as hallucinations and delusions. It is important to be extremely vigilant in distinguishing what are true hallucinations and delusions from other perceptual and thought experiences. For example, a man who reports seeing a ghost outside of his bedroom window may be hallucinating. However, because hallucinations require *no external stimulus*, whether he is simply misinterpreting another stimulus, like a tree blowing in the wind, is crucial to evaluate. If he is actually misperceiving one thing as another, the perceptual phenomenon is actually an *illusion*, not a hallucination.

Similarly, a delusion is a fixed, false belief held as true despite concrete evidence to the contrary, so beliefs that seem odd to you need to be probed carefully to see if there might be any validity to them. For example, whereas it may be a delusion for some of us to think we are being followed constantly (this would be an example of a paranoid delusion), a man who is going through a divorce and whose soon-to-be ex-wife has hired a private investigator may not be delusional in thinking he is being followed. There is actually evidence that his belief may be true (e.g., seeing the same man in the same car everywhere he goes), rather than evidence to the contrary.

Additionally, depressive, manic, aggressive, suicidal, and homicidal ideation should be noted. Much of this information will have been reported by the individual being assessed during the symptomatic evaluation. Often, however, much of this ideation will come out in the interview or assessment process more organically. For example, a man asked specifically about depressive ideation may deny it, but later in the process, after struggling with a cognitive task (e.g., block design on a Wechsler intelligence scale), may say to himself, "I am always *so* stupid! I'm always failing at stuff—I'm just so worthless." This would qualify as depressive ideation, despite the fact that he directly denied it previously. Similarly, a woman going through a divorce and undergoing a custody evaluation may deny any aggressive ideation toward her ex-husband when asked initially, but later in the assessment it may become clear that she "hate[s] the jerk" and actually has thoughts of harming him. These are clear examples of how the mental status evaluation requires the consideration of both the report of the individual being assessed and the observations of you as the assessor.

Cognition

Although you will be testing cognitive functioning later, clinical impressions of different domains of cognitive functioning should be noted from the interview, so that any suspected abnormalities can be included in the hypotheses generated later. Additional testing may be required as a result of these noted abnormalities. The major areas of cognition captured in the MSE are alertness, attention, concentration, and memory. Just like the other domains, you should be most interested in what is clinically outside of normal limits. For example, with alertness, note whether the individual looks sleepy, slumped in his or her chair and looking at the floor throughout the clinical interview (noted as "lethargic" in the MSE), or is particularly alert to everything you are doing and follows all of your movements and writing with great attention (noted as "hypervigilant" in the MSE). Similarly, with attention, concentration, and memory, make note of any conspicuous problems that seem to be interfering either with the assessment process itself or the individual's life in general. For example, while you will often test short-term memory in the assessment, it would be notable if a woman does not remember seemingly important details of her childhood or schooling. This impairment in memory may have organic or more dynamic roots, but either way it is important information when creating hypotheses of what could currently be impairing her functioning. Moreover, if a person cannot concentrate on the questions you are asking in the interview, it is likely that his or her concentration in other situations may be compromised as well.

Prefrontal Functioning

The final domain of the MSE is concerned with those higher-order skills and functions associated with the functioning of the prefrontal cortex area of the brain. Although attention and concentration are largely associated with the prefrontal cortex, the functions in this prefrontal functioning section are more related to personality variables such as judgment, planning, and insight. Your clinical evaluation of these domains will inevitably fall short—these domains of functioning are complex and difficult to assess, especially with clinical observation alone. It is nevertheless useful to evaluate them broadly. Specifically, in considering the self-report of the clinical interview, you should evaluate how appropriate you think the individual's judgment has been in the past. An individual who has been arrested multiple times for selling drugs likely does not have the best judgment (either for continuing to commit the act or continuing to get caught). Consider a woman who comes in for a custody evaluation and is extremely belligerent, oppositional, and caustic in her interaction with the assessor. While she may be angry about the situation (and perhaps rightly so), this strategy is a very bad one for getting the assessor to "be on her side," hopefully ultimately to report that she would be the best choice for the child. Frustrating or angering the person who will help decide whether you get your child back shows poor judgment, even though the assessor may understand why the woman is upset in general.

Planning refers to how well the individual seems to consider the future when acting; additionally, how well you feel he or she controls impulses is important in understanding the capacity for planning. Planning and impulse control are thus highly intertwined, and both constitute prefrontal functioning. Consider a client mandated for an assessment because of extreme delinquent behavior—vandalizing public property. It will be important to assess whether these acts of delinquency were planned and premeditated or were the result of poor impulse control. The same behaviors can have very different roots, and potential treatment for either of these situations would look very different.

Insight refers to how aware the person is (a) that he or she has difficulties and needs support or help, (b) that he or she plays a part in his or her own problems, and (c) of the specific issues that need addressing. A man currently mandated to a drug rehabilitation program by the court may report that he understands that his drug use served as a way of coping with negative emotions, which would constitute high insight. Alternatively, he may simply see his current situation as an impediment to his being able to enjoy himself on drugs again; this would constitute low insight.

This section of the MSE can be especially useful in determining how an individual is functioning developmentally. For example, children are not expected to have extremely high insight—it is not expected for a child to understand the role he or she plays in his or her own difficulties. This capacity generally develops throughout adolescence. An adult man who has extremely low insight into his problems, however, may be conceptualized as functioning, at least in this domain, as a preadolescent. It may then be important to begin to think about his other areas of functioning in terms of normative development, especially judgment, planning, and impulse control. It would not be unusual for that adult man with extremely poor insight also to have what could be considered preadolescent-level functioning in other domains, including extremely naïve judgment and difficulty delaying gratification.

TABLE 1.14	FORM FOR RECORDING MENTAL STATUS EVALUATION DATA

Mental Status Evaluation

Appearance: _____   Grooming: _____

Motor activity: _____

Coordination: _____

    Gross motor: _____

    Stance/posture: _____

    Gait: _____

    Balance: _____

    Fine motor: _____

Abnormal movements/
repetitive behaviors: _____

Relatedness (circle):

Normal	**Abnormal**	
Cooperative	Hostile	Uncooperative
Relaxed	Guarded	Unrelated
Friendly	Seductive	Withdrawn
Good eye contact	Poor eye contact	Clinging

Comments: _____

_____

Speech/Language (circle):

Receptive: **Normal**   **Abnormal**

Expressive:

	Normal	**Abnormal**		
Volume:	Low	Normal	Loud	
Pitch:	Monotone	Normal	Exaggerated	
Quality of voice:	Hoarse	Normal	Harsh	Nasal
Articulation:		Normal	Abnormal	
Rhythm:	Clutter	Normal	Stutter	Pauses
Rate:	Slow	Normal	Rapid	Pressure/push

(Continued)

TABLE 1.14   (*CONTINUED*)

Vocabulary/Grammar

Age appropriate:	Yes	No
IQ appropriate:	Yes	No
Idiomatic (slang):	Yes	No

Comments: _____

_____

Affect/Mood (circle):

Affect:	**Normal**	**Abnormal**		
Range:	Expressive/Good range	Flat	Constricted	Labile
Type:		Angry	Irritable	
		Anxious	Sad	
	Appropriate to situation	Inappropriate to situation		
Mood:	**Euthymic**	**Abnormal**		
	Happy	Elevated	Depressed	Angry
		Mild	Mild	Mild
		Moderate	Moderate	Moderate
		Severe	Severe	Severe
	Appropriate to situation	Inappropriate to situation		
Congruent:	Yes	No		

Comments: _____

_____

Thought Process (circle):

Normal	**Abnormal**	
Goal directed	Tangential	Flight of ideas
Logical	Circumstantial	Slow thinking
Abstract reasoning	Magical thinking	Rapid thinking
	Concrete thinking	Loose associations

Comments: _____

_____

TABLE 1.14	(CONTINUED)

Thought Content (circle):

	Normal	Abnormal
	Hallucinations	Delusions
	Not present	Not present
	Auditory	Paranoid
	Visual	Grandiose
	Olfactory	Body image
	Tactile	Ideas of reference
	Mood incongruent	Mood incongruent
	Mood congruent	Mood congruent
		Other: _____

Depressive Ideation	Suicidality	Aggressiveness	Homicidality
Not present	Not present	Not present	Not present
Worthlessness	Ideation	Ideation	Ideation
Excessive guilt	Plan	Plan	Plan
Self reproach	Intent	Intent	Intent
Low self-esteem			
Helplessness			
Hopelessness			

Comments: _____

_____

_____

_____

Memory (circle):   Normal   Abnormal

Comments: _____

_____

_____

_____

Attention and Concentration (circle):   Normal   Abnormal

_____

(Continued)

TABLE 1.14   (*CONTINUED*)

Comments: _____

_____

_____

_____

Alertness (circle):

Lethargic/sleepy   Alert   Hypervigilant

Judgment and Planning (circle):

Judgment: Poor   Fair   Good

Impulse control: Poor   Fair   Good

Comments: _____

_____

_____

_____

Insight (circle):

Poor   Fair   Good

Comments: _____

_____

_____

_____

Hypothesis Building

Once data have been gathered through completion of the clinical interview, the collection of background information from other sources (e.g., from the person who referred the individual, from other collateral sources, from medical records, etc.), and the mental status evaluation, it is time to pose the question: What *could* be going on for this person? To answer this question effectively, you need a clear and comprehensive knowledge of psychodiagnosis. If, for example, you do not remember that impairment in attention can be a symptom of depression, you may forget to include this as a viable hypothesis for an individual who presents with poor attention. If your only hypothesis is that the person may have a disorder of attentional ability (i.e., attention-deficit/hyperactivity disorder), then you may not choose to test for depression or any other possible cause of impaired attention. For extra assistance on the potential causes of symptoms, from a DSM-IV-TR perspective, consult the *DSM-IV-TR Handbook for Differential Diagnosis* (First, Frances, & Pincus, 2002), which includes a list of symptoms with all their likely diagnostic causes. That being said, a DSM-IV-TR perspective is only one of many perspectives.

Also important is a thorough knowledge of cognitive, personality, and emotional functioning from whichever theoretical perspective you subscribe to. The process of generating hypotheses for what is impairing an individual's functioning applies to any theoretical orientation. Consider a man who presents with interpersonal difficulties, for example. A hypothesis from a psychodynamic perspective may include the possibility that his object representations are chaotic and thus impairing interpersonal relations. A hypothesis from a cognitive perspective may include the possibility that he has an underlying schema of worthlessness, feeling that he does not deserve positive relationships, which sabotages his interpersonal relations.

The same presentation, considered from a multicultural perspective, may generate a hypothesis that a combination of racial discrimination and acculturation issues may be impairing interpersonal functioning, as social norms and conventions may be very different here from his culture of origin. The important point is that you should generate hypotheses for *all* the likely causes of the functional impairment. One hypothesis should *always* be that the individual's functioning is normative and functional—that nothing is wrong: This is the null hypothesis. In most cases, though, you will reject this hypothesis on the basis of the simple fact that the individual was referred, either by himself or herself or by someone else, for difficulties in functioning, as well as the clinical interview, which usually reveals significant impairment.

Identify Impairments

The first task in the process of hypothesizing is to clearly lay out the precise impairments in functioning. This often requires some degree of simplification (at times even oversimplification). Whereas you have amassed many pieces of data from different sources, at this point it is important to take a step back and try to understand, as broadly as possible, in what domains this individual's functioning is impaired.

For example, a woman going through a divorce may complain of the stress of the separation and elaborate on what a "jerk" her soon-to-be ex-husband is. She may complain of a lack of support and unfair treatment by her husband's attorney and the judge. She may complain that her own attorney has no idea what he is doing and "obviously hates women." And these complaints may only be the tip of the iceberg! When taking a step back, however, a complicated picture of a woman clearly in distress can be made clearer and simpler. The first step is to list the impairments in functioning. Currently, she has reported one major impairment—"stress" related to the divorce. We can also ascertain another major impairment from our clinical observation: interpersonal difficulty (we may also feel that her insight is somewhat impaired). While "interpersonal difficulty" is a broad term, she has reported a lack of support in general, has blamed others for her current situation,[4] and has reported generally negative feelings toward even those individuals who are trying to help her. Thus, there is substantial reason to believe that she has interpersonal difficulty, at least enough so that it merits further investigation during the assessment.

Enumerate Possible Causes

The next step of the hypothesis-building process is to try to enumerate all the logical possible causes for each of the broad areas of impairment in functioning. First and foremost, we must consider the fact that there may be nothing

---

[4]Remember, this is only a hypothesis. It may turn out that others truly are victimizing her. But given her global insistence that others are against her, it stands to reason that she may be playing a significant part in her interpersonal difficulties.

abnormal occurring—our null hypothesis posits, for this woman, that she is reacting as anyone would to a divorce and that her functioning is unimpaired in any domain. Considering the alternative, that she does have functional impairments, generates several other hypotheses as well. She reported "stress" related to her divorce, and while this term is vague, it should raise a red flag of possible anxiety, depression, and, most likely, adjustment difficulties. It is important not to jump to the conclusion that this is an adjustment disorder, even if this is likely our best hypothesis. Because we have not yet taken into consideration her functioning prior to the divorce, the duration of her symptoms, or many other factors, we cannot confidently say that this definitely does not constitute a mood or anxiety disorder.

As with any assessment, there are two hypotheses that must be ruled out across the board. The first is a substance-related disorder. There is a possibility that her current anxious state, above and beyond her situation, is exacerbated by the use of a substance—cocaine, for example. It is important to note that hypotheses may not be mutually exclusive—she could very easily have both an adjustment disorder and a substance abuse disorder, which exacerbates the former. The second hypothesis that must be considered for *every* assessment is that the impairment in functioning is due to a general medical condition. For example, a brain tumor can cause both mood and anxiety symptoms. While it is unlikely in this case (since we seem to have a logical precipitating external event), because we are not medical doctors, we cannot confidently rule out this possibility without at least current medical records (a recent physical can be extremely useful).

Another major hypothesis, given her interpersonal difficulties, would be a personality disorder. Regardless of your personal feelings about Axis II and personality disorders, it must be considered that this is one thing that can get in the way of interpersonal functioning. That being said, it is only one thing. As we will be testing this woman for depression in our assessment anyway, knowing that depression can also interfere with socialization, we will need to be mindful of whether the interpersonal impairment exceeds what would be expected of a woman with depression. Other hypotheses of what could impair interpersonal relationships could include social anxiety, systematic discrimination by society as a whole, or even psychosis (in the form of paranoid delusions, such that others are conspiring against her). This list of possibilities is hardly exhaustive (for example, Asperger's Disorder can impair interpersonal functioning, though it is unlikely in this case because of her history of significant relationships and no evidence of the other symptoms of the disorder). But when generating hypotheses, you want to try to be as expansive as possible, enumerating as many possibilities as you can come up with for each impairment in functioning. Many of these will be ruled out quickly and easily in the testing process, but each will help inform what tests you choose for the assessment battery. These hypotheses are crucial for the next step in the process, selecting tests—you must know what you are trying to rule in or rule out in order to decide how to proceed with testing.

Summary

The task of generating hypotheses as to what may be impairing an individual's functioning requires the synthesis of a large amount of information. Beginning with the referral questions, whether they come from the individual himself or herself or from someone else who referred the person for the assessment, clues as to what may be happening will begin to emerge during your first encounter. This is merely the beginning. The bulk of information about the person comes from (a) the clinical interview and (b) your clinical observation, including the mental status evaluation. From all of the information gathered, a picture of the individual's functioning will begin to emerge, though it may seem, at least initially, to get more and more complex (rather than clearer) as data accumulate.

After gathering all the data from collateral resources (medical records, consulting previous treating clinicians, etc.), the clinical interview, and your own clinical observations and mental status evaluation, the next task is to consolidate the data into coherent themes so that you can begin hypothesizing a cause. This begins with taking a step back and looking at what are truly the areas of impaired functioning, including subjectively felt distress, reported impairments, and other problems that may be outside of the person's awareness, such as a pattern of difficulties with other people. Finally, once the major areas of impairment have been identified, using your comprehensive knowledge of psychodiagnostics and personality and emotional functioning, a list of as many potential causes as possible for each of the impairments should be generated. This list will inform the next step of the assessment process. That next step is to choose a battery of tests to help you evaluate the validity and probability of each hypothesis you are considering.

CHAPTER 2

Selecting Tests

Central to the process of psychological assessment is the appropriate selection of psychological tests to assess specific areas of an individual's current functioning. Selecting the appropriate tests allows the assessor to gather data beyond simply what the assessor can observe and what the individual being assessed can directly report. A clear and deep understanding of exactly what different tests measure, as well as how they go about measuring it, is crucial to building an assessment battery that will most accurately illuminate an individual's functioning. This chapter presents a comprehensive, though not exhaustive, overview of important considerations involved in making appropriate and informed test selections.

GENERAL CONSIDERATIONS

At this point in the assessment (after the clinical interview and review of collateral information), you should have generated some hypotheses to explain the functional impairment of the individual being assessed. It is important to note that human functioning is complex, and testing these hypotheses, therefore, is most often complicated and multifaceted, which is why all assessments should include evaluations of both cognitive and personality/emotional functioning. In other words, it is impossible to understand an individual's emotional functioning without a clear picture of his or her cognitive functioning and vice versa.

Why Test?

The primary question when determining how to match the choice of tests to the hypotheses generated is: Why test? It is important to understand precisely what information you need to gather in order to evaluate the validity of each of your hypotheses. It is just as important, though, to understand what kind of information would be better obtained from tests than from clinical observation, self-report, or others' reports. For example, an individual may report difficulties with attention (*self-report*), and you may also have noticed that his or her attention wandered during the clinical interview (*clinical observation*). Obviously, it would be insufficient to leave it at that.

It would be important in this case also to obtain an *objective measure* of attention to determine just how serious (i.e., impairing his or her functioning) the difficulty is. Using a measure such as the test of everyday attention (TEA) or the Conners' Continuous Performance Test, 2nd Edition (CPT-2) will provide much more precise and accurate data than self-report or clinical observation alone. Additionally, because attention difficulties can be symptomatic of many disorders, the likely source of the poor attention could be one of several things. As the causes may range from a mood disorder to an anxiety disorder to attention-deficit/hyperactivity disorder (ADHD), more tests will be needed to rule out erroneous hypotheses and to identify those in strong contention.

The Multimethod Approach

Every effort should be made to approach each hypothesis from as many different angles as possible. Within constraints of time and resources, the more data that can be gathered using the largest possible selection of methods will increase confidence in the strength and validity of the conclusions drawn. This approach is known as the multimethod approach to psychological assessment (Meyer et al., 2001), and its goal is comprehensiveness. Not only does the use of multiple tests to evaluate many separate areas of functioning increase the scope of the assessment, but it can provide convergence of evidence across tests to create stronger arguments for some hypotheses over others.

For example, if an individual complains of feeling "depressed"—which can mean very different things to different people—further inquiry may be needed. Support for this hypothesis of depression will likely come from self-report, symptom-focused measures (e.g., the Structured Clinical Interview for DSM-IV Axis I Disorders [SCID-I] or the Beck Depression Inventory [BDI]), as these ask questions that are likely very similar to what would be asked in the clinical interview. You can be much more confident in the likelihood of an actual clinical depression (as opposed to, for example, nonpathological sadness) if evidence of the depression also emerges from self-report personality inventories (e.g., the Minnesota Multiphasic Personality Inventory, 2nd Edition [MMPI-2] or the Personality Assessment Inventory [PAI]) and on non–self-report, performance-based projective measures (e.g., the Rorschach Inkblot Test, Comprehensive System or the Thematic Apperception Test [TAT]).

If evidence of depression comes from the patient's self-report during the interview and from use of the BDI, the MMPI-2, the Rorschach, and the TAT, there is a great deal of convergent evidence that the hypothesis of depression is strongly supported, and you can confidently state that the individual is likely experiencing a depressive episode. Moreover, while all these tests converge on the broad category of depression, each specific test can offer a more nuanced picture of the quality of the depressed episode. For example, the BDI and MMPI-2 may qualify the depression as specifically melancholic, while strong themes of loss and loneliness may emerge in the responses to the Rorschach, MMPI-2, and TAT—a seemingly small but important quality that can be extremely important in terms of treatment. This type of depression is very different from a depression that is centered primarily on low self-esteem, for example, and will be treated very differently by a mental health professional.

When asking the question "Why test?," consider the fact that these small nuances, though they could likely be obtained through clinical interviewing and through the process of psychotherapy, may take much longer to emerge in these conditions, especially if the individual is not necessarily aware of them himself or herself. In this example, an answer to the question "Why test?" could include determining both whether the individual is clinically depressed or just nonpathologically sad and how the depression would be categorized (e.g., rooted in loneliness, hopelessness, low self-esteem, etc.), so that specific, targeted treatment recommendations can be made.

Very often, it is considerably easier to rule *out* a hypothesis than to confirm it. For example, if "poor attention" is a hypothesis and the individual's working memory index (WMI) on the Wechsler Adult Intelligence Scale, 4th Edition (WAIS-IV) is in the very superior range, it is extremely unlikely that there is an attention deficit. This is because the WMI taps several cognitive abilities, the most basic of which is auditory attention. For example, one of the subtests that makes up this index, Digit Span, requires the individual being assessed to take in a list of numbers read aloud to him or her and either repeat them back or reorder them in a specific way and produce the new list aloud. While the latter task requires much more than just attention, neither of these tasks would be doable if a functional impairment in attention were present. Someone who cannot attend to the numbers being read aloud has no way to repeat them back, let alone to manipulate them to produce a different output order. Thus, with the use of a test that is generally part of the standard battery of any assessment, attention deficit can be ruled out.

However, though a high score on WMI can *rule out* a hypothesis of attention deficit, low performance on this scale is insufficient to *confirm* the same hypothesis. Poor performance on that same Digit Span subtest *may* be due to poor attention, or it may be due to any other number of cognitive processes that are required to complete the task adequately, such as numerical ability or fluid mental flexibility. Thus, to confirm a hypothesis of impairment in attention, additional tests would need to be chosen (again, tests like the CPT-2, TEA, or the repeatable battery for the assessment of neuropsychological status [RBANS] may be useful in considering the hypothesis of attention in much greater depth).

A Standard Battery

Very often, psychologists will have a standard battery of tests that constitutes the base of most of the assessments they conduct. In addition to a thorough clinical interview, a good standard battery will include the following:

- A screening test for gross neurological impairment, such as the Bender Visual-Motor Gestalt Test, 2nd Edition (Bender-2) or the Beery-Buktenica Developmental Test of Visual-Motor Integration (Beery-VMI)
- A broad measure of cognitive ability, such as a Wechsler intelligence scale or the Stanford-Binet Intelligence Scales, 5th Edition (SB5)
- Several multimethod measures of personality and emotional functioning, including
  - A self-report, symptom-based measure, such as the SCID-I

- A self-report inventory, such as the MMPI-2 or the Millon Clinical Multiaxial Inventory, 3rd Edition (MCMI-III)
- Some projective measures, such as the Rorschach and the TAT

This kind of standard battery will address a number of basic hypotheses from different angles, as well as paint a comprehensive picture of how an individual is currently functioning. For example, a common standard battery for adults could be the Bender-2, WAIS-IV, MMPI-2, Rorschach, TAT, and Projective Drawings (such as the House-Tree-Person). Many general assessments of functioning, including those of individuals who present with mood, anxiety, and psychotic disorders, will be mostly adequately addressed with this standard battery, without the need to supplement with additional tests. The Bender-2 and WAIS-IV can rule out gross neurological and cognitive impairment, as well as exhibiting an individual's cognitive strengths and weaknesses. The MMPI-2 and projective techniques (Rorschach, TAT, and Projective Drawings), in combination with the clinical interview and clinical observation, can broadly evaluate an individual's emotional functioning. Specifically, mood, anxiety, and psychotic symptoms can be reliably captured by these different personality and emotional functioning measures.

It is important to note that new hypotheses may develop during the testing itself. For example, notable and interesting results from the WAIS-IV may warrant further investigation into a specific area of cognitive functioning. Even if there were no presenting complaint about attention, a significantly low score on the WMI warrants further investigation to see whether attentional impairment is the underlying cause of the poor performance on these WMI tasks. Additional tests of executive functioning (such as the Wisconsin Card Sorting Test [WCST] or the Trail Making Test) may prove useful as well, especially if attention is examined and determined to be unimpaired. Similarly, some evidence for a personality disorder may emerge from some of the projective tasks, so adding a self-report inventory that is more sensitive to Axis II pathology than the MMPI-2, such as the MCMI-III, can be useful in building evidence for or ruling out some sort of personality pathology.

Test Characteristics

It is extremely important when conducing psychological assessments to be vigilant as to the currency of your knowledge of what tests are available to use, what each test tests, and how each test tests what it tests (this sentence alone may serve as an assessment of vocal articulation!). Resources such as the *Mental Measurements Yearbook* and *Tests in Print* provide descriptions and reviews of most available tests. Additionally, Strauss, Sherman, and Spreen's (2006) *A Compendium of Neuropsychological Tests* and other similar texts can be useful for specific subdomains of assessment. Reviewing the *Journal of Personality Assessment*, the *Journal of Psychoeducational Assessment*, and other similar journals can also help keep you current on the state of psychological tests.

Different tests are differentially sensitive to varied aspects of personality and emotional functioning. For example, self-report, symptom-focused measures generally identify current states of functioning and overt characteristics that individuals are themselves aware of. For example, states such as current anxiety and characteristics such as low self-esteem are easily identified by self-report measures such as the SCID-I and the Symptom Checklist-90-Revised (SCL-90-R).

More enduring personality traits, including underlying motivations, biases, attitudes, and dispositions that may not be entirely consciously understood by the individual being assessed are better uncovered by self-report personality inventories and performance-based measures such as projective tests. For example, while an individual may be largely unaware of the fact, he or she may have a predisposition toward self-sabotaging behaviors in the face of success. Although self-report, symptom-focused measures will likely not uncover this trait, measures such as the MCMI-III and Rorschach are much more sensitive to these types of data.

Reliability

When deciding upon tests to use in a battery, you must ensure that each test has adequate psychometric properties. That is, each test used should be both reliable *and* valid. Reliability has to do with the consistency with which a test measures whatever it measures. A test that measures depressive symptoms, for example, if given to the same person with the same symptoms at a different time, should consistently detect the symptoms; this is one type of reliability. While this may be difficult to assess personally (because an individual's symptoms are not, in fact, consistent over time), statistics on a test's reliability should be able to be found both in the test's manual and in the major publications of test materials: *Mental Measurements Yearbook* and *Tests in Print*. There are four major types of reliability to consider when looking at tests.

The first is *inter-rater reliability*. Inter-rater reliability is the consistency with which multiple examiners obtain the same data from a given test. For example, if clinicians are trying to rate the quality of warmth during an interaction between a parent and her infant child playing together using some kind of warmth rating system, inter-rater reliability would be extremely important—that is, the system should be set up such that independent raters give relatively the same warmth ratings to the interaction they are watching. If the raters vary drastically on their warmth ratings, even though they are watching the exact same interaction (and this variation occurred consistently), the rating scale would be said to have low inter-rater reliability, and thus the ratings themselves would not be meaningful. For these types of measures, where clinician rating or scoring is integral to the measure itself, inter-rater reliability must be adequate.

The second type of reliability is *split-half* or *alternative forms reliability*. Split-half reliability refers to taking half the items of a single test (usually every other item) and correlating it with the other half of the items. If the test is meant to measure a single construct (e.g., the Beck Depression Inventory is made up of items that are all supposed to be assessing depression), then correlating two halves of the test should yield very good split-half reliability. This type of reliability is harder to assess when the test itself is not meant to yield a measure of a single construct. For example, the MMPI-2 has many different constructs that it attempts to measure (e.g., clinical scales range from somatic signs to depression to antisocial tendencies, among many others). Thus, it is not assumed that all the items should relate to each other in a consistent way.

Similarly, alternative forms reliability relates to giving two different versions of a test to a single individual (though, obviously, a whole sample of these would be needed to calculate a test's reliability). For example, many cognitive tests have alternative forms, including the PPVT-IV. The Peabody Picture Vocabulary Test, 4th Edition consists of a list of vocabulary words increasing in difficulty along with corresponding picture items for the client to choose from. Alternative forms of this test simply include different test items (vocabulary words and corresponding picture items) of approximately equivalent difficulty throughout. Giving the same individual the two different forms of this test should theoretically yield very similar scores, as the task is the same, the construct is clear, and the test itself has alternative forms reliability.

The third form of reliability to consider is *test-retest reliability*. The idea behind test-retest reliability is that the exact same test given twice to the same person should yield very similar results. Like the other forms of reliability, this type makes sense in connection with some tests but not others. One assumption that must be made about any test scrutinized for test-retest reliability is that the construct that it is measuring should not have changed drastically. For example, a test of how well a client slept the night before, given on two separate occasions several weeks apart, may not have good test-retest reliability, because the construct (sleep quality) is not one expected to be necessarily stable. Just because the assessor gets two drastically different outcomes from this same test given within two weeks does not mean that the measure is unreliable. The client's sleep may actually have changed during the past two weeks.

It makes more sense to use tests that measure more enduring traits, however, to evaluate this type of reliability. Tests of cognitive ability (IQ tests), for example, purport to measure a relatively stable trait. Thus, if an assessor gives a WAIS-IV to a client twice within six months, the results should be relatively consistent. The major limitation, however, is that on many performance-based tests, there is a practice effect—that is, taking the test once actually allows a client to practice and get better at some of the tasks (e.g., Block Design). Therefore, his or her performance the second time, if not enough time has passed, will likely improve. Nevertheless, measures that test supposedly enduring or consistent traits should have good test-retest reliability.

The final kind of reliability is *internal consistency* (α). This type of reliability, without getting too technical, basically takes each item of a single test and correlates it with every single other item on the test. Again, tests that measure a single construct should be able to yield high internal consistency (as should single scales from tests that measure multiple things). For example, the narcissistic scale from the MCMI-III should have good internal consistency (a high α). All the individual items from this scale should be highly intercorrelated. If they are not, then they are not consistently measuring whatever they are measuring.

When it comes to reliability, it is important to understand which type of reliability each individual test you are considering using should logically have. Inter-rater reliability does not make sense for a computer-administered (and scored and interpreted) test such as the Continuous Performance Test,

2nd Edition (CPT-2), nor does internal consistency make sense for a performance-based psychomotor task such as the finger tapper (during which the client taps his or her finger as many times as possible in a given time limit, to test for psychomotor speed). Additionally, reliability is a prerequisite for validity—that is, there is generally no discussion of whether a measure is valid (measures what it says it measures) if the test has not yet been proven to be reliable. However, reliability alone does not imply validity. Validity must be measured separately.

Validity

Also found in publications like *Mental Measurements Yearbook* and *Tests in Print* and in individual tests' manuals are statistics on validity. Validity refers to how accurately and precisely a test measures what it is supposed to measure. For example, a test that measures depressive symptoms should in fact measure symptoms related to depression, as opposed to symptoms related to anxiety (or ability in mathematics). As with reliability, because validity is a difficult concept to prove, there are multiple types of validity to consider when looking at tests.

The first type of validity to consider is not really a true measure of how valid a test is. This type of validity is called *face validity*. Face validity has to do with how valid a test *seems* to the person taking it; that is, does the test itself seem as though it is measuring what the assessor claims it is measuring. For example, a self-report measure that is supposed to measure level of depression and asks questions about sadness, feeling "blue," and lack of interest in usual activities is high in face validity—all of those questions *seem* to be measuring depression. Face validity should not be confused with actual validity, however. Many tests may seem valid, but when actually tested for validity (i.e., compared with other measures that have been deemed valid), they do not hold up. Additionally, a lack of face validity can be an asset of a test. Malingering is much more difficult with a test that has low face validity, for example. Self-report inventories vary in their face validity (and many have validity scales), and projective measures generally have the lowest face validity. The actual validity of a measure, however, is independent of its face validity.

Content validity refers to whether the items of a test cover the range of items that are necessary to test the construct the test is supposed to measure. For example, a test of depression should obviously include items on sad mood, but it should also include items related to appetite, sleep, psychomotor and vegetative symptoms, enjoyment of activities, and all the other symptoms known to be related to depression. Most generally, content validity is evaluated by independent experts in the field, and a measure is often assumed to be content valid when it has been evaluated for other types of validity. That is, content validity is assumed to be taken care of during test development, whereas the other types of validity are generally evaluated once a measure has been completely created.

Criterion-related validity is probably the most common type of validity used to evaluate psychological tests, perhaps because it is relatively easy to understand and measure. Criterion-related validity is measured by comparing the test of interest with other, outside measures of the same construct. For example, that new test of depression can be given to a sample of clients within a clinic who are also evaluated using a SCID-I, independent clinician ratings, and a BDI. If the new measure relates well to these other measures known to accurately diagnose depression (this is even better because it includes both self-report and an independent examiner's rating), it would be said to have high criterion-related validity. Specifically, this is referred to as *concurrent validity*, because the new measure is given at the same time as the established ones.

Predictive validity relates to the new measure being administered now and the criterion (outside, valid measure of some sort) being administered in the future. A good example of this is looking at whether or not tests of cognitive ability (e.g., the Scholastic Aptitude Test [SAT]) are predictive of academic functioning in the future (e.g., as reflected by college grades). If the SAT claims to measure potential for success in college, then it should in fact do so. It should thus have predictive validity.

The final type of validity to consider when choosing tests is *construct validity*. Construct validity is generally the hardest type of validity to prove, and it is the most convincing argument that a test measures what it says it measures. Harder to assess, construct validity means that research has shown that a test is significantly associated with the theoretical trait it claims to measure. This goes beyond criterion-related validity, which relates the new test to another measure. This type of validity relates the new test to the theoretical construct itself. That test of depression should in fact measure the construct of depression (not just correlate to a BDI, which is a single self-reported measure of depression).

One of the most common ways researchers try to establish construct validity is through a multitrait, multimethod matrix. This matrix compares the new measure with established measures that test for the same construct but in a different way (a different method), as well as measures that test different constructs but in the same way as the new measure. For example, consider a new measure of depression that is performance-based (for this hypothetical new measure, it is posited that depressed individuals will respond to puzzles a certain way, so this measure uses puzzles to test for depression). A multitrait, multimethod matrix would need the new measure to be compared with (a) several measures that measure depression but in a non–performance-based way, perhaps a BDI, SCID-I, and a psychiatrist evaluation; (b) measures that specifically do *not* measure depression, but use the same method (e.g., performance-based tests such as Matrix Reasoning and Visual Puzzles from the WAIS-IV); and (c) ideally at least one measure that measures a different construct using a different method—for example, a self-reported inventory of vocational interest. The matrix would then look at associations between the new test and each of these other tests.

The new test, in attempting to establish construct validity, would need to have a high correlation with the same-trait, different-method measures (the BDI, SCID-I, and psychiatrist evaluation) and low correlation with any test that measures a different construct (Matrix Reasoning, Visual Puzzles, and the vocational interest test), even if the same method (performance-based) is used. By establishing that it is the construct that is driving the scores on the new test and not the way it is being measured, researchers can argue that they have established good construct validity of their new test. Again, research on individual tests' validity should appear in their individual test manuals, and they can also be found in publications like *Mental Measurements Yearbook* and *Tests in Print*. Tests used in the individual assessment process should be both reliable and valid.

Test Types

As has been previously presented, there are three major types of psychological test.

Self-Report, Symptom–Based Measures   The first is the self-report, symptom-based measure. These measures can take several forms, most often as surveys or structured or semi-structured interviews. The most widely used examples of such tests are the Symptom Checklist 90-Revised (SCL-90-R),

the Brief Symptom Inventory (BSI), the Structured Clinical Interview for DSM-IV Axis I Disorders (SCID-I), and the Structured Clinical Interview for DSM-IV Axis II Disorders (SCID-II). These are broad-based measures of multiple symptoms that cut across different diagnostic presentations. For children, similar measures include the Child Behavior Checklist (CBCL), the Conners Rating Scales-Revised (CRS-R), the Schedule for Affective Disorders and Schizophrenia for School-Aged Children (Kiddie SADS), and the children's version of the SCID-I (KID-SCID).

In addition to broad measures of symptoms, targeted measures of symptoms of specific disorders are widely used. Common examples of these measures include the Beck Depression Inventory (BDI), the Beck Anxiety Inventory (BAI), the Hamilton Rating Scale for Depression, and the Alcohol Use Inventory (AUI). It should be noted that there are *many* such measures that assess specific symptoms as understood by the individual being assessed. Again, it is extremely important to be aware of all the different aspects of these measures, including their appropriate use, the populations on which they were normed, and their psychometric properties, to ensure that you are using them properly.

Self-Report Inventories   The second type of psychological test is the self-report inventory. These measures, while they are still based on self-report, are qualitatively different from symptom-based measures. They take into consideration the combined responses to items on the inventory and use them to create a profile of the individual being assessed. Rather than placing importance on any one individual item (as do the symptom-based measures), these measures cluster many responses together to discern the *type* of person being evaluated. Included in these responses may indeed be individual symptoms. For example, on the Personality Assessment Inventory (PAI), there is a depression scale that has some items that ask specifically about low mood. However, many items on the depression scale of the PAI are not simply DSM-IV-TR–defined symptoms of a major depressive episode. Because the measure has many items that do not clearly fit on a single scale and because responses are on a 4-point scale (from false to very true), it is much less likely than self-report, symptom-focused measures to be biased either by the level of insight of the person being assessed or by intentional skewing of presentation. That is, many individuals being assessed may purposely skew their presentations either toward more pathological (if, for example, they are applying for disability benefits and want to appear worse off than they actually are) or toward the less pathological (which is much more common, as many individuals may be somewhat guarded when meeting an assessor, a stranger, who is probing into very personal matters).

It is important to note that one of the greatest benefits of these self-report inventory measures is that they almost invariably have safeguards built in to assess the validity of the individual's approach to the test. For example, if an individual is responding randomly to items on the measure (due to low motivation for testing or poor reading ability, for example), these self-report inventories have scales that look specifically at this style, considering pairs of items that should always be answered in the same direction. If an individual has several pairs of these items answered in opposite directions, there is evidence that he or she was responding randomly to items. Similarly, many inventories (e.g., the MCMI-III) include scales of defensiveness, exaggeration, and a tendency toward presenting oneself in an overly favorable light.

The most common examples of these self-report inventory measures are the Minnesota Multiphasic Personality Inventory, 2nd Edition (MMPI-2), the Millon Clinical Multiaxial Inventory, 3rd Edition (MCMI-III), and the Personality Assessment Inventory (PAI). Each of these measures has a slightly different focus. While the MMPI-2 has the longest history and the widest use (Butcher & Rouse, 1996), each has a slightly different focus and different strengths. For example, the PAI maps much more clearly and easily onto the DSM-IV-TR, because it was developed to discriminate between Axis I disorders. The MCMI-III is much more sensitive to personality disorders (Axis II) and character styles than the other measures, because it was developed to characterize how an individual approaches the world, including interpersonally. For adolescents, each of these measures has forms created for and normed on younger populations, including the MMPI-A (adolescent version), the Millon Adolescent Clinical Inventory (MACI), the Millon Adolescent Personality Inventory (MAPI), the Millon Preadolescent Clinical Inventory (M-PACI), and the PAI-A (adolescent version). For children, inventory measures are generally completed by caregivers. The most widely used examples of these are the Personality Inventory for Children, 2nd Edition (PIC-2) and the Behavior Assessment System for Children, 2nd Edition (BASC-2).

Performance-Based Measures   The third and final type of test for psychological assessment is the performance-based measure. These measures require the individual being assessed to perform some type of task that is evaluated by the assessor, most often by comparing performance to norms of a large sample of same-age individuals who were administered the same measure in the same way. These tests are inherently less biased by insight and motivated skewing of self-report, but they are generally indicative only of the functioning of the individual at that very moment in time, which, in turn, is highly influenced by many factors, including many that are transient. For example, if a man being assessed gets very little sleep one night, which may be unusual for him, his performance on a measure of attention may be severely compromised, while on any other day he may perform quite well on the same measure. It is important to understand this fact when interpreting all performance-based measures.

Included in the general category of performance-based measures are tests of cognitive and neuropsychological functioning and projective emotional and personality measures. General cognitive measures such as the Wechsler Adult Intelligence Scale, 4th Edition (WAIS-IV), the Stanford-Binet Intelligence Scales, 5th Edition (SB5), and the Woodcock-Johnson Tests of Cognitive Ability (WJTCA), as well as their child and adolescent counterparts, require individuals to perform multiple tasks that assess many discrete areas of cognitive functioning. Neuropsychological measures, such as the Repeatable Battery for the Assessment of Neuropsychological Status (RBANS), the Wechsler Memory Scale, 3rd Edition (WMS-III), and the Bender Visual-Motor Gestalt Test, 2nd Edition (Bender-2), along with countless other measures of specific neuropsychological functioning, similarly require performance of relatively brief tasks that assess very specific areas of functioning.

Perhaps most controversially, projective measures of personality and emotional functioning constitute the final measures that are considered performance-based. Included in this category are the Rorschach Inkblot Test, storytelling techniques such as the Thematic Apperception Test, incomplete sentence techniques such as the Rotter Incomplete Sentence Blank (RISB), and projective drawings such as the Draw-a-Person, House-Tree-Person, and Kinetic Family Drawings. Additionally, children's projective measures include the Children's Apperception Test (CAT), the Roberts Apperception Test for Children (RAT-C), HART incomplete sentence stems, and a host of other brief measures. While psychologists (and, indeed, researchers) disagree on the psychometric properties and clinical utility of projective measures, it is important to understand their strengths and weaknesses clearly before making your final judgment of them. While many are not standardized in terms of scoring and interpretation (for example, the TAT has many coding schemes, but not one widely used and accepted method of interpretation), attempts are being made to make these measures empirically stronger.

For example, with the introduction of the Comprehensive System (Exner, 2002), the Rorschach became much more standardized in terms of administration, scoring, and interpretation. With this standardization comes empirical inquiry, and again there is much support for this system's validity (though the controversy lives on; see the following section on the controversy over projective measures). The strength of projective techniques lies in their ability to bypass common defenses in psychological assessment to reveal underlying emotional and personality content. For example, because of a lack of face validity (i.e., because clients will not easily understand how the assessor will evaluate their responses), it is much harder to fake responses on the Rorschach than on a self-report measure.

Another strength of projective techniques is their ability to obtain more nuanced clinical information than standardized objective measures. For example, while a Personality Assessment Inventory (PAI) can give you levels of depression (including levels of cognitive, affective, and physiological aspects of depression), projective measures may be able to help the assessor determine the *quality* of this depression. The TAT and Rorschach, for example, may be able to uncover whether the depression is highly related to low self-esteem, loneliness, loss, helplessness, hopelessness, or some other dynamics. Even though there are objective measures of hopelessness, an assessor may not think to include it in the battery (and, in fact, an assessor could not realistically include objective measures of *every possible dynamic* that may underlie a depression); therefore, projective measures may be useful in this way. Because of the controversy over the reliability and validity of projective measures, however, they should generally *never* be used alone; their usefulness is truly within a larger battery of tests that includes objective measures and clinical impressions. One advantage of the hypothesis-testing model for psychological assessment is that each piece of data from any measure, including projective measures, is evaluated only in terms of how well it converges with data from other measures; this way, projective data are not relied on in isolation of other data.

THE CASE (CONTROVERSY) OF PROJECTIVE MEASURES

Projective techniques are controversial, and it seems they may always be controversial. Research has both supported and refuted the use of projective measures in the study of personality and emotional functioning, but perhaps more important is their origin, rooted in psychoanalytic theory focused on projecting parts or pieces of the self onto ambiguous stimuli. Somehow this concept of projection has become both taboo in the eyes of more empirically minded psychologists (at times, perhaps, so much so that the emotional reaction does not allow for fair appraisal of the research literature) and heavily relied on in clinical practice (again, perhaps at times to the point that practitioners turn a blind eye to evidence against their validity).

Despite all the controversy in the literature on projective techniques, they are simply in high clinical demand—clinicians use and rely on them frequently (Hammer, 1997; Pattee, 1994). Even the strong proponents of their utility, however, must understand that their usefulness and validity improve significantly when used not in isolation but in conjunction with other measures of personality and emotional functioning (Weiner, 1966). Finding a way to appreciate what they can add, while remaining humble, skeptical, and conservative about the data they produce, is extremely difficult (perhaps again because of the emotional reaction psychologists tend to have about projective measures), and this is where the hypothesis-testing model, aggregating data across tests to build evidence for themes, can be most helpful.

The four most widely used projective measures of personality and emotional functioning are sentence-completion tasks (e.g., the Rotter Incomplete Sentence Blank), the Thematic Apperception Test (TAT), projective drawings (including the Draw-a-Person, the House-Tree-Person, and Kinetic Family Drawings), and, of course, the (notorious) Rorschach Inkblot Test. Research has proven, unequivocally, that establishing the validity or invalidity of these measures is extremely difficult. For each published article establishing some valid use of one of them, there is an equally compelling article criticizing its validity, and vice versa. However, researchers seem to be actively trying to *improve* the validity of these measures, most often by creating and researching a more standardized approach for coding, scoring, and interpreting them.

(Continued)

A good example of this attempt to improve validity of a widely used projective measure is the Rotter Incomplete Sentence Blank (RISB), one of several projective measures that use sentence stems as the stimulus and clients' completion of these sentence stems as the projective data. While most often used to provide nuanced, intuitive data for assessments such that clinicians glean what they imagine to be significant from responses or interpret them based on their own, generally psychoanalytic, theory, this method is extremely difficult to evaluate for reliability or validity, as it is so necessarily unstandardized. Even unstandardized, researchers found that they could consistently discriminate between certain pathological and non-pathological populations, including youth who are delinquent as opposed to those who are not and individuals who use drugs as opposed to those who do not (Fuller, Parmelee, & Carroll, 1982; Gardner, 1967), suggesting some degree of reliability, validity, and utility for the test itself.

More recently, however, Rotter and his colleagues have created an objective scoring system that is proving to have both good reliability (Rotter, Lah, & Rafferty, 1992) and good validity (Haak, 1990; Lah, 1989). While this scoring system is not yet widely enough used to evaluate its util-ity, it represents significant progress toward establishing a more reliable and valid method for using the RISB.

In some ways easier and in some ways more difficult to evaluate is the Thematic Apperception Test (TAT). The TAT utilizes black and white, some-what ambiguous prints that for the most part include pictures of people within them as stimuli and stories produced by the client as the projective data. With a long and varied history of use, the TAT has spawned countless different scoring and interpretive methods, so many that evaluating the psychometrics of the TAT as a test itself becomes extremely difficult. While the sheer number of systems can be frustrating, the fact that so many researchers have attempted to improve the test's reliability and validity is heartening. Historically, the psychometric properties of the TAT have been found to be extremely weak (e.g., Winter & Stewart, 1977); however many attempts have been made to rectify this by creating standardized, researchable methods of interpretation (Bellak & Abrams, 1997; Groth-Marnat, 2009; Meyer, 2004). Certainly progress has been made toward this end (Tuerlinckx, De Boeck, & Lens, 2002).

Less hopeful and more frustrating have been attempts to validate projec-tive drawing tasks, such as the Draw-a-Person, the House-Tree-Person, and the Kinetic Family Drawings. Projective drawing tasks have no presented stimulus; rather, they require the client to produce drawings from scratch (of a person and another person of the opposite sex; of a house, tree, and person; or of a family doing something together) and use this as interpretable projective data. While some researchers have found this technique to be valid in discriminating between individuals with and without mental illness and to predict psychological adjustment in general (Cohen, Hammer, & Singer, 1988; Hammer, 1997; Lehman & Levy, 1971; Yama, 1990), others have found it to fail to discriminate even between patients with severe schizophrenia and those without any mental illness (Wanderer, 1969). In fact, in general, researchers have found interpretation to be highly affected by nonprojective influences, such as artistic ability and general intellectual functioning (Feher, VandeCreek, & Teglasi, 1983). In addition, most research has uncovered the poor psychometric properties of projective drawings in general and has failed to produce any evidence of their validity (Killian & Campbell, 1987; Piotrowski, 1984).

Regardless of these failures to validate the technique, clinicians still widely use the drawings within assessment batteries, and many clinicians and even researchers believe that they can help evaluate a client's general level of adjustment (Hammer, 1997). Projective drawing tasks are widely used, and there is no evidence that their use will stop at any point soon. Thus, finding a way to incorporate data produced by them into a larger battery that includes objective measures is extremely important.

By far the most controversial projective measure in the literature is the Rorschach. Although several coding/scoring and interpretive systems have been developed, the most widely used is the Comprehensive System (CS), developed by Exner and his colleagues (2002). Although they genuinely seem to have attempted to make the Comprehensive System as psychometrically sound as possible, researchers have found significant flaws in their methodology and in fact in validity studies in general. Some have found that approximately half of the variables in the CS have suboptimal reliability (Acklin, McDowell, Verschell, & Chan, 2000) and that many of the scores are not valid (Lilienfeld, Wood, & Garb, 2000). In fact, entire books have been dedicated to questioning the validity of the CS (Wood, Nezworski, Lilienfeld, & Garb, 2003).

Additionally, many have contended that the CS tends to overpathologize individuals, which would be related to real problems with the normative sample used in Exner's original norming process (Grove, Barden, Garb, & Lilienfeld, 2002; Shaffer, Erdberg, & Haroian, 1999; Wood, Nezworski, Garb, & Lilienfeld, 2001). Others, however, contend that the CS has good inter-rater and test-retest reliability (Grønnerød, 2003; Viglione & Hilsenroth,

(Continued)

2001) and good incremental and broad validity (Bornstein & Masling, 2005; Exner & Erdberg, 2005; Viglione, 1999; Viglione & Hilsenroth, 2001). International studies have found scores in different countries (including some in Europe and Central America) to be similar, suggesting at least some consistency across culture.

Meyer (2004) found that the CS had validity similar to other instruments, including both medical and psychological measures, and others found it on average to be as valid as the MMPI-2 (Hiller, Rosenthal, Bornstein, Berry, & Brunell-Neuleib, 1999; Rosenthal, Hiller, Bornstein, Berry, & Brunell-Neuleib, 2001), finding that it had greater validity than the MMPI-2 on criteria that were objective, whereas the MMPI-2 demonstrated greater validity on criteria using self-report scales and psychiatric diagnoses. Grønnerød (2004) found it to have validity equivalent to other instruments based on self- or clinician-reported ratings.

To reconcile all these disagreements in the literature, some have proposed reconceptualizing the Rorschach not as a projective measure but rather as a performance-based information-gathering method (McGrath, 2008). While this does not solve the problems in the literature with reliability and validity, it seems to align with a way of treating the data produced by the Rorschach CS as not without possible error, data that should be considered along with multiple other measures of emotional and personality functioning.

Unfortunately, the controversy over projective techniques in psychological assessment seems unlikely to be reconciled any time soon. The reality of clinical practice of assessment is that many, if not most, practitioners use projective measures, even if they find them only anecdotally useful and employ their own intuitive methods for interpreting them. The research literature on projectives is nowhere near clear-cut enough to recommend either adopting or abandoning the measures, though it is certainly convincing enough to warrant careful and conservative use of them. Data should be understood clearly within the context of where they came from—knowing that the Rorschach can potentially overpathologize, for example, can help the assessor take extreme results that are found on the Rorschach and no other measure slightly less seriously. The Hypothesis Testing Method necessarily incorporates a conservative and humble use of projective techniques, given that data that converge on other tests' results are viewed as more convincing and useful.

PRACTICAL CONSIDERATIONS

In addition to the specific characteristics of tests, deciding what tests to use often depends on practical considerations. Most important are the time and cost associated with the use of the tests under consideration. A balance must always be struck between getting *enough* data from tests and creating an assessment protocol that is not overly cumbersome and ultimately prohibitive. Although more data is always better, there comes a point in every assessment when you can make confident conclusions without the addition of extra information. Some tests (e.g., the Wechsler intelligence scales) have shorter forms. The Wechsler Abbreviated Scale of Intelligence (WASI) is a four-subtest cognitive measure that assesses cognitive functioning in a much less specific way than the WAIS-IV; entire domains of functioning (working memory and processing speed) are not included. However, if it is clear that the presenting problem has nothing to do with cognitive functioning, it may be worth using this significantly shorter measure, because the extra information obtained by the WAIS-IV is unlikely to be significantly more useful in the conclusions drawn.

For example, an extremely cognitively high-functioning individual who was recently bereaved may require more emotional testing than cognitive, and a full WAIS-IV is unlikely to add critical information to the fact that his educational and occupational functioning is extremely good. Other measures have short forms as well; the most important caveat when considering short forms of measures is to check the psychometric properties of the short forms, as they will have been assessed separately from the longer forms. In addition to time, the cost of tests can also affect the decision of which to use. Although this chapter will not address specifics about test cost, it is important just to note that this is a factor involved in the decision process.

Other practical considerations in test selection include the age and functional capacity of the individual being assessed. Every test is developed and normed on a specific age group, and this should be presented clearly in the test's manual. Using a test with an individual who is outside of the age range it was normed on means you will be comparing his or her performance inappropriately with that of others of different ages. Similarly, you must consider the level of functioning of the individual to make sure each test will be appropriate. An adult whose cognitive functioning is extremely impaired and who has a second-grade reading level should not be administered the PAI, for example, because the items were written at a fourth-grade reading level.

Multicultural Concerns

This text does not specifically address the multicultural concerns associated with individual tests, but it is important to note that much research has been conducted on many psychological tests to determine specific cultural biases and whether there are specific populations for which certain tests are less effective. For an excellent survey of cultural considerations for specific tests, see Suzuki, Ponterotto, and Meller's (2008) *Handbook of Multicultural Assessment (Clinical, Psychological, and Educational Applications) (3rd ed.)*. It is important to note that, as stated in the Introduction, no test is perfect. No individual measure can be entirely free of cultural bias, and no test is optimal for use with every single population. Thus, it is important to be vigilant about the research on use of individual tests on different cultural populations. Because with the hypothesis testing model you are simply building up data from which to draw conclusions, the data based on interpretations of individual tests should be tempered by the consideration of how well the tests perform within the culture of the individual you are assessing. This topic is discussed further in Chapter 3, "Testing."

Familiarity

The final practical concern of import when deciding which tests to use in a battery is your own specific knowledge, training, and familiarity with the tests themselves. Ethical use of measures requires specific training on each individual measure, including supervised use of the tests. Even when an update to a measure is introduced (e.g., when the WAIS-IV was introduced as an update to the WAIS-III), you must undergo specific training on the measure, no matter how apparently similar it is to the original. There may be subtle differences that can easily go unnoticed but are extremely important in the administration, scoring, or interpretation of the new tests, so specific training must be undertaken. The more tests you are trained in, the more options you will have in your future career as an assessor for building effective assessment batteries. For example, many psychologists are trained only in the MMPI-2, which leaves them with only one option for selecting a self-report inventory measure, leaving out options that might be equally or more appropriate such as the MCMI-III or the PAI. These clinicians are limited in how well they can perform assessments in the future, especially if an assessment specifically calls for one of these other self-report measures. While all psychologists will have preferences, even *favorites*, when it comes to test selection, simply having the *option* to use more and different tests is an important part of being a well-rounded assessor.

PSYCHOLOGICAL ASSESSMENT MEASURES

This section presents some of the most widely used measures of psychological assessment in the broad domains of adult and child cognitive and personality/emotional testing. The purpose of this list is to give a broad overview of the utility of individual tests. The list is by no means exhaustive, and (obviously) training in each of these tests is absolutely necessary before it can be used in a psychological assessment.

Cognitive Assessment

When assessing cognitive functioning in adults, there are various performance-based measures from which to choose. Some are broad measures of overall abilities (such as the WAIS-IV), whereas some are more direct, individual measures of specific cognitive abilities (such as the Trail Making Test). It is important to note that many cognitive abilities are discrete, such that performance in one area of cognitive functioning may be relatively independent from performance in another area. Think about verbal functioning and nonverbal functioning. There are many individuals who are extremely "intelligent" when it comes to verbal functioning (they are able to use and understand language to a very high degree), but many of these people struggle when trying to read a map (this example is made without judgment about asking for directions). These cognitive abilities, verbal and map-reading, are relatively independent.

However, there are many cognitive abilities that are hierarchical and dependent on one another. For example, consider memory. Memory is a complex cognitive process that includes many steps. When considering the cognitive abilities of memory and attention, for example, you would not expect an individual with extremely poor attention to perform well on a measure of memory. If the information presented originally did not enter into the individual's mind because he or she was so distracted by other stimuli (as is often the case with poor attention), then how would he or she be expected to remember that information? These kinds of relationships are what make cognitive assessment of individuals complicated.

Table 2.1 lists some of the most widely used tests of cognitive functioning. Again, for comprehensive discussions of each of these tests, see either their respective manuals or such texts as Groth-Marnat's (2009) *Handbook of Psychological Assessment (5th ed.)* or Sattler's (2008) *Assessment of Children: Cognitive Foundations (5th ed.)*.

Personality and Emotional Assessment

As discussed previously, there are many measures of personality and emotional functioning. Whereas cognitive assessment is almost exclusively performed using performance-based assessments, personality and emotional assessments generally include self-report, symptom-focused measures, self-report inventory measures, and some performance-based measures. Additionally, whereas many of the individual domains of cognitive functioning can be assessed using a single test (or even a subtest), assessment of personality and emotional functioning necessitates the use of multiple measures in order to rule out or confirm hypotheses about individual functioning. That is, a single performance-based measure such as the CPT-2 can rule out the likelihood of attention problems, but in order to rule out depression, several measures using different methods are needed.

For example, using *only* a SCID-I to assess depression will provide little more information than a clinical interview asking about depressive symptoms. Because the SCID-I is a self-report, symptom-focused measure, if an individual wants you to know that he or she is depressed, he or she will tell you so. If not, though, the individual can simply hide the fact that he or she is depressed. Inventories and performance-based measures are less susceptible (though not impervious) to these individual, situation-specific motivational factors. On the other hand, performance-based measures such as the Rorschach or TAT have debatable validity and certainly have more potential for error. Thus, in order to assess for depression, using multiple measures

TABLE 2.1	**WIDELY USED COGNITIVE ASSESSMENT INSTRUMENTS AND TESTS**	
	Adult Assessment	**Child Assessment**
General Intellectual Functioning	• Wechsler Adult Intelligence Scale, 4th Edition (WAIS-IV) • Stanford-Binet Intelligence Scales, 5th Edition (SB5) • Woodcock-Johnson Tests of Cognitive Ability (WJTCA)	• Wechsler Intelligence Scale for Children, 4th Edition (WISC-IV) • Wechsler Preschool and Primary Scale of Intelligence, 3rd Edition (WPPSI-III) • Stanford-Binet Intelligence Scales, 5th Edition (SB5) • Woodcock-Johnson Tests of Cognitive Ability (WJTCA)
Mental Status	• Mini-Mental State Exam (MMSE)	• Mini-Mental State Exam (MMSE)
Visual-Motor Integrative Functioning (Note: Most broad measures of intellectual functioning also have measures of visual-motor integrative functioning)	• Bender Visual-Motor Gestalt Test, 2nd Edition (Bender-2) • Beery-Buktenica • Developmental Test of Visual-Motor Integration, 5th Edition (Beery-VMI)	• Bender Visual-Motor Gestalt Test, 2nd Edition (Bender-2) • Beery-Buktenica Developmental Test of Visual-Motor Integration, 5th Edition (Beery-VMI)
Verbal Functioning (Note: Most broad measures of intellectual functioning also have measures of verbal functioning)	• Peabody Picture Vocabulary Test, 4th Edition (PPVT-4)	• Peabody Picture Vocabulary Test, 4th Edition (PPVT-4)
Nonverbal Functioning (Note: Most broad measures of intellectual functioning also have measures of nonverbal functioning)	• Test of Nonverbal Intelligence, 3rd Edition (TONI-3) • Raven's Progressive Matrices	• Test of Nonverbal Intelligence, 3rd Edition (TONI-3) • Raven's Progressive Matrices
Attention	• Test of Everyday Attention (TEA) • Conners Continuous Performance Test, 2nd Edition (CPT-2)	• Test of Everyday Attention for Children (TEA-Ch) • Conners Continuous Performance Test, 2nd Edition (CPT-2)

(Continued)

TABLE 2.1   *(CONTINUED)*

	Adult Assessment	Child Assessment
Memory	• Repeatable Battery for the Assessment of Neuropsychological Status (RBANS) • Wechsler Memory Scale, Fourth Edition (WMS-IV) • Rey Auditory Verbal Learning Test • California Visual Retention Test • Bender Visual-Motor Gestalt Test, 2nd Edition (Bender-2)	• Bender Visual-Motor Gestalt Test, 2nd Edition (Bender-2) • Children's Memory Scale (CMS) • NEPSY, 2nd Edition (NEPSY-II)
Academic Achievement	• Wechsler Individual Achievement Test, 2nd Edition (WIAT-2) • Woodcock-Johnson Tests of Achievement, 3rd Edition (WJ III ACH)	• Wechsler Individual Achievement Test, 2nd Edition (WIAT-2) • Woodcock-Johnson Tests of Achievement, 3rd Edition (WJ III ACH)
Working Memory/ Executive Functioning (Note: Many broad measures of intellectual functioning also have measures of working memory functioning)	• Trail Making Test • Wisconsin Card Sorting Test (WCST)	• Trail Making Test • Wisconsin Card Sorting Test (WCST)

improves the confidence of your findings. Table 2.2 presents many of the most widely used tests to assess personality and emotional functioning.

Other Assessment

Not included in these lists of tests are more complex neuropsychological tests; for a list of these, see Lezak, Howieson, Loring, Hannay, & Fischer's *Neuropsychological Assessment (4th ed.)* (2004). Additionally, a comprehensive list of vocational assessments, including the Myers–Briggs Type Indicator (MBTI), the Strong Interest Inventory (SII), and the Self-Directed Search (SDS) can be found in texts like Kapes and Whitfield's *A Counselor's Guide to Career Assessment Instruments (4th ed.)* (2001).

TABLE 2.2	**WIDELY USED PERSONALITY AND EMOTIONAL INSTRUMENTS AND TESTS**	
	Adult Assessment	**Child Assessment (most of the self-report measures are completed by a guardian, teacher, or other adult figure)**

Self-Report, Symptom-Focused Measures

	Adult Assessment	Child Assessment
General Symptomatology	• Structured Clinical Interview for the DSM-IV Axis I Disorders (SCID-I) • Structured Clinical Interview for the DSM-IV Axis II Personality Disorders (SCID-II) • Symptom Checklist 90-Revised (SCL 90-R) • Brief Symptom Inventory (BSI)	• Schedule for Affective Disorders and Schizophrenia for School-Aged Children (Kiddie SADS) • Children's Version of the SCID-I (KID-SCID) • Child Behavior Checklist (CBCL)
Specific Psychopathology	• Beck Depression Inventory (BDI) • Beck Anxiety Inventory (BAI) • Anxiety Disorders Interview Schedule (ADIS) • State-Trait Anxiety Inventory	• Conners Rating Scales, Revised (CRS-R) • Children's Depression Inventory (CDI)
Self-Report Inventory Measures	• Minnesota Multiphasic Personality Inventory, 2nd Edition (MMPI-2) • Millon Clinical Multiaxial Inventory, 3rd Edition (MCMI-III) • Personality Assessment Inventory (PAI)	• Personality Inventory for Children, 2nd Edition (PIC-2) • Behavior Assessment System for Children, 2nd Edition (BASC-2) • Minnesota Multiphasic Personality Inventory, Adolescent Version (MMPI-A) • Millon Preadolescent Clinical Inventory (M-PACI) • Millon Adolescent Clinical Inventory (MACI)
Performance-Based Measures	• Rorschach Inkblot Test, Comprehensive System (Rorschach) • Thematic Apperception Test (TAT) • House-Tree-Person, Draw-a-Person, Kinetic Family, and other Projective Drawings • Rotter Incomplete Sentence Blank (RISB)	• Rorschach Inkblot Test, Comprehensive System (Rorschach) • Children's Apperception Test (CAT) • Roberts Apperception Test for Children, 2nd Edition (RATC) • House-Tree-Person, Draw-a-Person, Kinetic Family, and Other Projective Drawings • Rotter Incomplete Sentence Blank (RISB)

SUMMARY

When selecting tests, there are two overarching issues to consider:

1. What questions do you need answered to address your hypotheses? and
2. Do you know and trust everything about the tests themselves?

There is no substitute or replacement for specific training on the appropriate administration, scoring, and interpretation of individual measures. Part of this training should include a clear understanding of all the different psychometric properties, practical considerations, benefits, and potential "blind spots" of each test. No test is perfect, and no single test will prove a hypothesis definitively (which is why you need a degree to conduct psychological assessment). Taken together, though, in conjunction with clinical and collateral information and clinical observation, individual tests can help you build a solid argument in order to rule out some hypotheses and support others.

CHAPTER 3

Testing

There are several textbooks that focus exclusively on the testing step of the psychological assessment process. This step includes the administration, scoring, and interpretation of individual psychological assessment measures. These texts are generally either organized such that each chapter is a specific test (e.g., Groth-Marnat, 2009; Lezak, Howieson, Loring, Hannay, & Fischer, 2004; Sattler, 2008; Weiner & Greene, 2007) or focus entirely on a single test (e.g., Exner, 2002; Graham, 2006; Millon & Bloom, 2008; Morey, 1996), and without thorough knowledge and skill in this most primary step of the assessment process, no psychological assessment can be valid. While the entire process of psychological assessment has been and will remain relatively consistent, tests themselves change constantly due to improvements, updated norming, and advancements from research. As such, competence in psychological assessment is often equated with updated knowledge of exactly how to use the most recent tests and versions of tests. Again, you cannot be competent at psychological assessment without being extremely knowledgeable and skilled at the testing process. This chapter presents a few general considerations for testing, rather than detailed information about specific testing instruments.

PREPARING FOR TESTING

Cultural Considerations

Psychological tests do not measure constructs consistently across every person from every culture. Consequently, it is extremely important to understand the impact culture can have on performance of any test. For example, when the MMPI-2 is given to samples of clients with the same diagnoses, clients from different ethnic backgrounds, even from similar national cultures, register differently on individual scales (Suzuki, Ponterotto, & Meller, 2008). Even this nuanced, small detail is important in understanding how to interpret a test given to any client. At times, the cultural background of the client may even preclude you from giving a specific test, simply because it has not been appropriately normed on that population. You cannot blindly assume that a test's normative sample is representative of the entire national population—it is even less so for the entire international population. You should read the test's manual carefully to understand the cultural makeup of the normative sample; then you should look for the empirical research on use of those individual tests on clients with cultural backgrounds similar to the background of the client you are testing. Suzuki, Ponterotto, and Meller's (2008) book is an excellent resource for understanding the impact of culture on the assessment process.

Age Considerations

Assessing individuals of different ages entails very different approaches to testing. Obviously, the tests themselves are different for testing adults and for testing children (e.g., a WAIS-IV vs. a WISC-IV). Beyond different tests, though, age considerations can impact even the type of information you gather for an assessment. When assessing adults, you are often limited to self-report and individual testing measures; occasionally, you may have other resources available, such as a case worker, a spouse, a current therapist, or previous medical records. Most often, however, you must rely almost entirely on the client himself or herself for background information.

When assessing children and adolescents, however, assessments generally include a much more complex matrix of reporters of background information. Collateral interviews with parents are most common, but interviews and collateral-report measures with teachers, principals, counselors, and other important figures in the children's lives are common. In addition, many assessors conduct school visits to observe child clients in their school environment (it is rare, though not unheard of, that an assessor would visit an adult client's place of work to observe him or her there). Strategizing about how to collect as much data as possible on child cases is important when preparing to assess children, and engaging as many sources of information as possible is usually the best strategy.

The other major consideration that differentiates preparing to assess a child client from assessing an adult is the structure of the testing itself. Children become fatigued and lose concentration much more easily than (most) adults. As a result, you should prepare to both shorten sessions as needed, as well as to balance the measures administered to child clients as much as possible. That is, you must take into consideration what is likely to hold a child's attention, as well as to produce the most motivation from him or her. For example, administering a Bender-2, WISC-IV, and WIAT-II in the same session will likely prove unmanageable for most children (not to mention most assessors). Three cognitive tests in a row (especially long ones like the WISC-IV and the WIAT-II) will likely produce wandering attention, waning motivation, and flat-out fatigue by the end. You would expect a child to perform more poorly toward the end of the testing session than at the beginning.

Three strategies are most useful for addressing this problem: shortening sessions, providing interim activities for reinforcement, and varying the types of tests administered. At times, sessions must simply be cut short because the child has lost interest or motivation. However, having several games or activities at the ready before the testing session begins may prove extremely useful; some children need a quick game of toy basketball or running around in between tests to motivate them to continue, while others need different reinforcement—drawing or writing on a chalkboard, for example. Board games with quick, easy play can be invaluable (e.g., Connect 4), but board games that require longer, extended play may distract too much from the testing session. Plan carefully what may reinforce, in between tests, the child's ability to concentrate on the tests when he or she is supposed to.

Finally, varying the types of tests administered as you go will help reduce fatigue from the monotony of taking the same type of test over and over. For example, after administering a WISC-IV (if there is still time left in the session, and the child is not too exhausted), consider giving a drawing task (e.g., Projective Drawings) or a projective storytelling task (e.g., the Children's Apperception Test or the Roberts Apperception Test for Children). This way, after having had to concentrate and use their "school brain" for one test, they can switch to a more imaginative, playful measure. While this is also not a bad strategy to use when testing adults, it is almost necessary when testing most children.

When and Where to Test

Most testing occurs in therapy offices, consultation rooms, or specifically designated testing rooms. However, there are times when this is not necessarily possible. Some considerations are important when deciding where to test a client, and this generally has to do with normative procedures of the majority of the testing instruments available. Specifically, as you are generally trying to get the optimal performance out of the client (optimal, in this case, meaning that the client gives effortful attempts with a minimum of error caused by the client, the assessor, or the environment), you should find a *neutral* area in which to test. Neutral areas generally consist of rooms with very little distraction, including intrusive noises, excessive decorations, or some sort of emotional connection with the client. Testing a client in his or her home, for example, opens the testing itself to a great deal of error—phones are more likely to ring and distract the testing; people are more likely to walk in and affect the performance of the client; and being in a certain, familiar room may impact the way the client responds to certain measures. In general, most tests are normed in neutral places, so introducing such emotional attachment and familiarity to the place of testing may introduce a systematic source of error. As such, it is best to find an unfamiliar, quiet, calm, *neutral* place in which to administer tests.

Deciding when to do testing can be tricky. Choosing the optimal times of administering tests may simply not be feasible, given your and your clients' schedules, so at times you must simply settle for whenever you can meet. However, you must understand how this could impact the testing itself. For example, it is always best not to do testing before or during mealtimes—you do not want clients to be impacted by hunger, low blood sugar, or tiredness. However, this may simply not be possible. Children have school all day and may be able to meet only at 4:00 or 5:00 P.M. Adults may not be able to miss work and may be able to meet only at 6:00 P.M. These are not optimal times, because they overlap with mealtimes and follow a long day of work or school; as a result, the client may be tired. While this may be unavoidable, you should (a) do everything you can to make the conditions of testing such that the client is less likely to be tired, such as asking him or her to bring a snack and having shorter, less ambitious testing sessions; and (b) understand, during interpretation, that this may impact the client's performance on the tests. As stated previously, test order can help counteract the effects of being tired or hungry, such that you do not have a 4-hour session beginning with easier measures and ending with measures that require concentration. For example, when giving the Repeatable Battery for the Assessment of Neuropsychological Status (RBANS), which requires great concentration, short- and long-term memory, and active mental processing, it is best to give this at the beginning of any given session, rather than after several other measures. Projective storytelling tasks, such as the TAT, however, are less affected by fatigue, so they can occur later in a session.

Building Rapport

While, in general, rapport is built during the clinical interview (usually the first phase of the assessment process), it is important to understand your role as an assessor, which is different from the role of a therapist. When testing, it can often seem robotic and harsh (usually because you must read directions verbatim out of a manual), and this can be a stark contrast from your demeanor during the clinical interview. What is important to understand about your role, however, is your own professional boundaries when you are conducting an assessment. Again, this can be a balancing act between warmth and structure. A client may not be open, even in projective and objective personality measures, with an assessor he or she finds cold, or simply does not like. However, too much empathy may make a client uncomfortable, as it is coming from a stranger. Rapport is extremely important in assessment, though finding the balance between warmth and structure is not always easy.

Your primary role during the testing phase of an assessment is to administer the tests as accurately as possible—that is, your administration of the tests should be by the book and standardized so that they are comparable to how the normative sample received them. Consider, for example, that you decided during the WAIS-IV to both inform and congratulate a client every time he arrives at a correct answer (which is *not* part of the standard administration). This could impact the approach the client takes to the test in significant ways—for example, becoming so discouraged when an answer is incorrect that he loses motivation to continue, "beating himself up" about it. This makes it impossible to compare him directly with the normative sample, who were administered the test in a different way. While this might improve rapport, your primary role as an assessor is to administer the tests in a valid way.

There are times, however, when you must flip to the other side of the continuum of structure. Consider, for example, that an individual is filling out a Personality Assessment Inventory (PAI) and endorses items that he or she is having suicidal thoughts. At this point during the testing, after the standard administration of the test, you would likely become more of a therapist in your role with the client, assessing for suicidality and empathizing with his or her difficulty. You may choose to postpone any more testing for that day and spend the rest of the session simply processing the suicidality (and what it was like for him or her to reveal it to you). Your professional boundaries in a situation like this may shift from the standard administrator of tests to the caring professional that you are. Warmth, empathy, and humor, while they may not be as present during the actual test administration, are absolutely appropriate between tests, at the beginning and ending of sessions, and at any other point during the assessment.

TESTING

Standard Administration

The first and most fundamental skill in the testing process is standard and accurate administration of the tests themselves. The importance of standardized administration cannot be overstated. Because performance on tests is almost always gauged by comparing the score achieved by an individual client with the scores achieved by a large normative sample, you must ensure that the way the person you are assessing receives the test is the same as everyone in that normative sample received it. This is the only way that you can confidently compare the individual's performance with that of his or her peers (i.e., the normative sample). In the best-case scenario, an error in administration of a test is minor and will likely not affect the score drastically.

Take, for example, administration of the Similarities subtest on the Wechsler Intelligence Scale for Children, 4th Edition (WISC-IV). A minor administration error might be over-querying on a single response. That is, because some responses to questions require queries (prompts for further information, in order to give the respondent an opportunity to improve his or her response) and some do not, if you queried a response that explicitly does not need a query, this would constitute a minor error. But this error could be easily corrected in the next stage of the testing process—you would simply score the response as if you had not queried, and it would not affect the subtest score. More subtly, making multiple errors of this kind could still affect the test. For example, if you consistently over-query, the individual being assessed may get frustrated or may feel that he or she is performing worse than he or she actually is. This may subtly affect his or her subsequent performance.

At its worst, poor administration can cause a test to be completely invalid or unscorable. Take, for example, the Letter-Word Identification subtest of the Woodcock-Johnson Tests of Achievement, 3rd Edition (WJ-III). This is a relatively straightforward subtest in which the individual being assessed is visually presented a list of written words to pronounce aloud. There are specific rules to reach basal (getting a certain number of consecutive items correct, such that there is a great possibility that all the unadministered items below that, which are theoretically easier, would likely be correct, and thus the individual is given credit for them) and ceiling (getting a certain number of consecutive items incorrect, such that it is likely that the unadministered items above that, which are theoretically harder, would be incorrect, and thus the subtest is discontinued). From the start point, the individual must get six consecutive items correct in order to reach basal for this subtest and receive credit for the lower unadministered items.

If he or she does not reach basal, lower items must be administered, until either the lowest six consecutive items administered are correct or the first item is administered. An error in administration for this subtest could include not reaching basal but not reversing appropriately. Not reaching basal invalidates a subtest because you cannot get an accurate score for it—you can no longer assume (by convention) that all of the items below the first administered item would have been correct, so you cannot get an accurate score to compare with a normative sample. Thus, there would be no way of knowing, compared to others his or her age or in his or her grade level, how well the individual reads words.

In between these best- and worst-case scenarios lie many errors in administration that can affect either an individual's performance on a test or the ultimate score of it. Incorrect placement of stimulus items, not reading the directions verbatim, errors in recording the responses, and countless other minor errors can affect the testing. This is the reason that training focuses (and rightly so) intensely on the testing process.

As an illustration, while you are training on specific tests, you should try an exercise that is analogous to the effects of improper administration (though it is truly an exercise on problems with scoring tests). The first time you administer a WAIS-IV, calculate all of the Index and IQ scores before your teacher or supervisor has helped you correct the scores of the individual items or subtests. Compare the final scores with those you calculate from the same WAIS-IV after it has been corrected for minor scoring errors. Sometimes it may even out, but you may be surprised just how much minor errors can affect the ultimate scores.

A similar exercise may come up when you are learning the Comprehensive System for the Rorschach. The first time you try to code a protocol on your own, enter those scores into the scoring program you are using (e.g., the RIAP-5 or the Ror-SCAN). Then enter the corrected protocol into the same program and see just how much difference those small errors make in the conclusions drawn from the test. Although these are really exercises about errors in scoring, they are analogous to what can happen with small administration errors, as these administration errors can easily affect scoring in a small way. These exercises emphasize just how important correct and standardized administration of tests is for the tests to give accurate, reliable, and valid information about the person being assessed.

Cultural Considerations

There may be rare occasions when slight variations from the standardized procedure may be warranted, though this should be done thoughtfully and avoided if possible. When a client comes from a group underrepresented by the normative sample of a specific test, for example, the standardized administration becomes less important, as interpretation will be conducted within the context of understanding that comparing the client to the normative sample is not necessarily valid. Additionally, in certain cases, especially when for cultural reasons a client is not entirely acquainted with the assessment or psychotherapeutic process, slight alterations in the standardized administration procedure may be necessary in the service of maintaining or building any sort of alliance. Whenever standardized procedures are altered, it is extremely important that the assessor understand exactly how that might affect the scores on the test, such that interpretation is consistent with these alterations.

Testing the Limits

The testing process can be affected by many factors. It is hoped that tests are *most* affected by whatever they are measuring. For example, it is hoped that cognitive tests are most affected by the level of cognitive functioning of the individual being tested; similarly, it is hoped that emotional measures are most affected by the emotional state of the person and that a memory test is affected by his or her memory functioning. However, there are many other factors that can impact performance on individual psychological tests. Performance can be affected by very transient state factors, such as tiredness from not sleeping well the night before. It can also be affected by motivational factors, such that boredom, carelessness, purposely trying to perform poorly (even as far as malingering), and other factors can alter performance on individual tests.

Because many factors can impact performance on any one test, there are times when you may need to "test the limits." That is, you may need to go back and alter the standard administration of a test (a) to assess whether something is getting in the way of the individual's performance, (b) to find out whether the individual has potential for higher functioning, or (c) to evaluate the meaning of some responses more deeply. There are many different ways to test the limits, so many things fall under the testing-the-limits umbrella. For example, if you think that an individual being tested knows a word presented in the Vocabulary subtest of the WAIS-IV but earned 0 points, you could later go back and ask specifically about that word in several different ways, such as asking the individual to use it in a sentence or asking about related forms of the word (this would be a type of testing the limits to find out whether there might have been motivational factors involved originally or if the problem originally was with expressive ability, rather than knowledge of the word itself).

Another example would be if an individual reached ceiling on a subtest, and you went back later and administered some items that are above the ceiling that were originally unadministered, to see if there is in fact potential for higher functioning than the subtest score itself reported. If you had questions about the specific content of a response, you could test the limits by later going back to the response itself and asking specific probing questions about it. For example, if a child's response to an item on the Vocabulary subtest of the WISC-IV or to a Thematic Apperception Test (TAT) card related to a very in-depth description of fear, you may go back to the response later and ask whether the child has ever experienced that type of fear and in what situation. Because all of these procedures are outside of the standard administration of the tests, they are considered testing the limits. But they can each yield extremely important data to use when you are interpreting everything together. Testing the limits illustrates one major reason that the process of psychological assessment has not been entirely computerized from beginning to end—computers can reliably administer, score, and now even interpret many tests, but nuanced clinical data and interpretation cannot be adequately obtained without a trained assessor.

The most crucial aspect of testing the limits is the fact that it is *outside of the standard administration* of the test itself. That is, you must complete the *entire* standardized administration of a test *before* you can go back and test the limits. Testing the limits could significantly affect how the individual performs on the rest of the test if it were conducted in the middle of the test's administration; it could affect his or her confidence level, emotional state, level of fatigue or any other minor (or major) factor that could affect the rest of the testing. Therefore, testing the limits must happen only after you have completed the entire, standard administration of the test. This way, you have *both* the results of the comparison-based, normative results of tests *and* more nuanced, clinical data that can help you in interpreting those normative results and in conceptualizing all the data together later in the assessment process.

Scoring Tests

Coding Versus Scoring

Although this is not a general convention in the testing process, it may be helpful to differentiate between the processes of coding and scoring. In general, coding is the process of applying a coding system to the responses of an individual being assessed. Scoring, in contrast, is the computation of scores based on cumulative and composite numbers derived from coded responses. For example, on the WAIS-IV Vocabulary subtest, you will have to decide whether an individual response merits 0, 1, or 2 points. To do this, you must apply the coding scheme that was developed for the subtest and is presented in the manual, so that you can be confident that everyone in the normative sample had his or her responses coded in the same way. When you add up all the points of the Vocabulary subtest to arrive at the subtest raw score and when you convert this raw score into a standard score and build composite index and IQ scores, you are scoring the test.

This distinction can be important because when you consider that you are coding individual items, rather than scoring them (i.e., you are applying the coding scheme given to you), you can feel better about leaving your personal judgment somewhat more out of the process. For example, on the Wechsler Abbreviated Scale of Intelligence (WASI), one of the Vocabulary items is "Alligator." When asking individuals what an alligator is, there are many possible responses, and thus the WASI manual presents a coding scheme to determine which responses earn 0, 1, and 2 points. One response that is listed as a 2-point response is "Crocodile." That is, when an individual is asked what an alligator is, it is considered an optimal response to say that an alligator is a crocodile. Personally, you may have a reaction to this (obviously, I do)—an alligator is specifically and explicitly *not* a crocodile. These two animals are not the same thing at all. If I were coming up with a score by myself, I might consider giving this type of response 1 point, if I were feeling generous. But 2 points? It is at these moments when it is helpful to remember that you are merely applying the Wechsler coding scheme to the responses—you are not trying to come up with a score by yourself. From the exercises presented previously, you can understand why standardized scoring of tests is just as important as standardized administration, so applying the coding schemes of individual tests is crucial.

INTERPRETING TESTS

Perhaps one of the most important skills that sets psychologists apart from members of all other professions is the ability to interpret testing instruments. This is likely the major reason that this is the focus of most of the best texts on psychological assessment. Although this book does not discuss interpreting individual tests, there are some important considerations that are important for interpreting all tests. First and foremost, it is important to understand that you, as the assessor, are the one who is interpreting the test. You should be confident that you are adequately trained and competent to interpret each test. You should make sure you have the appropriate training and, as needed, supervision on interpretation of tests.

This is especially important in view of the current prevalence of computer-interpreted tests. While these are extremely useful, no computer interpretation program will understand the nuances of the individual you are assessing better than a psychologist. Take, for example, the MCMI-III interpretation software. It is invaluable for scoring and giving interpretive hypotheses—it even gives diagnostic considerations based on the measure. However, books have been written and new research comes out all the time about nuanced interpretation of the MCMI-III. As helpful as the interpretative software is, it does not replace the expertise of a well-trained psychologist who is current on the literature.

One of the most important reasons that it is important to remember that you are the one interpreting tests is to use additional information that is available to you in the interpretation of each test. For example, as presented previously, the timing of testing can impact a client's performance on certain tests, and it is important to remember this information and integrate it into your overall interpretation of the measures. Additionally, you must always revisit the cultural considerations previously discussed. Knowing that most tests' validity varies by culture, you must understand and integrate how this may have affected the results that emerged from the tests.

Perhaps one of the most important reasons for remembering that it is you who interprets tests is that you can monitor your own biases and preconceptions. Supervision and consultation can be extremely useful in this regard, but it is important to understand your own biases—about culture, about tests, about certain diagnoses, and about any other factor that may impact your interpretation of tests. As well-trained a psychologist as you may be, you are still a human with (perhaps unconscious) biases, attitudes, motivations, and personality characteristics that may affect the way you interpret tests. While there is no way to eliminate this, simply being mindful of it can go a long way toward minimizing its effect on your interpretation.

Summary

You cannot conduct psychological assessments without knowing the ins and outs of the process of psychological testing, including appropriate administration, scoring, and interpretation of individual testing instruments. You will likely spend much of your assessment coursework training on individual tests, which is the foundation of any valid, ethical assessment. Many excellent texts focus on this aspect of the assessment process, and the importance of understanding the standard administration, coding and scoring, and interpretation of tests cannot be overstated.

CHAPTER 4

Integrating Data

Perhaps the most mystifying (some say "intuitive") stage within the psychological assessment process is integrating the data from multiple, extremely varied sources into a coherent picture of the individual being assessed. If you are merely listing strengths, weaknesses, and symptoms, the process is rather straightforward. Similarly, if you report your findings test by test, there is very little room for error. However, both of these strategies, listing symptoms and reporting findings alone, lack the coherence and explanatory power to support your conclusions. Presenting an explanatory model for the impairment in functioning by truly integrating the data in a coherent and interesting way makes the process more complex, but the results are more meaningful. This chapter will present a *method* for taking data from all sources and integrating the data clearly and logically.

It should be noted that the complexity of integration of data and conceptualization constitutes a major reason why only accredited professionals are legally allowed to conduct psychological assessment. Whereas administration and scoring of tests could be learned relatively easily by many people, this part of the process requires a much higher level of thinking that is based on a comprehensive understanding of personality functioning and psychodiagnosis. Such an understanding can derive from a range of theoretical perspectives.

Using the method outlined in this text, you can just as easily conceptualize a case from a cognitive, psychodynamic, or developmental perspective. Regardless of orientation, excellent supervision is necessary to hone and improve these skills of conceptualization. While the process outlined in this chapter will help organize the method for integrating data and conceptualizing the case, it is not intended as a substitute for good supervision and feedback. Professional supervision is essential to support you in your efforts to present a clear and logical "argument" that backs up your conclusions and recommendations.

It is important, once again, to bear in mind the limitations of individual tests and the results they provide. While the current text is not meant to be a survey of individual tests, it is essential to the process of conceptualization that you ultimately have confidence in the measures you are using. Without this confidence, you cannot be confident about the data that you are now trying to integrate. It is extremely important during this conceptualization process to approach the data with humility, understanding that no single finding from any single test should be given as much weight as the results that emerge consistently across tests, especially across methods (i.e., in both objective and projective measures).[1]

STEP 1: ACCUMULATING THE DATA

The first step of the integration process is to accumulate your data in a single place. To begin with, this simply means creating a list, by test, of all the results of the personality and emotional functioning testing, regardless of their apparent usefulness or importance. You should include in this list any symptoms or issues that came from the clinical interview, as well as salient behavioral observations. Writing out all the evidence in a single list accomplishes several goals (besides overwhelming you with a very long list). Primarily, it allows you to pull together your individual data in a common place so that you can begin to see how they may all fit together. An assessment is like a puzzle, with the data as the individual puzzle pieces. This step allows you to lay out all the pieces of the puzzle on the table before you begin to put them together to form a picture. In addition, this step will make the ultimate task of writing up the report much easier, because you will have laid out all the evidence from the tests in a single place for easy reference. The creation of this list also sets you up for the next step— identifying themes that have emerged from the amassed evidence.

---

[1]For more detailed information on the strengths and limitations of individual tests, so that you can know which results to afford even slightly greater weight, consult texts that focus on the measures themselves (e.g., Groth-Marnat, 2009; Lezak, Howieson, Loring, Hannay, & Fischer, 2004; Sattler, 2008; Weiner & Greene, 2007).

THE CASE OF PAUL—ACCUMULATING THE DATA (STEP 1)

Paul was a 30-year-old, mixed-race male who presented for an assessment at the urging of a family member in the mental health field, and because he was "generally frustrated with life." He had an extensive drug and legal history, having been to drug rehabilitation several times and having been in prison several times, both for drugs and for robbery. He had a long history in the foster care system but had lived with both his mother and father at different points in his childhood, though he had been taken away from them, as they were abusive and neglectful. At the time of the assessment, he was mostly unemployed, except for occasional jobs as a stuntman and in shows during which he would mutilate himself (piercing and cutting himself in many areas on his body). His cognitive testing revealed that he was functioning in the Average range compared to others his age, with High Average verbal comprehension. Table 4.1 presents the data that emerged from Paul's testing.

TABLE 4.1	ACCUMULATION OF PAUL'S DATA

MCMI-III
Drug dependence
Depression
Disinhibited tendencies
Emotional dysregulation
Antisocial behaviors
Anger
Passive-aggressive tendencies
Shallow interpersonal interactions
Identity diffusion

MMPI-2
Family problems
Views relationships with others as dangerous
Depression
Disorganization in thinking
Extremely high anger score
Tightly guarded emotions
Disregards others' rights and needs

TABLE 4.1 *(CONTINUED)*

PAI

Drug abuse
Aggression
Depression
Suicidality
Antisocial attitudes and behavior
Weak identity
Manipulative interpersonal behaviors
Erratic emotionality

RORSCHACH

Oppositional tendencies
Acts out
Unmet needs for closeness
Intellectualizes
Emotionally guarded
Underlying anger and resentment
Depression
Views future pessimistically
Loneliness and neediness
Currently experiencing painful emotions
Insecure about himself
Confused thinking
Preoccupied with own needs at the expense of others
Difficulty establishing and maintaining close and lasting relationships
Mistaken impressions of people
Excessive attention paid to how others react to him

TAT

Drugs
Interpersonal relationships are composed of games
Does not understand others well
No clear understanding of who he is
Sadness, which turns to anger and "blowing up"
Guarded about emotions
Qualified negative emotions with overly happy/idealistic ones
Anger about life
Rapid shift in emotion
Loneliness
Helplessness
Thrill about breaking rules

(Continued)

TABLE 4.I	*(CONTINUED)*

PROJECTIVE DRAWINGS

Weak identity

Family is disconnected/confusing

Other people can be frightening and confusing

Currently overwhelmed with sad thoughts

Restriction of emotions

BEHAVIORAL OBSERVATIONS/OTHER DATA

Long drug history

Few friends/close relationships

Reported being "frustrated" with life, but no more detail

Self-mutilation

Score of 65 on the Dissociative Experiences Scale (DES), which suggests high likelihood of dissociative experiences

History of aggressive behavior

Previous imprisonment

Self-mutilation

At times illogical in his presentation

Reported transient suicidal ideation

Reported that he is "searching for myself"

THE CASE OF BRANDON—ACCUMULATING THE DATA (STEP I)

Brandon was a 13-year-old, Caucasian male who was referred for an assessment by his psychiatrist, who had tentatively diagnosed him with attention-deficit/hyperactivity disorder (ADHD) and prescribed him Adderall. He was "being disruptive" at school and at home, including being aggressive toward his mother, and he was struggling significantly in his academic work. Until a few months before the assessment, Brandon had been living with his father, who was reportedly physically and emotionally abusive, hitting Brandon to the point that he bruised and bled, withholding food from him for days at a time, and using going to school "as a punishment." Because of one of these bruises, his school had called the state child protective services agency, and Brandon had been placed into his mother's custody. His mother also reported that she suspected he might have a learning disability. Table 4.2 presents the data that emerged from Brandon's testing.

TABLE 4.2	ACCUMULATION OF BRANDON'S DATA

Cognitive Functioning

WISC-IV

Full-Scale IQ: 102
Verbal Comprehension Index: 108
Perceptual Reasoning Index: 108
Working Memory Index: 97
Processing Speed Index: 83

WIAT-II

Total Composite: 111
Mathematics Composite: 110
Oral Language Composite: 114
Reading Composite: 107
Written Language Composite: 113

Emotional Functioning

MACI

Extremely introverted and turned inward on himself
Inhibited
Tries to deal with emotions on his own—but there are too many
Views himself very negatively
Family discord
Identity diffusion
Peer insecurity
Depressive affect
Oppositional tendencies

Rorschach

Current adaptive capacities are overloaded
Painful internalized affects
Current situational stress
Feelings of loss (object loss)
Guilt/shame/remorse/regret
Limited interpersonal ability
Can form close relationships
Indifference to interpersonal involvement
Capable of adaptive interpersonal behavior
Negative self-rumination

(Continued)

TABLE 4.2   *(CONTINUED)*

May be oppositional
Unclear identity
Emotional stress—interfering with pleasure in life
Loneliness
Stringent control over his feelings
Unsophisticated way of viewing the world—thinks dichotomously
Tends to misinterpret the actions/intentions of others
Intrusive ideation

Projective Drawings
Feels vulnerable
Weak sense of self
Low self-esteem
Depressed
Highly attuned to others
Guarded
Views his environment as unsafe
Fears father

AID
Wants to run away/escape
Fear of his own aggression
Acts out at times
Mistrust of others

Three Wishes
Negative view of himself
Depression
Anger toward his father

Behavioral Observations/Other Data
Abusive father
Change of environment to live with mother
Aggressive toward mother
Disruptive and belligerent toward teachers at school
Getting into fights with peers
Academic difficulties
Anger toward father
Anger toward psychiatrist
Anger toward having to do the assessment
Oppositional behavior in the testing sessions

It is recommended that when you are listing the major results from the tests, you do so in a table with a small, empty column on the left and each individual piece of data constituting a row in the column on the right. After completing your list, you are ready to begin the next step of the process.

STEP 2: IDENTIFYING THEMES

The next step in the integration process involves categorizing the data and results into coherent themes. At times, the themes emerge obviously and easily. Most often, however, it is more difficult to begin to categorize all of the results into themes that are meaningful. Themes can include specific symptoms, such as low self-esteem or feelings of worthlessness. Themes can include environmental factors, such as feeling lack of support from family or others. Themes can include personality or character styles or characteristics, such as the tendency to hold in emotions or a bias toward negatively interpreting all ambiguous stimuli. A good theme is clearly and straightforwardly described by the data.

This is an important point—make sure that the data are *explaining* the theme, not just related to it. For example, if one of the tests reveals a strong need for approval and you already have a theme of low self-esteem, you need to decide whether this piece of evidence really fits within the "low self-esteem" theme or not. While it is closely related, the need for approval may better fit into a theme of social desirability and behaving according to external validation needs, rather than the theme of low self-esteem itself, which is much better supported by specific pieces of evidence for low self-worth—for example, comparing himself or herself unfavorably with others, along with similar results. If no other data emerge to support this new "social desirability" theme, however, it may make sense to put this piece of evidence back within the "low self-esteem" theme.

When thinking about themes, if they do not emerge naturally or easily from the data, you might begin by trying to identify the (a) emotional and (b) thought processes of the individual. Scan the results first for any evidence that informs the emotional life of the individual, and then locate any evidence for what is going on cognitively and ideationally for him or her. You may not quickly and easily identify *what* the data are saying about the emotional world of the individual, for example, but after assigning these pieces of evidence a common label (i.e., "emotional stuff"), when you look at these data all at once, a more specific theme may emerge. Other domains that commonly help themes emerge include information about the interpersonal world of the individual, how the person feels about himself or herself, and the coping strategies and mechanisms of the individual. While these are only suggestions of what to look for in terms of themes, they are a good place to start if no themes immediately jump out.

The step of identifying themes may take several iterations. The reason for creating two columns in the first step of the integration process is to make this step clearer and easier to handle. As you go through the evidence, label the themes as best as you can, trying to fit each piece of evidence into a theme, even if you are not entirely clear on the theme itself. For example, if you begin by simply writing "emotion" next to all the evidence about the emotional world of the individual, you can look at all these data to see if a more specific emotional theme emerges. This theme may need to be revised or even split into several themes, but at least you have begun to identify which data go together. As you go through the data, even many times, you should begin to see which pieces of evidence fit together rather clearly. As with a puzzle, once the pieces are laid out on the table, this step is like sorting the pieces according to color, then within each color group sorting out pieces by shape.

There are some pieces of evidence that may not fit cleanly into any one theme. These may be pieces of contradictory information, or they may simply not fit into the themes you are constructing out of the data. Regarding the former, do not discount them immediately. For example, if you have a theme of low self-esteem, and one test reveals that the individual presents as highly self-confident, there may be merit to both. You will have to decide whether to incorporate them into a single theme (something like "self-concept") or to separate them into two differing but related themes. In this example, it is widely acknowledged in the literature on narcissism (e.g., Akhtar & Thomson, 1982; Horowitz, 1989; Kernberg, 1975; Raskin, Novacek, & Hogan, 1991; Rhodewalt & Morf, 1998) that highly presented self-esteem can simply be a defense against and a mask for low self-esteem. If there is enough evidence for the high self-esteem/narcissism element, then it may constitute its own theme, closely related to the theme of low self-esteem. If it emerges from only one or two tests, it may work within the theme of low self-esteem.

When a piece of evidence simply does not fit the themes you are generating from the rest of the data, leave it blank or label it "miscellaneous." When you have finished generating themes (or at least a first pass at them), look at those miscellaneous pieces of evidence together to see whether they constitute an additional theme. It should be noted that there are times when a single piece of evidence simply does not fit within or contradicts the other themes. Because of the nature of assessment, each test has a margin of error. Not every single piece of evidence has to be incorporated into the themes; that said, however, you should fit as much of the evidence into the themes as possible. Some assessments have as few as two or three themes, while others have as many as ten. Even though multiple themes make the assessment less manageable, at times there is simply so much test evidence that it becomes necessary to increase the number of themes. There are no rules as to the number of themes. The best guideline is to have the fewest possible themes that comprehensively account for all (or most) of the test evidence.

STEP 3: ORGANIZING THE DATA

The next step provides you with a visual means to identify the strongest arguments from the themes you have identified. Again, it is extremely important to take into account how much data, *across different tests and measures*, support each theme. Themes with evidence from only a single test, or not much evidence at all, should be reconsidered. If there are additional data that do not fit, try to combine them to create an additional theme. Also, perhaps most importantly, scan each of the themes individually to make sure all of the evidence you have categorized holds together conceptually. That is, it is extremely important to make sure that all of the individual pieces of data together truly describe the theme that you have identified.

This step of organizing the data is simply a matter of reformatting the results from the previous step. A table is created that lists themes in the first column and individual measures (including self-report, behavioral observations, and mental status information) in the top row. Each box within the table will contain individual pieces of evidence from each of the tests that support the themes. This step is like taking all the blue pieces of the puzzle and assembling them in a way that they naturally fit, so that you have a full blue puzzle section. Again, bear in mind the limitations of certain tests. Projective tests without widely accepted standardized, validated coding

THE CASE OF PAUL—IDENTIFYING THEMES (STEP 2)

The data from Paul's testing are presented in Table 4.3, with themes identified and labeled. It is important to note that it was necessary to make several passes at the data to identify and label all the themes before arriving at the final result as presented here.

TABLE 4.3	**LABELING OF PAUL'S THEMES**

Themes

	MCMI-III
Drugs	Drug dependence
Depression	Depression
Behavior	Disinhibited tendencies
Emotion	Emotional dysregulation
Behavior	Antisocial behaviors
Anger	Anger
Interpersonal	Passive-aggressive tendencies
Interpersonal	Shallow interpersonal interactions
Identity	Identity diffusion
	MMPI-2
Family	Family problems
Interpersonal	Views relationships with others as dangerous
Depression	Depression
Thinking	Disorganization in thinking
Anger	Extremely high anger score
Emotion	Tightly guarded emotions
Behavior	Disregards others' rights and needs
	PAI
Drugs	Drug abuse
Behavior	Aggression
Depression	Depression
Depression	Suicidality
Behavior	Antisocial attitudes and behavior
Identity	Weak identity
Interpersonal	Manipulative interpersonal behaviors
Emotion	Erratic emotionality

TABLE 4.3	(CONTINUED)

Themes

	Rorschach
Behavior	Oppositional tendencies
Behavior	Acts out
Interpersonal	Unmet needs for closeness
Emotion	Intellectualizes
Emotion	Emotionally guarded
Anger	Underlying anger and resentment
Depression	Depression
Depression	Views future pessimistically
Depression	Loneliness and neediness
Depression	Currently experiencing painful emotions
Identity	Insecure about himself
Thinking	Confused thinking
Interpersonal	Preoccupied with own needs at the expense of others
Interpersonal	Difficulty establishing and maintaining close and lasting relationships
Interpersonal	Mistaken impressions of people
Interpersonal	Excessive attention paid to how others react to him
	TAT
Drugs	Drugs
Interpersonal	Interpersonal relationships are composed of games
Interpersonal	Does not understand others well
Identity	No clear understanding of who he is
Depression/Anger	Sadness, which turns to anger and "blowing up"
Emotion	Guarded about emotions
Emotion	Qualified negative emotions with overly happy/idealistic ones
Anger	Anger about life
Emotion	Rapid shift in emotion
Depression	Loneliness
Depression	Helplessness
Behavior	Thrill about breaking rules
	Projective Drawings
Identity	Weak identity
Family	Family is disconnected/confusing
Interpersonal	Other people can be frightening and confusing
Depression	Currently overwhelmed with sad thoughts
Emotion	Restriction of emotions

(Continued)

TABLE 4.3	(CONTINUED)

Themes

	Behavioral Observations/Other Data
Drugs	Long drug history
Interpersonal	Few friends/close relationships
Emotion	Reported being "frustrated" with life, but no more detail
Behavior	Self-mutilation
Misc.	Score of 65 on the dissociative experiences scale (DES), which suggests high likelihood of dissociative experiences
Behavior	History of aggressive behavior
Behavior	Previous imprisonment
Thinking	At times illogical in his presentation
Depression	Reported transient suicidal ideation
Identity	Reported that he is "searching for myself"

THE CASE OF BRANDON—IDENTIFYING THEMES (STEP 2)

The data from Brandon's testing are presented in Table 4.4, with themes identified and labeled. It is important to note that it was necessary to make several passes at the data to identify and label all the themes before arriving at the final result as presented here.

Cognitive Functioning

The cognitive functioning data do not need categorization as the emotional functioning data do. Instead, a careful comparison of Brandon's overall aptitude and ability (as measured by the WISC-IV) and his academic achievement in the broad domains of reading, writing, mathematics, and oral language (as measured by the WIAT-II) reveals that he is achieving at or above the level expected given his overall average aptitude. Two findings are of particular note from his cognitive testing. First, his average working memory suggests that it is unlikely that he suffers from ADHD of the inattentive type, as the ability to complete these tasks requires, at a minimum, adequate sustained attention and concentration. Second, his processing speed is significantly lower than the rest of his cognitive functioning, which may suggest one of several factors impairing his speed of processing information, including emotional disturbance (e.g., depression), anxiety, or personality factors such as perfectionism or hypervigilance. The emotional functioning assessment will help in understanding what is likely impairing his processing speed.

TABLE 4.4	LABELING OF BRANDON'S THEMES

WISC-IV

Average	Full-Scale IQ: 102
Average	Verbal Comprehension Index: 108
Average	Perceptual Reasoning Index: 108
Average	Working Memory Index: 97
Low Average	Processing Speed Index: 83

WIAT-II

High Average	Total Composite: 111
High Average	Mathematics Composite: 110
High Average	Oral Language Composite: 114
Average	Reading Composite: 107
High Average	Written Language Composite: 113

Emotional Functioning

Theme	MACI
Emotion	Extremely introverted and turned inward on himself
Emotion	Inhibited
Emotion	Tries to deal with emotions on his own—but there are too many
Self-esteem	Views himself very negatively
Family	Family discord
Identity	Identity diffusion
Interpersonal	Peer insecurity
Emotion	Depressive affect
Behavior	Oppositional tendencies

	Rorschach
Stress	Current adaptive capacities are overloaded
Emotion	Painful internalized affects
Stress	Current situational stress
Emotion	Feelings of loss (object loss)
Emotion	Guilt/shame/remorse/regret
Interpersonal	Limited interpersonal ability
Interpersonal	Can form close relationships
Interpersonal	Indifference to interpersonal involvement
Interpersonal	Capable of adaptive interpersonal behavior
Self-esteem	Negative self-rumination
Behavior	May be oppositional

(Continued)

TABLE 4.4	(CONTINUED)

Identity	Unclear identity
Emotion	Emotional stress—interfering with pleasure in life
Emotion	Loneliness
Emotion	Stringent control over his feelings
Misc.	Unsophisticated way of viewing the world—thinks dichotomously
Interpersonal	Tends to misinterpret the actions/intentions of others
Emotion	Intrusive ideation

Projective Drawings

Emotion	Feels vulnerable
Identity	Weak sense of self
Self-esteem	Low self-esteem
Emotion	Depressed
Interpersonal	Highly attuned to others
Emotion	Guarded
Family	Views his environment as unsafe
Family	Fears father

AID

Family	Wants to run away/escape
Emotion	Fear of his own aggression
Behavior	Acts out at times
Interpersonal	Mistrust of others

Three Wishes

Self-esteem	Negative view of himself
Emotion	Depression
Emotion	Anger toward his father

Behavioral Observations/Other Data

Family	Abusive father
Family	Change of environment to live with mother
Behavior	Aggressive toward mother
Behavior	Disruptive and belligerent toward teachers at school
Interpersonal	Getting into fights with peers
Misc.	Academic difficulties
Emotion	Anger toward father
Emotion	Anger toward psychiatrist
Emotion	Anger toward having to do the assessment
Behavior	Oppositional behavior in the testing sessions

In the process of restructuring the themes into a table, some of the themes that were loosely labeled before (e.g., behavior) become clearer in their meaning (i.e., antisocial behavior). Others seem to encompass too much (e.g., emotion). Interestingly, the one piece of evidence marked as "miscellaneous" seems somehow related to other categories, but it is in the conceptualization phase that, hopefully, it will become more obvious how. Also, the family theme was too sparse, so it was combined with the Interpersonal theme. Paul's data are presented in Table 4.5.

TABLE 4.5   PAUL'S ORGANIZED DATA

Concept/Test	MCMI-III	MMPI-2	PAI	Rorschach	TAT	Projective Drawings	Behavior/Other
Antisocial Behavior	Disinhibited tendencies	Disregards others' rights and needs	Aggression	Oppositional tendencies	Thrill about breaking rules		Self-mutilation
	Antisocial behaviors		Antisocial attitudes and behavior	Acts out			History of aggressive behavior
Substance Abuse/ Dependence	Drug dependence		Drug abuse		Drugs		Long drug history
Interpersonal Difficulties	Passive-aggressive tendencies	Views relationships with others as dangerous	Manipulative interpersonal behaviors	Unmet needs for closeness	Interpersonal relationships are composed of games	Other people can be frightening and confusing	Few friends/ close relationships

(Continued)

TABLE 4.5 (*CONTINUED*)

Concept/Test	MCMI-III	MMPI-2	PAI	Rorschach	TAT	Projective Drawings	Behavior/Other
	Shallow interpersonal interactions			Preoccupied with own needs at the expense of others	Does not understand others well		
				Difficulty establishing and maintaining close and lasting relationships			
				Mistaken impressions of people			
				Excessive attention paid to how others react to him			
Weak Identity	Identity diffusion		Weak identity	Insecure about himself	No clear understanding of who he is	Weak identity	Reported that he is "searching for myself"
Emotion	Emotional dysregulation	Tightly guarded emotions	Erratic emotionality	Intellectualizes	Guarded about emotions	Restriction of emotions	Reported being "frustrated" with life, but no more detail

Scale						
Anger	Anger	Extremely high anger score		Emotionally guarded Underlying anger and resentment	Qualified negative emotions with overly happy/idealistic ones Rapid shift in emotion Sadness, which turns to anger and "blowing up" Anger about life	At times illogical in his presentation
Confused Thinking		Disorganization in thinking		Confused thinking		
Depression	Depression	Depression	Depression Depression	Depression Suicidality	Depression Views future pessimistically Loneliness and neediness Currently experiencing painful emotions	Sadness, which turns to anger and "blowing up" Loneliness Helplessness	Currently overwhelmed with sad thoughts Reported transient suicidal ideation

(Continued)

TABLE 4.5 (CONTINUED)

Concept/Test	MCMI-III	MMPI-2	PAI	Rorschach	TAT	Projective Drawings	Behavior/Other
Miscellaneous							Score of 65 on the Dissociative Experiences Scale (DES), which suggests high likelihood of dissociative experiences
Emotionally Guarded*		Tightly guarded emotions		Intellectualizes	Guarded about emotions	Restriction of emotions	Reported being "frustrated" with life, but no more detail
				Emotionally guarded	Qualified negative emotions with overly happy/idealistic ones		
Erratic Emotions	Emotional dysregulation		Erratic emotionality		Rapid shift in emotion		

*Because the Emotion theme seems to be too inclusive, we will pull out two sub-themes (Emotionally Guarded and Erratic Emotions) related to how Paul seems to deal with his emotions. Interestingly, one seems like something he does, and one seems more like an outcome.

When the themes are restructured into a table, it becomes clear that there is pretty strong evidence for most of the identified themes. For example, there is evidence of low self-esteem across most measures administered. Of particular note, one of the pieces of data previously labeled as "miscellaneous" can be recategorized into the Interpersonal theme. Additionally, when the emotion data is assembled like this, it may seem that too much is being compiled into a single theme. Brandon's data are presented in Table 4.6.

TABLE 4.6   BRANDON'S ORGANIZED DATA

Test: Concept/ Theme	MACI	Rorschach	Projective Drawings	AID	Three Wishes	Interview/ Behavioral Observations
Emotion	Extremely introverted and turned inward on himself	Painful internalized affects	Feels vulnerable	Fear of his own aggression	Depression	Anger toward father
	Inhibited	Feelings of loss (object loss)	Depressed		Anger toward his father	Anger toward psychiatrist
	Tries to deal with emotions on his own—but there are too many	Guilt/shame/ remorse/regret	Guarded			Anger toward having to do the assessment

(Continued)

TABLE 4.6 (CONTINUED)

Test: Concept/Theme	MACI	Rorschach	Projective Drawings	AID	Three Wishes	Interview/Behavioral Observations
	Depressive affect	Emotional stress—interfering with pleasure in life				
		Loneliness				
		Stringent control over his emotions				
		Intrusive ideation				
Self-Esteem	Views himself very negatively	Negative self-rumination	Low self-esteem		Negative view of himself	
Family	Family discord	Current adaptive capacities are overloaded	Views his environment as unsafe	Wants to run away/escape		Abusive father
		Current situational stress	Fears father			Change of environment to live with mother
Identity	Identity diffusion	Unclear identity	Weak sense of self			
Interpersonal	Peer insecurity	Limited interpersonal ability	Highly attuned to others	Mistrust of others		Getting into fights with peers

		Can form close relationship		
		Indifference to interpersonal involvement		
		Capable of adaptive interpersonal behavior		
		Tends to misinterpret the actions/intentions of others		
Behavior	Oppositional tendencies	May be oppositional	Acts out at times	Disruptive and belligerent toward teachers at school
				Aggressive toward mother
				Oppositional behavior in the testing sessions
Misc.	Unsophisticated way of viewing the world—thinks dichotomously → interpersonal			Academic difficulties
Emotional Restriction*	Extremely introverted and turned inward on himself	Stringent control over his emotions	Guarded	
	Inhibited			

(Continued)

TABLE 4.6 (CONTINUED)

Test: Concept/ Theme	MACI	Rorschach	Projective Drawings	AID	Three Wishes	Interview/ Behavioral Observations
	Tries to deal with emotions on his own—but there are too many					
Negative Emotion	Depressive affect	Painful internalized affects	Feels vulnerable	Fear of his own aggression	Depression	
		Feelings of loss (object loss)	Depressed		Anger toward his father	
		Guilt/shame/ remorse/regret				
		Emotional stress— interfering with pleasure in life				
		Loneliness				

*When looking at the Emotion theme together, it seems that we have actually captured two separate themes in one. There are data that reveal his emotional *process*, and some data that focus on the *content* of his emotions at the moment. As such, being as flexible at this point as we can, we will separate the theme into two separate themes. What emerge are cleaner themes that look like emotional restriction—his tendency to hold in his emotions as tightly as he can—and what seems to be a great deal of current negative emotion.

systems (such as Projective Drawings) will likely fill fewer boxes in the chart, because the validity of these data are more easily challenged. More highly validated measures will yield results about which you can be more confident. However, given that no test is perfect, it is important to take into account results that are revealed *across multiple measures* when thinking about how confident you can be about the themes that emerge.

STEP 4: CONCEPTUALIZING

Once the themes have been finalized, the fourth and final step is to conceptualize what is going on for the individual. This is where the puzzle pieces are finally put together to create a larger picture. Rather than simply reporting the themes as the findings of the assessment, the hypothesis testing model requires the integration of the themes into a *narrative* describing what is occurring for the individual assessed. This narrative aims to make the results clearer, more coherent, and more understandable to the person being assessed (in addition to the referral parties or anyone else receiving the feedback). The more easily the results can be understood, the more likely the individual will follow up on the recommendations made as a result of the assessment.

As with pulling out the themes from the data, constructing the narrative occasionally happens quite easily, but more often it is not that clear. The important thing to note is that the narrative has only to make logical, intuitive sense. Although several different narratives could be created for the same set of themes, each one is as valid as the others as long as they proceed logically from the data. It is the themes that support the conclusions, diagnosis, and recommendations, while the narrative simply organizes these data in a more accessible way. If one of the themes is like the blue section of the puzzle being assembled, this final step is like connecting the larger blue section to the larger green section, as well as all the other sections, to create a full, coherent picture.

For example, if you have one theme labeled "low self-esteem" and another labeled "interpersonal isolation," they could be placed in a narrative in several different ways. In one case it could be asserted that the low self-esteem constricts social comfort and thus likely impedes the individual's ability to function interpersonally. The case could just as easily be made, though, that the lack of socialization contributes to feelings of inadequacy. There may even be a third variable that explains both the low-self esteem and the interpersonal isolation, such as early childhood abuse and a lack of family support. It could be argued that the low support, in the context of a history of abuse, has led to a lack of interpersonal trust, making it difficult to establish interpersonal relationships.

Additionally, the early abuse could lead to feelings of worthlessness and inadequacy if the individual feels somehow guilty about or responsible for it. Regardless of how the narrative is told, however, the low self-esteem and lack of interpersonal relationships, together with other supporting data, lend support to a conclusion and diagnosis of, for example, depression, and the subsequent recommendations of psychiatric consultation, psychotherapy, and possibly other means of support such as social clubs. Although this example is condensed and relatively straightforward, it illustrates the point that no one narrative is necessarily correct, and that multiple narratives can emerge from the same themes. Several examples of common narrative structures follow.

Diathesis-Stress Model of Conceptualization

The first, and likely the most straightforward, way to conceptualize how themes combine to explain the functioning of an individual is adapted from the diathesis-stress model (Zubin & Spring, 1977). Simply put, themes can often be categorized into the following three types:

1. *Diatheses*—what the individual contributes to the situation in terms of personality style or general approach to the world
2. *Stressors*—what is going on or has gone on in the environment
3. *Outcomes*—what symptoms or more temporary issues are currently occurring for the individual as a result of the interaction of stressors and diatheses

Simply put, this model posits that diatheses and stressors interact to cause the outcomes. For example, consider a teenage boy (not Brandon) who is referred for assessment because of behavior problems such as explosiveness at school. Testing reveals that he has a general style of inhibiting his emotions, and his parents recently divorced. The diathesis would be his emotionally inhibited style, the stress would be his parents' divorce, and the outcome (likely one of a few) would be his explosive behavior. The model is shown in Figure 4.1.

FIGURE 4.1   DIATHESIS-STRESS MODEL OF
                    CONCEPTUALIZATION

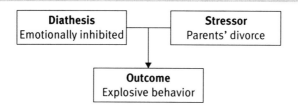

Developmental Model of Conceptualization

A second model for fitting themes into a narrative is a developmental model. In this model, themes constitute evidence of different developmental levels, such that there is either delayed or uneven development along some part of the individual's functioning. Most often, this model is appropriate when the current functioning (represented by the themes) is not adequate to meet the demands of the chronological age or life stage. In general, symptoms or current functioning occur as a result of the mismatch between the individual's current developmental level, including his or her coping capabilities, and the demands being placed on him or her.

For example, that same teenager with behavioral problems may be acting out for a very different reason. Suppose that rather than a theme of the parents' divorce, a theme emerged that in living in his newly divorced mother's home, this boy has had to take on the responsibilities of the adult male in the house, disciplining his younger siblings, earning money by taking a part-time job, and even serving as the primary means of emotional support for his mother. Other themes about his functioning might also emerge to help understand at what developmental level he is generally functioning, including what demands he should be able to cope with.

His developmental level, because he is an adolescent, is likely not equal to that of a fully developed adult male, who can handle the responsibilities of being the father figure to a family. For example, themes may emerge from the tests that reveal that he is actively trying to search for and find his identity (e.g., trying many different hobbies, questioning who he is in terms of his racial and spiritual identity, etc.). He has a strong need for

FIGURE 4.2   **DEVELOPMENTAL MODEL OF CONCEPTUALIZATION**

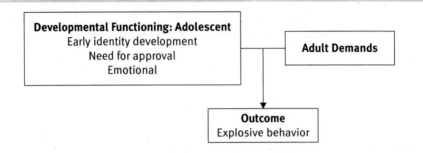

peer approval and erratic emotionality, despite his general tendency to restrict his emotion. These themes represent very normative developmental tasks and signs for a teenager.

However, the demands being placed on him at home are more than he can handle at the moment. While at home, coping with these adult demands, he acts "appropriately," helping his family cope with the transition of divorce. At school, though, where he does not have the same demands, expectations, or responsibilities as at home, he is acting out in an explosive way. It would be no surprise that an adolescent who had to hold all his impulses and emotions in at home might "spill" during school, seeming impulsive and oppositional. The model is shown in Figure 4.2.

Common Function Model of Conceptualization

A third model that is often suggested by the themes is the common function model. In general, this model applies when each of the themes seems to be contributing the same function (usually defensive) for the individual. For example, that same adolescent boy whose parents recently divorced may be employing several different techniques to avoid experiencing overwhelming emotions. In addition to the explosive behavior, themes may emerge such as somatic complaints, shallow relationships, and a preoccupation with video games. Each of these themes could be understood as a means by which this boy is working to keep emotions out of his awareness. In this model, each theme represents a defensive strategy employed to avoid having to feel the intense emotions that might be triggered by his currently turbulent home life. The model is shown in Figure 4.3.

FIGURE 4.3   **COMMON FUNCTION MODEL OF CONCEPTUALIZATION**

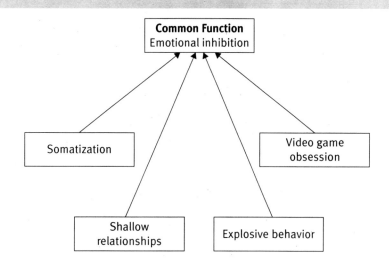

Complex Models of Conceptualization

Most often, the narrative model that emerges from the data is more complex than the three models just described, with multiple layers and feedback loops. However, the fact that narratives often do not fit perfectly into any of the three models previously presented does not preclude their use. Rather, they may serve as a baseline template from which to start, building other layers as needed. Consider this same adolescent boy. The themes that emerge may fit into a model based on the diathesis-stress model, but with more layers. He has a tendency to hold in his emotions, and his parents recently divorced; both are still viable as diathesis and stress, respectively. Perhaps acting out in school is not the only outcome.

Academic difficulty may be another theme that emerges in the assessment, though cognitive testing revealed no organic reason for any difficulty with school. Having used the diathesis-stress model as a starting place, you may notice that the "academic difficulty" theme does not seem to be a logical outcome of the diathesis (emotional inhibition) and stress (parents' divorce). However, it may be an outcome of the combination of the acting out in school and not having adequate time or support to do his homework, because of the divorce. The diathesis-stress model is still the basis for the narrative, but an added layer of complexity is necessary to explain the themes in a coherent and logical way. The model is shown in Figure 4.4.

FIGURE 4.4   **COMPLEX MODEL OF CONCEPTUALIZATION**

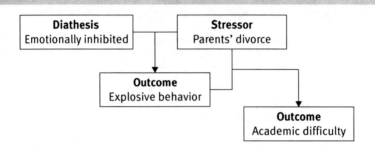

THE CASE OF PAUL—CONCEPTUALIZING

A few different options for conceptualizing the case of Paul are now given. These constitute only some of the many possible narratives. As always, the task at this point is to create a logical narrative among the themes so that it presents a coherent story. We have to connect the following themes:

- Antisocial behavior
- Substance abuse/dependence
- Interpersonal difficulties
- Weak identity
- Emotionally guarded state
- Erratic emotions
- Anger
- Confused thinking
- Depression
- (Dissociation)

Diathesis-Stress Model Conceptualization of Paul

In trying to apply the diathesis-stress model of conceptualization, we must try to divide the themes into (a) those *traits* that are inherent within Paul, traits that he likely developed at an early age and that he "brings to the picture" (diatheses); (b) those external issues that affect his functioning (stressors); and (c) those *states* that are more situational or transient (outcomes). As long as you can make a convincing argument for how each theme relates to the others, Paul will be more likely to receive feedback and take recommendations.

For Paul, no one of the themes seems purely to be a stressor. That is, no one of the themes is purely external to him (as would be the case if the testing had revealed some sort of current situational stress). However, there was some evidence of family difficulties (and we know that he had a difficult childhood in which he was passed around to many different homes), even though we ended up combining that with his interpersonal difficulties. Because of this evidence, though, it makes sense to conceptualize his interpersonal difficulties (including his difficult family history) as the stress part of the model.

What is more difficult in Paul's case is deciding which of the themes are part of the diathesis and which are part of the outcomes. Often it makes sense to think about interpersonal difficulties as an outcome of whatever else is going on, but in this case we have used that as the stress in the model. Other themes seem more likely to be outcomes, because they are more transient or situational in nature. Those include his drug use, his anger, his antisocial behaviors, and his depression. What are left are: erratic emotions, confused thinking, emotionally guarded state, and weak identity.

Any combination of these is arguable as either diatheses or outcomes, so the decision should be based more on your clinical intuition and your impression of Paul himself. While it could make sense that his erratic emotions, combined with stress, lead him to be emotionally guarded, it seems more intuitive that he generally tends to keep tight control over his emotions, but when faced with significant stress, he no longer does this effectively and his emotions become erratic. Consequently, erratic emotions will be added to the outcomes, and his emotionally guarded state will be part of the diathesis.

In terms of his confused thinking, during his testing sessions with the assessor, Paul does not seem to be, at his core, illogical or loose in his associations. At times his stories were somewhat incoherent, but this does not seem to be a trait that is fundamental to who he is. So his confused thinking will be added to the outcomes. On the other hand, when experiencing Paul during the assessment, his unclear sense of who he is *did* seem core to his personality functioning. Again, any combination of these four final themes could arguably be part of the diathesis in this model. Because of this clinical impression of him, we will add it to his emotional guardedness in the diathesis. The diathesis-stress model for Paul is shown in Figure 4.5.

(Continued)

FIGURE 4.5   **DIATHESIS-STRESS MODEL FOR PAUL**

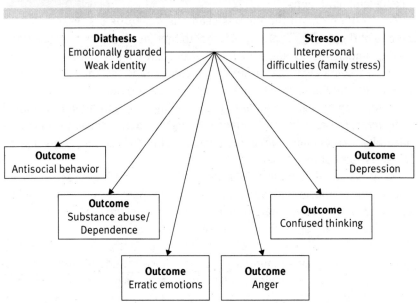

This model makes intuitive sense for the most part. In general, someone who keeps such tight control over his emotions when faced with stress is bound to "spill" in some way. In Paul's case, it seems to cause an array of chaotic thoughts and feelings. However, there are some problems with this model, which can be addressed later in a more complex model. For example, his substance abuse is more likely a way to escape the anger, depression, and erratic emotions, rather than an outcome alongside them. However, this model is logical and arguable, and it would contribute to an adequate report and feedback.

Developmental Model

When thinking developmentally about Paul, there does seem to be a mismatch in his general developmental functioning and his chronological age, which represents the developmental level of the everyday demands being placed on him. That is, as an adult, he must navigate adult relationships, work to earn a living, and live independently. However, many of his themes represent the normative functioning of an early adolescent. For example, an adolescent is not expected to have a clear identity yet, whereas an adult

FIGURE 4.6   DEVELOPMENTAL MODEL FOR PAUL

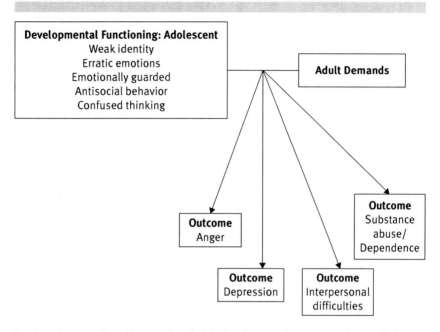

is. Erratic emotionality, antisocial behavior, and emotional guardedness are also traits associated normatively with adolescents. Even some confusion in logic is somewhat expected of an adolescent, whose executive functioning is not yet fully developed. Given this mismatch in his adolescent developmental functioning and the adult demands of his life, it makes sense that some of the outcomes have emerged. Anger, depression, and interpersonal difficulty can all logically be associated with this developmental mismatch. And his substance abuse, whereas it could be part of his adolescent functioning, is likely a way to cope with not being developmentally able to handle the demands of his life. The developmental model for Paul is shown in Figure 4.6.

Much like the diathesis-stress model for Paul, this model makes intuitive sense and would likely be easily understood by Paul. An additional benefit of this model is that it normalizes some of the themes that could be heard as rather pathological. For example, confused thinking can easily suggest psychosis or completely illogical ideation, but when it is conceptualized along the developmental continuum as somewhat normal for an adolescent to form mistaken impressions or jump to somewhat illogical conclusions at

(Continued)

times, the theme becomes much less frightening. However, before committing to this model, we will consider some others.

Common Function Model

The common function model for Paul is somewhat difficult to conceptualize, mostly because there are simply a great number of themes. However, especially given the antisocial behavior and the drug use, he does seem to be working hard to cope with his emotions. Specifically, he seems to be trying to keep tight control over his emotions, given his current anger and depression. That is, because of his erratic emotions, which are currently characterized by anger and sadness, he is employing many tactics to keep himself from having to consciously feel them. Certainly his antisocial behavior, substance abuse, and interpersonal guardedness are easily seen as serving this purpose. The harder themes to justify would be his somewhat confused thinking and his weak sense of identity. However, as long as in the narrative you can justify that these are also serving the purpose of dealing with his emotions, this model is viable. The common function model for Paul is shown in Figure 4.7.

FIGURE 4.7   COMMON FUNCTION MODEL FOR PAUL

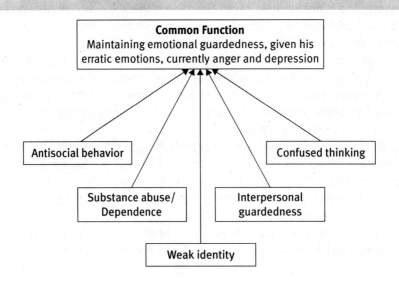

Common Function
Maintaining emotional guardedness, given his erratic emotions, currently anger and depression

Antisocial behavior

Confused thinking

Substance abuse/ Dependence

Interpersonal guardedness

Weak identity

While this model is not perfect, it has several advantages. Again, as with the two previous models, it makes intuitive sense to think about Paul in this way. In addition to this, however, in terms of recommendations for treatment, this model places specific emphasis on building healthier and more effective ways to deal with his emotions. While his use of drugs and acting out behaviors do help him avoid his loneliness and anger, they are far from the healthiest way to deal with these feelings, even though they may feel overwhelming to him. This emphasis may be a good one in terms of having him focus on his own treatment in the future.

Complex Model

When considering a more complex model for Paul's functioning, it helps to think about some of the strengths of the previous models. The diathesis-stress model for Paul places good emphasis on what seems to be most core to who he is, while the common function model emphasizes his style of coping. The added benefit of creating a more complex model for Paul is the fact that the piece of evidence about his dissociative tendencies can be incorporated more easily (though it easily could have been added to the common function model as another way he copes with his emotions). A more complex model will have several layers. In Paul's case, it makes sense to first think about what he brings to the picture: a weak identity and emotional dysregulation. Admittedly, one of the major reasons that these are being included in the first level of the model is that he seems to fit clearly into a Borderline Personality Disorder diagnostic category, and these are two clear criteria for this disorder. The other major reason they are coming first in this model is because, from the developmental model, they seem to be two areas that are developmentally somewhat lagging.

When considering the outcomes of his emotional dysregulation and his poor sense of who he is, the next logical level (again, taken from the common function model) includes his anger, depression, and confused thinking. Erratic emotions, especially for someone who does not have a clear sense of who he is and how to deal with them, can be extremely alarming and disruptive. They can influence both feelings and thinking. And returning to the strength of the common function model, the next layer of a more complex model would include how he attempts to cope with the anger, depression, and confused thinking. The major way he seems to cope is by dissociating and distancing, both from his emotions (guardedness)

(Continued)

FIGURE 4.8   COMPLEX MODEL FOR PAUL

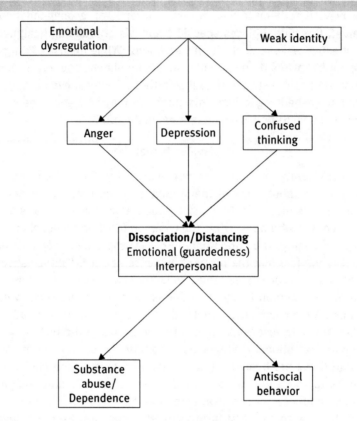

and from other people (interpersonal distancing). However, currently, this strategy does not seem to be working. As such, it results in his using substances and acting out. This complex model (and this is only one of many possibilities) for Paul is shown in Figure 4.8.

This model pulls together the strengths of the other three models. There is a developmental emphasis (given his normatively adolescent struggles at the top of the model), as well as emphasis placed on his ineffective strategies for coping with his negative emotions. Each layer of the model, when described in its narrative form, will flow logically to the next, so that Paul is more likely to connect with the story. This model will also flow well with the diagnosis (in this case there will be multiple diagnoses) and recommendations to address each of the levels of themes in the model.

THE CASE OF BRANDON—CONCEPTUALIZING

A few different options for conceptualizing the case of Brandon from earlier are given here. These constitute only some of the many possible narratives. As always, the task at this point is to create a logical narrative among the themes so that it presents a coherent story. We have to connect the following themes:

- Low self-esteem
- Oppositional behavior
- Poor sense of self
- Interpersonal difficulty
- Family stress
- Emotional restriction
- Negative emotion

Diathesis-Stress Model Conceptualization of Brandon

In trying to apply the diathesis-stress model of conceptualization, we must try to divide the themes into (a) those *traits* that are inherent within Brandon, traits that he likely developed at an early age and that he "brings to the picture" (diatheses); (b) those external issues that affect his functioning (stressors); and (c) those *states* that are more situational or transient (outcomes). It may be more difficult to figure out which themes are diatheses and which are outcomes in the case of a child or adolescent, as much of personality is not yet formulated. For example, a lack of clear identity could be a driving force behind current impairments, or it could be an outcome of other things. Always remember that as long as you can make a convincing argument for how each theme relates to the others, Brandon and his mother will be more likely to understand the feedback and take recommendations.

For Brandon, there is a clear theme that fits the stressor part of the model—the theme of family stress. This theme is slightly internal for him (i.e., it is causing him stress and taxing him more than his coping resources can handle), but the core of this theme is external, especially given his history of abuse by his father and the dramatic shift in his environment not too long ago. It is easy to understand that his turbulent family situation, in combination with the type of person he is, is causing him some problems currently. What is more difficult is figuring out which theme or themes describe "what type of person he is."

(Continued)

Looking at the rest of the themes, we might consider that some adolescents with very turbulent family and home lives do not develop functional impairments as Brandon did. But what kind of adolescents would fare better than he has? Would it be an adolescent who has a clearer identity, thus making the poor sense of self the diathesis? Might it be an adolescent who feels better about himself (and would that likely be possible), making low self-esteem the diathesis? When looking at all of the themes, what seems most core to who he is as a person and how he deals with the stress of his family and home situation is the fact that he spends much energy keeping his emotions tightly constricted. Although it would be difficult, an adolescent who could process his or her feelings more freely and perhaps use them to make his or her needs known to others around him or her may fare better with the turbulent family life. Thus, we will use emotional restriction as the diathesis, with all the other themes as outcomes of the interaction between restricting his emotions and suffering a very difficult family and home life. The diathesis-stress model for Brandon is shown in Figure 4.9.

While this model is arguable, it has some problems. Namely, the diathesis and stressor make sense, but some of the outcomes might be difficult to argue as the outcome of the diathesis and stress together. However, each could be argued separately. For example, oppositional behavior could be the result of an adolescent who holds his emotions tightly in but has

FIGURE 4.9   **DIATHESIS-STRESS MODEL FOR BRANDON**

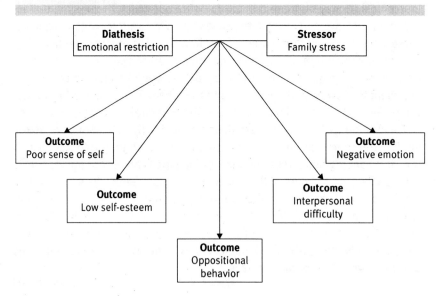

a difficult home life—this is not uncommon, actually. As we will see later, however, a slightly more complex model may be useful when thinking of some of the outcomes.

Developmental Model

When considering the developmental model for conceptualizing Brandon, we face a very interesting difficulty. When we think about some of the themes and at what developmental level they are appropriate, many of them are actually at the preadolescent or adolescent level. For example, developing a more solid sense of who you are is generally seen as a task of adolescence, so his poor sense of self (even though it is poor even in comparison to others his age) would be about on target with his chronological age. Similarly, family stress and navigating the interpersonal world with peers are traits not uncommon to preadolescents and adolescents (again, though his are likely more severe than what would be considered normative for his age). In this case, his developmental level is about on the same level as his chronological age, so the developmental model would not make sense. That is, the *developmentally appropriate* life demands being placed on him are not mismatched with his level of development to date, even though his life circumstances are clearly demanding more than he can currently handle. Thus, we will not even posit a developmental model for understanding what is impacting Brandon's functioning.

Common Function Model

As with the developmental model, we run into some difficulty when trying to apply the common function model to Brandon's case. The first step is to evaluate each of the themes to identify (a) what are the overall defensive or coping strategies of the individual and (b) what the individual is striving to do. This model is difficult to apply to Brandon, as the themes that emerged from the testing seem not to be clearly related to coping strategies. Therefore, it may be difficult to conceptualize each of the themes as serving a common purpose. The only common function that may make sense is a combination of two of the themes: He may be striving to keep stringent control over his emotions given his chaotic family life (emotional restriction and family stress). If this were the common theme, then an argument would have to be made that each of the remaining themes are present to serve the purpose of keeping his emotions restricted. Some of the themes, such as oppositional behavior, may be relatively straightforward to present in

(Continued)

FIGURE 4.10   **COMMON FUNCTION MODEL FOR BRANDON**

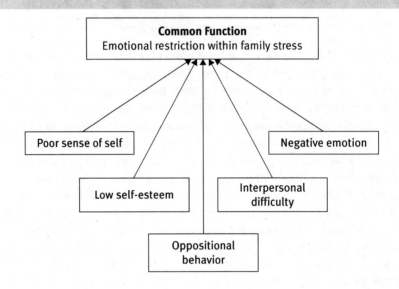

this way. Others, however, such as negative emotions and low self-esteem, would be more difficult to justify. That is, it may be difficult to explain that Brandon has low self-esteem *in order to* keep his emotions constricted. You would have to be a *very* convincing writer to justify this model. If you were brave enough to make this argument, the common function model for Brandon is shown in Figure 4.10.

This model focuses on a major dynamic that seems to be affecting Brandon's functioning currently—the fact that he works hard to maintain strict control over his emotions, which is not surprising, given his tumultuous family and home context. Again, however, this model is a difficult one to present, as arguing that some of the themes are serving the common function of restricting emotions is not intuitive to a reader. Thus, rather than stretching these logical connections, it is likely more useful to create a more complex model to explain Brandon's emotional functioning.

Complex Model

Thus far, the diathesis-stressor model has been the most logical and intuitive model to explain Brandon's functioning. However, some of the outcomes seem to be slightly more complex than presented in this pure

FIGURE 4.11   **COMPLEX MODEL FOR BRANDON**

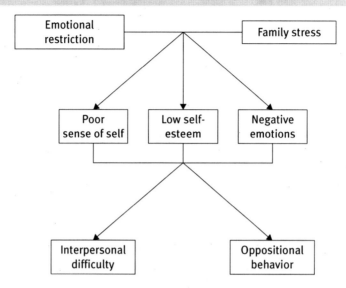

diathesis-stressor model. That is, for example, interpersonal difficulty does seem related to and is surely a result of his restricting emotions and his family stress. However, there may be some mediating steps between this interaction as a cause and interpersonal difficulty as an outcome. When thinking about what is most likely to stem from the diathesis-stressor interaction, three of the themes—low self-esteem, poor sense of self, and negative emotions—emerge as somewhat intuitive. Further, the remaining themes—interpersonal difficulty and oppositional behavior—can easily be seen as stemming from emotional distress, low self-esteem, and a weak identity. The model is shown in Figure 4.11.

As always, there are multiple ways to describe how the themes work together to explain an individual's current functioning, and this is simply one that seems to make intuitive sense to apply to Brandon. One strength of this model is that it situates his oppositional behavior as a result of negative stuff going on inside him, as a reaction to his not feeling good in general or not feeling good about who he is. It is common for negative emotions in children and adolescents to come across as irritability or oppositionality, and this seems to be the case with Brandon. The implication is that by addressing even the themes in the middle row, his oppositional behavior and interpersonal difficulty are likely to improve. This is very

(Continued)

different from placing his oppositional behavior as somehow more core to who he is (and diagnosing him with Oppositional Defiant Disorder or some other behavioral disorder).

We cannot be sure that his oppositional behavior is not independent from his negative emotions, but it is likely that he acts out because he does not feel good. If addressing his negative emotions, low self-esteem, and poor sense of self does not ameliorate his oppositional symptoms, they can be assumed to be independent, and, as such, they would constitute a behavioral disorder (like Oppositional Defiant Disorder) and should be addressed behaviorally.

Summary

The process of integrating test data and creating a coherent conceptualization of the issues presenting in an assessment case can easily be the most daunting, "mystical" part of the entire assessment process. This process need not be magical or scary. While it will become much easier with more clinical knowledge, supervision, and especially practice, breaking down the process into its basic steps can make it more manageable.

The first step in the process is collecting and recording all your data—from tests, the clinical assessment (including the clinical interview, collateral information, and a mental status evaluation), and behavioral observations—into a single place. The second step, one of the more challenging steps, is to go through the data to see what themes emerge; this is a process that becomes easier and clearer with practice. Themes can represent anything from symptoms to strengths, defenses to personality style characteristics, and coping mechanisms to evidence of maladaptive processes. These themes can illuminate how an individual organizes his or her emotional world, both his or her thought process and thought content, and how he or she feels about himself or herself and others, among other aspects of his or her functioning.

The third step is to lay out these data, which have been categorized into themes, in a chart, making it easy to determine (a) whether you have enough evidence to support each of the themes and (b) whether the themes make conceptual sense, such that all of the data used to support each theme truly do *describe* the theme. At this point, you may need to revisit the second step, adjusting the themes to make more sense.

The fourth and final step is to use the themes to conceptualize the case, using one of many models as a basis for conceptualization. At times, the conceptualization will be extremely evident from the themes. However, the conceptualization is often less obvious, in which case several template models can be useful in explaining how the themes fit together to describe the person. Each of the models may have different emphases, and thus different implications for treatment, but each one includes and explains each of the themes in a logical way that can be understood by those receiving feedback.

After completing this process, you will have a clear conceptualization that incorporates all the data you received from the tests, as well as your clinical observation. The clearer this conceptualization is to you, the easier it will be both to write up and to convey to others. The narrative structure of the conceptualization (and later, the write-up) gives the assessment face validity, such that the person being assessed is much more likely to understand and remember the results, as well as to follow through on recommendations made based on the results.

CHAPTER 5

Writing Reports

Although different authors, and indeed different supervisors, will have different expectations when it comes to writing up psychological assessment reports, most reports typically have general similarities and will differ only slightly according to the needs of the different placements and settings in which you will work. This chapter presents one format for writing up reports, but its ultimate goal is to provide useful guidelines for (a) the type of information that should be presented and (b) effective ways of presenting that information. These guidelines should be useful regardless of the write-up format you use. One of the most difficult tasks involved in writing a psychological report is to balance the language to make it both professional and easily understood by all parties who may read it. This means that the language used in reports should be relatively free of psychological jargon, unless you define terms explicitly and clearly within the report itself. However, language cannot be so informal that it undermines the psychologist's authority. Finding the balance in language and writing style between obtuse and authoritative is a challenging task indeed, and this chapter is meant to help make the process less daunting.

THE REPORT FORMAT

The format for psychological assessment reports presented in this chapter is designed to be a logical outgrowth of the hypothesis testing model. Specifically, each section is presented clearly and simply, building an argument first for the hypotheses generated, then for the conclusions drawn. While you will not report all hypotheses posited, nor the conclusions about each, the argument put forth in the report should explicitly support the diagnosis and recommendations. There are times when it will be useful to list some of the hypotheses that were ruled out. For example, a child who is referred for an ADHD evaluation may turn out instead to be depressed, which can similarly impair attention. Not only will the report make a strong argument for the diagnosis of depression, but it will clearly present the evidence that the hypothesis of an ADHD diagnosis was not supported by the findings of the testing and was therefore rejected. Ultimately, the report should present a cohesive, compelling argument that supports the conclusions drawn. The major sections of the report are presented in Table 5.1.

TABLE 5.1   MAJOR SECTIONS OF THE ASSESSMENT
             REPORT

The Psychological Assessment Report

Identifying Information
Source of Referral and Referral Questions
Measures Administered
Notes on Testing
Description of Patient*
Presenting Problem
Background Information
   History of Presenting Problem
   Symptomatic Evaluation
   Psychosocial Evaluation
Mental Status Evaluation
Behavioral Observations
Overall Interpretation of Test Findings
   Cognitive Functioning
   Personality and Emotional Functioning
   Vocational Functioning (if tested)
Summary
Diagnostic Impressions
Recommendations
Signatures
Appendices
   Test Results
   Feedback Addendum

* The term "patient" will be used throughout; however, the term "client" is also widely used. Whatever term you use, make sure it is consistent throughout the entire report.

Identifying Information

Sometimes presented as a template with different fields to be filled in according to each case, the identifying information section includes the bare essentials for identifying both the person being assessed and yourself as the assessor. Typically included in this section are name of the individual being assessed; the individual's sex, age, and date of birth; the individual's ethnicity; the name of the assessor/examiner and his or her supervisor, if applicable; the date of the report; and the dates of testing. One way to organize this section is presented in Table 5.2.

There are a few conventions for the information presented in this section. For example, the word "sex" is used instead of "gender," because gender can be considered a social construct, whereas sex is a biological term. Because this is a brief heading, rather than a discussion of gender identity, the more straightforward, biological term is more appropriate at this point. Additionally, the age reported should be the individual's age at the date of the report, not necessarily his or her age during the assessment. Because the date of the report is listed clearly at the beginning of the report, the convention is that it is easier to understand that the age listed is the age at this date. Also, follow all conventions related to titles and degrees when reporting your own and your supervisor's names (do not write Dr. So-and-So; report the name followed by the highest degree earned—Johann X. Supervisor, Ph.D., for example).

The trickiest field in the identifying information section is ethnicity. The best case is to use the term that the individual uses to describe him or herself. An American of Chinese descent, for example, may identify herself using Chinese American, Asian American, Chinese, or even Amerasian. If she identifies as any of these, use this term in the identifying information. If for any reason an individual being assessed does not self-identify his or

TABLE 5.2	IDENTIFYING INFORMATION	
Name:	Date of Report:
Sex:	Assessor:
Age:	Supervisor:
Date of Birth:	Dates of Assessment:
Ethnicity:	

EXAMPLE

Name:	Donald Q. Diddlewatt	Date of Report:	9/21/2008
Sex:	Male	Assessor:	A. Jordan Wright, PhD
Age:	34	Supervisor:	N/A
Date of Birth:	10/18/1973	Dates of Assessment:	8/28/2008; 8/31/2008; 9/4/2008; 9/7/2008
Ethnicity:	African American		

her ethnicity (this may be the case in settings in which you have extremely limited time for the assessment, for example), use general current social convention to identify his or her ethnicity. This same woman, if she did not identify her own ethnicity, would, according to current convention, be identified as Asian American. It is important to note that these sociopolitical conventions are subject to change, so if you are unsure of an ethnic designation, it would be wise to confer with a supervisor or colleague.

Source of Referral and Referral Questions

Just as these are most often the first points of information known to you as the assessor, the source and reason for referral are among the first pieces of information introduced to the reader of the report. As with the rest of the report, it is best to be as specific as possible. This section should include the specific relationship of the individual being assessed to whoever referred him or her for the assessment, as well as the reason given for the referral. While this is often similar to the presenting problem, which is described in further detail subsequently, a general statement of the referral reason is usually adequate. For example, if a therapist has referred a patient because treatment has stopped progressing, the referral question could be "The patient was referred by his therapist for treatment considerations, as progress during therapy has slowed unexpectedly." For someone who may be depressed or anxious, the referral question may simply be "To assess current emotional and psychological functioning." Most often, the general referral questions will be explained in further detail in the presenting problem section.

EXAMPLE

Source of Referral and Referral Questions

Mr. Diddlewatt was referred for an assessment by his current therapist, Fiona R. Snodgrass, LCSW, who has been working with him for about three years. Ms. Snodgrass reported that the patient has become "significantly more hostile" lately, with no apparent cause. The referral was made to assess his current emotional functioning and for treatment considerations.

If the individual being assessed is a child, state clearly that consent for testing was provided by his or her parent or legal guardian, and also that the child gave assent for being tested. These terms, consent and assent, are legal terms. Consent is written and signed by a person legally able to give consent (generally, adults give their own consent, unless they have been deemed by a court unable to make medical decisions for themselves; children are not legally allowed to give consent for themselves). Assent is a general agreement to receive services given by someone who is not legally able to give consent. The age of consent varies by state; make sure you know the law in whichever state you are practicing.

Measures Administered

Although "measures administered" is probably the most straightforward section of the entire report, keep a few conventions in mind. First and foremost, write the formal name of each test administered in its entirety, followed in parentheses by the abbreviation that you plan to use throughout the report. For example: Wechsler Adult Intelligence Scale, 4th Edition (WAIS-IV). Any reviews of records, collateral interviews, and the clinical interview should be listed here as well.

There are several choices for the format of this section. Some assessors prefer to list measures alphabetically, so that other professionals can search for specific measures quickly and easily. Others prefer to list them thematically, such that measures of background information (clinical interview, collateral interviews, reviews of records, etc.) come first, cognitive measures (aptitude,

EXAMPLE

Measures Administered

- Clinical interview—8/28/08
- Collateral interview with current therapist—8/28/08
- Bender Visual-Motor Gestalt Test, 2nd Edition (Bender-2)—8/31/08
- Wechsler Adult Intelligence Scale, 4th Edition (WAIS-IV)—8/31/08
- Minnesota Multiphasic Personality Inventory, 2nd Edition (MMPI-2)—9/4/08
- Rorschach Inkblot Test, Comprehensive System Scoring (Rorschach)—9/4/08
- Personality Assessment Inventory (PAI)—9/4/08
- Human Figure, House-Tree-Person, and Kinetic Family Drawings (Projective Drawings)—9/4/08
- Millon Clinical Multiaxial Inventory, 3rd Edition (MCMI-III)—9/7/08
- Thematic Apperception Test (TAT)—9/7/08

achievement, and neuropsychological tests) come next, and tests of personality and emotional functioning (checklists, objective measures, and projective measures) come last. This format mirrors the structure of the report, so it makes intuitive sense. A final option is to list measures in the order they were administered. Also optional is listing the date each measure was administered next to the measure itself.

Notes on Testing

The notes on testing section does not necessarily need to be in every psychological assessment report. The purpose of this section is to note any circumstances that might make the current assessment different from a standard assessment. That is, any circumstance that may impact the results of the assessment significantly that is different from what would generally be expected of any normal assessment, should be reported.

For example, any variation on standardized administration of tests should be noted, as should the reason for the variation. If you made an error while administering a subtest, for instance, you would indicate in this section that, due to assessor error, the score obtained from that subtest was rendered invalid and replaced by another subtest in the calculation of the index score. Specifically, for example, if the validity of the information subtest of the WAIS-IV was compromised for some reason, it could be replaced by the comprehension subtest when calculating the verbal comprehension index and the full scale IQ. Another example would be when an individual is assessed in front of a one-way mirror, behind which sits a class of graduate students studying assessment. In this case, the fact that the assessment is being conducted in front of the mirror may impact the results of the assessment. Another example might be the setting in which the testing takes place. If you are required to assess an individual on an inpatient unit at the patient's bedside, for instance, this would represent a significant variation from the standard administration of the tests being used.

At the end of this section, you should always include a statement of whether the results of the current assessment should be considered a valid representation of the individual's current functioning. Generally, minor variations in the testing circumstances will not alter the assessment enough to invalidate your conclusions. However, if an individual being assessed exhibits extremely low motivation or even oppositional behavior, such that he or she could be said to have been endeavoring to undermine the results of the assessment, it would be helpful to include a note indicating that, for this reason, the results of the current assessment should be interpreted with caution.

EXAMPLE

Notes on Testing

The current assessment was conducted in front of a one-way mirror, behind which sat a group of seven graduate students training in psychological assessment, as part of their requirements for a PhD in clinical psychology. The patient was notified of this and gave explicit consent to be observed during the assessment. It is possible that these circumstances may have altered the patient's responses slightly, but given his constant motivation and openness throughout the process, the current assessment should be considered a valid representation of his current functioning.

Description of Patient

The description of the patient should serve as a brief introduction to how the individual being assessed presented and appeared during the assessment. This description is a combination of factual information about his or her demographic profile as well as clinical observations. The purpose is to provide the reader of the report with a visual image of the person who sat across from you in the room during the assessment. You should pay special attention to a comparison of the person's physical appearance to what would be considered normative. For example, if a preteen girl being assessed is tall and more fully developed than would be expected given her age, then this should be stated clearly.

It is important to avoid judgmental language throughout this section. For example, if an adult woman is dressed provocatively, with tight-fitting and low-cut clothing, avoid saying she was dressed "inappropriately"; simply report the facts of her attire as objectively as possible. Other basic behavioral observations can be included in this section, if you think that they contribute to the reader's mental picture of the person being assessed. For example, if an adolescent boy made no eye contact with you and spoke in a barely audible volume throughout testing, providing these details can be very illustrative for the reader.

Presenting Problem

As previously stated in Chapter 1, the presenting problem may be significantly more complicated than what the individual presents as his or her chief complaint (if he or she complains of anything at all). At this point you have

EXAMPLE

Description of Patient

Mr. Diddlewatt is a light-skinned, African American man who was 34 years old at the time of testing. He is tall with a very thin, lanky build, and he looks slightly older than his stated age. He typically looked tired, with large dark circles under his eyes. He was dressed appropriately in baggy jeans and a tight T-shirt, though he wore the same outfit to all assessment sessions. He was very talkative and friendly, and he was extremely cooperative throughout the assessment process.

compiled all of the data collected from (a) the referral source; (b) the clinical interview; (c) collateral measures (including parent interviews for children, reviews of medical and psychiatric records, and consultations with previous mental health providers, whenever possible); and (d) your own clinical observations and a mental status exam and synthesized it into areas of functional impairment and hypotheses. Therefore, this section should flow easily and directly from the work you have already done.

A useful way of organizing the presenting problem section is to include a paragraph for each major area of functional impairment. The presenting problem includes *all* areas of problematic functioning, including subjectively felt distress (such as low mood or anxiety), concrete specific impairment (such as unemployment or divorce), and global areas of impairment (such as difficulties with interpersonal functioning or socialization in general). While there is no agreed-on formula for structuring this section, in general the most salient difficulty or most impaired area of functioning is listed first, followed by a listing of the somewhat less crucial difficulties.

It is important to reserve this section for the problems the individual is facing *currently*. There will be an opportunity in the background information section to discuss difficulties in the past, whether different from the current problems or simply historical information about them. Additionally, where necessary, make sure to include the sources of the different pieces of information. If the entirety of the information you have included in this section is derived from the self-report of the individual being assessed, there is no need to keep repeating that he or she reported the information. However, if some of the information was obtained through self-report and some was provided by the referring doctor, it is important to make this distinction known.

Background Information

The background information section can take many forms. Most importantly, however, it should include three major areas: the history of the presenting problem, the symptomatic evaluation, and the psychosocial evaluation. Using these three subheadings offers a relatively easy and clear way to organize what usually turns out to be an almost overwhelming amount of information. Another way of organizing it is to create subheadings for the history

EXAMPLE

Presenting Problem

According to his current therapist, Mr. Diddlewatt has recently become "more hostile" in general. When asked specifically about this issue, the patient described feeling angrier and "more keyed up" than usual. He stated that his anger tends to be focused on his boss, with whom he has always had a "difficult" relationship. Moreover, he reported yelling at one of his friends after what he, in retrospect, considered only minor annoyances, such as her being 15 minutes late for a dinner with him. Even when describing this incident, he seemed to become agitated, as indicated by increasing vocal pressure and volume.

In addition to his anger, the patient reported that he fears dying, more than he feels he should. In order to cope with this fear, he needs "everything to be perfect," including having all the furniture in his house facing in the exact same direction, so that as much as possible is predictable. Additionally, he has constant thoughts of death and dying, and he mentally plays out all the different ways in which he could die, "so that I won't be surprised when it happens."

The patient also reported difficulties sleeping, stating that his thoughts often race at night and he cannot get to sleep. Additionally, he reported some loss of energy, though during the interview he seemed extremely alert and energetic. He stated that he had stopped socializing recently, except for with his girlfriend, because he is afraid he will lose his temper with his friends and lose them entirely. He also reported that he is not eating very much lately.

of the presenting problem and all of the subsections of the symptomatic and psychosocial evaluations. However, this can be both tedious and overwhelming both for you and for the reader of the report. There may be times when a few paragraphs are sufficient to cover the major points of background information. You will invariably have more information than is useful for the purpose of the report; your challenge is to limit the information to what is most useful, while making it clear that you have evaluated all the different areas that are relevant to the individual's functioning.

A major note on this section (which will apply to all of the sections) concerns verb tense. The tense you use for verbs throughout a report can get confusing. It is best to keep clear in your mind exactly what is present and ongoing and what is in the past. Throughout the report, whenever discussing what the individual being assessed reported, use the past tense for the fact that he or she reported it in the past. However, you should evaluate the content of whatever was reported for its own proper tense. That is, if whatever was reported is ongoing, it should be written in the present tense. If it is in the past, use the past tense. For example, you may produce a sentence like this for a woman who is struggling with insomnia: "The patient reported that she has difficulty both falling asleep and staying asleep throughout the night." These sleep problems are ongoing, so although she reported it in the past to you, the present tense is used for the difficulty itself. However, how she used to cope with this may be put like this: "The patient reported that she used a prescription sedative in order to ensure that she fell asleep." Because she no longer employs this tactic, the entire sentence is presented in the past tense.

The history of presenting problem section is extremely important in that it provides a context for the individual's current problems and functioning. Specific issues that should be addressed here are the duration of the problems presented in the presenting problem section, as well as any history of similar difficulties. Any additional information that may further illustrate the nature of the presenting problem in a way that makes it more easily understood by the reader should be included as well. For example, if part of the presenting problem includes difficulty sleeping (insomnia), any information related to sleep throughout the individual's entire history can be considered for inclusion in the history of presenting problem section. Details such as when the individual began sleeping alone as a child, any previous difficulties with sleep, and even a history of a night-shift work schedule might be important in understanding what is happening for the individual. Additionally, this section can go into more detail about what exactly has happened during the course of the presenting problem. For example, it is a good idea to include what reportedly goes through the mind of the individual when he or she cannot sleep, as well as any history of similar thoughts or thought patterns. Again, this section is meant to provide a contextual and historical picture of the current problems in functioning, because this history may be extremely important in understanding why the current problems are occurring for the individual.

Background Information

History of Presenting Problem

Mr. Diddlewatt reported that he has struggled with his anger for many years. He reported that he had been expelled from several different middle schools because of getting into fights with peers and "blowing up" at teachers. While he was reportedly better during high school and beyond, he stated that he continued to feel angry, even if he did not express it as he had in middle school. When asked specifically what he was most angry about, he reported that it began with anger toward his parents, who he felt were unsupportive of him. This was compounded by the fact that he was the only Black student at any of his schools growing up in a small Southern town, and he faced much discrimination and "hate" from the other children, as well as the teachers.

The patient's anxiety about death "is relatively new." He reported that he had always been a bit of a perfectionist, liking everything "in its proper place." But the extent of his thinking about death and dying, which increases his need for things to be in place, reached its current level only several months ago. He could not identify any triggers—nobody close to him had passed away or was harmed, and he had not had a birthday or injury that may have spotlighted his mortality. "It just started randomly, and I know it's crazy, but I just can't stop it."

The patient further reported a period of about a year when he feels he was depressed, feeling "down" most of the time and feeling unable to accomplish even the most basic tasks, like brushing his teeth and washing dishes. When asked for details about this period, he reported that he was so depressed that he could not work, that he cut off contact with almost all of his friends and family, that he slept and ate excessive amounts, and that nothing made him happy. This period occurred about five years ago, but he managed to "pull myself out of it" and regain a normal level of functioning for him since that time. "I haven't been depressed again since then, thank God."

Symptomatic Evaluation

The patient reported that he had previously been in treatment only once before, in middle school, which was mandated by one of the schools he entered after being expelled from another one. He was

(Continued)

required to see the guidance counselor once a week for about three months, which he felt was not helpful. He has been in his current therapy for about three years, which he reports is "much more helpful" than his previous experience. Although he was evaluated by a psychiatrist as part of the intake process for his current treatment, the issue of psychotropic medication has never actually been considered, and he has not seen the psychiatrist since that first visit. He had been depressed for that year (about five years ago), but because he felt he had pulled himself out of the depression, he did not see the need to even consider medication.

His current therapy, by both his and his therapist's report, is interpersonally oriented and supportive. The major area of focus has been how his feelings about his parents have affected his current relationships with other people, which are very often characterized by a lack of trust, a lack of genuineness, and a tinge of anger and resentment. He reported liking his current therapist and finding the therapy "useful."

The patient denied any history of significant medical illness or substance abuse. He did report some experimentation with marijuana in college, though he denied using it since graduating. The patient drinks socially, rarely actually getting intoxicated. He reported drinking "a glass of wine with dinner if I go out with friends or on a date," but rarely more than that.

The patient reported very little history of medical or psychiatric illness in his family, "that I know of." He described his mother as "erratic," often rapidly fluctuating between "disengaged and overly energetic." Specifically, he recalled several periods in which she did not leave her bedroom for several weeks at a time. At other times, she seemed "almost frazzled," with so much energy that she could not seem to control herself. During these periods, she would volunteer for many different charities, rush the patient around from place to place in a way that did not make sense to him, yell excessively at the patient and his father, and declare loudly that she was "extremely disappointed" with all the people in her life. She was never diagnosed with any disorder and never received any treatment. The patient denied any other family history of erratic behavior or psychiatric treatment.

The patient reported no difficulties with his mother's pregnancy with him or during birth. Although he was not completely sure, he denied any delays in any developmental milestones, feeling he sat up, walked, talked, and potty trained at generally appropriate ages. He denied any abuse, by his parents or anyone else, and any other traumas as a child.

Psychosocial Evaluation

The patient is an only child of parents who are still currently married and residing in the small Southern town in which he grew up. They were reportedly one of the only Black families in the town, and he was the only Black student in every school he attended through high school. He reported difficulty with his parents, feeling they were never supportive of him or understanding of his difficulties in school. His mother did not work, and his father worked many hours in a factory. With his mother's erratic behavior and his father's hectic work schedule, the patient felt he had no significant relationships with adults when he was a child. Currently, he speaks to his parents about once a month, though he says these conversations are "always cold and businesslike."

Academically, the patient maintained decent grades in mainstream education throughout his schooling, going to college in a large New England city that was "more diverse and more accepting." He majored in business, receiving a BA from a small liberal arts college. He worked in banks most of his adult life, and he currently holds a position doing clerical and administrative tasks in a large bank, a job he has had for two years, which he reportedly does not like. He has "a racist boss," with whom he argues at least once a week. His boss's boss seemingly appreciates the patient's work and productivity, as he will not allow the patient to be fired, even after outright confrontations with his boss.

The patient denied any criminal or legal involvement, currently or in the past.

The patient is a heterosexual male who is currently not in a romantic relationship. He reported one significant romantic relationship with a woman while he was in college, but since then he has not had a serious relationship with a woman. He has "a group of friends," with whom he socializes on a regular basis, but he does not have a best friend or even a person he considers himself close to. He reported that he knows he has "issues" related to getting close to others. He has sex occasionally, with women he meets on the Internet, but none of these involvements ends up becoming a relationship beyond the sexual contact.

Much of the patient's past is characterized by feeling targeted and victimized by others because of his race. As an African American growing up in a small Southern town that was predominantly White, the patient struggled significantly with his own racial identity. He reported times growing up when he "pretended not to be Black," making sure his haircut,

(Continued)

clothes, and voice were as similar as possible to those of his White peers. His parents never discussed with him the struggle of being Black in an intolerant town, and he feels resentful that they never shared their own experiences. Although he found relief moving to a large New England city, which he experienced as more tolerant, he reported that since leaving his hometown, "I just don't think of my race anymore—it's just easier that way." On occasions when he is forced to consider his own race, such as when his boss calls him racist, derogatory names, he becomes extremely angry, and "I become that middle schooler who got into so many fights again."

Mental Status Evaluation

The mental status evaluation (MSE) is the only section of the entire report (other than the appendix of test scores, should you choose to include one) that is generally aimed toward other mental health professionals. As such, it is the only section of the report in which you can use psychological jargon without shame. Phrases like "Her affect was mood-incongruent and inappropriate to the situation" would be taboo anywhere else in a report, because most readers would have no idea what you are talking about, but in the MSE, this language is entirely appropriate.

The mental status evaluation section should be a concise paragraph that includes at least a note on *all* of the major areas of the MSE (which were presented in Chapter 1). That is, no matter how relevant or irrelevant the individual's functioning on any one domain appears, you must report on it. This is an area in which there can be a true balance of strengths and areas of concern. In many cases much of the MSE will appear "within normal limits"—this is a phrase that is used regularly to represent the fact that an area or domain of functioning is not significantly outside of the norm of behavior that is adaptive or functional. Usually only some of the MSE constitutes functioning outside of the norm of adaptive behavior, so the paragraph can include both positive and negative attributes. The MSE is almost entirely based on your clinical observation. This format, including both what is unimpaired and what seems unusual to you, forces you to consider the entire person sitting across from you, including his or her strengths.

Remember from Chapter 1 that there are six major areas of the MSE, each of which needs to be addressed. They are (1) appearance and behavior, (2) speech and language, (3) mood and affect, (4) thought process and content, (5) cognition, and (6) prefrontal functioning. As you proceed through each section, you will note in which domains your patient is functioning within normal limits, as well as those domains in which his functioning is outside of what would be considered normative. Including concrete examples of this non-normative functioning will both illustrate your point and lend a degree of seriousness to your argument. That is, it is important not to simply state that a domain is outside of the normal range, but to explain exactly how it is outside of the normal range with specific supporting examples.

EXAMPLE

Mental Status Evaluation

The patient arrived on time for appointments and called ahead of time to reschedule those he could not keep. He was casually and appropriately dressed, and he was cooperative throughout the assessment process. His motor activity was slightly agitated during sessions, shaking his leg repeatedly and fidgeting with his fingers, but was within normal limits. The patient spoke in an appropriate volume. His rate of speech was fairly quick and pressured. He used language well, but he expressed a lack of understanding in relation to certain emotions. For example, he asked what anxiety was and how it was different from being energetic. His mood was reportedly "fine," except for some reported anger at work, and his affect during testing was both mood-congruent and appropriate to the situation, as he smiled and laughed throughout sessions. The patient's thought process was goal-directed. His thought content centered primarily on thoughts of his own death, though he denied suicidality. Homicidality was also denied, though he reported feeling at times as though he wants to harm his boss—he denied that he would ever actually follow through on this feeling. No hallucinations were reported, and no delusions were elicited. His attention, concentration, and memory all seemed intact. The patient's insight was poor, as he struggled to identify anything other than the racism of others as causes for any of his current difficulties. His judgment and impulse control were within normal limits.

Behavioral Observations

The behavioral observations section is the place where you should describe, in greater detail than in the mental status evaluation, behaviors that occurred *during the process* of the testing. Note that behaviors that an individual reports he or she enacts outside of the testing sessions should be reported in the presenting problem or background information sections, rather than here. As this section is expressly concerned with how an individual behaves during the assessment process, it is extremely important to include *any and all* notable behaviors observed, even if they were also included in another section (such as in the description of patient, in the MSE, or in the overall interpretation of test findings). No test session behavior should be listed elsewhere that is not also covered in this section.

The behavioral observations section should always include at least some information on how well-related the individual was to you throughout the assessment. Behavioral observations that indicate relatedness include the degree to which the individual maintained eye contact, the appropriateness of conversation, his or her comfort in disclosing personal information, and his or her general cooperativeness and friendliness. In this section it is imperative that you support any claims you make about the individual's functioning with concrete, behavioral evidence. For example, if you state that someone "seemed anxious during the clinical interview," you must support that claim with the evidence that led you to that conclusion. In this case, you might state that the person shifted around in his or her seat constantly, made only sporadic eye contact with you, and seemed to stutter when trying to make a point, despite the fact that he or she does not seem to have a difficulty with stuttering in general. All of these behavioral observations serve as evidence of your claim that the individual "seemed anxious" during sessions. Feel free to employ the useful phrase "as evidenced by" throughout this section. Using this phrase will force you to include the concrete, behavioral evidence for any conclusions you have drawn.

In addition to general comments about relatedness, any other behaviors that you feel may constitute good illustrative information for a point you will make later in the report should be included here. For example, constant and persistent erasing on all tasks that involve drawing (e.g., Bender-2, Projective Drawings) may be salient to you, as it may seem excessive. Moreover, even if during testing it did not seem too important, if testing

EXAMPLE

Behavioral Observations

The patient was cooperative throughout the testing process. He maintained eye contact well throughout the entire assessment, even when discussing difficult topics. He frequently and comfortably initiated conversation. He gave concise answers to questions, and at times it was difficult to elicit more detailed responses. During the assessment, he at times seemed anxious or overly energized, as evidenced by his shaking his leg repeatedly and fidgeting with his fingers and cracking his knuckles. Additionally, during several cognitive tasks, he made self-deprecating remarks, stating that he was "bad at math" and making generally negative statements about his performance on the tasks. Despite this he displayed good effort on all tests administered.

reveals that the individual has extreme perfectionistic tendencies, then the constant erasing may be a good illustration of how this personality characteristic may impact his or her functioning. In either case, it is important to include this information here, so that you can use it later to illustrate exactly what you mean by a certain psychological construct or term.

Overall Interpretation of Test Findings

The structure of this section constitutes the bulk of the work you have done in the assessment and, as such, it is by far the most important section of the report. This is also the section that will vary the most from report to report and, especially, from psychologist to psychologist. The structure presented here represents one clear and logical way of organizing your interpretations. The presentation should include either two or three sections (depending on the referral questions): cognitive functioning, personality and emotional functioning, and vocational functioning. At times, again depending on the referral questions, as well as the findings that emerged from the testing, the personality and emotional functioning sectioning may be better organized into two separate sections—one for personality functioning and one for emotional functioning. Obviously, the vocational functioning section should be included only if vocational testing was administered and the question of work was a central part of the presenting problem or referral questions.

Cognitive Functioning

The cognitive functioning section is the first step to understanding how an individual relates to the world and what may be impacting his or her current functioning. Specifically, it offers a picture of cognitive strengths and weaknesses, all of which likely impact how the person is functioning. If a teenager is referred for an assessment because he is having behavioral difficulties in school, it may turn out that his ability to effectively use language to express himself represents a significant weakness for him. This, in turn, may help explain (a) why he may be having difficulties in school and (b) why he may express his frustrations by acting out, rather than expressing himself with words.

Alternatively, it could be very important to find that there is no cognitive weakness at all. In this case, we would want to focus more heavily on his emotional functioning to see how he is currently feeling and how his experience of these emotional states might be impacting his overall functioning. A third case may be that the cognitive functioning section reveals extreme strengths in intellectual aptitude, which may contribute to his being bored in classes that are moving too slowly for him. This boredom may translate to behavioral problems in class. Whatever the case, it is important to start with a basis of how the individual is functioning in terms of his or her cognitive abilities.

Depending on the referral questions and the types of testing conducted, the cognitive functioning section can generally take one of three forms.

When Cognitive Functioning Is Secondary   In general, when the cognitive testing is not the major focus of the assessment and you have given only an aptitude test (e.g., WAIS-IV) and perhaps a few neuropsychological screening instruments (e.g., Bender-2), the format can be a straightforward description of cognitive strengths and weaknesses by domain. In most cases, six paragraphs are necessary: one introductory paragraph, four subdomain/index paragraphs, and a final summary paragraph.

The first paragraph contains a general breakdown of broad domains of functioning. It is extremely important to know exactly how to interpret tests of intelligence. For example, there are instances in which you will not report a Full-Scale IQ (FSIQ), simply because it is misleading. That is, the subdomains that make up the FSIQ are so drastically (and significantly) different that the broader FSIQ is rendered meaningless. (If the verbal comprehension, perceptual reasoning, and working memory indices are high average, while the processing speed index is extremely low, reporting that the FSIQ is in the low average range would be misleading.) In these cases, this first paragraph will consist of a basic comparison of the four subdomains of cognitive functioning (from the WAIS-IV, these would be verbal comprehension, perceptual reasoning, working memory, and processing speed).

The final sentences of this paragraph should include conclusions drawn from any neuropsychological screening instruments used. For example, if a Bender-2 were given and the individual exhibited no weaknesses on the measure, a statement would be made that based on the Bender-2 there is no evidence of gross neurological impairment. These brief neuropsychological screening measures are important for ruling out major impairments in neurological functioning, though conclusions based on them should be limited to these broad areas of severe impairment. For example, adequate performance on the Bender-2, a measure of perceptual, motor, and visual-motor integration functioning, as well as short-term visual memory, may not necessarily rule out all neurological impairment. However, the Bender-2 can rule out gross and major brain damage, given that major cortical damage would likely impair perceptual, motor, visual-motor integration, or short-term visual memory functioning.

The second, third, fourth, and fifth paragraphs of this section will each represent a separate subdomain of functioning, as dictated by the cognitive test given. For example, if using the WAIS-IV, each of the indices (verbal comprehension, perceptual reasoning, working memory, and processing speed) would get its own paragraph, each with its own heading to make clear what the paragraph is about. The order in which you present these paragraphs will depend on the data that emerge from the test itself. If there are no interesting subdomains (e.g., if all the indices are in the average range, with no significant differences between any two), you would likely start with the domains that are most representative of overall functioning (verbal comprehension and perceptual reasoning), followed by those domains that are more susceptible to interference from emotional, personality, or situational variables (working memory and processing speed).

However, if there are findings that particularly stand out, you should start with the domain/index that is highest (the greatest strength), and the others should follow in decreasing order until the greatest weakness is presented last. For example, if an individual exhibits a significantly higher verbal comprehension compared to the other domains, with the working memory score being significantly lower, you would present the paragraphs in the order from greatest strength to greatest weakness, as follows: verbal comprehension, perceptual reasoning, processing speed, and working memory.

Each of these four paragraphs should have the same structure. They should each start with a general statement of the individual's performance on that index as compared with others his or her age. This sentence should not include the name of the index (which is the heading of the paragraph), but should rather be a clear description of what exactly the domain is assessing. For example, for the verbal comprehension index, you might state: "The patient's performance on tasks that assess her ability to both understand and use language fell within the average range of functioning compared to others her age." This sentence makes clear exactly what the domain assesses. The use of a qualitative range, rather than an index score, allows anyone who is reading the report to understand how the individual performed.

Following this statement of general functioning in the domain, you should report any *interesting* subtests (i.e., subtests that are meaningful because of how the individual performed on them). That is, any subtest that is a significant normative strength or weakness (i.e., a strength or weakness compared to same-age peers) or a significant ipsative strength or weakness (i.e., a strength or weakness compared to the individual's own functioning) should be described. If there are no "interesting" subtests, you can make a general statement that all the subtests that make up this domain fell within the same range of functioning. Similar to the description of the domain, the descriptions of the subtests should be made in clear terms that can be understood by anyone reading the report.

An optimal sentence will be structured to include (a) a description of what the task required of the individual, (b) the skills assessed by the task, and (c) how the individual performed on the task (i.e., whether it was a strength or a weakness, or the qualitative range of his or her score). For example, a significant ipsative strength on the vocabulary subtest may be reported like this: "The patient exhibited a significant strength compared to her own overall functioning on a task that required her to define words, which assesses her word knowledge, long-term memory, and ability to express herself clearly." This sentence clearly defines the precise area of her functioning that constitutes the strength.

The final sentence of each of these four subdomain paragraphs should be a general statement of what these findings might indicate. While this may vary from report to report, in general it is important to state why the individual may have performed the way he or she did on that index. For example, good performance on verbal comprehension is often an indicator of intellectual ambition and good schooling. A closing sentence for this paragraph may be written like this: "This strong performance in the verbal domain likely reflects that she has taken advantage of both formal and informal educational opportunities and is ambitious about her education." While this sentence is tentative (using words like "likely"), it is a good hypothesis about why an individual may be strong in the verbal domain.

The final paragraph of the cognitive section should be a cognitive summary. While similar to the first paragraph of the section, it should report only "interesting" findings rather than describing all subdomains of functioning, whether or not they are interesting. The first half of this paragraph should be dedicated to a reiteration of salient strengths and weaknesses. The second half of this paragraph should clearly state the possibilities for why these significant variations in functioning may have been exhibited. For example, consider an individual who performs within the high average range on verbal comprehension, perceptual reasoning, and working memory, but falls within the low average range on processing speed.

There are several reasons this may occur. While there may be perceptual or motor difficulties, these can be verified or ruled out with the Bender-2. So in the second half of this paragraph, possibilities for why processing speed may be lower than the rest of his or her functioning will be presented: "Slowed speed of processing information can be due to several factors. While it could be due to motor difficulty, her high average performance on the Bender-2 showed that she has no impairment in motor functioning. Other factors that can impair processing speed include emotional disturbance (e.g., depression), anxiety, low motivation, and certain personality factors, such as perfectionism." Because psychomotor slowing is one of the criteria for depression, it should at least be presented among other possibilities to explain low processing speed. Because you have not yet presented the emotional functioning of the individual, it would be inappropriate in this section to definitively state that the observed deficit is likely due to emotional difficulties such as depression. Instead, simply set out your hypotheses, which you will revisit later after you have presented the personality and emotional functioning section.

EXAMPLE

Cognitive Functioning

On the WAIS-IV, the patient exhibited varied performance across his different domains of functioning. Specifically, while his perceptual reasoning and working memory both fell within the Average range of functioning compared to others his age (50th and 57th percentiles, respectively), he exhibited a significant strength in his verbal comprehension (76th percentile). He exhibited a weakness compared to his own overall functioning in his processing speed (14th percentile). The client exhibited no soft signs of neurological damage as evidenced by his High Average to Superior performance on the Bender-2.

Verbal Comprehension. On measures of general verbal skills, such as verbal fluency, ability to understand and use verbal reasoning, and verbal knowledge, the patient's performance fell within the High Average range of functioning compared to others his age (Verbal Comprehension Index, 76th percentile). He exhibited a significant strength on a task requiring him to explain the conceptual similarities between terms, which assesses his abstract verbal reasoning (Similarities, 98th percentile). His good verbal ability reflects intellectual ambition and knowledge gained from both formal and informal educational opportunities.

Perceptual Reasoning. On tests that measure nonverbal reasoning, visuospatial aptitude, and induction and planning skills, the patient performed within the Average range compared to others his age (Perceptual Reasoning Index, 50th percentile). Tasks in this domain involve nonverbal stimuli such as designs, pictures, and puzzles and assess the individual's abilities to examine a problem, draw upon visuospatial skills, organize thoughts, and create and test possible solutions. All of the subtests that make up this domain fell within the Average range of functioning.

Working Memory. On tasks that assessed the ability to memorize new information, hold it in short-term memory, concentrate, and manipulate the information to produce some result or reasoning outcome, the patient's performance fell within the Average range compared to others his age (Working Memory Index, 57th percentile). All the subtests that make up this domain fell within the Average range of functioning, suggesting adequate attentional and fluid reasoning skills.

Processing Speed. The patient's performance on tasks that measure the ability to focus attention and quickly scan, discriminate between, and respond to visual information within a time limit fell within the Low Average range of functioning compared to others his age (Processing Speed Index, 14th percentile). Specifically, on a task assessing processing speed and visual motor coordination, which required the patient to match a series of numbers to shapes as quickly and accurately as possible within a limited period of time, his performance represented a weakness relative to his same-age peers and his own overall functioning (Coding, 9th percentile).

Cognitive Summary. The patient's performance across domains of cognitive functioning was varied, with High Average verbal ability and a significant weakness in his speed of processing nonverbal information, which fell within the Low Average range. Significant weakness in processing speed can be due to several factors, including emotional disturbance, psychomotor slowing, attentional problems, and personality factors like perfectionism. As he exhibited no motor difficulty on the Bender-2 and no attentional deficit in working memory, it is likely that his lower processing speed is secondary to emotional or personality factors.

When Cognitive Functioning Is Primary When cognitive questions are primary to the referral, specifically when there is the possibility of a learning disorder, the structure of the cognitive functioning section will change slightly. In this case, the specific strengths and weaknesses within cognitive ability and aptitude may not be very important. It is generally more important in this case to compare and contrast cognitive *ability* with academic *achievement*—that is, you will make a comparison between what an individual *should* be able to achieve and what he or she actually *is* achieving, specifically in school domains. The cognitive functioning section on these reports should have three major sections: cognitive ability, academic achievement, and cognitive summary.

The cognitive ability section can be identical to the format presented previously (the first format presented), with six subsections related to subdomains of functioning. However, when there is a question of a learning disability, being so specific within this ability section is often less important than the *comparison* between the ability section and the achievement section. Because much of school achievement is highly dependent on verbal functioning, it may be more important to delineate how the individual performed verbally compared to his or her other subdomains of functioning (as was done in the previously presented structure of the first paragraph). Verbal ability is especially important for reading and writing. Mathematics achievement, however, can be dependent on several areas of ability, including perceptual reasoning and working memory. Thus, it is important to report the results of these indices. However, it may be less important to report specific subtest strengths and weaknesses, again because the *comparison* of achievement and ability is more important than the minor variations within the ability domains. As such, the cognitive ability section may be significantly shorter than the cognitive functioning section of the previously presented report type.

The academic achievement section is based on achievement testing (e.g., WIAT-2 or Woodcock-Johnson Tests of Achievement) and is often included when an individual is having difficulty in one or more school or academic domains. This section refers to how well the individual has learned and can apply skills in reading, writing, mathematics, and oral language. The academic achievement section can have a subsection for each of these four domains of school achievement. Within each subsection/ domain of achievement, a concise report of how the individual performed on the tests of achievement should be presented in a similar way to the cognitive ability subdomain paragraphs. It should first state generally how the person performed across all tasks (e.g., a general comment on overall reading achievement, such as that the patient's reading achievement fell within the average range), then reporting any interesting differences within the domain subtests (e.g., any differences between phonetic word reading and reading comprehension, such as reading comprehension being average, but phonetic reading being low average). Finally there should be a sentence that summarizes what the findings may mean (e.g., the patient is likely reading by word recognition more than phonetically, as he or she is comprehending adequately despite poor phonetic reading).

At times, some of these subsections/domains may be collapsed into a single subsection. For example, if the individual's performance on reading tests is low average, and his or her performance on writing tasks is also low average, it may make sense to combine these into a reading/writing subsection. The rationale is that with low average reading ability, the expected level of performance on writing tasks would be low average; therefore, by combining these two sections, you place less emphasis on the poor writing ability, as it is seemingly due to the poor reading ability. That is, it would be rare for an individual to have difficulty reading but to be exceptionally good at writing (though when this does happen, it merits the use of separate subsections for each). It is likely that poor reading achievement is the major reason for the poor writing achievement. Mathematics should generally be separated into its own section, as it is conceptually separate from the other, more verbal domains of achievement.

The final section is the cognitive summary. This is where you can make preliminary conclusions about the likely presence or absence of a learning disorder. Although you cannot make the diagnosis based on the aptitude and achievement testing alone—other factors that *must* be considered include educational opportunity and sensory impairment—you can state clearly whether the achievement performance on the school domains is significantly lower than would be expected given the individual's measured aptitude or ability. If achievement in all academic domains is equal to what would be expected, given ability, you can confidently rule out a learning disorder.

EXAMPLE

Cognitive Functioning

Cognitive Ability. On the WAIS-IV, the patient exhibited varied performance across his different domains of functioning. Specifically, while his perceptual reasoning and working memory both fell within the Average range of functioning compared to others his age (50th and 57th percentiles, respectively), he exhibited a significant strength in his verbal comprehension (76th percentile). He exhibited a weakness compared to his own overall functioning in his processing

(Continued)

speed (14th percentile). The client exhibited no soft signs of neurological damage as evidenced by his High Average to Superior performance on the Bender-2.

On specific measures of general verbal skills, such as verbal fluency, ability to understand and use verbal reasoning, and verbal knowledge, the patient's performance fell within the High Average range of functioning compared to others his age (Verbal Comprehension Index, 76th percentile). Verbal skill is an important factor in an individual's ability to function in school and learn reading, writing, and the verbal use of language.

Academic Achievement. On the WIAT-II, the patient exhibited significant differences between the different domains of academic achievement. He exhibited a strength in his mathematics skill, but he showed some difficulties with his reading and writing ability. His use of oral language was adequate, falling within the Average range compared to others his age (Oral Expression, 73rd percentile).

The patient's mathematics skill fell within the Superior range of functioning compared to others his age (Mathematics, 97th percentile). He exhibited a specific strength in his ability to solve computation problems involving mixed fractions, negative two-digit integers, and linear equations (Numerical Operations, 97th percentile). His performance on these tasks suggests no deficit in his ability to learn math.

When it comes to reading and writing, however, the patient exhibited some difficulty. His ability to read phonetically was adequate (Pseudoword Decoding, 50th percentile), but his understanding of entire passages falls below what would be expected, given his High Average verbal ability (Reading Comprehension, 12th percentile). Additionally, his writing ability was Low Average (14th percentile), which is also lower than would be expected of someone with his verbal ability, but is expected given his Low Average reading ability.

Cognitive Summary. The patient's cognitive ability was generally Average, with a weakness in his speed of processing information and a strength in verbal ability. Low processing speed can be due to several factors, including emotional disturbance, psychomotor slowing, attentional problems, and personality factors like perfectionism. As he exhibited no motor difficulty on the Bender-2 and no attentional deficit in working memory, it is likely that his lower processing speed is secondary to emotional or personality factors.

On tests of academic achievement, the patient performed well in mathematics and adequately in oral expression. However, he showed weakness in both reading and writing ability, suggesting the possibility of a learning disorder. Because his writing ability is at a level expected given his reading ability, it is likely that the patient has a reading disorder.

When Cognitive Functioning Includes Neuropsychological Screening When cognitive questions are primary and you have given a neuropsychological screening battery, a third and final format for the cognitive functioning section is most appropriate.[1] A neuropsychological screening report contains many subsections and has a significantly different structure for the cognitive functioning section. This different structure is primarily due to the fact that, rather than assessing four major subdomains of functioning, you have assessed many separate areas of cognitive and neuropsychological functioning. Not only is the overall structure different from the previously presented cognitive functioning sections, but the format within each subsection is different than in the other cases presented previously.

Evidence of Cognitive Decline. Similar to the report structures previously presented, the first paragraph of this cognitive functioning section provides a general preview of the major areas of functioning. The purpose of the testing is often to assess the possibility of a decline in cognitive functioning. As such, general indicators of current cognitive functioning (e.g., the four indices of the WAIS-IV), an estimate of premorbid level of functioning (e.g., the WTAR or the AMNART), and a comparison of the two are included in this section. This comparison makes it clear whether there is evidence for a decline in overall functioning. That is, if your measure of current intellectual functioning is significantly lower than your measure estimating premorbid functioning, then there is evidence of a possible decline in functioning. This section needs less detail than subsections presented earlier (i.e., there may be no need to report the patient's performance on the different indices of the WAIS-IV), because the report will go into much more detail of specific domains of functioning following this introductory paragraph.

Motivation. The second paragraph is a short section on "Motivation" (and should be titled as such). Having used measures of malingering and motivation, you will make a presentation of whether or not poor motivation or the potential for faking were likely factors affecting the testing. As with the

---

[1]It should be noted that neuropsychological screening refers to the use of a battery of cognitive tests to identify areas of neuropsychological impairment. Neuropsychological testing is much more detailed and targeted, and it both takes much more training and uses a different format for writing up than a neuropsychological screening report. For further information on neuropsychological testing, see Lezak, Howieson, Loring, Hannay, and Fischer, 2004.

sections to follow, a detailed presentation of performance on the individual tests is unnecessary. A simple statement of general performance and the interpretation of the results is sufficient for this section. For example, if performance on two measures of motivation and malingering was adequate, it could be presented as: "The patient's adequate performance on two brief memory tasks measuring motivation (Double Digits and TOMM), both falling within the average range compared to others her age, suggests that motivational factors likely did not interfere with her performance on the testing." Note that the specifics of the tests and her performance on them are secondary to the conclusion drawn from her adequate performance.

Orientation. The third paragraph, titled "Orientation," is a statement regarding the individual's orientation to person, place, and time, most often as measured by the Mini-Mental State Exam (MMSE). Unless the individual is *not* adequately oriented, a single sentence stating that he or she is oriented to all three domains (person, place, and time) will suffice here. When an individual is not oriented, you will state this clearly and use it as evidence later in your cognitive summary section.

Attention. The next paragraph addresses "Attention." Attention is addressed early on in the write-up because it informs many of the other skills to be assessed. For example, an individual who cannot attend to information will not be able to encode that information into memory. Therefore, memory functioning is expected in this case to be at least partly dependent on attentional functioning. Depending on the measures administered, you may have information on selective attention, sustained attention (concentration), and attentional switching. These terms should be defined clearly if they are used in this section. Again, similar to all the other subsections, specific details about the tests themselves, and how the individual performed on each subtest, may not be necessary. Simply stating (a) what was assessed, (b) how the individual performed on that assessment, (c) whether or not there is evidence of impairment, and (d) implications of any impairment is adequate for the attention subsection (and the others) of the cognitive functioning section.

Motor Functioning. Again, motor functioning is a basic skill that may underlie other domains of functioning and their assessment. For example, processing speed (which is explained in the following paragraph) is most often assessed utilizing pencil-and-paper tasks, such as Trails A and the

Coding and Symbol Search subtests of the WAIS-IV. Thus, impairment in motor functioning will affect performance in tasks assessing speed of processing. In order not to erroneously report a deficit in processing speed when the problem is actually in motor coordination, this section should be presented first. Similar to the preceding section, a presentation should be made of any areas of impairment and the implications of these deficits on other areas of functioning.

Processing Speed. Again, processing speed is a domain of functioning that may affect domains presented later. For example, memory may be adequately encoded, but because an individual is slow to process the incoming information, not as much will enter his or her awareness, which may result in what could appear to be poor memory functioning. Measures of processing speed are presented, again focusing on evidence of any impairment and implications of that impairment.

Memory. Memory is an extremely important domain of cognitive functioning in neuropsychological screening assessments, given that memory impairment is one of the most common complaints you will likely receive for this type of assessment. It is extremely important to distinguish between the concept of memory and the domain of working memory, which, while related to memory, should not be included here. Whereas memory is a process of taking in information and encoding it for future retrieval, working memory requires manipulation of that information and involves more prefrontal cortex operations than memory. In this section, a clear comparison of the different types of memory (e.g., immediate auditory memory, delayed visual memory, etc.) should be presented. More importantly, implications of variation across these different types of memory should be explained clearly, focusing on the implications of the impairment or deficit for the cognitive functioning of the individual being assessed.

Language. Language functioning consists of different areas of skill, including verbal fluency, vocabulary, expressive ability, and comprehension. Many broad measures of intellectual ability and neuropsychological status (such as the WAIS-IV and RBANS, respectively) will provide broad measures of verbal functioning. What is most important in this section is to "tease apart" all of the different components of verbal functioning and present them clearly, so that any area of deficit is clear and specific. For example, if an individual performs poorly on the vocabulary subtest of the WAIS-IV, a task that requires him or her to define words presented both aloud and in written form, there are several possible implications. First, the individual's word knowledge may simply be poor. However, he or she may have difficulty with verbal expressive ability, despite knowing intuitively what each word presented means. As this subtest is a measure of expressive vocabulary, another test of receptive vocabulary may be given (such as the Peabody Picture Vocabulary Test, 4th Edition, PPVT-IV), which assesses word knowledge separate from expressive ability. If performance on the PPVT-IV is adequate, then you can make a clear conclusion about the deficit being more specifically in expressive ability, rather than word knowledge or long-term word memory. Each subdomain of verbal functioning should be presented clearly and separately, again always including implications of these deficits.

Visuospatial Functioning. Visuospatial functioning represents nonverbal information processing. Similar to verbal functioning, there are tests that measure complex visuospatial and visual-motor skills which rely on combinations of several more basic visuospatial skills. For example, the Bender Visual-Motor Gestalt Test, 2nd Edition (Bender-2) has a Copy Phase, which requires an individual to use a pencil and paper to copy designs presented visually to him or her. This task requires basic perceptual skills, basic motor skills, and higher order coordination and integration of these two skills. As such, the Bender-2 also includes subtests of pure perception and pure motor skills, so that if an individual performs poorly on the Copy Phase, you can look at the component skills separately to see where the deficit occurs. Similarly, many perceptual tasks on broad intellectual measures, such as Block Design on the WAIS-IV, actually tap multiple basic skills and higher order integrative ability. As with the language section, you should make every effort to present, as clearly as possible, exactly where in the complex process of visuospatial functioning any deficits occur, as well as their implications for functioning.

Executive Functioning. Executive functioning is a measure of those processes related to the prefrontal cortex. The term executive functioning generally needs a note of introduction and definition in the report, as it is not as clear as the other terms, such as language and attention. Included in this domain are measures of working memory (especially the more complex tasks, like the Letter-Number Sequencing subtest from the WAIS-IV) and measures of the ability to switch strategies and inhibit one's own behavior (e.g., Trails B or the Wisconsin Card Sort). This section represents the highest order and most sophisticated of the skills assessed, all of which rely on intact functioning in many of the other domains. For example, performance on tasks in the executive functioning subdomain will almost always be compromised if an individual's attention is impaired. If he or she cannot maintain attention to the task presented, the more complex "executive" skills of switching strategies during task performance will not even come into play.

Cognitive Summary. Finally, the last paragraph of this form of the cognitive functioning section is the "Cognitive Summary." This summary is extremely important in pulling together all of the strengths and weaknesses presented in the previous paragraphs to make clear what is going on cognitively with the individual overall. Similar to the previous cognitive summary sections presented, this paragraph provides an opportunity to explain what the pattern of strengths and possible impairments may *mean*, including implications for diagnosis, prognosis, and treatment. Only "interesting" findings should be reported again, in order to simplify and clarify the picture being presented in the report.

EXAMPLE

Cognitive Functioning

Based on the results of testing, the patient's estimated IQ, prior to emotional or physical factors interfering with his functioning, falls within the High Average range compared to others his age (WTAR, 79th percentile). His current Full Scale IQ on the WAIS-IV fell within the Average range compared to others in his age range (45th percentile). He exhibited a significant strength in his verbal ability (Verbal Comprehension Index, 76th percentile), but his processing speed fell within the Low Average range (14th percentile). Based on the difference between his High Average estimated previous IQ and his Average current IQ, there is evidence of some decline in overall functioning.

Motivation. Two brief memory tasks (Double Digits and TOMM) were administered in order to assess the patient's motivation for testing. The

(Continued)

patient's adequate performance, both falling within normal limits, indicates that motivational factors did not interfere with his performance on the testing.

Orientation. The patient was alert and oriented to place, person, and date, based on his Average performance on the MMSE.

Attention. The testing revealed that the patient's selective attention is intact; however, his sustained attention is inconsistent. More specifically, the patient performed within normal limits on tasks requiring him to attend to information with alternative information distracting him, which are measures of selective attention (Letter Cancellation, 64th percentile; WAIS-IV Cancellation, 50th percentile). However, on tasks in which he was required to keep his attention focused for an extended amount of time, he performed poorly compared to others his age (Digit Span Forward, 14th percentile; RBANS Attention Index, 8th percentile).

Motor Functioning. The patient's motor functioning was within the Normal range, as evidenced by his ability to quickly tap his finger repeatedly within a time limit (Finger Tapping, 90th percentile). Additionally, the patient displayed no unsteadiness of motor functioning and was able to fluidly manipulate a pencil during drawing tasks (Bender-2 Motor, 76–100th percentile).

Processing Speed. The patient displayed significant weakness on tasks that required him to act within a time limit. Specifically, his ability to solve a verbal and motor task quickly and efficiently fell within the Borderline range compared to others his age (Trails A, 4th percentile), and his ability to solve nonverbal motor tasks within a time limit was Low Average (WAIS-IV Processing Speed Index, 14th percentile).

Memory. The patient displayed some variation in his memory functioning, with some impairment in his ability to learn and recall complex information. Specifically, his ability to learn meaningful information was intact (RBANS Story Memory, 50th percentile; RBANS Story Recall, 59th percentile). However, less interesting information, such as a list of random words and geometric designs, was more difficult for him to learn and remember (RBANS List Learning, 4th percentile; RBANS List Recall, 1st percentile; RBANS Figure Recall, 0.7th percentile; Bender-2 Recall, 14th percentile). The fact that he also struggled on a task to recognize whether words presented had been part of the word list learned earlier (RBANS List Recognition, 1st percentile) suggests that his memory deficit is primarily due to difficulty learning the information in the first place.

Language. Overall, the patient demonstrated a relative strength in his language abilities when compared to other areas of cognitive functioning. His general ability to use and understand language fell in the High Average range of functioning compared to others his age (WAIS-IV Verbal Comprehension Index, 76th percentile), as was his ability to respond verbally to either naming or retrieving learned material (RBANS Language Index, 76th percentile). His general command of vocabulary fell within the Average range (PPVT-4, 59th percentile).

Visuospatial. The patient exhibited no deficit in his visuospatial ability, as evidenced by his Average performance on tasks assessing his ability to solve visual puzzles and recreate nonverbal pictures. Specifically, his ability to integrate his visual perceptual ability with his motor skill, copying in pencil geometric figures presented to him was Average (Bender-2 Copy, 50th percentile; RBANS Visuospatial/Constructional Index, 64th percentile). Additionally, his ability to solve nonverbal puzzles and abstract visual tasks also fell within the Average range (WAIS-IV Perceptual Reasoning Index, 50th percentile).

Executive Functioning. The patient performed well on a task requiring him to switch his mental strategy to a new set of directions, as well as hold and process two mental constructs simultaneously within a time limit (Trails B, 69th percentile). He also demonstrated adequate ability to hold information in his head and manipulate it to produce a different outcome (WAIS-IV Working Memory Index, 57th percentile).

Cognitive Summary. The patient's estimated possible IQ, prior to emotional or physical factors interfering with his functioning, falls within the High Average range, while his current measured IQ falls within the Average range, suggesting a likelihood of some cognitive decline. Specifically, he showed deficits in his ability to sustain his attention and in his speed of processing information. Additionally, he showed deficit in memory, though this is likely due to his poor attention, as he exhibited difficulty learning non-meaningful information. He showed strength in his ability to understand and use language.

Deficit in processing speed and sustained attention can be the result of several different factors. Included in the possible causes of these weaknesses are attentional deficit, emotional disturbance, anxiety, low motivation, and personality characteristics like perfectionism. As motivation was assessed and appears adequate, and because his measures of executive functioning, which require attentional capability, were adequate, it is likely that emotional disturbance, anxiety, and/or personality factors are currently impairing his cognitive functioning.

Personality and Emotional Functioning

The personality and emotional functioning section of the report is one of the most difficult to write. Even after you have pored over all the data and conceptualized what is currently going on with the individual you have assessed, being able to present it in a clear and cohesive way poses a difficult challenge. For example, it is here that the balance between not using too much jargon, but at the same time making it sound professional, is absolutely vital. The purpose of this section is not only to present the conceptualization (which was discussed in depth in Chapter 4), but to do it in a way that makes sense to the reader and is compelling enough to support the recommendations that will be made later in the report.

The first paragraph of this section should always address the overall characterization of the individual's current functioning—no test information should be included. Rather, you should simply present the story of all the themes and how they interact. Ideally, if someone were to read only this single paragraph of the report, the reader should come away with a good idea of what is occurring within the individual you assessed—that is, this paragraph should comprehensively present the narrative of what is going on for the individual that is affecting his or her functioning. Extremely important to this paragraph is that it should set out the structure for the remainder of this section. The story should flow clearly from theme to theme, and the subsections below this paragraph should flow directly from the story. For example, if the narrative explains that the combination of the person's low self-esteem and lack of social support is leading to depression, the subsections that follow should be (a) low self-esteem, (b) lack of social support, and (c) depression. The evidence for each of these will be presented in the subsequent subsections, but this opening paragraph has created a clear, logical structure for the rest of the personality and emotional functioning section.

The subsequent paragraphs, each with its own subheading, should address the individual themes. Parallel to the cognitive functioning section, each paragraph should have the same structure, with a general opening sentence briefly outlining the *entire* theme, followed by the evidence supporting the theme itself. Each individual subsection, based on each individual theme, should include a synthesis of test evidence in support of its conclusions. The key here is *synthesis*. While it may be easier to list all of the evidence by test (such as all the evidence from the MMPI-2, followed by all the evidence from the Rorschach, and so on), similar themes from each of the tests should be compiled and reported together.

In effect you are presenting the reader with a concise synthesis of your conclusions, such that the reader does not have to do the work of sifting through all of the evidence to understand your reasoning. Often general themes from one test (e.g., the MMPI-2) can be elaborated on or illuminated by themes from another (e.g., a projective test such as the TAT). For example, the MMPI-2 may reveal sadness, but the TAT may further indicate the nature and quality of that sadness by, for example, identifying themes of helplessness or hopelessness. In this way, you can present general themes first, then provide more specific details, even within a single paragraph or subsection on a major theme.

It is important in these paragraphs that evidence comes clearly and directly from the tests administered. If the PAI reveals something specific, simply state that your conclusion was supported by data from the PAI. Make it absolutely clear where each piece of new information came from. That being said, you should then present an integration and synthesis of these findings—do not make the reader interpret! Additionally, test evidence should be primary in these paragraphs. While behavioral observations and clinical information (from the presenting problem or background section) may be directly related to the theme, use these data only as supporting evidence later in the section.

An even better strategy is to use the test evidence to *explain* why or how either the individual may have reported something or you may have observed something. For example, if testing revealed that a man has a personality tendency toward passive-aggressive behavior, and during the testing he made sarcastic remarks about how "stupid" testing is, you might state toward the end of the paragraph: "This passive-aggressive tendency may explain why throughout testing he made sarcastic remarks and rolled his eyes when new tasks were presented." This way, the behavioral observation is presented as an additional piece of data to support the theme, but it is secondary to test data, which should always take precedence.

These theme paragraphs should be fair and tempered, such that you are not overstating your conclusions. Do not be afraid to present both positive and negative attributes within each theme subsection. While you may feel strongly about a certain conclusion and interpretation, make sure that the test evidence truly supports it. If not, temper your conclusions with words such as "likely" and "may." For example, if the examinee exhibits feelings of worthlessness on several tests and you feel strongly that the feelings are probably longstanding and pervasive because of what she has reported about the nature of her early childhood environment, you could state, "It is likely that these feelings of worthlessness began early in her life, given her family circumstances." Or you could state, "These current feelings of worthlessness may have begun early in her life, given her challenging family circumstances."

The final sentence of each of these paragraphs should connect the themes back to the overall narrative or to the following theme, such that it places the entire subsection back into the context of the individual's overall functioning. For example, the final sentence of a paragraph on a theme about anxiety may place it in the context of the theme of social isolation that follows it: "This anxiety not only causes internal discomfort but makes it difficult for her to interact comfortably with others."

EXAMPLE

Personality and Emotional Functioning

The results of the assessment revealed that the patient is harboring extremely resentful and angry feelings about the very real racist society in which he was raised. However, given his upbringing, he adopted an avoidant style of coping with the world, such that he tends to deal with his emotions and difficult external situations by avoiding thinking about or engaging with them. Additionally, in order to decrease the number of situations he needs to avoid, he adopted a style of perfectionism, so that he can control as much as possible and not be surprised by external events. Thus, his anger and resentment toward the racist world he grew up in is avoided. Avoiding dealing with his anger, however, has led to several difficulties. Namely, because he works so hard to keep his angry feelings out of his awareness, he has become anxious that he will have to deal with these difficult emotions. This anxiety has generalized to many fears. Additionally, he harbors low self-esteem and some emptiness, again because his avoidant style has impeded the development of a healthy, positive identity. While his avoidant style was useful growing up, to cope with the racist treatment he experienced and his unsupportive parents, his anger is now so great that it is coming out in angry outbursts. His anxiety, low self-esteem, and explosive outbursts are also impairing his ability to relate to and become close with other people.

Anger. The patient is harboring a great deal of anger toward the world around him, specifically because he feels that he has been discriminated against his whole life. His MMPI-2 and Rorschach revealed a pervasive feeling of anger and resentment toward the world in general. Additionally, his MCMI-III and Rorschach revealed a desire to be oppositional and "lash out" at others he thinks are treating him unfairly. Specifically, his TAT suggested that his anger stems from racial sources. From years of actually being dis-criminated against and treated unfairly, growing up in a predominantly White Southern town, he began to harbor resentment for the fact that he was treated differently and, in actuality, unfairly. His Projective Drawings revealed that he has ambivalence about being Black, as it has been the source of so much tension in his life. He reported feeling discriminated against while growing up, as well as currently having a "racist" boss, which is stirring up his longstanding feelings of anger. However, he never learned how best to express his anger, and he does not generally process it, given his avoidant style of coping with it.

Avoidant Style. The patient developed a style of dealing with the world and his own emotions by avoiding thinking about or engaging with them, a strategy that served him well growing up but may be breaking down somewhat now. His Rorschach revealed that, rather than deal with situations, difficulties, and feelings that come up in his life, he tends to avoid them and distract himself. His MMPI-2 further suggested that he tends to distract himself often rather than dealing with his own emotions. In fact, his Projective Drawings and TAT revealed that he likely does not have the resources to cope with his own emotions, even if he wanted to. Having grown up with parents who encouraged him not to process his emotions and to "buckle down" and focus on his studies rather than discuss diffi-culties in school, it was adaptive and appropriate for him to develop this avoidant style. The result now, however, is that his anger continues to build up inside him, and he avoids dealing with it.

Perfectionism. One of the ways the patient manages to avoid dealing with negative emotions or circumstances in his life is by being extremely perfectionistic. His MCMI-III revealed a tendency to be overly concerned with being correct and perfect, overly bound by rules and regulations in

(Continued)

everything he does. The Rorschach and MMPI-2 revealed that this tendency serves the purpose of making sure he is rarely surprised by anything; the more control he has over situations and the less error there is in what he does, the more predictable his life can be. His TAT revealed that this tendency is present across contexts, from work to interpersonal relationships, over which he tries to maintain strict control. When his control over situations fails, it often brings up either emotions that he is unwilling or unable to cope with due to his avoidant style or significant anxiety.

Anxiety. The patient's avoidance of emotions, especially his anger, has led to significant anxiety; the more he avoids dealing with his anger, and the more it increases with everyday instances of discrimination, the more he fears that he will have to at some point cope with this scary emotion. Anxiety was a constant theme revealed in his MMPI-2, Rorschach, MCMI-III, and TAT. Specifically, his MMPI-2 and TAT suggested that he fears all the complexities of the outside world, and his Rorschach revealed that he spends much mental energy trying to simplify situations in his mind and make them more concrete and easier to understand. The complex world, full of difficulties to cope with, is overwhelming to him, as revealed by his TAT. This general anxiety about the unpredictable nature of the world likely explains his reported fears of dying and constant thoughts of how it might happen.

Low Self-Esteem. In addition to anxiety, his avoidant style and general anger have led to low self-esteem and feelings of emptiness; because he was unable to process his emotions and situations growing up, he was unable to create a positive and stable self-image, including a healthy racial identity. His MMPI-2 and Rorschach revealed significantly low self-esteem. However, his MCMI-III suggested that he tends not to show this low self-esteem to others, trying to avoid it by employing a defensive technique of appearing self-confident and self-assured. This self-confidence, however, is merely a mask for his low self-image, as revealed by his Projective Drawings. His Rorschach and TAT also revealed an underdeveloped identity, especially his racial identity, which can contribute to poor self-image. His low self-esteem explains his self-deprecating remarks during the testing, when he seemed to genuinely feel that he was performing poorly and saw himself negatively because of that poor performance.

Explosiveness. The patient's way of coping with his own anger and negative emotions, avoiding them and not addressing them at all, is currently not working; his level of anger is too great for him to hold in, and it is coming out explosively in different situations, beyond what the situations actually deserve. His MCMI-III and Rorschach revealed a tendency to act impulsively when he feels out of control of situations, and his MMPI-2 revealed that these impulsive acts likely take the form of exaggerated anger. Moreover, his TAT exhibited a fear that he cannot control his anger, due to experiences when he felt out of control. This supports his report that he has been getting disproportionately angry with others, including his friends, for relatively minor annoyances. This explosiveness has also contributed to his anxiety and low self-esteem, and together these contribute to difficulties with other people.

Interpersonal Difficulties. Due to the patient's avoidant style, perfectionistic tendencies, resentment toward the world, and the resultant anxiety, low self-esteem, and explosive behaviors, he has difficulties maintaining significant relationships with others. It should be noted that he has good social skills and a highly developed understanding of social norms and appropriate behavior, as evidenced by his Rorschach, MMPI-2, and MCMI-III. However, his Rorschach and MMPI-2 revealed difficulties sustaining significant relationships. His TAT suggested that he both finds it difficult to trust people and also fears the strong feelings associated with interpersonal relationships. Given his avoidant style and perfectionistic tendencies, the unpredictable nature of relationships and the feelings they provoke create anxiety within him, as exhibited by his TAT and Rorschach. While he is able to sustain his relationship with some friends, currently, his angry outbursts at them may reflect both his anger exploding out of him and a way of distancing himself from these significant relationships.

Vocational Functioning

In reports in which there is a vocational question and you have administered vocational interest (and even aptitude) tests, you will likely want to include a separate, short section on vocational functioning. Major tests of vocational interest (e.g., Strong Interest Inventory) often include professions of individuals with similar profiles to the person being assessed, a breakdown of vocational area priorities (such as with the RIASEC model), and even priorities in terms of work environments. All of these are important to include in this section, though later (in the summary section), you will synthesize these findings with the cognitive and personality findings in order to make a realistic recommendation based both on interests (presented here) and capabilities (both in terms of cognitive abilities and personality style). This section is particularly straightforward in terms of reporting what emerges from whatever vocational tests you have given. As you can see from the example that follows, not much interpretation is necessary when reporting the vocational interest findings.

It should be noted that, although this section seems relatively straightforward, assessments that include vocational testing are more complicated. The ultimate goal of vocational assessments is to synthesize data from four areas—vocational interests, cognitive aptitude, work-style preferences, and personality functioning—in order to make recommendations for jobs and careers in which the client is most likely to succeed. The interest and work-style section presented here is only the first step of this entire process.[2]

EXAMPLE

Vocational Functioning

The patient was given the Strong Interest Inventory, a test of interest in different domains of work functioning. In terms of general occupational themes, not only does he tend toward jobs that involve researching and analyzing, but he feels that he wants to be in a position to manage others and their work as well. In terms of his preferences for his work environment, he prefers to work alone and dislikes taking risks, but he is highly comfortable taking charge and motivating others, expressing his opinions easily. The testing suggested careers of possible interest like computer analyst positions, teaching math or science, or working in the medical field.

The patient was also given the MBTI, a test of personality style to match preferred work settings. His profile of ISTJ suggests that he thrives on organization, logic, and the ability to consider jobs completed, disliking unfinished business. He sees himself as thorough and dependable when it comes to clearly-defined tasks. He enjoys responsibility and being held accountable for his actions, so he would likely thrive in a supervisory or teaching position.

---

[2]For a more detailed and comprehensive review of vocational assessment, see Walsh and Savickas (2005).

Summary

If individuals read only one section of a report, it is most often the summary section. The most important "rule" of the summary section is that it should *not include any new information*. Without exception, any statements made about current functioning, behavioral observations, or anything else *must* have been presented previously in the report. Even though you may be synthesizing information in a slightly new way—for example, by integrating the emotional findings with the cognitive findings— the information presented about each of the individual domains (emotional and cognitive) should have been presented previously in their respective sections.

The structure of the summary should mirror the structure of the report. The first paragraph should include a few points of description of the individual being assessed, as well as the referral questions and presenting problems. The second paragraph should clearly restate the most important cognitive findings. The third paragraph should be a retelling of the narrative that began the personality and emotional functioning section. At the end of this paragraph can be a synthesizing statement pulling together the cognitive and emotional findings. If there was vocational testing, the next paragraph should restate the most important findings from the vocational interest testing, as well as integrating the cognitive and personality findings into a coherent presentation of what the individual would be both interested in and have aptitude for doing.

The following paragraph should be a clear description of diagnostic impressions. Specifically, any diagnosis that you are giving should be presented in a way that clearly supports the diagnosis. That is, you should justify the diagnosis you have made by listing the DSM-IV-TR criteria that emerged from the assessment that support that diagnosis. If there was a question about another diagnosis that you ended up ruling out, you should include exactly why the individual does not meet criteria for the ruled-out diagnosis. Additionally, it is occasionally useful to list some of the other diagnoses that were considered and why the person does not meet the criteria for them. This will flow directly into the diagnostic impressions section that follows.

EXAMPLE

Summary

Mr. Diddlewatt is a light-skinned, 34-year-old African American man who was referred for an assessment by his current therapist of three years because he has reportedly become "more hostile" lately. He also reported constant fears of dying and thoughts about ways it may happen, in addition to difficulties sleeping, some loss of energy, poor appetite, and recently having stopped socializing with everyone except some close friends.

The patient's performance across domains of cognitive functioning was varied. His nonverbal reasoning ability and ability to concentrate on and manipulate information is Average. He exhibited a significant strength in verbal ability and a significant weakness in his speed of processing nonverbal information, which is likely due to his current emotional functioning.

The patient is currently harboring long-standing feelings of anger and resentment toward the world, rooted in feeling unfairly treated and discriminated against growing up as one of few Black people in a small Southern town. However, rather than process this anger, he has developed a personality style of avoiding difficult situations and emotions, including his own resentment toward the world. Additionally, he has developed perfectionistic tendencies in order to minimize any unpredictable and potentially difficult situations or emotions in his life. Because of his avoidant style and unprocessed anger, he is currently experiencing much anxiety in his life, poor self-esteem, and sporadic, explosive behavior when he cannot avoid his anger anymore. All of this together is causing him difficulties sustaining relationships, despite the fact that he has the capacity and skills to be close to others.

In terms of work, the patient tends toward jobs that involve researching and analyzing, but he feels that he wants to be in a position to manage others and their work as well. Although he prefers to work alone, he is highly comfortable taking charge and motivating others, expressing his opinions easily. Careers that he is most interested in include computer analyst positions, teaching math or science, or working in the medical field. Given his strong verbal functioning and his perfectionistic tendencies, it is likely that he would succeed in careers like these.

The patient currently meets criteria for Major Depressive Disorder. Specifically, he is currently struggling with low self-worth, a decrease in appetite and sleep, loss of energy, and a loss of interest in socializing with others. Although he did not report depressed mood, he is exhibiting agitation and anxious preoccupation, thinking constantly about dying and how it might happen. Additionally, he reported a previous episode of depression, so his depression is recurrent.

Diagnostic Impressions

A full, 5-axis diagnosis should be included for each individual assessed. Regardless of your personal feelings about DSM-IV-TR diagnosis, this is the standard professional language we currently use to communicate with others in the psychological community. Avoid using "diagnosis deferred" on Axis I and Axis II, as this might indicate that you simply did not do enough testing. A thorough assessment should always yield a clear diagnostic picture, and if it does not, then you should consider doing more testing in order to accomplish this goal. The format for the diagnostic impressions can be found in the *DSM-IV-TR* (American Psychiatric Association, 2000).

Recommendations

In the end, the entire purpose of psychological assessment is to provide clear, direct, specific, and useful recommendations for improving an individual's functioning and life. It is vitally important to make this section extremely clear such that it can be easily followed by any reader, remem-

EXAMPLE

Diagnostic Impressions

Axis I	296.32	Major Depressive Disorder, Recurrent, Moderate
Axis II	V71.09	Avoidant personality traits
Axis III		None
Axis IV		Limited social support
Axis V	GAF =	60

bering that your audience may include other mental health professionals, the individual who was assessed, parents or guardians, or school personnel, among others. Much like other sections, the format of this section will vary from psychologist to psychologist. However, the overarching question you should ask yourself when rereading the recommendations you are making is: Are these clear, specific, and useful?

A secondary question is how reasonable the recommendations are. For example, if you recommend that an individual take a four-month vacation, that may be clear, specific, and useful; however, in most cases it will not be feasible, given the constraints of a working person's life. While this example may seem clear-cut, many times it may be more difficult to discern. Frequently recommendations are made for types of treatment that individuals may not have access to. For example, recommending a dialectical behavior therapy (DBT) program for someone who has borderline personality disorder may, in theory, be the best course of action. But if there are no DBT programs available to the person, for geographic or financial reasons, the recommendation is not a reasonable one.

To make recommendations clearer, it is useful to use a bullet-point format. The more specific the recommendation, the more likely an individual is to follow it. For example, if you recommend ongoing, one-on-one talk therapy, the recommendation could be improved simply by providing a specific referral, including a name and telephone number to contact for an intake.

One final note on recommendations is to endeavor to make recommendations in an unbiased way. For example, you may have mixed feelings about medicating an individual who is depressed. While the research on treatment of depression can be overwhelming, there is increasing empirical support to suggest that the most effective treatments for depression include both a medication component and a talk therapy component (Barlow, 2008; Roth & Fonagy, 2005). Regardless of your feelings about medication, given this evidence, you are ethically responsible to recommend a consultation with a psychiatrist to determine if pharmacotherapy may be beneficial (keeping in mind it will ultimately be up to the psychiatrist and the patient whether or not to include medication). As a psychologist, you should of course never recommend a specific medication. Even in extreme cases of ADHD, for example, when you think a psychostimulant is absolutely necessary, you can only recommend a psychiatric consultation to assess how helpful medication may be. For further information on the research of treat-

EXAMPLE

Recommendations

Given the patient's current functioning, the following recommendations are being made:

- The patient should consult with a psychiatrist regarding his depression and anxiety. Although medication is not being recommended, a consultation with a psychiatrist should be undertaken to see if psychotropic medication may be helpful with his current depression.
- The patient should continue in his current talk therapy. Issues that should be addressed in therapy include
    - ○ Processing negative emotion, especially his anger. Anger toward his parents and toward the racist world he both grew up in and currently lives in should be addressed.
    - ○ Helping build a positive self-identity, including his racial identity.
    - ○ Decreasing his anxiety through cognitive-behavioral techniques.
    - ○ Decreasing his perfectionistic tendencies and increasing his ability to cope with less-than-perfect results.
    - ○ Increasing his capacity for closeness with others. Interpersonal therapy can help him tolerate the unpredictable nature of close relationships.
- Career counseling may be useful in terms of helping the patient decide if he wants a career change and how best to go about it.

ments and interventions, see Barlow, 2008; Carr, 2009; Christophersen and Mortweet, 2001; Roth and Fonagy, 2005; Seligman and Reichenberg, 2007.

Signatures

All reports should be signed and dated, both by you as the assessor and by your supervisor, who should be a licensed psychologist (if applicable). The only major concern is that signatures should not be on a separate page by themselves. For legal reasons, there must be at least some other content text on the page with the signatures, as this ensures that the signature page cannot simply be detached and placed onto an altered report.

> **EXAMPLE**
>
> **Signatures**
>
> _____   _____
> Emily B. Student, MA   Date
> Assessor
>
>
> _____   _____
> A. Jordan Wright, PhD   Date
> New York State Licensed Psychologist
> Supervisor

Appendices

Although you may or may not choose to include an appendix to your report, should you elect to include one there are two types that may be particularly useful. First, you might include an appendix with the scores from each of the cognitive measures. This is especially useful for neuropsychological screenings and when the referral source is another psychologist, who may be interested in looking at the raw data as a quicker "language" for how the individual is functioning than reading the entire report. However, where this is not the case, you should exercise caution in including these scores, given that their interpretation is legally and ethically reserved for licensed psychologists and those under their supervision. Consider an example of a man with a Full Scale IQ from the WAIS-IV of 90. You may not have reported this within the report, especially if his verbal comprehension is a 130, and the Full Scale IQ is being pulled down by presently impaired processing speed, which in this case was impaired due to depression. The Full Scale IQ of 90 is an underestimate of this man's functioning, but he may not realize this if he looks at the appendix and sees this number. In this case, listing the data from the cognitive tests could actually do more harm than good. As you would in other areas of clinical practice, you should exercise sensitivity and consideration when deciding whether or not to include an appendix of cognitive scores.

The second appendix that may be useful is actually more accurately referred to as an addendum. This addendum is a general progress note regarding the feedback session, and it is useful when the individual being assessed had a strong, specific reaction to the assessment feedback (others who read the entire report, such as the individual's therapist, may find this information useful). You should include the reactions of the person being assessed, including any areas that he or she disagreed with or reacted poorly to. The general demeanor of the individual during the feedback, as well as a plan for any follow-up regarding recommendations should also be included. This addendum should take the form of a progress note, in whatever structure is appropriate for the setting in which you are conducting the assessment.

SUMMARY

The psychological assessment report should present a clear, cohesive, and comprehensive argument that supports your conclusions and, most importantly, your recommendations. The recommendations made in the report

EXAMPLE

Appendix: Addendum—Feedback Session

9/25/08: Feedback Session, 45 minutes

Mr. Diddlewatt came in for his feedback session. He was in generally good spirits, smiling and friendly toward the assessor. While receiving feedback, he paid very good attention, interrupting to ask questions throughout whenever he did not understand a concept. While he reported agreeing with most of the report, he reported disagreeing with the idea that he may need psychotropic medication. While he remained mostly resistant to this idea, he did agree to follow up with his therapist about the possibility of consulting a psychiatrist, "if she agrees that it would be helpful." He agreed to all other recommendations and was given two copies of the report, one for himself and one for his therapist. Further, he gave consent for the assessor to call his therapist and give her the feedback verbally, in addition to the copy of the report.

should stem directly from (a) what you know about the patient and what is going on for him or her and (b) what you know about the research on treatments of choice for different difficulties. Taken all together, the report from start to finish should flow and be relatively easy to read, such that you have minimized anything disjointed within it. Perhaps the greatest challenge is the balance between making the report readable and accessible, but also making sure it sounds professional. Supervision is key in terms of editing first reports. Once you have written a good number of reports, however, you can use statements and even entire sections from previous reports in writing up new reports. There is no ethical dilemma when plagiarizing your own past reports—there simply is no need to reinvent the wheel. If you have stated before that someone has a weakness in verbal functioning, for example, there is no need to find a new, interesting way to say this. Find your old report, and copy and paste that section into your new report. The only danger is that you *must* reread and edit these sections to make sure they make conceptual sense for the individual you are *currently* assessing.

CHAPTER 6

Providing Feedback

Providing feedback on psychological assessments can be a very delicate and difficult process. As with the rest of the assessment process, it requires both the technical skill of an assessor and the therapeutic skill of a clinician. The feedback session, more than any other session in the assessment process, is a *hybrid* between a testing session and a therapy session. This chapter outlines the technical decisions to be made before the session takes place, and it is these decisions that drive the *content* of the feedback session.

However, the key to effective feedback resides less in the content of the feedback than in the process, which requires all the skills of an effective therapist. This process is made particularly challenging by the fact that it is unlikely that a therapeutic alliance has been firmly established over the relatively brief course of the testing. An effective feedback session will include clear and specific feedback from the assessment, all of which should culminate logically in useful and specific recommendations.

Just as important, an effective feedback session will include constant checking in with the individual receiving feedback to ensure that he or she is adequately comprehending and following the results and recommendations and to empathically gauge any reactions and feelings that he or she may be having. Receiving feedback about your functioning from a relative stranger who purports to know things about you that you might not even be aware of is an understandably bizarre and awkward process. For this reason, many individuals receiving feedback will have feelings about the feedback ranging from ambivalent to strongly negative. The most effective feedback sessions both permit and encourage this dynamic interplay between the information being presented and the individual receiving it.

The process that takes place between the time of finishing the assessment and report and actually providing live feedback should be characterized by conscious, deliberate, and thoughtful planning. There are several decisions to be made about how the feedback session will occur. You should always think about each of these issues carefully, doing your best to anticipate how each may affect the individual receiving the feedback.

To Whom Am I Giving Feedback?

In general, you will give feedback to the person you assessed. There may be exceptions to this rule, but when there are, the circumstances generally dictate to *whom* you give the feedback. That is, you will generally give feedback to whoever your client is, whether that is the individual you are assessing, a court, an agency, or someone else. For example, if you are doing a forensic evaluation for the court, the court is your client and will receive the feedback. If you are charged to do a custody evaluation, an inpatient evaluation, or some other assessment by a third party, this third party generally dictates to whom you give feedback.

Considering What Will Be Most Helpful

Often when you do a psychological assessment of an individual, he or she has come in for help and specific recommendations, which may include providing beneficial feedback not only to the individual but to others involved in that person's care. Specifically, in consideration of what might be of greatest benefit to the person being assessed, you might ask yourself, Are there others who can be enlisted to assist in the goal of improving this person's overall functioning? If so, then you might consider giving feedback to these individuals as well. For example, if you are making a recommendation for psychotherapy to address specific issues, the current or eventual therapist would likely find the specifics of the report (provided in written or verbal format at the assessor's discretion) to be useful in the treatment of the individual. If you are recommending a psychiatric consultation, giving the psychiatrist the feedback would likely improve the care of the individual by providing him or her with additional information to assist in diagnostic clarification, for example.

If there are medical issues in addition to psychological problems and your recommendations include the coordination of medical and mental health care, giving feedback to the individual's doctor will improve the likelihood of this outcome. For example, a diabetic individual who presents with somatic symptoms beyond what would be expected from the diabetes alone can truly benefit if his or her primary care physician and mental health professional communicate often and openly. Because it is often very difficult to parse out which symptoms are related to the diabetes and which may be more psychosomatic in nature, coordinating between health-care providers, each of whom has expertise in different areas of this individual's functioning, improves the chances of treating him or her effectively.

For all of the providers to "be on the same page," giving feedback to each of them (in addition to the individual who was assessed) may be warranted. Obviously, to provide this kind of additional feedback you must get permission from the client (which again could be the individual being assessed, a court or agency, or someone else), generally in the form of a signed release form. This ensures that you may legally give feedback to someone other than your client, and ideally it ensures that the client understands why giving feedback to a third party would be useful.

If a colleague has requested the assessment, whether it is to help inform a treatment that has stalled for some reason or to provide clarification on the issues impacting his or her client, you may be able to provide feedback to the individual you are assessing and to his or her therapist concurrently. Having a person's therapist in the feedback session with you and the person you have assessed has several benefits. First and foremost, the assessment feedback can serve as the basis of a shared language and experience between the individual and the therapist, such that, regardless of how they feel about the feedback itself, they at least know what exactly was said in the feedback session.

In addition, as the therapist and the client will generally have a stronger working alliance, the therapist can help to clarify any aspects of the feedback in a way that can be more easily heard by the individual. Furthermore, this process can help avoid any "splitting" between providers, which can often happen when there are two distinct mental health providers involved; if you and the therapist appear as a clear, collaborative team in the feedback session, there is less room, as a result of the feedback, for the person who was assessed to idealize one and devalue the other. This is not foolproof, obviously. This risk is always present when a third person is involved in the therapeutic dyad.

But the more collaborative and cooperative the two mental health providers can be, the less likely this splitting will occur.

Diagnostic Considerations

When deciding to whom you should give feedback, diagnosis may also be a consideration. Although this is a complicated matter worthy of a more extensive explanation than this chapter affords, a general rule of thumb is that the decisions as to who gets feedback and exactly how become more difficult when a personality disorder is involved. Again, as some form of psychotherapeutic treatment will likely be recommended, providing feedback to the mental health provider can enable him or her to use feedback to provide better treatment, in general.

Including the mental health provider in the feedback session may be especially important in the case of personality disorders. This is because the individual who was assessed and given feedback may often disagree with, take offense to, or somehow distort the feedback to fit in with his or her self-image. The feedback can often be distorted as it is passed verbally from him or her to his or her provider (it can become a game of telephone, in which whispers are passed from one person to the next, becoming increasingly distorted until the content itself is almost unrecognizable). Thus, the more direct feedback you can give to the client's providers, the better.

What makes this difficult in the case of several personality disorder diagnoses (most notably the Cluster B personality disorders) is the fact that the person you assessed may simply not *want* the feedback given to his or her providers. Legally and ethically, you cannot give feedback to anyone other than the individual you assessed without his or her willing, informed consent (with the exception of special cases, such as court-mandated evaluations). Thus, an additional task and challenge in feedback sessions becomes providing a clear and concise rationale to the individual for how he or she will benefit from your extending the report or verbal feedback to his or her mental health providers.

Developmental Considerations

When the individual assessed is a child, there are several key factors to consider when deciding who should receive feedback. First, you will always want to give some form of feedback to the child assessed. As many children do not clearly understand the purpose of the assessment, you want to avoid making it even more mysterious by having no clear outcome. Bearing in mind the age of the child, you must strategize carefully as to how best to give the feedback. For very young children, for example, it generally makes sense to give feedback to parents or guardians alone first, without the child present, so that you can be clear with the feedback and the parents or guardians can ask candid questions. Then, it may be useful to give feedback to the child with the parents in the room with you. In this case, the parents can hear exactly what kind of language you are using with their child, so that they know how to talk about it later with him or her. Additionally, having parents in the room may make feedback less frightening for the child.

On the other hand, for preadolescents and adolescents, although both the child and his or her parents or guardians will need to receive feedback, the structure of the sessions will likely be quite different from that required for younger children. One option that tends to work well is to give feedback to the adolescent first, alone, followed by inviting the parents into the room with the adolescent to give them the feedback all together. This can mitigate some of the adolescent's typical fears that you will be disclosing something different to his or her parents than you did to him or her; the parents will never receive feedback without the adolescent present.

You can also enlist the adolescent to help give his or her parents feedback in a way that he or she thinks they will best be able to understand and take in. This strategy can empower the adolescent to have some control over how feedback is given to his or her parents, so that he or she will hopefully feel less undermined or betrayed by the information you must disclose to the parents. The first half of the session, with the adolescent alone, can also be treated as a "heads-up" for what you will be disclosing to the parents, constantly checking in with him or her to see how he or she will react to this information being shared with his or her parents. Again, the key is anticipating how it *may* affect the individual who was assessed, especially given his or her age and level of development, for you to give feedback to other important people.

DO I GIVE A COPY OF THE REPORT?

Although there is no ethical or legal rule about whether or not to give the written report to the person you have assessed (though the setting in which you work may have some guidelines), one guiding principle that may be helpful is to err on the side of transparency and disclosure by providing the written report unless there is a compelling reason not to. Although there may be many reasons that giving a written report to the person you assessed may be unwarranted, there are a few reasons that seem to come up more often than others. The first and most important reason for not providing the individual assessed with a copy of the report is that you have determined that doing so is likely to be harmful or unduly distressing.

Determining whether or not giving the report will harm an individual is a clinical judgment call that can benefit from supervision or consultation. Most often the consideration of potential harm is related to something that emerged in the content of the report or the diagnosis given. Although mental health professionals differ on their views on diagnosis (e.g., stigmatizing as opposed to informative and supportive of better treatment), there are times when giving an individual a specific diagnosis may be damaging, and you should consider both the nature of the diagnosis and the individual whom you have come to know during the course of the assessment. Similarly, if a theme emerged on the assessment that you feel would truly be harmful for the person to hear (and see and keep), then you may be best advised to find a way to frame and convey that theme verbally rather than in writing. Providing a verbal context for a particularly sensitive theme will likely allow the person being assessed to better take in and understand the feedback. As in all clinical work, you will do well to allow yourself to be guided by the "do no harm" ethic.

The other major consideration when deciding whether or not to give a copy of the written report to the individual being assessed has to do with the level of his or her functioning. Specifically, a comprehensive written report may simply be too overwhelming and complicated for some individuals to understand and be able to tolerate. An individual who is cognitively functioning within the borderline intellectual functioning range, for example, may not be able to make use of a full written report. In these cases, the person may benefit from receiving a brief breakdown of the full report. You may create a "cheat sheet," a one-page summary of the report with the major findings and themes and the recommendations. The "cheat sheet" provides the individual with an easily comprehensible written account of the assessment findings that he or she can revisit later as a reminder of the most salient details of the feedback session.

How Should the Session Be Structured?

There is no single optimal way to structure a feedback session for all individuals assessed. In general, though, there are two major structures to apply to the session that can help organize the content from the assessment into a presentation that will be heard effectively by the person you assessed. Which one of these you choose, or whether you choose a different structure entirely, will depend on your own personal style, the nature of the feedback being given, and the specific functioning of the person receiving the feedback. The key to deciding what format the session should take lies in anticipating what will be most readily heard and understood by the individual in a way that will encourage him or her to follow up on the recommendations being offered.

The first—and most straightforward—way to structure a feedback session is to follow the format of the assessment report. Often, when you have decided to give a copy of the written report to the individual who was assessed, it simply makes sense to structure the session around the structure of the report. You can begin by checking in with the person, giving him or her the report, and orienting him or her to it by explaining its structure, its sections, and how it is presented to support clear recommendations. After orienting the person to the major headings, you can then go back to the beginning and go through the report together, section by section, giving a verbal explanation of everything that is written and clarifying anything that is unclear (obviously, all the while constantly checking in with the person to gauge his or her understanding and reactions). This structure will naturally lead to the recommendations, which will be emphasized in the session, followed by a plan for follow-up (which is discussed subsequently).

An alternatively useful structure for the feedback session is to organize the entire session around the recommendations. That is, as you provide the results from the assessment, you immediately follow each individual result with the specific recommendation that relates to that finding. (Clearly, if the result is something positive or that does not need addressing, then there may be no specific recommendation connected to it.) This structure can be useful if you think that, for whatever reason, the individual may be overwhelmed by hearing all the results or if you anticipate resistance to the recommendations that would be best addressed by more explicitly emphasizing their rationale.

While it may be more challenging to present your findings clearly, using this structure does a particularly effective job of emphasizing the recommendations aimed at improving the person's functioning, which after all is the ultimate goal of the assessment. By summarizing each of the recommendations again at the end of the session, you have simply presented the recommendations more times than you would if the session were structured linearly around the report. Simply repeating the recommendations a few times may actually work wonders with individuals ambivalent about following them!

Should I Disclose the Diagnosis?

Perhaps the most controversial decision to make before doing a feedback session is whether to disclose your diagnostic impressions with the person you have assessed. This may be moot if you have decided to provide the individual with a copy of the report, which clearly states the diagnosis. Without getting into a philosophical discussion of the merits of diagnosis (and you may have your own personal opinions about diagnosing, which is perfectly appropriate), you should simply let yourself be guided by the same consideration as when deciding whether or not to give a copy of the written report: (Try to) do no harm. Diagnosis can be stigmatizing. Depending on the setting you work in, a diagnosis can follow an individual for a lifetime. Diagnosis can also be extremely organizing and informative (and many people find themselves relieved to be able to place a name on their suffering), especially when it comes to deciding which treatments will likely be effective. You must simply weigh, as best you can, the pros and cons of disclosing the diagnosis. Again, in the service of transparency and genuineness, you may consider disclosing your diagnostic impressions unless there is a compelling reason not to.

One challenge of disclosing diagnosis is finding a way to explain exactly what the diagnostic label means, beyond what it *sounds like* it means. For example, a woman who was clearly depressed was given a diagnosis of major depressive disorder (MDD), and although she knew she was depressed, she had a very strong reaction to the word "major." These are the sorts of labels and details that we in our profession use so often that we begin to take for granted how this might sound to someone who is not in our field. Once it was explained exactly what the MDD label meant (including the fact that there is no such thing as a minor depressive disorder), her anxiety reduced significantly. Psychoeducation about exactly what different diagnostic labels mean is absolutely crucial in a good feedback session. Again, showing empathy for a person receiving a diagnostic label as part of the assessment feedback will help you avoid taking these labels for granted.

How Is the Session Going?

When thinking about the feedback session as a "hybrid" of assessment and psychotherapy, gauging how the session is going on a moment-to-moment basis becomes extremely crucial. Just as you were attuned to behavioral observations during the assessment, you should remain observant of any and all reactions, even if they are nonverbal, on the part of the person receiving feedback. Often the sheer volume of the information being provided can make the feedback overwhelming, such that individuals cannot process it quickly enough to verbalize their reactions. However, very often people cannot hide even minor reactions on their faces or in their bodies, so you should stay aware of any change in demeanor, posture, affect, or any other nonverbal signs indicating that he or she may be having a reaction to something you have said. If you notice behavioral reactions, you should stop and make sure that the individual is following what you are saying and provide answers to any questions he or she might have.

Although they can feel a bit halted and stop-and-start, the best feedback sessions include regular checking in with the person receiving feedback to make sure he or she, firstly, understands everything that is being said. But this is merely the first step. A good feedback session will include providing an atmosphere that communicates to the person receiving feedback that it is entirely acceptable, and even encouraged, for him or her to have reactions to what is being presented. It should feel okay for him or her to be surprised or disappointed and even to disagree with what is said, and you should make every effort to minimize any shame on his or her part for asserting his or her reactions, feelings, and opinions. It is not hard to empathize with these reactions when you take time to understand how foreign and bizarre this process is—almost any reaction is reasonable to have in what is an unusual and uncomfortable situation. Individuals being assessed should be encouraged to share their reactions freely and openly within the session (as well as in the future, potentially, with his or her therapist, if that is consistent with the recommendations you are providing).

When gauging the flow of the session, there may come a point when a reaction to the feedback is so strong that it may be necessary to stop the feedback part of the session and shift into a more psychotherapeutic stance. If at all feasible, you should be flexible enough to hold off on the feedback and reschedule it for a future date, while using the rest of the current session to process whatever emotions and thoughts were elicited by the feedback so far. Remember that it should be acceptable for the person to be angry with you, as well as feeling hurt or sad. Your clinical training will have prepared you to tolerate these emotions and to process them empathically with the person in whatever way you feel is appropriate.

Again, the ultimate goal is to work toward recommendations in a way that will allow the person to hear them, understand them, and ultimately follow through on them. If reactions to some of the content of the report are potentially getting in the way of the person taking the recommendations, you should shift the flow of the session to make sure that he or she can emotionally prepare to come back for another session to complete the feedback. Although this may sound relatively straightforward, an individual's reactions to feedback can be unpredictable, and you should be prepared for anything to happen within the session.

How Will I Follow Up?

An ethical and logistical piece of the feedback session is collaborating with the individual you assessed about how best to follow up on the recommendations made. There may be instances in which you feel that the recommendations are clear enough that the person needs no further assistance in following through on them. For example, if you make a recommendation for psychotherapy at the clinic in which you work, and together with the person you assessed you fill out the necessary forms during the feedback session, there is probably no need to follow up with the person himself or herself (though you may want to follow up with the clinic to ensure that the referral has been made appropriately). Additionally, if the individual can easily (and will readily) take the recommendations (e.g., if someone were referred for vocational testing in order to help with career decisions, and the recommendations included discussing certain aspects of the decision with his or her therapist, whom he or she already sees), again there may be no need to follow up with the individual.

However, there are times when it is necessary to follow up with the individual to make sure that recommendations are understood and followed through. Even with the most specific recommendation (e.g., you may have provided the name and number of an appropriate therapist or clinic), because it is presented along with a potentially overwhelming amount of additional information during the feedback session, you may arrange with the person to speak on the phone during the following week to check in and make sure there were no difficulties with the referral process. Sometimes individuals will have delayed reactions to the feedback that may render them ambivalent about taking the recommendations. Moreover, referrals do not always go smoothly—the person may be turned down by the recommended treatment provider for a host of reasons (e.g., medical insurance, a long waiting list, etc.). Thus, to ensure that the person is not left with deep ambivalence or a lack of alternative resources, you should make sure to find a way to follow up with him or her so that the recommendations can be followed through.

Some individuals will choose not to follow through on the recommendations; this is entirely acceptable (unless they are mandated for some reason). However, the reason that a person does not follow through should *never* be because they did not understand the recommendations, did not have a chance to discuss reactions to the recommendations, or did not have alternatives if one of the recommendations ended up being unfeasible. Make the plan to follow up a collaborative process with the person who was assessed, and be sure to make the plan before the end of the feedback session. This conveys a caring and empathic stance, ensuring that the person will have support from you until the recommendations are carried out successfully, while it still maintains the boundary that you are doing the psychological assessment and not psychotherapy with the individual.

SUMMARY

The feedback session is the culmination of the process of psychological assessment. It constitutes the entire purpose of assessment—to give some sort of feedback and recommendations to improve an individual's life or functioning in some way. More than any other session in the assessment process (including the clinical interview, which can often bring up a great deal of conflicting emotion), people have strong reactions to the feedback session. The session requires spontaneity and flexibility on the part of the person who is giving the feedback, such that the need to convey the content of the feedback is balanced with the real, live needs of the real, live individual receiving the feedback.

There are times when feedback sessions simply do not go well (or are subjectively felt not to have gone well by the assessor, at least), and sometimes the information that emerges from the assessment is very difficult for a person to hear. An angry, hurt, disappointed, sad, or even cut-off reaction does not necessarily mean that the feedback session went poorly. Remembering that the ultimate goal of the feedback session is to have the person hear, understand, and hopefully take the recommendations, allowing them to be angry or sad may actually contribute to this goal being met.

Case Studies in Psychological Assessment

Introduction to Part II:

CASE STUDIES IN PSYCHOLOGICAL ASSESSMENT

The following six case studies present the entire process of psychological assessment from beginning (referral) to end (feedback and follow-up). The cases were chosen not to represent exhaustively all the types of cases possibly referred for assessments; such a collection of cases would be impossible to compile. Instead, they were chosen merely as illustrations of the assessment *process* itself. Three adult and three child cases were chosen, with varied referral reasons, presentations, and amounts of information available.

The cases are presented as closely as possible to the way they were actually conducted (except, of course, for details that were changed for the purpose of protecting the identities of the actual clients assessed). In addition to trying to present the process as it unfolded, an attempt was made to present the logic and thinking behind each step, including consideration of alternatives when appropriate. For example, when deciding on a model for conceptualizing personality and emotional functioning, rather than just presenting the final model, an attempt is made to discuss each of the possible models that were considered before deciding on the one that was chosen. In doing so, it is hopefully clear that the final conceptualization chosen by the assessor is one of several viable options and is in no way a "correct" version. More important than the final product (the report) is the process the assessor goes through, systematically, for each individual assessment.

CHAPTER 7

An Underachieving Woman

Lorraine Ryder was referred for an assessment by her therapist who had been seeing her weekly for psychotherapy for about a year. She had recently been sent for a neuropsychological evaluation to determine whether she had attention-deficit/hyperactivity disorder (ADHD), but her therapist and psychiatrist were not pleased with the report obtained from this testing, because it did not (a) state clearly or definitively whether or not she likely had ADHD or (b) make clear recommendations. Thus, she was referred for a comprehensive psychological evaluation to determine "what's really going on with her," as she was "not meeting her potential." This information was the extent of the referral information, and it was requested that she bring a copy of her neuropsychological evaluation with her to her first psychological assessment appointment.

THE CLINICAL INTERVIEW

Lorraine Ryder came in to the office on time, dressed casually and appropriately. She was an extremely friendly looking and charming young woman, who looked to be in her mid-20s. She was a White woman of average height and weight. She made good eye contact and smiled genuinely as she came into the office and began the interview. There was nothing remarkable about her appearance or the way she related to the assessor from the beginning of the assessment process.

Before beginning the open-ended clinical interview, the assessor asked her a few factual identifying information questions. She reported that she was 24 years old, giving her date of birth. When asked her ethnicity, she reported that she is a "White mutt, Jewish on my mother's side, but not my father's." Her native language is English, having been born and raised in Virginia. She is currently single and has no children.

As a note on the presentation of this clinical interview: The sections presented here are not categorized into symptomatic evaluation and psychosocial evaluation, as the flow of the clinical interview did not follow this structure. The subsections are presented in the following text so as to present the clinical interview as closely as possible to the way it actually unfolded, rather than artificially grouping sections of information that did not present themselves sequentially. That is, the presentation that follows is how the clinical interview happened chronologically, along with the overarching questions the assessor asked Lorraine. Clarifications were occasionally necessary throughout the interview, but those questions and comments are not presented here.

Presenting Problem: What Would You Like to Get Out of a Psychological Assessment, and Why Now?

As is almost always the case, the assessor began the clinical interview by assessing the presenting problem from the perspective of the individual being assessed. When asked in general why she wanted to have a psychological assessment, she began to explain how she felt there was a "gap between my drive and knowledge and ability to do things," stating that she knew she had knowledge and skills, but that she was "for some reason" unable to accomplish things she would like to accomplish. "Something is getting in the way of me doing what I know I can do." When asked to clarify, she reported that she has some anxiety around work tasks, and that she becomes frustrated with even day-to-day, basic functions. "Every day I'm reinventing how to do everything." She also reported some attention difficulty, racing thoughts, and severe problems making decisions.

These presenting problems were relatively vague, so the assessor probed and tried to get more specific information out of Lorraine. She specified that in the mornings, for example, she gets somewhat confused when it comes to doing simple tasks like brushing her teeth—she feels that instead of "just going through the motions," she needs to think very hard about the steps involved in brushing her teeth, "reinventing the wheel every day." She stated that this confusion was not debilitating, in that she knows that she knows how to brush her teeth, but rather it frustrates her that she gets confused and has to think through these tasks so purposefully.

Further, she specified that during job tasks, for example, she always thinks there are better ways to do things than the way she does them, which prevents her from doing any of them at all. She spends time researching whether or not there are these "better ways," never quite completing things adequately. When she does complete tasks, she is consistently unsatisfied with the outcome. She reported that "if someone holds my hand through things," she can complete tasks on time and adequately.

When asked about suicidal ideation, she reported passive ideation: "I sometimes think that it would be okay if I died." She reported that she had had this ideation at times in her past, though she could not recall specifically when. Because she endorsed ideation, the assessor assessed her intent by asking whether she thought she would ever actually harm herself. She reported that she did not think she would ever harm herself, and that the ideation occurred "only when I'm depressed." She reported that she did not actually want to die, and that she only thought about it occasionally. She denied any thoughts of harming anyone else.

History of Presenting Problem: Tell Me More About How All These Problems Started and Affected You in the Past

The logical next step, once the presenting problem had been clarified, at least somewhat, was to assess the history of this presenting problem. When asked about the history of these varied problems, she reported that she was "definitely like this in college." She received a BA in creative writing from a prestigious liberal arts college in California. She reported a good GPA (about 3.4 in college), but she stated that she had difficulty finishing work and handing assignments in on time. She received many Incompletes in classes because of this problem. She stated that her problem handing in final products was largely because she was unhappy with the results, especially for creative writing assignments. She reported that these problems with handing in assignments varied, however, revealing an inconsistency that made her extremely anxious. "My performance was emotionally affected," such that she became overwhelmed at times, especially when she was feeling depressed, but she performed better when she was challenged and in a good mood.

She reported that before college, and specifically in high school, she was "like this," but that circumstances were somehow different. She reported taking on "a million different activities," keeping herself extremely busy, "always going, stressed out," but she somehow "kept afloat." She feels that having so many different activities gave her less opportunity to scrutinize her performance in any one area. Before high school, she could not recall whether or not she struggled with these issues. She also reported previous bouts with "depression," though her memory was vague about specific symptoms, timing, duration, or any other details about these episodes.

Important to note is that through her description of the history of the presenting problem, her educational history was reported. There is then no need to ask specifically about educational history when going through the rest of the clinical interview. This is a good illustration of the flexibility required when conducting open-ended, unstructured (or even semi-structured) clinical interviews. General questions about why an individual wants or needs the assessment, as well as about the history of the presenting problems, can actually uncover more in terms of sections needing assessment than just the presenting problem and history of presenting problem sections.

Occupational History: So These Problems Have Clearly Affected You at School—Tell Me More About Your Work History

Rather than go into the symptomatic evaluation part of the clinical interview, because she had already begun to report on her educational history, it made logical sense to assess how, if at all, her presenting problem was affecting her ability to work or perform job tasks. She reported immediately that she is currently unemployed and has recently decided to become an actress. So far, as an aspiring actress, work had been "inconsistent and sporadic," and she was both living with and being supported by her parents.

When asked about her work history, she reported that she had had one job since graduating from college. She worked at an advertising agency for about two years, a job that she enjoyed and found creatively satisfying. After about a year, she began missing work regularly and being consistently late when she did show up. Because she reportedly produced high-quality work, her agency afforded her some flexibility, including the ability to work from home on projects. Even with this flexibility, however, she continued to have difficulty submitting projects on time or at all, and she was eventually fired from her position. When asked what she felt "got in the way" with this job, she reported that it was likely "the same stuff" as with her schoolwork in college. She felt consistently unsatisfied with the quality of her work, and at times she would spend so much time researching alternatives to her process that she would not even begin to work on the content of the project.

Psychiatric Symptoms: I'm Going to Ask You More Specifically About Some of the Symptoms You've Reported; Let's Start With Your Mood—How Have You Been Feeling Emotionally?

Because Lorraine's presenting problem was relatively vague, and because she mentioned several times that she has a history of what she considered depression, it was decided to ask more specifically about areas of functioning and symptoms related to depression, in order to clarify her presenting problems. The assessor warned her that he was going to ask more probing, specific questions, and that at any point, if she did not feel comfortable answering a question, she should just let him know. First, the assessor asked about her mood more specifically. "It's been decent in the last year," though she reported that it shifts rapidly, going from happy to sad to angry quite frequently. She again reported that she had been depressed in the past.

She was then asked about other specific symptoms, including her appetite, her sleep, enjoyment of usual activities, hobbies, libido, crying, and specific feelings like hopelessness, helplessness, and worthlessness. She reported a good appetite ("massive, actually") and no problems with enjoyment of usual activities and hobbies or her libido. Her energy level was "okay," though she reported difficulty waking up in the morning and getting herself going, feeling as though she wanted to go back to sleep for a long time. Her sleep "has been an issue for a long time." In fact, she reported having gone to a sleep center to assess and treat her abnormal sleeping patterns. She used to sleep about 13 hours a night, and at times would sleep for about 28 hours straight, about once a month. Currently, however, she sleeps about 8 hours a night and feels relatively refreshed when she wakes up and finally gets herself going. When asked, she endorsed a constant, low-grade level of helplessness, feeling as though she could not handle her own problems and her own life. However, she denied any hopelessness, feeling instead as though she was actually taking steps to help with her problems. She also reported that she cries excessively, though not only when she is sad: "Any emotion makes me cry—when I'm angry, frustrated." She related a story about being on the phone with the phone company, discussing a billing issue, and becoming extremely frustrated and beginning to cry uncontrollably.

Because the assessor was examining her mood history, he asked specifically about symptoms of mania as well. This is an example of when it is extremely important to be very familiar with psychopathology and the DSM-IV-TR; whenever a depression is suspected, symptoms of bipolar disorder (i.e., manic and hypomanic symptoms) should also be assessed. When asked if there were ever times when she needed less sleep or felt extremely good about herself, she reported that she would occasionally stay up all night but not feel tired the next day, and that at times she felt extremely "high on myself," feeling that she was special and "queen of the world." She reported that these instances were brief, however, and she generally took no action when she was feeling this way. When asked directly, she denied hallucinations (seeing or hearing things that were not actually there) and delusions (ever thinking strange thoughts or feeling as though people were against her or out to get her).

Psychiatric History: Tell Me More About Your History in Therapy and With Psychiatrists

Reasonably comfortable that he had gotten some more clarity on her current psychiatric state, the assessor moved on to the psychiatric history. She reported that she currently has diagnoses of depression, anxiety, and ADHD, for which she sees her therapist weekly and her psychiatrist monthly. She reported that she is currently prescribed extended-release Wellbutrin, Lexapro, and Lamictal. She had been prescribed Adderall as an adolescent, but she no longer took this ADHD medication. As a psychologist, and not a psychiatrist, the assessor need not necessarily be concerned with all the details and interactions of psychotropic medications prescribed to a patient. However, the assessor should always have a working knowledge of commonly prescribed medications. Wellbutrin is a common medication for depression, and Lexapro is a common medication for depression and anxiety; Lamictal, however, is a medication generally prescribed for bipolar disorder (or epilepsy), not one of the diagnoses she self-presented. Consequently, a "red flag" for bipolar disorder should be raised, and it will automatically become one of our hypotheses later in the assessment process.

Although she had been seeing her therapist only for about a year, she reported that she had been seeing her psychiatrist since the eleventh grade, when she was first diagnosed with ADHD and depression and was medicated. She reported not being aware of any significant side effects of any of her current medications.

Family Psychiatric History: Are There, or Have There Been, Any Known Mental Illnesses in Your Family?

Because she was reporting specific psychiatric symptoms and history, as well as having begun seeing mental health professionals as an adolescent, the assessor chose next to assess her family's psychiatric history. While she had been talking for quite awhile, this is an example of why it is extremely important to keep in mind the information that needs to be gathered in a clinical interview. She did not, in an unstructured way, disclose her family's psychiatric history; it was only through asking directly and specifically about this topic that she disclosed an extensive history of mental illness in her family. She reported that her mother was being treated for obsessive-compulsive disorder, her sister was being treated for an anxiety disorder, and all of her grandparents had been medicated for various mental illnesses. She reported that her paternal grandmother had had several psychotic breaks. Although mood and anxiety disorders would have been likely hypotheses anyway, because of the heavily genetic component of these disorders, her significant family history of anxiety and mood disorders (and possibly psychotic disorders) lends more evidence to the possibility that they may be at play within Lorraine's presentation.

Medical and Family Medical History: Can You Tell Me More About Your Medical History, and Any Serious Medical Problems in Your Family?

The assessor moved on to other possible factors that could affect psychiatric functioning. First, he assessed medical history, including history of significant medical illness in Lorraine's family. She reported that at 2 years old, she was hospitalized with chickenpox because of suspicion that she might have Reye Syndrome. Because the assessor was unfamiliar with Reye Syndrome, he took the opportunity to engage Lorraine in teaching him about her understanding of the disorder (which he later researched to verify the details). The syndrome is a sudden-onset disease of the brain and liver, sometimes fatal. Related symptoms include lethargy and vomiting. Lorraine turned out not to have had Reye Syndrome, though this hospitalization (for whatever the medical problem) may have impacted her development in some way. She denied any other major medical problems or hospitalizations. It was specifically asked when she had her last physical examination and blood workup; she had been sent by the neuropsychologist who did the neuropsychological evaluation two months before, and she was found to have no medical illnesses. She also denied any major medical illnesses in her family.

Alcohol/Substance Use History: Tell Me About Your Use of Alcohol and Other Drugs, Now and in the Past

The other factor that can affect psychiatric functioning to be assessed is use of alcohol and other substances. While she denied overuse of alcohol, reporting that she drinks socially and rarely gets or has ever gotten drunk, she reported occasional use of marijuana in college. Further, she reported a two-week period in her freshman year of college during which she snorted her Adderall in order to get high. However, frightened that she might become dependent, she stopped this substance abuse. She denied any family history of substance use or abuse.

Developmental History: I'm Going to Ask You Some Questions That You May or May Not Know the Answer to About Your Early Childhood; Let's Start With Your Mother's Pregnancy With You—Were There Any Problems or Anything Notable About When She Was Pregnant With You?

Satisfied with the general content and history of psychiatric functioning, the assessor decided to move on to completing the rest of the core of the symptomatic and psychosocial evaluation, beginning with Lorraine's early development. She was asked about anything remarkable or any problems related to her mother's pregnancy, her birth and delivery, her developmental milestones, and her educational and cognitive development. She reported that while pregnant her mother "tumbled down a staircase," but there had been no apparent harm to either her or her mother. At birth, she reported that she was noticeably cold, so the doctor put a hat and mittens on her, in addition to the blanket in which she was wrapped (she, half-jokingly, commented that she looked like she was isolating herself with her blanket). She reported no known problems with developmental milestones or intellectual or cognitive development, except that she often daydreamed in elementary school. Additionally, she reported that she cried every first day of school throughout elementary and middle school—"I'm not good with transitions." She also reported that during high school she was "depressed," spending days sleeping in the nurse's office. Otherwise, she reported nothing notable about her development.

Family History: Tell Me More About Your Family and the Environment You Grew Up In

When asked about her family and growing up, she reported that she is the youngest of three children, having an older brother and sister, neither of whom currently lived at home with her and her parents. She reported a "normal, dull" childhood, remembering nothing remarkable about how she was raised. Her parents were still married, and she reported feeling that they loved and supported her and her siblings. Notably, not only was she vague when reporting about her childhood and family context growing up, but she explicitly reported that her memory of growing up was vague and unspecific. She had difficulty recalling any specific events that occurred within her family before graduating high school.

Social and Psychosexual History

When describing her family history, without prompting, she naturally flowed into a description of her social history. Although she could not remember specific family details growing up, she could remember details about her friends in middle and high school vividly. She stated that she felt that her memory was "odd," as she remembered events and people from the past "in surprising detail," while she sometimes struggled to remember what happened the day before. She reported a "great" social network, currently and in the past, including four very close girlfriends who have been close for many years. Included in this group are two "best friends." At times in her life, however, she reported having difficulty "getting myself to things," like group dinners and other social engagements. She reported that these friends have stuck with her "even through my antisocial phases," when she went long periods of time without seeing them.

She reported dating and being sexually active ("I guess the normal amount") in college, though since then she has not had a significant romantic relationship. She denied any history of sexual abuse or early sexual behavior.

Criminal/Legal History: Have You Ever Had Any Involvement With the Legal System or Been in Trouble With the Law?

This was perhaps one of the easiest areas of the current assessment (though definitely not of all assessments); when asked, she denied any history of criminal or legal involvement.

Multicultural Evaluation: Can You Tell Me a Bit About Your Cultural Identity and How It Has Developed?

Knowing that she is a White, half-Jewish female born and raised in the South (the current assessment was conducted in New York City, where she now lived), the assessor knew that language and acculturation to the country were not major issues. However, acculturation to a different area of the country, as well as her spiritual and cultural identities, were assessed. With all the best intentions of trying to understand how her cultural context influenced her development and current functioning, she generally and categorically denied that they had any impact on her life. She was not currently or in the past religious, and she reported having no difficulty transitioning out of Virginia or into California for college or to New York City afterward. She jokingly reiterated that she was "just an average White mutt" culturally.

REVIEW OF NEUROPSYCHOLOGICAL EVALUATION

A thorough review of the neuropsychological assessment report was necessary, especially because the evaluation had taken place only a few months before the current assessment. While many measures were included in the neuropsychological assessment, of particular note was the Wechsler Adult Intelligence

Scale, 3rd Edition (WAIS-III), as it is a standard measure of current intellectual functioning that would likely have been included in the present psychological assessment. She performed in the high average to superior ranges as compared with others her age in almost all measured domains. Her only slight weakness was in working memory, which was still in the high average range.

In addition to the WAIS-III, Lorraine was administered the Wechsler Memory Scale, 3rd Edition (WMS-III). She was found to have no major impairment in memory functioning; however, she exhibited significantly weaker performance when asked to learn a second list of 16 words than when she was asked to learn the first list of 16 words, which "suggests a strong effect of proactive interference and variable attention overall," according to the report. This finding suggests that her level of attention seems to shift from one task to the next, depending on other factors.

Finally, the neuropsychological assessment included the Minnesota Multiphasic Personality Inventory, 2nd Edition (MMPI-2). Her results from this test suggested an "overly critical" view of herself, a "high level of situational and psychological distress," a "tendency to feel worthless and inadequate," and included characteristics of passivity, apathy, and indecisiveness. The recommendations from the neuropsychological evaluation included reevaluation of her prescribed Adderall, with indication that it should be increased due to her apparent ADHD; structured, goal-oriented, cognitive-behavioral therapy "to address her organizational and time management needs"; and follow-up with the sleep clinic to address her sleep disorder.

MENTAL STATUS EVALUATION

Appearance and Behavior

Lorraine's appearance and behavior were unremarkable. She was adequately groomed and well-related interpersonally, and she exhibited no odd or repetitive movements or behaviors. She made good eye contact throughout the clinical interview, and she was friendly and cooperative.

Speech and Language

While she seemed to comprehend all of the questions asked of her (exhibiting adequate receptive language ability), there were times when her speech became somewhat confused, tangential, and hard to follow. Her volume, articulation, and vocabulary were all appropriate, but her rate of speaking was often very rapid, causing her to clutter some of her words together, making them difficult to understand. Her train of thought, while logical to follow (i.e., her thinking did not consist of loose associations), rarely stayed on point, and although she answered direct questions logically, after giving the answers she often kept talking and becoming somewhat confused in her speech.

Mood and Affect

She reported euthymic mood currently, with a history of depression, and her affect was appropriate to both the situation and to the reported mood. She smiled freely and showed some variation in affect, seeming generally happy, without evidence of current elevated, depressed, anxious, or angry mood.

Thought Process and Content

As previously stated, her thought content was free of hallucinations and delusions, though it had some depressive ideation in the form of helplessness. Suicidality, aggressiveness, and homicidality were not present. Her thought process, however, was notably tangential and confused at times. This confusion was exhibited in the sessions to a mild degree, and she reported that her thought process in her everyday functioning is at times so confusing that she cannot perform simple routine tasks.

Cognition

Lorraine was alert throughout the clinical interview, and her attention and concentration seemed unimpaired. She reported some abnormalities in her memory functioning: She has only vague memories of her childhood, at times has difficulty remembering details from the previous day, and at the same time has extremely vivid memories of certain aspects of her past. Other than these slight abnormalities, however, her memory seemed generally intact.

Prefrontal Functioning

Lorraine's judgment and insight seem mostly adequate, but her planning ability seems to be one of her greatest impairments. She reported significant difficulty making decisions, and there is a seeming immobility in her life currently because of this difficulty and her other problems.

Hypothesis Building

Now that the clinical assessment (clinical interview, review of previous reports, and mental status evaluation) is complete, the information gathered can be used to create hypotheses for what is going on for Lorraine. It is important to note that no collateral information was gathered in this case for several reasons. First and foremost, there were no previous hospitalizations and no indicators that anyone, including a child, was in danger. She seemed to be open and honest throughout the interview, and her reported presenting problems were very much in line with the referral questions sent by the referring therapist. It was not felt that anything would be gained by interviewing any other interested parties (e.g., her therapist or her parents), and because of time and money limitations, it was decided to move forward with the assessment.

Identify Impairments

For Lorraine, the task of identifying the specific impairments is not a simple one. Her presenting problems are somewhat vague and diffuse, and she is having global difficulties in functioning across different domains in her life. Additionally, some of what could be considered functional impairment seems to be justified or justifiable in her present circumstances. For example, she is unemployed, but she has changed her career goals significantly to be an actress, and many actresses are unemployed, which in most cases would not be considered an impairment in functioning based on psychological factors. However, in Lorraine's case, because she was fired from her last job, has reported difficulty with job-related tasks, and has so drastically changed her career goals, it would be naïve not to consider her job difficulties part of functional impairment due to psychological factors.

Unemployment, itself, however, is not a useful impairment to identify in terms of building hypotheses. There are simply too many factors that could cause job difficulties (in fact, there are very few diagnostic criteria, if any at all, that could not impair job functioning). So we must look more specifically at areas of her life that are impaired and the symptoms that are presenting.

Enumerate Possible Causes

First and foremost, she seems to have significant mood-related symptoms. She reported that much of her functioning is mood dependent. Additionally, she exhibited many symptoms related to a depressive disorder (e.g., sleep disturbance, depressed mood, helplessness, fatigue), as well as potential symptoms related to a bipolar disorder (e.g., decreased need for sleep, elevated mood). Thus, a major first hypothesis is a *mood disorder* (which includes dysthymic disorder, major depressive disorder, bipolar I disorder, and bipolar II disorder, among several others).

Additionally, Lorraine reported several anxiety symptoms, as well as displaying some symptoms that could be related to an anxiety disorder (e.g., excessive worrying about perfectionism, preoccupying thoughts). It is important to note that some of the presenting symptoms, like the rapid speech, could be related to several disorders (this is why the diagnostic process is so difficult), so to be safe we will include all the possibilities. As such, another hypothesis would be an *anxiety disorder*, including generalized anxiety disorder, obsessive-compulsive disorder, and anxiety disorder not otherwise specified (there is no evidence of such anxiety disorders as specific phobia, social phobia, panic disorder, or agoraphobia, so we will not include them as hypotheses).

Although she no longer uses marijuana and uses alcohol only socially and in moderation, because of her history of snorting Adderall to get high, a *substance use disorder* must be considered. In her case, however, it seems extremely unlikely that her current impairments in functioning are due to the effects of using (or withdrawing from) substances.

Perhaps most difficult to understand are the odd symptoms related to her confusion, difficulties making decisions, and bizarre patterns of memory functioning. Based on our knowledge of the DSM-IV-TR, there are several possibilities as to what could be causing these bizarre impairments. First, these could be symptoms related to a *psychotic disorder*, such that they represent a possible thought disorder. Additionally, however, they could be symptoms of some sort of *dissociative disorder*, such that there is a bizarre depersonalization or derealization causing the confusion. The third possibility is that the strange phenomena are due to one of several *personality disorders*, including schizotypal personality disorder and dependent personality disorder.

Of particular note in this assessment is the question of attention-deficit/hyperactivity disorder (ADHD). Both because she has difficulty in concentration and attention and because the neuropsychological evaluation diagnosed her with ADHD (not to mention that she has been prescribed Adderall), the diagnostic question of whether or not she has ADHD is a central one. However, it is not a major hypothesis in this assessment. Although she has some evidence of poor attention, there are some details of this symptom that suggest it is due to something other than ADHD.

Specifically, in her neuropsychological evaluation, there were two findings that would suggest that she does not have ADHD. First, she exhibited high average performance on the Working Memory Index (WMI) of the WAIS-III. The WMI requires extremely good attention, in addition to other skills. Second, on the WMS-III, she exhibited unexpectedly varied performance across tasks that require the same amount and type of attention. This finding suggests that her attention is not globally impaired across domains (as would be the case in ADHD), but rather that it is dependent on something else, such as her mood or anxiety. It is much more likely that her poor attention is secondary to one of these other diagnoses; thus, ADHD will not be a central hypothesis in this assessment.

As part of every hypothesis consideration, you should *always* consider (a) that the presenting problems have an etiology in substance use and (b) that the presenting problems have an etiology in a medical condition. In Lorraine's case, both are easily ruled out as hypotheses given that (a) she is not currently using any substances and the pattern of problems are not consistent with a substance etiology, and (b) she recently had a physical examination and blood tests and was found to have no medical problems. The bizarreness of some of the symptoms, however, is an indication that neurological tests may be helpful, to make sure that the attention, memory, and procedural impairments are not due to some sort of brain injury or an agent affecting the brain (e.g., a tumor). At this point, however, especially because the symptoms do not seem to be new or different from any other point in her life (though perhaps more salient), it will be assumed that the symptoms are psychological in nature.

SELECTING TESTS

In some ways, selecting tests for the current assessment is somewhat easier than normal, given the fact that Lorraine very recently had a neuropsychological evaluation. While many measures were given previously, two would have likely been chosen for this assessment, and the data from the neuropsychological evaluation can be used and integrated in the current assessment. These two tests are the WAIS-III and the MMPI-2. The former is part of the standard battery I use for every adult assessment, and the latter is one of a few choices for objective personality inventories for possible use.

Selecting tests for the current assessment will flow directly from the hypotheses generated. Although she had no impairment in memory functioning as measured by the WMS-III in the neuropsychological evaluation, because one of our minor hypotheses is some sort of gross neurological impairment (for which a neurological evaluation would be extremely useful), it is important to supplement the understanding of intellectual functioning (i.e., the WAIS-III) with a screening of overall neurological functioning. Therefore, the Bender Visual-Motor Gestalt Test, 2nd Edition (Bender-2) was chosen. The Bender-2 very quickly and easily assesses four domains of neurological functioning: visual perceptual ability, fine motor skill, visual-motor integration, and short-term visual memory. Although adequate performance on the Bender-2 cannot completely rule out neurological impairment, it can provide us with evidence that there may be neurological damage with lower scores.

The major hypotheses for the current assessment are general Axis I disorders, including mood disorders, anxiety disorders, and possibly a psychotic disorder. With mood and anxiety disorders, differential diagnosis can be tricky. Anxiety symptoms can come with a mood disorder, mood symptoms can come with an anxiety disorder, and both mood and anxiety disorders can exist as comorbid disorders. The pattern is similar with mood and psychotic disorders. Luckily, much of the rest of my standard battery is aimed at teasing apart differential diagnosis of Axis I disorders.

Taken together, the Rorschach Inkblot Test (Rorschach), the Thematic Apperception Test (TAT), and the Projective Drawings should offer enough projective evidence to understand what is diagnostically going on for Lorraine. In addition, as part of my standard battery, one of the objective measures of personality and emotional functioning will be chosen. Although we already have data from the MMPI-2 from the neuropsychological evaluation, adding the Personality Assessment Inventory (PAI) will be important in order to distinguish between the Axis I disorders. The PAI is a good measure in this case because Lorraine is cognitively high functioning and thus can reliably respond to the PAI questions with the

4-point scale and because the PAI maps well onto the DSM-IV-TR for Axis I disorders. Altogether, the PAI, Rorschach, TAT, and Projective Drawings should provide enough evidence for diagnosis on Axis I.

The one exception is the possibility of a dissociative disorder. While these measures may rule out the possibility of dissociation, if they do not rule it out, another measure looking specifically at dissociation may be used, such as the dissociative experiences scale (DES) or the dissociative disorders interview schedule (DDIS). However, because the standard battery measures can rule out the possibility of a dissociative disorder, one of these measures will be used only if the other measures do not rule out this possibility.

The final hypothesis generated from the clinical assessment was the possibility of a personality disorder. While the battery thus far may be helpful in understanding the personality dynamics (especially the Rorschach), the PAI tests only for two types of personality disorders—borderline and antisocial. Neither one of these is a hypothesis, so it will be extremely useful to add an additional objective measure that better taps personality (Axis II) functioning. For this, the Millon Clinical Multiaxial Inventory, 3rd Edition (MCMI-III) will be used. This measure's strength is its sensitivity to personality and character styles; together with the projective measures, it can provide a comprehensive picture of Lorraine's personality functioning.

Thus, our assessment's battery of tests will consist of

- Bender-2
- MCMI-III
- PAI
- Rorschach
- TAT
- Projective Drawings
- (If needed: DES)

ACCUMULATING THE DATA

A table of results follows (Table 7.1), displaying each individual measure administered. Note that the DES was not administered, because the battery as given ruled out the likelihood of a dissociative disorder.

TABLE 7.1   ACCUMULATION OF LORRAINE'S DATA

MMP I-2 (from neuropsychological evaluation)
Overly critical view of herself
High level of situational and psychological distress
Tendency to feel worthless and inadequate
Passivity, apathy, and indecisiveness

MCMI-III
Submissively dependent
Self-effacing
Noncompetitive
General avoidance of autonomy
Resents others she depends on because they are critical/disapproving
Underlying anger—rarely shown
Anger—toward people who fail to appreciate her need for affection/nurturance
Need for security threatened by her own anger
May withdraw to moderate anxiety and sensitivity to rejection
Anger—leads to loneliness, though this is rarely divulged
Calm/pleasant on the surface, but with underlying tension
Underlying tension—anxiety, sadness, guilt
Acts weak, self-doubtful, and needy for reassurance
Behaves in ways either to be left alone or to evoke nurturance
Some somatic depression symptoms—weakness, fatigue
Feels life is empty but draining
Some manic symptoms—rushed speech, accelerated thinking
Bipolar symptoms

PAI
Grandiosity
Inflated self-esteem
No irritability or hyperactivity
Confusion, distractibility, and difficulty concentrating
Problems communicating clearly
Tangential and/or circumstantial thinking
Current worry and anxiety
Overconcern with issues she has no control over
Generally positive but at times fluctuating self-evaluation
External locus of control
Bipolar symptoms
Possible personality disorder indicated

(Continued)

TABLE 7.1   (CONTINUED)

Rorschach

Problems with thinking clearly

Intrusive ideation—needs not being met and unable to prevent others from determining her destiny

Situational stress—seems to be impeding her thinking clearly

Coping strategy—escapist—goes into fantasy

Coping—tends to imagine how other people and outside events will make decisions for her

Some evidence of distorted reality

Pessimistic

Discouragement

Misperceives events at times

Confusion between reality and fantasy at times

Impaired social perception

Overincorporation—takes in more information than she can effectively organize and make sense of

When under time pressure—becomes anxious and dissatisfied and underachieves

Excessive openness to experience—aware of way too much around her

Small things feel big to her

High achievement orientation and good IQ

Poor decision-making skills

Tendency toward impulsive action at times

Loneliness and neediness

Confused by her own emotions

Current affective disturbance

Tends to internalize pain and affect—does not express it

Resentment and anger toward people and the world around her

Chronic state of irritation

Difficulty being happy—confused by even this feeling

Self-avoiding, because of general self-criticism and self-consciousness

Identity diffusion

High dependency needs

Resents those who do not meet her needs; is easily disappointed

Bipolar symptoms

Projective Drawings

Hypercritical of self and others

Overly aware of information in her environment

TABLE 7.1   (*CONTINUED*)

Hidden true self
Low self-esteem
Feels damaged in some way
Is overwhelmed by the world
Poor social perception

TAT
Discouraged easily
Disappointed
Copes with the world by being paralyzed and making no decisions
Unmet needs for affection
Overincorporation of information from the world
Restricted feelings
Feels abandoned
Others can never meet her needs
Wears a "mask"
Copes by withdrawing
Hopelessness
Ambivalence about relationships—both wants and fears closeness
Gets confused easily when anxious/overwhelmed/under stress

IDENTIFYING THEMES

Because there is so much information to go through, it may be necessary to be somewhat vague when identifying themes in the current assessment. For example, I chose simply to label one theme "thinking" to begin with, as there were many results on her thought process, but without labeling it yet as to what it actually says about her thinking ability. Similarly, there are many results about her emotional functioning that say many different things, so I simply labeled them "emotion" during this step, and when I look at all the emotional data together, it will hopefully become clearer what the results are saying about her emotional functioning. The preliminary themes for Lorraine are listed in Table 7.2.

TABLE 7.2   **LABELING OF LORRAINE'S THEMES**

Themes	
	MMPI-2 (from neuropsychological evaluation)
Self	Overly critical view of herself
Current (symptoms)	High level of situational and psychological distress
Self	Tendency to feel worthless and inadequate
Passive (and paralyzed)	Passivity, apathy, and indecisiveness
	MCMI-III
Need (for nurturance)	Submissively dependent
Self	Self-effacing
Need	Noncompetitive
Need	General avoidance of autonomy
Resentment (and anger)	Resents others she depends on because they are critical/disapproving
Emotion	Underlying anger—rarely shown
Resentment	Anger—toward people who fail to appreciate her need for affection/nurturance
Emotion	Need for security threatened by her own anger
Passive	May withdraw to moderate anxiety and sensitivity to rejection
Current	Anger—leads to loneliness, though this is rarely divulged
Emotion	Calm/pleasant on the surface, but with underlying tension
Emotion	Underlying tension—anxiety, sadness, guilt
Need	Acts weak, self-doubtful, and needy for reassurance
Passive	Behaves in ways either to be left alone or to evoke nurturance
Current	Some somatic depression symptoms—weakness, fatigue
Current	Feels life is empty but draining
Current	Some manic symptoms—rushed speech, accelerated thinking
Current	Bipolar symptoms
	PAI
Self	Grandiosity
Self	Inflated self-esteem
	No irritability or hyperactivity
Thinking	Confusion, distractibility, and difficulty concentrating
Thinking	Problems communicating clearly
Thinking	Tangential and/or circumstantial thinking
Current	Current worry and anxiety
Overincorporation	Overconcern with issues she has no control over
Self	Generally positive but at times fluctuating self-evaluation

TABLE 7.2   (*CONTINUED*)

Themes

Need	External locus of control
Current	Bipolar symptoms
	Possible personality disorder indicated
	Rorschach
Thinking	Problems with thinking clearly
Current/Need/ Resentment	Intrusive ideation—needs not being met and unable to prevent others from determining her destiny
Current/Thinking	Situational stress—seems to be impeding her thinking clearly
Passive/Thinking	Coping strategy—escapist—goes into fantasy
Thinking/Need	Coping—tends to imagine how other people and outside events will make decisions for her
Thinking	Some evidence of distorted reality
Current	Pessimistic
Need/Resentment	Discouragement
Thinking	Misperceives events at times
Thinking	Confusion between reality and fantasy at times
Thinking/Resentment	Impaired social perception
Overincorporation	Overincorporation—takes in more information than she can effectively organize and make sense of
Overincorporation	When under time pressure—becomes anxious and dissatisfied and underachieves
Overincorporation	Excessive openness to experience—aware of way too much around her
	Small things feel big to her
	High achievement orientation and good IQ
Passive	Poor decision-making skills
	Tendency toward impulsive action at times
Need	Loneliness and neediness
Emotion	Confused by her own emotions
Current	Current affective disturbance
Emotion	Tends to internalize pain and affect—does not express it
Resentment	Resentment and anger toward people and the world around her
Resentment	Chronic state of irritation
Emotion	Difficulty being happy—confused by even this feeling
Self	Self-avoiding, because of general self-criticism and self-consciousness
Self/Need	Identity diffusion
Need	High dependency needs

(*Continued*)

TABLE 7.2 *(CONTINUED)*

Themes	
Resentment	Resents those who do not meet her needs; is easily disappointed
Current	Bipolar symptoms
	Projective Drawings
Self/Resentment	Hypercritical of self and others
Overincorporation	Overly aware of information in her environment
Emotion	Hidden true self
Self	Low self-esteem
Self	Feels damaged in some way
Thinking	Is overwhelmed by the world
Thinking/Resentment	Poor social perception
	TAT
Resentment	Discouraged easily
Resentment	Disappointed
Passive	Copes with the world by being paralyzed and making no decisions
Need	Unmet needs for affection
Overincorporation	Overincorporation of information from the world
Emotion	Restricted feelings
Need/Resentment	Feels abandoned
Resentment	Others can never meet her needs
Emotion	Wears a "mask"
Passive	Copes by withdrawing
Current	Hopelessness
Need/Resentment	Ambivalence about relationships—both wants and fears closeness
Thinking	Gets confused easily when anxious/overwhelmed/under stress

ORGANIZING THE DATA

When identifying themes, there were clearly some data that would not yet easily fit into the broad categories. Those data will be placed at the end of the organizational table to see whether they together create a coherent theme. Also, some of the theme titles can become much more specific once all the data have been examined together. Lorraine's reorganized data are presented in Table 7.3.

TABLE 7.3

LORRAINE'S ORGANIZED DATA

Test: Concept/Theme	MCMI-III	PAI	Rorschach	Projective Drawings	TAT	Interview/ MMPI-2
High Need for Nurturance	Submissively dependent	External locus of control	Intrusive ideation—needs not being met and unable to prevent others from determining her destiny		Ambivalence about relationships—both wants and fears closeness	
					Feels abandoned	
	Noncompetitive		Discouragement			
	General avoidance of autonomy		Coping—tends to imagine how other people and outside events will make decisions for her			
			Loneliness and neediness			
			Identity diffusion			
			High dependency needs			
Resents When Needs Not Met	Resents others she depends on because they are critical/disapproving		Intrusive ideation—needs not being met and unable to prevent others from determining her destiny	Hypercritical of self and others	Discouraged easily	
	Anger—toward people who fail to appreciate her need for affection/nurturance		Discouragement	Poor social perception	Disappointed	
			Impaired social perception		Feels abandoned	
			Resentment and anger toward people and the world around her		Others can never meet her needs	

(Continued)

TABLE 7.3   (CONTINUED)

Test: Concept/Theme	MCMI-III	PAI	Rorschach	Projective Drawings	TAT	Interview/ MMPI-2
			Chronic state of irritation		Ambivalence about relationships—both wants and fears closeness	
			Resents those who do not meet her needs; is easily disappointed			
Low Self-Esteem	Self-effacing	Grandiosity	Self-avoiding, because of general self-criticism and self-consciousness	Hypercritical of self and others		MMPI-2: Overly critical view of herself
		Inflated self-esteem	Identity diffusion	Low self-esteem		MMPI-2: Tendency to feel worthless and inadequate
		Generally positive but at times fluctuating self-evaluation		Feels damaged in some way		
Thinking Problems		Confusion, distractibility, and difficulty concentrating	Problems with thinking clearly	Is overwhelmed by the world	Gets confused easily when anxious/ overwhelmed/ under stress	

	Problems communicating clearly	Situational stress—seems to be impeding her thinking clearly	Poor social perception	Hidden true self	Restricted feelings
	Tangential and/or circumstantial thinking	Coping strategy—escapist—goes into fantasy			
		Coping—tends to imagine how other people and outside events will make decisions for her			
		Some evidence of distorted reality			
		Misperceives events at times			
		Confusion between reality and fantasy at times			
		Impaired social perception			
Restricted/ Confused Emotion	Underlying anger— rarely shown	Confused by her own emotions			
	Need for security threatened by her own anger	Tends to internalize pain and affect—does not express it			Wears a "mask"
	Calm/pleasant on the surface, but with underlying tension	Difficulty being happy— confused by even this feeling			

(Continued)

TABLE 7.3   (CONTINUED)

Test: Concept/Theme	MCMI-III	PAI	Rorschach	Projective Drawings	TAT	Interview/ MMPI-2
	Underlying tension—anxiety, sadness, guilt					
Overincorporation		Overconcern with issues she has no control over	Overincorporation—takes in more information than she can effectively organize and make sense of	Overly aware of information in her environment	Overincorporation of information from the world	
			When under time pressure—becomes anxious and dissatisfied and underachieves			
			Excessive openness to experience—aware of way too much around her			
Passive/ Paralyzed/ Withdrawal	May withdraw to moderate anxiety and sensitivity to rejection		Coping strategy—escapist— goes into fantasy		Copes with the world by being paralyzed and making no decisions	MMPI-2: Passivity, apathy, and indecisiveness
	Behaves in ways either to be left alone or to evoke nurturance		Poor decision-making skills		Copes by withdrawing	

Current Affective Disturbance	Anger—leads to loneliness, though this is rarely divulged	Bipolar symptoms	Intrusive ideation—needs not being met and unable to prevent others from determining her destiny	Hopelessness	MMPI-2: High level of situational and psychological distress
	Some somatic depression symptoms—weakness, fatigue		Situational stress—seems to be impeding her thinking clearly		
	Feels life is empty but draining		Pessimistic		
	Some manic symptoms—rushed speech, accelerated thinking		Current affective disturbance		
	Bipolar symptoms		Bipolar symptoms		
Other		No irritability or hyperactivity	Small things feel big to her		
		Possible personality disorder indicated	High achievement orientation and good IQ		
			Tendency toward impulsive action at times		

Note that the data in the "other" category are interesting, but not particularly useful. Information such as there being no indication of hyperactivity, there being a possible personality disorder, and there being some impulsiveness may be useful diagnostically, but none of these gives us additional interesting information on any specific areas of functioning of interest in the current assessment. Similarly, a finding about her IQ from the Rorschach is somewhat superfluous, as we have an actual measure of intellectual functioning (the WAIS-III). The result that small issues feel big to her may make sense later diagnostically, but it does not seem to fit easily into any of the thematic categories, so we will simply treat it as "noise" or "error" in the data.

Another important point when looking at the organized table of results is that even though the Rorschach seems to give more data than some of the other measures, it carries no more weight than any other test. The strength of each theme comes with the evidence coming up on multiple different tests—that is, the more tests a single theme emerges on, the more confident you can be about the validity of that theme.

CONCEPTUALIZING

The task at this point is to try to fit the themes together in a way that tells a coherent story, a convincing narrative that will have logical validity to anyone who reads the report or receives feedback, especially to Lorraine herself. Specifically, we have the following eight themes to connect:

1. High need for nurturance
2. Resenting others when her needs are not met
3. Low self-esteem
4. Problems with logical thinking
5. Confused by and restricts emotions
6. Overincorporation of information from the world
7. Passivity, paralyzed, withdrawal coping
8. Current affective disturbance

Before deciding on the most logical way to fit all these themes together, we will first consider the model templates presented in Chapter 4: the diathesis-stress model, the developmental model, and the common function model for conceptualization.

Diathesis-Stress Model

In trying to apply the diathesis-stress model of conceptualization, we must try to divide the themes into (1) *traits* that are inherent within Lorraine, that she likely developed at an early age, and that she "brings to the picture" (diatheses); (2) *external issues* that affect her functioning (stressors); and (3) *states* that are more situational or transient (outcomes). It is important to categorize each of our eight themes into these three types. Some may be arguable, but as long as the final model is logical, it is not as important to be "correct" as it is to be convincing. Remember that the point of creating our narrative is not to change our conclusions or diagnoses, but rather to frame them in an acceptable, understandable way for those receiving feedback. The way I categorize these themes here may differ from how others would, but I will give justification for each. Also, the order in which I am presenting them is entirely arbitrary.

High need for nurturance is easily recognizable as a trait. When thinking developmentally, this is a need that comes very early on. It is very likely that, because of her temperament and early childhood experiences, Lorraine developed a high need for nurturance that seems to have gone unmet for much of her life. This need may not be greater than normal or excessive, but what is notable is that her need for nurturance is greater than the nurturance she receives. Thus, this need is a diathesis.

Resentment and anger toward others when her needs are not met is a bit more complicated. While it makes sense that resentment and anger are states and thus outcomes, when the theme is examined more closely, it seems that the fact that her needs are not met is more like an external stress. If there were no more themes, it would make sense that a high need for nurturance (diathesis), in combination with her needs not being met (stress), would lead to resentment and anger (outcomes). Thus, for the sake of the diathesis-stress model, this theme may need to be split into (a) her needs being unmet and (b) anger and resentment about her unmet needs. So this theme of resentment toward others will fill the roles of both a stress and an outcome.

Low self-esteem, while some may disagree, is almost always best viewed as a state, rather than a trait. Part of the reason for this is a sense of hope that low self-esteem is transient and easily addressable. This is not to imply that it is any less serious than other, more trait-like issues; there is some sense of judgment (a bias I will admit to) that nobody is born with or develops early a chronic, trait-like lack of confidence and poor regard for himself or herself. Thus, low self-esteem will be considered an outcome for Lorraine.

Problems with logical thinking is another theme that is somewhat difficult to categorize and depends on the particular judgments of the psychologist who is conceptualizing. Some disorganized thinking can be biologically based and innate. Some can be a result of situational stress and disorganizing circumstances. The decision about confused thinking can be based on several factors. One is how serious the problem is. It is likely that if the thought problems are profound (extremely psychotic), they are *causing* many more problems and can be considered a trait. In Lorraine's case, however, she is extremely high functioning, and her confused thinking does not seem to have impacted her life from childhood; therefore, it makes more sense to conceptualize it as an outcome, less serious and more transient.

Emotional restriction and confusion is a style of being, a trait. While being confused by emotions could be situationally based, restricting emotions as a general style is learned early on and affects how personality develops. As such, this theme will be considered a diathesis.

Overincorporation, similarly, is a style of interacting with the world. While in many reports the word "overincorporation" may be too "jargony," there are times when it is simply such a strong theme that it can be defined within the report itself and used throughout. This seems to be the case with Lorraine. She simply takes in way too much information from the world around her, much more than she can effectively or efficiently organize or handle. This style of connecting to the external world is a trait she is bringing to the picture, so it will be considered a diathesis.

Passivity, being paralyzed, and withdrawal are coping strategies or results of whatever else is happening with her. While this is not yet a good name for the theme (which will be addressed during the report-writing step of the process), these three things conceptually make sense together, such that they all have to do with how she likely reacts to difficulty or stress. As such, they are considered outcomes.

Current affective disturbance, even in the label itself, is necessarily a state. That is, because it is "current," it is not chronic. Emotional disturbance is not part of the core of Lorraine's personality. Therefore, this theme will be considered an outcome. The diathesis-stress model for Lorraine is shown in Figure 7.1.

FIGURE 7.1   DIATHESIS-STRESS MODEL FOR LORRAINE

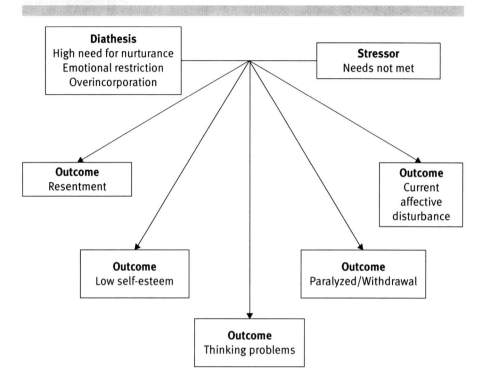

This model is not too complex, and it seems that it could be arguable. The key would be writing it up in a way that makes this model make absolute sense. The challenge would be to explain how each of the outcomes is a logical result of the interaction between Lorraine's style of interacting with the world and the fact that her needs are not being met. Before deciding on using this model, however, consider other models as well.

Developmental Model

The first step of the developmental model for conceptualizing is to look at the themes and see what they say about how Lorraine is functioning developmentally. For example, does she display feelings, needs, and attitudes normal for an adolescent (e.g., emotional lability, high need for peer approval, and a hazy identity)? Or does she more resemble a child (with high dependency need, difficulty telling fantasy from reality, and an inability to care for herself)? Or does she resemble an adult (with healthy independence, emotional maturity, and good decision-making skills)? Remember that the developmental model will work only if there is a discrepancy between the level at which she is functioning and the actual age-demands being placed on her. It is not interesting to say that she is functioning at the level of an adult and has adult demands being placed on her; this scenario should not lead to any problems. This model is relevant only when her level of functioning falls below what is being expected of her, such as being an adult with adult demands but functioning as a child. This mismatch between functioning and demands would likely lead to problems.

For Lorraine, there is mixed evidence of her level of developmental functioning. Cognitively, she is clearly functioning extremely well as an adult. Emotionally, her high needs for nurturance indicate that she may be functioning at an earlier developmental stage than an adult, as need for nurturance and care, while it is seen in most people, is prominent in childhood. Additionally, she is confused by emotions, suggesting that her emotional development may have been arrested at an early age, before she learned to understand, integrate, and tolerate feelings. Similarly, her ideational development seems to be more childlike, in that she has difficulty with logical thinking (at least at times). Also, shutting down when faced with difficulty (i.e., being paralyzed or withdrawing) is not a healthy adult coping mechanism. Thus, it could be argued that psychologically, she is functioning at a much younger level than the adult that she is. When thinking about Lorraine as a person, this hypothesis makes sense; she is not currently gainfully employed, lives with her parents, and displays what could be considered some regressive behavior at home, including an inability to make decisions. The developmental model for Lorraine is shown in Figure 7.2.

Again, this model is not too complex, but the emphasis of the argument in the report would be slightly different. In terms that are not too psychological, it would be necessary to explain how the themes that represent more childlike developmental functioning do so. This would make a part of the assessment report psychoeducational, such that it informs the reader about human development. The difficult part, if we choose this conceptual model for Lorraine, would be explaining how the childlike developmental functioning, in interaction with the adult demands, leads specifically to some of the outcomes. While it is logical that resentment, low self-esteem,

FIGURE 7.2   DEVELOPMENTAL MODEL FOR LORRAINE

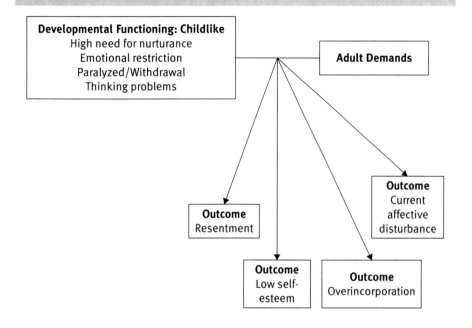

and current affective disturbance could be due to the mismatch between her functioning and the demands being placed on her, the style of taking in too much information from the world (overincorporation), while it does not represent a childlike developmental trait, may be harder to consider a logical outcome. This task is not impossible, as it could be argued that she has adopted this style of taking in too much information as a result of needing more and more nurturance and searching to find it everywhere, but it is not as straightforward and logical as the other outcomes.

Common Function Model

The common function model explains the themes together as all serving a common purpose (often this purpose is reflected in one or two of the themes). Generally, the first step is to evaluate each of the themes to identify the overall defensive or coping strategies of the individual. This is relatively straightforward with Lorraine, in that her major defensive strategy is to restrict her emotions, which are overwhelming and confusing to her. The difficult part, then, becomes explaining that the other themes serve the purpose of helping her restrict her emotions. While her resentment, over-incorporation, withdrawal, and even thinking problems could arguably serve this purpose, it would be a very difficult claim to make that her current affective disturbance, low self-esteem, and high need for nurturance are serving this same purpose. However, if we rethink how some of the themes work and make our common function model a bit more complex, the common theme could be more specific, such that she needs to restrict her emotions because of her high need for nurturance and her low self-esteem. This makes the model a bit more viable, though the current affective disturbance is still hard to explain with this pure common function model. The common function model for Lorraine is shown in Figure 7.3.

This model becomes compelling when discussing the difference between *how* she goes about trying to restrict her emotions (all the themes that have this common function, many of which are maladaptive) and *why* she wants or needs to restrict her emotion (the nurturance needs, the fact that they confuse her, and her low self-esteem, arguably). However, because of the logical problems presented previously, it is likely that a more complex model is necessary for understanding Lorraine's functioning.

FIGURE 7.3   **COMMON FUNCTION MODEL FOR LORRAINE**

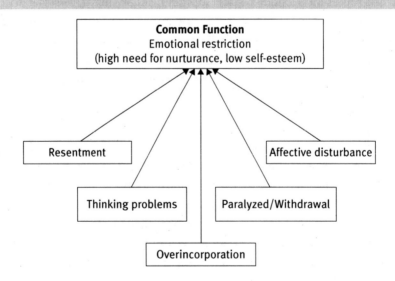

Complex Model

Although each of these three models might be adequate, with so many themes and some problems with each of the models, it is useful to consider a more complex model. Any of the three models previously presented could serve as the basis for a more complex model. For example, to address the problem with the common function model, a complex model could use the same common functions, but could also add outcomes to her style of using those functions. For example, while she may employ overincorporation, withdrawal, and resentment toward others to serve the purpose of restricting her emotions, these patterns have currently led to affective disturbance and problems in thinking clearly. The model is shown in Figure 7.4.

Similarly, the diathesis-stress model could be used as the basis for a more complex model. Given Lorraine's current functioning, one area of functioning that could be emphasized more in the model is the interpersonal domain. In order to play up the interpersonal domain more, greater importance can be placed on the resentment theme, as, together with the high need for nurturance, it leads to interpersonal ambivalence. Therefore, the diatheses stay the same (overincorporative style, high need for nurturance, and emotional restriction), and the stress remains her unmet needs (though instead of separating this out as its own theme, it can be subsumed into the high need for nurturance and resentment themes again), and the

FIGURE 7.4   COMPLEX MODEL FOR LORRAINE

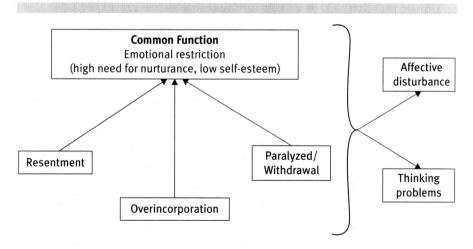

FIGURE 7.5   ANOTHER COMPLEX MODEL FOR LORRAINE

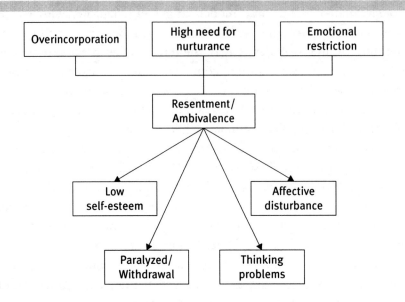

outcome becomes the resentment and ambivalence about interpersonal relationships. From this resentment and ambivalence come the other current problems, as secondary outcomes. The model is shown in Figure 7.5.

While both of these complex models are adequate, and there are many more that could be created to explain what is happening with Lorraine, this is the one that will be used in the write-up of the report.

REPORT WRITING

Before the report is written, one final step is necessary—the determination of diagnosis and recommendations. Our original hypotheses included a mood disorder, an anxiety disorder, a psychotic disorder, a dissociative disorder, a substance-related disorder, and a personality disorder. Given the evidence that emerged on the tests, a few of these hypotheses can be ruled out relatively easily. While she reports anxiety, no evidence of anxiety emerged on any of the tests. "Anxiety," as reported by individuals being assessed, may mean different things; one meaning could be an anxiety disorder, but it is just as likely that "anxiety" reveals general discomfort, which could be related to any number of other problems. So in this case, we will not diagnose an anxiety disorder. Similarly, there was no evidence of any dissociative disorder. That leaves us with a mood disorder, a psychotic disorder, a substance-related disorder, and a personality disorder as possible hypotheses.

For Lorraine, there is much that is impairing her functioning. Specifically, there are significant signs of mood and thought disturbances getting in the way of optimal functioning, including bipolar tendencies (low self-esteem and depressive symptoms, as well as evidence of manic symptoms, including accelerated thinking, rushed speech, and some periods of inflated self-esteem) and impaired logical thinking. Together, these suggest either (a) Bipolar I Disorder with Psychotic Features or (b) Schizoaffective Disorder, Bipolar Type. The difference between the two is whether or not she has the psychotic symptoms (impairment in logical thinking) outside of a mood episode (when there are no mood symptoms). If she does have psychotic symptoms independent of mood symptoms, it is schizoaffective disorder. If she does not, she is struggling with Bipolar Disorder with Psychotic Features.

This differential diagnosis is one of the only instances in which it is acceptable to have a "rule-out" in the diagnosis, as there is no definitive way to distinguish between the two from an assessment, except for a more detailed history of these symptoms, which Lorraine was unable to give. Thus, her diagnosis on Axis I will include the Bipolar I Disorder, with a rule-out of Schizoaffective Disorder. Additionally, because of her substance abuse in college, she will be given an Axis I diagnosis of substance abuse (but not dependence), in remission, as it is not a problem anymore.

While many of the themes are adequately accounted for by the Axis I diagnoses, there are a few that seem to be impairing her functioning above and beyond the mood and/or psychotic disorder. Specifically, her extremely high need for nurturance, her resentment when her needs are not met by others, and her being paralyzed and unable to make decisions are indicative of a Dependent Personality Disorder on Axis II.

Recommendations, as will be presented in the assessment report that follows, will stem directly from the diagnoses and the themes. Because of the mood and/or psychotic disorder, a recommendation for her to continue to see her psychiatrist will be made. Additionally, specific recommendations for the focus of her psychotherapy will be made, including building more realistic interpersonal expectations, narrowing her focus of attention so as not to take in more information from the world than she can handle, tolerating experiencing and expressing emotions, improving her self-esteem, and addressing her depressive symptoms.

Identifying Information

Name:	Lorraine Ryder	**Date of Report:**	6/22/2007
Sex:	Female	**Assessor:**	A. Jordan Wright, PhD
Age:	24	**Supervisor:**	N/A
Date of Birth:	1/1/1983	**Dates of Assessment:**	6/1/2007, 6/8/2007, 6/15/2007
Ethnicity:	Caucasian		

Referral Questions

The patient was referred by her therapist for diagnostic clarification and treatment considerations. Specifically, patterns of behavior which seem to impede her functioning, especially related to work, were a focus of examination.

Measures Used

- Clinical Interview
- Review of Neuropsychological Evaluation (11/20/2006)
- Bender Visual-Motor Gestalt Test, Second Edition (Bender-2)
- Millon Clinical Multiaxial Inventory, Third Edition (MCMI-III)
- Rorschach Inkblot Test—Comprehensive System (Rorschach)
- Thematic Apperception Test (TAT)
- Projective Drawing Tests (Projective Drawings)
- Personality Assessment Inventory (PAI)

Presenting Problem

The patient reported that there is a significant "gap between my drive and knowledge and the ability" to execute tasks and follow through. She reported that "something is getting in the way of me doing what I know I can do." Specifically, she seems to be suffering from anxiety, as well as some cognitive difficulties that frustrate her and her ability to do "everyday, basic functions." She reported decision-making and attentional problems, as well as a pervasive feeling that there are better ways to do things she tries to do, which in turn stops her from doing them in any way.

Currently, the patient is diagnosed with depression, anxiety, and Attention-Deficit/Hyperactivity Disorder (ADHD). She sees a psychotherapist weekly and a psychiatrist once a month. Currently, she takes Lamictal, Wellbutrin, and Lexapro; she previously took Adderall for ADHD. She reported a good appetite ("massive, actually") and no problems with enjoyment of usual activities and hobbies or her libido. Her energy level was "okay," though she reported difficulty waking up in the morning and getting herself going, feeling like she wants to go back to sleep for a long time. Her sleep "has been an issue for a long time." In fact, she reported having gone to a sleep center to assess and treat her abnormal sleeping patterns. She used to sleep about 13 hours a night, and at times would sleep for about 28 hours straight, about once a month. Currently, however, she sleeps about 8 hours a night and feels relatively refreshed when she wakes up and finally gets herself going.

She reported a constant, low-grade level of helplessness, feeling like she cannot handle her own problems and her own life. However, she denied any hopelessness, feeling like she was actually taking steps to help with her problems. She also reported that she cries excessively, though not only when she is sad: "Any emotion makes me cry—when I'm angry, frustrated. . . ."

She reported that she would occasionally stay up all night but not feel tired the next day, and that at times she felt extremely "high on myself," feeling that she was special and "queen of the world." She reported that these instances were brief, however, and she generally took no action when she was feeling this way.

Background Information

History of Presenting Problem

The patient reported that her problems with decision making, attention, and anxiety were present in college. She received a Bachelor of Arts in creative writing from a prestigious liberal arts college in California. She reported a good GPA (about 3.4 in college), but she stated that she had difficulty finishing work and handing assignments in on time. She received many Incompletes in classes because of this problem. She stated that her problem handing in final products was largely because she was unhappy with the results, especially for creative writing assignments. She reported that these problems with handing in assignments varied, however, revealing an inconsistency that made her extremely anxious. "My performance was emotionally affected," such that she became overwhelmed at times, especially

(Continued)

when she was feeling depressed, but she performed better when challenged and in a good mood.

She reported that before college, and specifically in high school, she was "like this," but that circumstances were somehow different. She reported taking on "a million different activities," keeping herself extremely busy, "always going, stressed out," but she somehow "kept afloat." She feels that having so many different activities gave her less opportunity to scrutinize her performance in any one area. Prior to high school, she could not recall whether she struggled with these issues. She also reported previous bouts with "depression," though her memory was vague about specific symptoms, timing, duration, or any other details about these episodes.

Symptomatic Evaluation

The patient has been seeing a therapist for about a year, but she has been seeing a psychiatrist since the 11th grade, when she was first diagnosed with ADHD and depression and was medicated. She reported that at 2 years old, she was hospitalized with chickenpox because of suspicion that she may have Reye Syndrome; she did not have the illness. She denied any other major medical problems or hospitalizations. Her last physical examination and blood workup was two months ago, and she was found to have no medical illnesses.

While she denied overuse of alcohol, reporting that she drinks socially and rarely gets or has ever gotten drunk, she reported occasional use of marijuana in college. Further, she reported a two-week period in her freshman year of college during which she snorted her Adderall in order to get high. However, frightened that she may become dependent, she stopped this substance abuse.

While she denied any major medical illnesses in her family, she reported an extensive history of mental illness in her family. She reported that her mother was being treated for Obsessive-Compulsive Disorder, her sister was being treated for an anxiety disorder, and all of her grandparents had been medicated for various mental illnesses. She reported that her paternal grandmother had had several psychotic breaks. She denied any family history of substance use or abuse.

She reported that while pregnant her mother "tumbled down a staircase," but there had been no apparent harm to either her or her mother. At birth, she reported that she was noticeably cold, so the doctor put a hat and mittens on her, in addition to the blanket in which she was wrapped. She reported no known problems with developmental milestones or intellectual or cognitive development, except that she often daydreamed in elementary school. Additionally, she reported that she cried every first day of school throughout elementary and middle school—"I'm not good with transitions." She also reported that during high school she was "depressed," spending days sleeping in the nurse's office. Otherwise, she reported nothing notable about her development.

Psychosocial Evaluation

The patient is a single, 24-year-old, Caucasian female who is the youngest of three children, having an older brother and sister, neither of whom currently lived at home with her and her parents. She reported a "normal, dull" childhood, remembering nothing remarkable about how she was raised. Her parents are still married, and she reported feeling that they loved and supported her and her siblings. She reported that her memory of growing up was vague and unspecific. She had difficulty recalling any specific events that occurred within her family before graduating high school.

She reported a "great" social network, currently and in the past, including four very close girlfriends who have been close for many years. Included in this group are two "best friends." At times in her life, however, she reported having difficulty "getting myself to things," like group dinners and other social engagements. She reported that these friends have stuck with her "even through my antisocial phases," when she went long periods of time without seeing them. She reported dating and being sexually active ("I guess the normal amount") in college, though since then she has not had a significant romantic relationship. She denied any history of sexual abuse or early sexual behavior.

She reported that she had had one job since graduating from college. She worked at an advertising agency for about two years, a job that she enjoyed and found creatively satisfying. After about a year, she began missing work regularly and being consistently late when she did show up. Because she reportedly produced high-quality work, her agency afforded her some flexibility, including the ability to work from home on projects. She continued to have difficulty submitting projects on time or at all, and she was fired from her position. She reported that she felt consistently unsatisfied with the quality of her work, and at times she would spend so much time researching alternatives to her process that she would not even begin to work on the content of the project. She is currently unemployed and has recently decided to become an actress. So far, as an aspiring

(Continued)

actress, work has been "inconsistent and sporadic," and she is both living with and being supported by her parents.

She denied any history of criminal or legal involvement.

She reported that as a half-Jewish female born and raised in the South, she is not currently, nor was she in the past, religious, and she reported having no difficulty transitioning out of Virginia or into California for college or New York City afterward.

Mental Status Evaluation

The patient was cooperative and friendly, and she made good eye contact. While she exhibited adequate receptive language ability, at times her speech became confused, tangential, and hard to follow. Her volume, articulation, and vocabulary were all appropriate, but her rate of speaking was often very rapid, causing her to clutter some of her words together. She reported euthymic mood currently, with a history of depression, and her affect was appropriate to both the situation and to her reported mood. She smiled freely and showed some variation in affect, seeming generally happy, without evidence of current elevated, depressed, anxious, or angry mood. Her thought content was free of hallucinations and delusions, but had some depressive ideation in the form of helplessness. Suicidality, aggressiveness, and homicidality were not present. Her thought process was notably tangential and confused at times. The patient was alert throughout the clinical interview, and her attention and concentration seemed unimpaired. She reported some abnormalities in her memory functioning, as she only has vague memories of her childhood, at times has difficulty remembering details from the previous day, and at the same time has extremely vivid memories of certain aspects of her past. Other than these slight abnormalities, however, her memory seemed generally intact. The patient's judgment and insight are adequate; however, her planning and decision-making abilities are impaired.

Behavioral Observations

The patient was extremely friendly and cooperative throughout testing. She gave effortful attempts on all tests administered. She required several reminders and clarifications related to the time and place of testing, as well as following some directions in order to copy and send her previous evaluation to the assessor. She became visibly anxious when she felt she was not portraying herself in the way she wanted to, and she often had difficulty articulating herself appropriately, especially to a degree that was satisfactory to her. When discussing herself, she alternated between flippantly joking and being genuine and tearful. In the short amount of time in the accessor's presence, her "moodiness," or emotional lability, was very apparent. She did not exhibit any overt signs of inattention or hyperactivity, and it is believed that this testing is a valid representation of her current functioning.

Overall Interpretation of Test Findings

Cognitive Functioning

Note: The results of the WAIS-III are based on review of the Neuropsychological Evaluation (11/20/06). The percentile scores are not included, as they were not reported in the original evaluation.

Overall, on the WAIS-III, the patient is functioning within the Superior range compared to others her age. Both her Verbal IQ and Performance IQ fell within the Superior range, suggesting that her cognitive functioning is relatively consistent across domains. On the Bender-2, which examines visual-perceptual, motor, visual-motor integrative, and short-term memory functioning, the patient performed within the Very High range (around the 98th percentile on each subtest) compared to others her age. This excellent performance suggests that there is no evidence of neurological damage or deficit.

Verbal Comprehension. On measures of general verbal skills, such as verbal fluency, ability to understand and use verbal reasoning, and verbal knowledge, the patient's performance fell within the Superior range of functioning compared to others her age (Verbal Comprehension Index). Specifically, she exhibited a significant strength compared to same-age peers and to her own overall performance on a task requiring her to define words presented to her, which assesses word knowledge, long-term memory, and ability to express herself (Vocabulary). Strong verbal functioning suggests that she is intellectually ambitious and has made good use of both formal school and other educational opportunities.

Working Memory. On measures assessing the ability to memorize new verbal information, hold it in short-term memory, concentrate, and manipulate that information to produce some result or reasoning outcome, the patient's performance fell within the High Average range compared to others her age (Working Memory Index). All subtests that make up this

(Continued)

domain fell within the Average to High Average ranges. Good working memory suggests that not only does she have unimpaired attention and concentration skills, but she can work through and manipulate information in her mind well.

Perceptual Organization. On tests that measure nonverbal reasoning, visuospatial aptitude, and induction and planning skills on tasks involving nonverbal stimuli such as designs, pictures, and puzzles, the patient performed within the Superior range of functioning compared to others her age (Perceptual Organization Index). All of the subtests that make up this domain fell within the High Average to Superior ranges. Her nonverbal reasoning ability also seems to be unimpaired and quite strong compared to others.

Processing Speed. On tasks that measure the ability to focus attention and quickly scan, discriminate between, and respond to visual information within a time limit, the patient's performance fell within the Average range compared to others her age (Processing Speed Index). Although it is her weakest domain of functioning, the speed at which she processes information does not seem impaired.

Cognitive Summary. Overall, cognitively, the patient is functioning extremely well compared to others her age. Her strong verbal functioning suggests that she will likely succeed in efforts that require the use of language. Her one area of slight weakness compared to her own overall functioning is the speed at which she processes information. It should be noted that her processing speed does not constitute a weakness compared to others her age, but rather only to her own overall Superior functioning.

Personality and Emotional Functioning

The patient was administered several standardized measures of emotional functioning. The results of these tests suggest that she has a style of taking in too much information from the world around her, much more than she can efficiently and effectively organize and use. This style of overincorporation, combined with restricted, internalized, and confusing emotions and unmet extreme needs for nurturance, have led her to develop strong mixed feelings about interpersonal relationships. Specifically, she has both a high need for closeness and involvement with others and resentment toward others when she feels they do not meet her needs, which has led to a fear of being disappointed by others. Together, her style of taking too much information in, restricting her emotion, and having unmet needs for closeness and a resultant ambivalent style have led to several outcomes she is currently struggling with: low self-esteem, impairment in her ability to think logically and coherently, emotional disturbance, and a style of withdrawing or being paralyzed when needing to make decisions.

Overincorporative Style. The patient has a general style of taking in too much information, more than she can effectively organize or use in day-to-day life. This may be an asset in some areas of her life, such as creative writing; however, it can be detrimental as well. Her Rorschach revealed that she is exceedingly open to experience, being aware of and taking in everything from her environment. This overly broad focus of attention leads her to take in details others may not view as important, that they might selectively screen out in order to efficiently process the world. Her Rorschach also revealed that this style may leave her anxious and dissatisfied with the product of tasks in which she is under time pressure. She will be acutely aware of her hastiness and all the faults of her product. This may lead her to generally underachieve. Additionally, because she is taking in so much information, issues that would be minor annoyances to others likely become somewhat paralyzing and overblown to her. Her PAI revealed that she is overconcerned with issues over which she has no control. Additionally, her Projective Drawings suggested that she is overly aware of minor details and hyper-aware of what she views as small insults or disappointments from others, whether intended or not. Her Rorschach also revealed that she has an underdeveloped method for coping with the demands of the world, showing no consistency in relying on intellectual or emotional resources. Her style of taking in the world, on its own, likely paralyzes her when she has to make decisions or is under time pressure, but it also affects her interpersonal relations and her view of herself.

Emotional Confusion and Restriction. The patient is easily overwhelmed and confused by her own emotions, and, as such, she has adopted a style of restricting and internalizing them. Her MCMI-III, Rorschach, Projective Drawings, and TAT each suggested that she tends to restrict her emotions, opting to "wear a mask," which helps her appear generally calm and pleasant on the surface. Her Rorschach revealed that this is likely due to being generally confused about emotions and disoriented by strong feelings. Her underlying tension, however, is characterized by her MCMI-III as anxiety, sadness, and guilt feelings. Her Rorschach revealed that because she is so confused by her emotions, she has difficulty being happy, even when she feels she should be. Her MCMI-III specified that much of the inner turmoil she suppresses is related to anger and resentment toward others in her life and the world

(Continued)

around her, even though this anger is rarely shown publicly. Specifically, she holds in anger toward others she feels do not meet her need for nurturance and affection. Her MCMI-III revealed that this anger threatens her need for security, which is why she chooses to restrict it. Her Rorschach revealed that she is prone to occasional impulsive or angry outbursts, which would constitute a "leak" in her emotional constriction. Her restriction of emotion, possibly in reaction to taking in too much information from a confusing world, contributes to her interpersonal ambivalence.

Excessive Need for Nurturance. The patient has unusually strong needs for nurturance and affection from others, needs that easily go disappointed, especially given her tendency to take in even slight cues she views as insults from others and conceptualize them as failures to be nurturing. Her PAI and Rorschach both revealed that she generally feels that her life is overly determined by external forces, that she does not have the power to steer her own life. As such, as revealed in her MCMI-III, Rorschach, and TAT, she has become overly dependent on others in her life, leaning on them for support, imagining that they will make decisions for her, and fearing their abandonment of her. Her Rorschach revealed that this, to an extent, has impeded her forming of a clear identity and sense of purpose in life. Her own self-doubt and discouragement, as well as profound loneliness, as revealed in her Rorschach, have led to several behavioral styles identified in her MCMI-III, including being interpersonally submissive, noncompetitive, and acting weak, self-doubtful, and needy, all in order to evoke nurturance. Her MCMI-III also revealed that she generally avoids autonomy; her lack of clear identity and her self-doubt have led her to fear making clear decisions that impact her life.

Interpersonal Ambivalence. Because of her significantly unmet needs for closeness and nurturance, the patient has become extremely ambivalent about relationships, continuing to need affection and closeness on the one hand, but also fearing the inevitable rejection and disappointment (much of which is related to her hyper-awareness of minor cues from others that are likely generally unintended) on the other. Her MCMI-III, Rorschach, and TAT all revealed an acute awareness that although she is dependent on others to determine her destiny, she generally resents others for disappointing and discouraging her, as well as for being critical or disapproving of her. In fact, her Rorschach and TAT revealed a generally pessimistic view that others will ultimately never fulfill her needs for closeness. Her Rorschach suggested that this leads to a chronic state of low-grade irritation, another reason she has difficulty ever being truly happy. Her

Rorschach and Projective Drawings, however, suggested that this interpersonal ambivalence is largely based on judgments made from impaired social perception, and her TAT revealed that she is much too easily discouraged and disappointed interpersonally. Specifically, she has difficulty perceiving the actions of others realistically and making appropriate judgments and decisions based on this. This is likely due to her overincorporative style, as well as her becoming somewhat disorganized when strong emotions are involved, which they often are in interpersonal relationships.

Low Self-Esteem. The patient currently suffers from low self-esteem, resulting from her unmet needs for intimacy and closeness and her unclear personal identity. Her Projective Drawings and Rorschach revealed general self-doubt and a sense of being damaged or unworthy. More specifically, however, her PAI suggested a generally fluctuating view of herself, marked by sometimes positive aspects, but often highly self-critical. This extreme self-criticism also appeared on her Rorschach, which suggested that it is a chronic state of criticizing herself in a maladaptively self-conscious way, and her Projective Drawings, which revealed a hypercritical view toward herself. Her MCMI-III additionally revealed a general style of self-effacement. Her Rorschach revealed that at times she avoids self-focusing, in order to cope with her low self-esteem. Her PAI suggested that at times she may actively become grandiose and show inflated self-esteem, again in order to cope with her inner inadequacy.

Impaired Logical Thinking. Currently, likely as a result of her overincorporative style and being overwhelmed by emotions, the patient is struggling with impairment in her ability to think entirely logically and coherently. Her Rorschach and MCMI-III suggested that her thinking at times is not only confused, but also rushed and accelerated, even faster than she herself can keep up with. Her Projective Drawings revealed that in general the world is overwhelming to her, not surprising given her tendency to take in inordinate amounts of information from it. Her TAT revealed that when she is overwhelmed, however, her thinking becomes confused, similar to what the Rorschach and MCMI-III suggested. More specifically, her PAI revealed that she struggles with confusion, distractibility, and difficulty concentrating, symptoms she reported in the clinical interview. Additionally, her PAI revealed tangential or circumstantial thinking at times, as well as problems with communicating clearly. Her Rorschach reinforced the finding that situational stress can impede clear thinking, specifying that she has impairment in her

(Continued)

logic, significantly misperceives events, and at times confuses reality and fantasy. She has adopted a coping style that is escapist, retreating into fantasy when she becomes overwhelmed, imagining how others or external events will make her decisions for her and at times significantly distorting reality. It is unclear how aware of these problems in thinking she currently is, though they significantly impact her functioning, including her ability to make decisions and effect changes in her life.

Emotional Disturbance. Currently, the patient is struggling with emotional difficulties consistent with a diagnosis of Bipolar Disorder. Her MCMI-III, PAI, Rorschach, and TAT suggested signs of depression, including sadness, loneliness, pessimism, hopelessness, and significant intrusive ideation, specifically about her unmet needs and her inability to prevent others from determining her destiny. Her PAI also suggested a moderate degree of current worry. Her MCMI-III suggested, however, that she rarely divulges these negative feelings to others. Additionally, her MCMI-III and Projective Drawings revealed that she views life as somewhat empty, but significantly draining and effortful. As such, her MCMI-III revealed some physical signs of depression, including weakness and fatigue. Also revealed in her MCMI-III, PAI, and Rorschach, however, were physical signs of mania or hypomania, including grandiosity, rushed speech, accelerated thinking, and inflated self-esteem. It is significant to note that there was no evidence of irritability or hyperactivity, though some moodiness was revealed in her MCMI-III. Additionally, her sleep pattern, while unclear the underlying cause for its irregularity, is somewhat consistent with a manic state.

Withdrawal and Impaired Decision-Making Ability. Two major effects of her current functioning are a coping style of withdrawing from others and from situations and becoming paralyzed when needing to make decisions or follow through on plans. Her TAT, MCMI-III, and Rorschach all revealed a style of withdrawing when overwhelmed. Specifically, she may withdraw from others in order to moderate her anxiety about being disappointed and her sensitivity to rejection. Her retreat into fantasy, revealed in her Rorschach, also constitutes a withdrawal tactic. Her MCMI-III further suggested that her needy behaviors at times serve to distance herself from others, prompting them to leave her alone. Her Rorschach and TAT further suggested that because of her overincorporative style, her restriction of emotion, and her dependence on others, she can become paralyzed when making decisions, leading her to make no decision at all. Because she is so often disappointed by her own efforts, as revealed in the Rorschach, she avoids putting herself in a position to judge her own output. This process, however, also becomes judged, and it reinforces her low self-esteem and feelings of inadequacy.

Summary and Recommendations

Lorraine Ryder is a single, 24-year-old, Caucasian female who currently lives with her parents. She was referred for a psychological assessment to assess the reason for her difficulties with decision making and execution of plans, as well as diagnostic clarification and treatment considerations. Cognitively, she exhibited no evidence of neurological damage or cognitive deficit.

Emotionally, she has a style of taking in too much information from the world around her, much more than she can efficiently and effectively organize and use. This style interacts with restricted and confusing emotions and unmet needs for nurturance, having led her to develop strong ambivalent feelings about interpersonal relationships. Specifically, she has both a high need for closeness and involvement with others and resentment toward others when she feels they do not meet her needs, which has led to a fear of being disappointed by others. Together, her style of taking in too much information, restricting her emotion, and having unmet needs for closeness and a resultant ambivalent style have led to several outcomes she is currently struggling with: low self-esteem, impairment in her ability to think logically and coherently, emotional disturbance, and a style of withdrawing or being paralyzed when needing to make decisions.

Currently, she is struggling with significant emotional disturbance characterized both by depression—including sadness, loneliness, hopelessness, fatigue, and weakness—and mania—including grandiosity, inflated self-esteem, rushed speech, and accelerated thinking. These, together with significantly impaired thought processes and confusion, are consistent with a diagnosis of Bipolar I Disorder, with Psychotic Features. If the disorder in thinking (i.e., psychotic features) occurs outside of a mood episode (i.e., depressed or manic state), then a diagnosis of Schizoaffective Disorder should be applied. Additionally, her presentation of difficulty with decisions, needing others to assume responsibilities or coax her through processes, extreme need for nurturance and discomfort and disappointment related to this need not being met, and difficulties initiating or completing projects is consistent with a diagnosis of Dependent Personality Disorder.

(Continued)

Diagnostic Impression and Recommendations

Axis I	296.54	Bipolar I Disorder, Most Recent Episode Depressed, Severe with Psychotic Features
	295.70	Rule-Out: Schizoaffective Disorder, Bipolar Type
	305.90	Substance Abuse, in Sustained Full Remission
Axis II	301.6	Dependent Personality Disorder
Axis III		Sleep Disorder
Axis IV		Unemployment, limited support
Axis V	GAF =	50

Given the patient's current functioning, the following recommendations are being made:

- The patient should continue to be seen by a psychiatrist, in order to find the optimal balance of medications for her Bipolar Disorder.
- The patient should continue in individual psychotherapy in order to address some of the underlying issues related to her Bipolar Disorder, as well as her Dependent Personality Disorder. Specifically, areas of focus can include:

  ○ Becoming more realistic in her understanding of interpersonal interaction, such that she is not disappointed by small failures on the part of others to meet her needs for nurturance and affection.
  ○ Helping her understand what parts of the world are more meaningful and impactful than others, such that her focus of attention can begin to become less broad and all-encompassing.
  ○ Beginning to find more appropriate and adaptive ways to both feel and express her emotions, such that they do not become overly internalized and restricted, and such that they do not "spill" as impulsive outbursts or crying with every emotion.
  ○ Resolving her feelings of ambivalence toward interpersonal relationships.

- ° Improving her self-esteem through a more realistic view of who she is and what she does.
- ° Improving her reality-testing abilities, in order to become more effective and realistic in judging the world.
- ° Addressing her current feelings of depression, including loneliness, hopelessness, and sadness.
- ° Beginning to make decisions and not judge herself too harshly on the product of those decisions, in order to facilitate her finding more of a sense of who she is and a direction for the future.

_____   _____

A. Jordan Wright, PhD   Date
New York State Licensed Psychologist

FEEDBACK

Preparation for Feedback

Obviously, the current assessment is very dense, with a great deal of information learned from the testing to relay back to Lorraine, her therapist, and her psychiatrist. The feedback to her psychiatrist would have to rely entirely on the report, and the feedback to her therapist consisted of sending her the report (with Lorraine's consent), then following up with a phone call to discuss any questions or concerns. Feedback to Lorraine herself was the primary focus, as feedback sessions balance giving information and providing a safe, therapeutic environment to process the information relayed. Luckily, Lorraine and the assessor had built good rapport throughout the assessment process, so the groundwork for a good feedback session had already been laid.

The major considerations when deciding exactly how to give feedback to Lorraine were (a) her level of cognitive and intellectual functioning, (b) her level of insight, and (c) the specific type and amount of information that needed to be relayed to her. Regarding her intellectual capacity, because she is so intelligent, especially in the verbal domain, it was decided that she would be given the report and taken through it verbally as is. There was no need to create a summary sheet of the results for her, because she can easily take in and comprehend even the most complex ideas presented in the report. Regarding her level of insight, there are definite areas of concern of which she is entirely aware, and much of the feedback was geared toward using the findings from the assessment to explain the impairments she knows she has. For example, the odd symptoms related to her awareness and "reinventing" of simple tasks is explained by the psychotic features revealed in the testing. As such, each area of functional impairment and complaint made by her would be addressed throughout the feedback to explain their underlying causes.

Regarding the type and amount of information in the feedback, there is simply a great deal of information. Moreover, while the mood disorder may not surprise her, a bit more time will likely need to be taken to discuss the personality disorder, including some psychoeducation about its meaning, treatment, and prognosis. Ultimately, the flow of the feedback session will take its pace both from the assessor and from Lorraine, as the assessor will constantly check in with her reactions and feelings about the feedback presented.

Feedback Session

The feedback session began with an exploration of how Lorraine found the process of the assessment—she reported that it was "interesting," and she was "anxious" to get the results. Exploring this anxiety, she reported that she has been struggling with these problems for a while and that therapy and medication were helping somewhat, but she wanted to "get this all sorted out as quickly as possible." Understanding that discussing this further may easily make her more anxious, the assessor gave her a copy of the report, rather than just presenting the results.

The first task was to orient her to the structure of the report. Sitting next to her and using her report throughout, the assessor quickly took her through the major sections of the report, explaining which would be of interest and why. Pausing at the background information section, he explained that this was "all the stuff you presented to me," that she may not find it as interesting, but that it was important to go through, at least briefly, to restate the problems and confirm that they were captured accurately in the report. Then the rest of the report was gone through very briefly to explain that it all builds up to the recommendations at the end.

After she was oriented to the report structure, the session was brought back to the presenting problem and background information sections, which were paraphrased for her as she skimmed along with them. She had no comments or concerns with these sections, even after probing, so the assessor moved on to the overall interpretation of test findings section. The cognitive functioning section was relatively straightforward, as it was based on a report and feedback she had already received, so again it was addressed only briefly.

The bulk of the session focused on the personality and emotional functioning section. The assessor explained that he would first tell her all the results (i.e., the narrative from the first paragraph), and then he would go through each of the parts of the results individually to explain and discuss them further. During the presentation of the overall narrative, she seemed to have a "glazed over" look in her eyes, as if overwhelmed, so she was reassured that all of the information would be repeated and explained as much as needed until she was comfortable with it all. The session then moved to the individual themes.

Several of the initial (diathesis) themes resonated extremely well with her, eliciting positive reactions. These included the overincorporation, emotional restriction (apparently a theme she had heard often from her current therapist), and the interpersonal ambivalence. She had more difficulty with the high need for nurturance, so more time was spent processing that theme. It was clear from the look on her face when this theme was presented that she was unsure or somewhat confused about it; the assessor noted, "you seem to be having a reaction to this one," which began a dialogue about her thoughts of this theme.

She reported that she did not remember much about her needs as a child or her parents' reaction to them and that at times she does not trust others to be there for her. However, many of her sentences began with "Is it unreasonable to expect" or "Is it unrealistic to want" with regard to interpersonal relationships. The high need for nurturance was reframed slightly: Instead of focusing on her needs as being excessive or unrealistic, it was emphasized that whatever her needs were, they were not being met. She linked this to her "uncertainty" about other people, which was a perfect transition into the interpersonal ambivalence theme.

Similarly, most of the outcome themes made sense to her, including low self-esteem, affective disturbance, and withdrawal and impaired decision-making ability. However, the impaired ability to think logically caused her some concern. Although she knew she had some bizarre problems in her thinking, seeing it written clearly as impaired logic "frightens me a bit." Again, understanding the hybrid nature of feedback as an assessment session *and* a therapy session, the assessor had to balance empathizing with the difficulty seeing this in print and educating her on the specific meaning of the theme. To do this, the assessor asked Lorraine to describe again the bizarre phenomenon she experiences each day related to "reinventing" simple tasks; then he asked her to describe how she understands the title of the theme related to impaired logical thinking. Noting that her latter description "does sound a lot scarier," the assessor refocused this latter description on explaining the former phenomenon. Additionally, psycho-education about the treatment and prognosis of psychotic features was presented, in order to give her hope. After checking in with her and probing further to ensure that she was comfortable, the session moved to diagnosis and recommendations.

Although her psychiatrist seemingly suspected bipolar disorder as a diagnosis (having prescribed her a mood stabilizer), she had never heard this diagnosis from the psychiatrist or her therapist. When hearing what the diagnosis means, specifically focusing on how it explains her days of feeling extremely good about herself, needing less sleep, and accelerated thinking, she reported that she was "relieved" that it can be addressed more specifically in therapy and with medication. She additionally had a reaction to the substance abuse diagnosis, but it was explained why this needed to be included, focusing on using it as a warning sign for both herself and for her treatment team of the possibility of misusing substances in order to cope with difficulties.

As expected, extra time and attention needed to be paid to the dependent personality disorder diagnosis. However, this was not because she disagreed or had issues or was confused about the diagnosis. Rather, when hearing exactly what the diagnosis meant, she became tearful, revealing that "I see myself in that description totally." Again, focused on building hope, balanced with empathy, the assessor allowed her to express her thoughts about the diagnosis and her overreliance on others, as well as her ambivalence about trusting others, and then discussed how important it is for these tendencies now to have a name, a label. Knowing what is going on will inform her treatment. This therapeutic conversation transitioned naturally into the recommendation list, which she attended to and repeated back with explanations to ensure her understanding of each point and why it was important.

To conclude, the assessor again asked Lorraine about her experience of the assessment overall and the feedback session specifically. She sighed loudly, looked at the assessor with a half smile, and stated that "it's just important." After processing for a few minutes, the assessor encouraged her to call him if she had any questions or concerns, assured her that he would call her therapist to discuss the feedback, and wished her luck. She thanked him and half-jokingly asked if she could refer all her friends for an assessment.

SUMMARY

Lorraine Ryder is a good example of the power and utility of psychological assessment. While her therapist and psychiatrist (and she) had a relatively good understanding of *part* of the reasons for her functional impairments (the mood disorder, specifically), many of her symptoms were unexplained (or seemingly erroneously explained with ADHD). While this is not always the case, because the assessor has an ongoing relationship with the referring therapist, with Lorraine's permission the therapist gave the assessor occasional updates on their treatment together.

Additionally, about a year after the feedback session, Lorraine called the assessor and left a message on his voicemail, thanking him for the assessment and reporting her progress in treatment because of the change in focus due to the recommendations from the report. Especially interesting in this case is how easy it is for a therapist to collude with the symptoms of dependent personality disorder, when therapists want to be helpful and help push for certain decisions to be made, even subtly and not consciously.

Because the diagnosis was made, however, special attention was paid in therapy to making sure that Lorraine was making all decisions in the therapy herself, as practice for decision making in her everyday life. Her medication had been switched to include an antipsychotic medication, which "dramatically changed" her ability to function day to day. She was still reportedly working on "being okay with emotions," but her progress to date was exceptional, and the psychological assessment had a great deal to do with pushing the treatment forward.

CHAPTER 8

A Recovering Alcoholic

ati Lai's sponsor from Alcoholics Anonymous (AA) encouraged her to seek out mental health services. When she found the clinic online, she filled out the application requesting multiple services, including individual counseling and a psychological assessment. On her application, she reported that she was "an alcoholic" with "blockages" in her life. Her psychological assessor was the first to contact her, having coordinated at the clinic that she would begin individual counseling concurrently with the assessment, and she reported being very eager to begin both services. She scheduled to have two individual counseling sessions before her first scheduled psychological assessment session.

THE CLINICAL INTERVIEW

Tati Lai came in to the office on time, dressed casually and appropriately. She was a petite and friendly young woman who smiled broadly throughout introductions. She looked mid-20s in age, with long, straight dark hair and a moderately dark complexion, clearly not Caucasian, but not clearly another distinct ethnicity. She made good eye contact as she came into the office and began the interview. There was nothing remarkable about her appearance or the way she related to the assessor from the beginning of the assessment process, other than her seemingly extreme openness to the experience.

Before beginning the open-ended clinical interview, the assessor asked her a few factual identifying information questions. She reported that she was 25 years old, giving her date of birth. When asked her ethnicity, she reported that she is "mixed race, it's complicated." Her native language is English, having been born and raised in Florida. She is currently single and has no children.

As a note on the presentation of this clinical interview, the sections that follow are not categorized into symptomatic evaluation and psychosocial evaluation, as the flow of the clinical interview did not follow this structure. The subsections presented in the text reflect as closely as possible the clinical interview as it actually unfolded, as opposed to artificially grouping sections of information that did not present themselves sequentially. That is, the presentation that follows is how the clinical interview happened chronologically, along with the overarching questions the assessor asked Tati. Clarifications were occasionally necessary throughout the interview, but those questions and comments are not presented here.

Presenting Problem: So What Is It That Brings You in for an Assessment Now?

Once basic identifying information had been gathered, the assessor began the clinical interview with an assessment of the presenting problem. Tati approached the question as if the assessor had asked why she wanted mental health services at this time, and she began by explaining that she is "skeptical" of therapy because she did it in college. She reported that she was an "active alcoholic" in college, and she became sober when she moved to New York, where she is currently "working the 12 steps." She explained that the fourth and fifth steps include taking a "moral inventory of myself" and "looking at my defects of character," so her AA sponsor recommended that she enter therapy to help her with these processes.

After explaining why she was seeking services at this point, she began to list off, in a rapid and mechanical way (even counting them off on her fingers), what she thought were the issues she needed to work on. She included: "why I am so closed off to relationships with men"; "I create blockages at work, like procrastinating"; "I overthink things"; "I beat myself up for little things"; and "I have a huge perfectionist problem." She reported that she just turned 25 years old, and she "always saw myself being somewhere else by now." When probed, she reported that she is not happy in either her work situation or her personal life at the moment.

When asked, she denied both suicidal and homicidal or aggressive ideation.

History of Presenting Problem: You Seem to Be Struggling With a Lot Right Now; Can You Tell Me More About How All of This Started and Affected You in the Past?

Because she had listed so many difficulties, the assessor decided to ask Tati about her history in a broad way, not yet knowing what he was going to get from her. She began immediately by stating that, while she had many boyfriends in high school, they were all "immature little boys," and she has only had one "real" romantic relationship in her life, during college. However, as she continued to speak, which she did without pause (and seemingly without taking breaths at some points), she did not elaborate on any one subject. Immediately after stating that she had one significant romantic relationship, she reported that she grew up in Florida, but is very "anti-Florida in my views, so I wanted out ASAP." Her father is still in Florida, married to her stepmother, but her mother, who was reportedly an alcoholic, "died at 30 from an overdose." She reported this without significant affect. Again, seemingly without pause for breath, she moved rapidly away from this subject, reporting that she has always been "achievement-oriented," not wanting relationships to get in the way of her success. She reported that she has only ever had one good friend, but again she moved quickly off this topic before the assessor was able to probe more deeply into this or any other topic.

It is important to note the tone of the interview thus far. Tati was speaking somewhat rapidly; the assessor felt as if she were trying to relay as much full information as possible during the interview, but because she was speaking without pause, the assessor was not able to interrupt easily her flow of thought, which seemed slightly overwhelming. It was clear that Tati was trying to be open during the interview, seemingly nondefensive. The assessor, for the sake of building rapport, allowed her rapid flow of associations to continue, even though there was much information missing, and he took notes to make sure he went back to ask more specifically about important details.

She rapidly shifted to the fact that she moved from one city in Florida to another for college, but that she graduated in three years "because I am very driven and wanted to get out of Florida." She stated that she formed some friendships in college, but that she was "always afraid of a serious relationship and intimacy," as she felt that a romantic relationship "would hold me back." Although normally the assessor would probe for more specifics about what exactly she felt a relationship would hold her back from, she quickly turned the conversation (or monologue, more accurately) to another topic, which the assessor allowed, again for the sake of rapport.

During her last semester in college, she said, "I met a woman." Although she came back to this later, she immediately shifted to reporting that she then graduated. Then, "One night, I drank a lot of Everclear [an extremely potent grain alcohol beverage] and almost died—I woke up in the hospital." She then returned to speaking about the woman she met her last semester in college, almost as though she had not interrupted this line of thought with other, extremely important information. "She became my world." She reported that she felt she was no longer focused on herself or achieving academically: "I took a backseat." She then began a story about her relationship with this woman, how the woman left the country for an internship in France, how Tati moved to Washington to live with her aunt after graduating from college, how she went to visit the woman in France six months later, and how when she arrived, the woman told her that she was back together with her ex-girlfriend. This experience reportedly "triggered my abandonment issues from my mom," and she got drunk, left France to return back to Washington (reportedly drunk the entire journey), and remained drunk for three weeks, at which point she impulsively moved to New York. "I'm very extreme with my reactions."

At this point in the interview, she stopped and looked at the assessor with wide eyes. It was the first silence in the room since the beginning of the session (and the assessor's hand was getting tired from taking notes). It was at this point the assessor had to decide in which direction to take the interview, as there were many pieces of information that needed following up. The assessor decided to begin to probe seemingly one of the most important pieces of information disclosed thus far, her family history.

Family History: You Said That Your Mother Passed Away When You Were Young; Tell Me More About Your Family

Tati reported that she was 9 years old when her mother passed away. When discussing this topic, she displayed an especially wide smile. She was told on a Friday that her mother had died, the funeral was on the Monday after, and she begged to go back to school on Tuesday. In what was becoming clear to the assessor as her style of relating information, Tati went off topic and began to talk about her emotions. She reported that she is "in touch with" her emotions for the most part, able to cry at movies and other sad things. "But I'm cut off from them in another way. I don't take time to metabolize—I just distract myself." She used her wanting to go back to school so soon after her mother's death as an example of how she chooses to distract herself to cope with negative emotions in her own life, rather than to "metabolize" them.

She reported that her father is of Chinese descent, and her mother was of Italian descent. They divorced when Tati was 7 years old, and her father remarried a woman from China soon after that. Although the circumstances of her mother's death were not yet clear, the assessor chose to probe another area of her history before returning to this topic, as he did not want to frustrate or offend Tati by making it clear that she had not yet fully answered his questions about her family. The assessor chose to begin a multicultural evaluation because it was coming up naturally in the flow of the interview.

Multicultural Evaluation: Growing Up in Florida as a Half-Chinese, Half-White Woman Must Have Been Interesting; Can You Tell Me About That?

Tati chuckled for a moment when asked about her cultural background, reporting that "people always thought I was Hispanic," given that she looked as though she might be and that was the most common type of minority in Florida. She reported that she did not "fit the mold" in Florida and she tried to "fit in" in several different ways throughout her childhood and adolescence. She was a cheerleader for one year in high school, but she reported hating it. She also joined the Fellowship of Christian Students, despite the fact that she was not actually Christian, and she found some social satisfaction in this group.

The assessor then probed a bit about her spiritual identity, as she brought up the fact that she had some conflicting religious feelings growing up. She reported that her mother was Catholic and her father is Muslim, so her religious identity growing up was unclear. She reported that her spirituality "always helped me through tough times." Interestingly, rather than continuing to discuss her religious or spiritual identity, at this point Tati returned to the topic of her mother's death.

"I remember the day my mom died." She reported that her father was "acting weird" all day and that she had a "knot in my stomach" as well. A friend of her parents picked her up from the after-school program she took part in, which was unusual. She thought at that point that her father had died. At that moment, she reported feeling guilty because she had treated her stepmother badly. When she arrived home, though, there were many family members there, and they told her that her mother had died. She reported that, to this day, she is unclear about how or why her mother passed away. She overheard some family members speaking on that day, saying that it was an overdose of cocaine. But she was never told, nor did she ever really ask, the real story surrounding her mother's death. She continued to smile throughout this part of the clinical interview.

At this point she returned to the topic of her spiritual identity. She reported that at times she went to mosque with her father, but she "didn't *get* that religion." She became Southern Baptist for about two years in high school, again to fit in with her friends in Florida. Once more veering off topic, she discussed having a "great relationship" with her aunt, who is currently also in AA and is "very spiritual." When Tati went to college (a small, private, Catholic college), she reported that she was "drawn to the social justice aspects of Catholicism." She spoke about a weeklong "plunge" she undertook with her Catholic peers, spending a week in a homeless shelter to help understand the needs of that community. She reported that she became "very close" to the peers she did the plunge with (in contrast to her earlier statements that she has not been very close to anybody except one friend from childhood). Because of this discrepancy, the assessor chose to ask more in depth about her social history.

Social History: You Mentioned Earlier That You Had One Good Friend Growing Up

Tati did not need an actual question to begin discussing her friend. She reported that she really had only this one friend growing up, a girl who lived a block away from her. She began by saying that it was difficult for her to talk about, as they are no longer friends. When asked why, she reported that they have "different political views, so we took different paths." She reported that this girl was "a good influence" on her, as she was highly motivated and achievement-oriented as well. Tati reported that at times she would find out that her friend was doing her homework on a Friday evening, so Tati would also do her homework that night to keep up with her friend.

"Oh, and my stepmom wasn't nice to me." This phrase literally came in the middle of her discussion about her social history, followed by a continuation of her current social situation.

Currently, she has a roommate in New York that she did not know before moving in with her. She became a very close friend when she first moved to New York, but she related a story about how the roommate had a male classmate who "became like a brother to me," who then moved to the South, after which Tati stopped drinking. This story obviously contained more information than she shared, but she quickly jumped to the fact that currently most of her close friends are "AA friends," and she is not very close to her roommate anymore. The assessor made a note to return to this topic at some point. To help organize the rest of the time in the clinical interview, the assessor warned Tati that he would be asking her a few very specific questions to make sure he had enough background information.

Psychiatric History: Can You Tell Me About Your Previous Therapy?

Tati explained that she had been mandated to therapy in college by her school after her experience of being hospitalized because of her alcohol abuse. She saw the therapist only a few times. Her therapist told her to go to AA, which she did, but she then quit therapy. She never saw a psychiatrist or was prescribed any medication. She denied any other psychiatric history.

Medical History: What About Any Significant Medical History?

Tati denied any serious illnesses or hospitalizations, except for the one hospitalization for alcohol abuse in college. Although it had come up repeatedly, the assessor chose not to probe this hospitalization yet, as he felt it might evoke a lengthy response from Tati. For that reason, he chose to continue with relatively benign areas of the assessment.

Developmental History: Now I'm Going to Ask You Some Questions About Your Early Childhood; Was There Anything Notable About Your Mother's Pregnancy With You or Your Early Development?

In what was beginning to be characteristic of Tati's style of communicating, she began to relate information that was potentially important in a rather offhanded way. She reported that her mother required a C-section to give birth to her, but that otherwise she does not know details around the pregnancy or birth. Specifically, she is unaware of any use of alcohol or other substances during the pregnancy. She reported that everything else was fine, except that she was "extremely colicky," to the point that her parents had to bring her several times to the emergency room for fear that something was wrong with her. She also "vaguely" remembers needing some sort of walker to help her start walking, which may or may not have been delayed, but by school she walked fine. Her toileting was uneventful.

Family Medical (and Psychiatric) History: Were There Any Significant Illnesses in Your Family?

Although only asking about family medical history, this question ended up tapping family psychiatric history as well. "There was a lot of alcoholism on my mom's side of the family." Tati spent some time listing family members who were either alcoholics or in AA, focusing on her great-grandmother, her grandmother, and her aunt, all of whom were or are in AA. She cited them as role models for her. She also reported diabetes on her father's side of the family, but no other major medical or psychiatric problems.

Occupational History: Tell Me a Bit About Your Work History

Currently, Tati is finding employment through a temp agency. When she moved to New York, she found a job at a television station. Interestingly, when she reported this, she stated that she got a job with a "network affiliate," not reporting which network she worked for. About two sentences later, she "slipped" and said the name of the station, laughing and getting obviously embarrassed that she had said the name of the station. She reported that she worked for that network for almost two years and that she had a "demanding boss, who was difficult, but I learned a lot." She decided to leave that job to pursue stand-up comedy.

Just after quitting her job, she auditioned for and was accepted to do stand-up in a New York theater and comedy festival. She reported being amazed that she got a gig from her first audition. She has not been as successful since, and she currently takes temp jobs "as crutches." She is currently studying stand-up comedy as well.

Psychosexual History: Okay, and About Your Sexual History

Clearly having built some rapport up to this point in the interview, the assessor was unashamed when asking Tati about her sexual history. She reported that she had been "really closed off" sexually, having had sex only with the girlfriend from college who moved to France. When she moved to New York, she reported that there were several episodes where she would "black out drunk" and wake up in the morning with random men. She quickly stated that there were not many of these, continuing to smile broadly. She clearly became somewhat embarrassed, turning red, so the assessor tried his best to put her at ease, treating this information like any other information gathered during the interview.

Educational History: And About Your Educational History

Tati reported that she was "an okay student," really focusing only on "what inspired me." Included in this category was history—she was "a huge history buff." Immediately after stating this, however, she again jumped to a drastically different topic, stating that she "blacked out my parents' divorce." When probed, she reported that she really has very little recollection of it at all, even though she knows it happened and was old enough that she should remember. She stated that in fourth through sixth grades, she tried to keep her mind off of "things," getting bored and distracted easily in class. "Oh, math was challenging for me—I always had tutors. And I had bad test anxiety." Sensing that she was getting off topic again, the assessor decided to interrupt and ask her a bit more about her family history.

Family History (Revisited): Can You Tell Me a Bit More About Your Family Growing Up, Like Any Brothers and Sisters?

Tati reported that she was the only child from her mother and father's relationship, but that she has one half-brother, who is 12 years younger than Tati, from her father's remarriage. She reported that she is not as close with him as she would like to be, partially because he is so much younger than she is, and partially "because of my stepmother." This phrase clearly needed some probing, so the assessor asked Tati about her stepmother.

Tati began by explaining that her stepmother had been abused. She reported that this is "probably why she took all her frustrations out on me." She reportedly did not know much about American culture when she came to Florida to marry Tati's father, and she reportedly said to Tati, "If I knew you were gonna live here, I wouldn't have married your father." Tati and her stepmother had a "difficult relationship," and they did not interact much, never eating meals together with the family or spending time together. In fact, Tati reported that growing up she had "a sensitive stomach," not being able to tolerate Chinese food. Now, however, she likes Chinese food: "I think it was because I hated my stepmom."

She reported that for all her vacations growing up she would go to Washington to be with her aunt, with whom she was very close.

Psychosocial and Psychosexual History (Revisited)

Without prompting, Tati returned to the topic of romantic relationships. "I go for emotionally unavailable men," she reported. She seeks out men "as closed off as I am." She looked at the assessor and said that he must be a bit confused because of the woman she dated in college, but she stated that she was the only woman she had ever been attracted to, and she identifies as heterosexual. She then began to retell the story of the roommate she was very close to when she moved to New York but is no longer friends with. Tati again described her roommate's male classmate that she became close to as "an unrequited love—he was unavailable." She reported that she was resentful of her roommate, who also became close to this man. When he moved away, Tati's resentment grew so much (despite the fact that she neither dated this man nor told her roommate how she felt) that she cut ties with her roommate.

Alcohol/Substance Use History: Okay, You've Talked a Lot About Your Alcohol Use—Can I Ask About That and Any Other Drugs You've Used?

Comfortable that he had gotten most of the necessary information other than her substance use history, the assessor finally chose to revisit her alcohol use, knowing that this part of the clinical interview might take awhile. She reported that she tried marijuana one time in college, but that she did not like it. She also denied using any other drugs.

Tati reported that she had "sips of alcohol" as a child, but that she truly started drinking when she was in college. She reported that she "drank everything with alcohol in it," blacking out (not remembering large periods of time while drunk) often. She parenthetically reported that her uncle is also a long-time, chronic alcoholic—she said this almost apologetically, as she had forgotten to mention it when discussing her family history of alcoholism. She reported that she drank primarily on weekends, but that she always "drank to get drunk." She then related the story of when she required hospitalization.

When she was 20 years old, she had a big final exam for one of her classes. She reported that she spent the 72 hours before the exam studying, only taking "catnaps here and there." Just before she had started studying for the exam, a "stupid boy" she had been dating for a few weeks broke up with her. After completing the exam, despite the fact that she was exhausted, rather than going home and going to sleep, which was her intention, she went to a friend's apartment to have a drink. "One drink turned into lots of drinks," and the next morning she woke up in the hospital with a blood alcohol level near .40, "almost dead." It was not at this point that she decided to stop drinking, but she now cites it as evidence of the danger of her drinking.

Criminal/Legal History: Have You Ever Been in Trouble With the Law?

Tati denied any legal difficulty in her past.

Presenting Problem (Revisited)

Interestingly, at the very end of the final session of assessment (weeks later), Tati reported that she wanted to make sure the assessor knew a few things about her that she had not yet disclosed. She pulled out a sheet of paper with a list on it and began reading it, very rapidly. She reported that she felt as a child she "acted out of spite" when her mother died, especially because of her "emotionally abusive stepmother." She reported feeling she struggles with complacency; a fear of intimacy and overthinking things; a fear of failure and a fear of success; trouble trusting people; and trouble "balancing things in my life."

She also reported that she feels a great deal of resentment in her life, at the moment especially toward her roommate, who had left a birthday party with that man that Tati had begun to feel close to. She reported that her resentment increases "when I just sit in quiet," but when she is busy it is not a problem. She reported wanting to "let it go." Of note is that, other than the specific story of her roommate leaving a party with the man she liked, she had previously reported everything on this list to the assessor. There was in actuality no new information about her current struggles, though it appeared she anxiously feared that she may have left out some details or information.

MENTAL STATUS EVALUATION

Appearance and Behavior

Tati's appearance was unremarkable. She was adequately groomed, well-related interpersonally, and made good eye contact throughout the clinical interview. She was friendly and cooperative. She exhibited some fidgeting behaviors at times during the clinical interview.

Speech and Language

Tati clearly understood all of the questions and comments made by the assessor. Her speech, however, was low in volume at times, as well as rapid and with some stutter because of the fast rate of speech. Her pitch and articulation were normal, and her vocabulary was age- and culture-appropriate.

Mood and Affect

Tati reported mostly euthymic mood currently, with only current mild depression. Her affect was mildly anxious, with constant smiling, some fidgeting behaviors, and at times her complexion turning red. Her affect was not sad or depressed at all throughout the clinical interview.

Thought Process and Content

Tati's thought content was free of hallucinations and delusions, though she exhibited excessive guilt and some depressive ideation. She denied any suicidal or homicidal/aggressive ideation. Her thought process was characterized by rapid and somewhat circumstantial thinking. At times she was tangential, but she generally came back to the point she was trying to make.

Cognition

Tati was alert throughout the clinical interview, and her attention and concentration seemed unimpaired. She reported some abnormalities in her memory functioning, including "blacking out" parts of her childhood. Other than these slight abnormalities, however, her memory seemed generally intact.

Prefrontal Functioning

Tati's judgment and insight seem mostly adequate; however, she reported a history of impulsivity (including moving to New York impulsively, not having a plan once she was there and not knowing anybody).

Hypothesis Building

Now that the clinical assessment (the clinical interview and the mental status evaluation) has been completed, the information gathered can be used to create hypotheses for what is going on for Tati.

Identify Impairments

For Tati, there seem to be multiple impairments in her functioning, despite the fact that, overall, she is functioning quite well. She reported some depressed feelings and guilt, and she exhibited some anxious behaviors, so her first impairment is subjectively felt distress. While this is a vague impairment in functioning, it is likely one of the most salient to Tati herself. Additionally, it seems pretty clear that her alcohol use has been a problem in the past, even though it is not currently affecting her actively.

In addition to her subjectively felt distress and alcohol abuse, however, there seem to be several other areas of functional impairment. Primarily, she reported a significant history of interpersonal and social difficulty, to the point that it seems she does not have any stable, close friends. She cited only one good friend ever, though she is no longer friends with her. And her "best friend in New York" was her roommate, but she has cut ties with her. Her other friends seem to be primarily from AA. Further, even though it seems not to be her fault, her family relationships are significantly strained.

Currently, Tati does not have a stable job. It is difficult to ascertain whether or not this constitutes impairment in functioning, as it is the result of a willful decision to pursue stand-up comedy. However, for the sake of building hypotheses, it is safer to assert that this *may* be an area of impairment, especially as it seems to have resulted from a history of impulsivity, along with restlessness with where she is at any given moment of her life.

Enumerate Possible Causes

Because of Tati's subjectively felt distress, two hypotheses should be a *mood disorder* (which includes dysthymic disorder, major depressive disorder, bipolar I disorder, and bipolar II disorder, among several others) and an *anxiety disorder* (including possible generalized anxiety disorder). More specifically, however, there is evidence of depressed mood and some possible manic behavior, related to her impulsivity and her story about studying for 72 hours straight in college without the need for much sleep.

Another obvious hypothesis, given her presenting problems, is a *substance use disorder*, specifically alcohol dependence. Although there was no evidence given in the clinical interview about withdrawal or tolerance symptoms, the amount of psychological dependence, as well as how seriously it impaired her functioning, should be assessed with testing.

To account for some of the other minor symptoms related, including her lack of focus (growing up and now) and her impulsivity, one hypothesis of what could be happening with Tati is *attention-deficit/hyperactivity disorder* (ADHD).

Finally, given her interpersonal difficulties, a safe hypothesis is the possible presence of a *personality disorder*. Given the clinical assessment, only one of a few personality disorders is likely, including obsessive-compulsive personality disorder (related to her self-identified perfectionism), border-line personality disorder (given her history of rapid and rocky interpersonal relationships), and histrionic personality disorder (given her history of drinking and her avoidance of deep emotions).

As part of every hypothesis consideration, you should *always* consider (a) that the presenting problems have an etiology in substance use and (b) that the presenting problems have an etiology in a medical condition. For Tati, the possibility that her mood, anxiety, or interpersonal symptoms are secondary to lasting effects of her alcohol use should be considered. Because her interpersonal issues constitute patterns that began before she started using alcohol, an alcohol-related etiology for these symptoms can be ruled out. However, there is a possibility that her mood and/or anxiety symptoms are related to her previous alcohol abuse. There is no evidence of any medical condition that could be contributing to her current difficulties, as ruled out by a recent physical exam. At this point, it will be assumed that the symptoms are primarily psychological in nature.

SELECTING TESTS

Selecting tests for the current assessment flows from the hypotheses generated. Cognitively, Tati had no apparent impairment in functioning, aside from the possibility of attention difficulties. Even so, a screening for neurological impairment and a general assessment of current intellectual functioning is always part of a good psychological assessment. Thus, the Bender Visual-Motor Gestalt Test, 2nd Edition (Bender-2) and the Wechsler Adult Intelligence Scale, 4th Edition (WAIS-IV) were chosen and administered. The WAIS-IV has one index of functioning that is helpful in ruling out ADHD, the Working Memory Index (WMI). The WMI has subtests that require sustained attention, in addition to higher-level mental manipulation processes. While poor performance on the WMI cannot, in and of itself, diagnose an attention deficit, good performance on the WMI can rule out ADHD (inattentive type), as the subtests require, at a minimum, sustained attention. Thus, depending on Tati's performance on the WMI of the WAIS-IV, additional tests may be necessary. If she performs poorly on the WMI, two tests will be added to the battery: The Conners Continuous Performance Test, 2nd Edition (CPT-2) and the Test of Everyday Attention (TEA).

If she performs adequately on the WMI of the WAIS-IV, thus ruling out attention difficulties, these measures will be unnecessary.

The rest of the major hypotheses for the current assessment are general Axis I disorders, including mood disorders, anxiety disorders, and a substance abuse disorder. Again, utilizing the standard battery presented in this book (which includes both objective and projective measures of personality and emotional functioning), differential diagnoses between and within mood and anxiety disorders should be relatively clear. Thus, the Rorschach Inkblot Test (Rorschach), the Thematic Apperception Test (TAT), and the Projective Drawings should offer enough projective evidence to understand what is diagnostically going on for Tati. For the objective measure of the battery, both for the mood/anxiety disorders question and for the question of a substance abuse disorder, the Personality Assessment Inventory (PAI) will be utilized, as its strength lies in its ability to map onto Axis I of the DSM-IV-TR. Altogether, the PAI, Rorschach, TAT, and Projective Drawings should provide enough evidence for diagnosis on Axis I.

The final hypothesis generated from the clinical assessment was the possibility of a personality disorder. While the battery thus far may be helpful in understanding the personality dynamics (especially the Rorschach), the PAI tests for only two types of personality disorders—borderline and antisocial. Because other personality disorders are also hypothesized, it will be extremely useful to add an additional objective measure that better taps personality (Axis II) functioning. For this, the Millon Clinical Multiaxial Inventory, 3rd Edition (MCMI-III) will be used. This measure's strength is its sensitivity to personality and character styles; together with the projective measures, it will provide a comprehensive picture of Tati's personality functioning.

Thus, our assessment's battery of tests will consist of

- Bender-2
- WAIS-IV
- MCMI-III
- PAI
- Rorschach
- TAT
- Projective Drawings
- (If needed: CPT-2 and TEA)

Accumulating the Data

Table 8.1 shows the results from each individual measure administered. Note that because she performed well on the WMI of the WAIS-IV, the CPT-2 and TEA were not administered. This good performance rules out the likelihood of ADHD, so additional measures of attention are unnecessary.

TABLE 8.1	ACCUMULATION OF TATI'S DATA

MCMI-III

Erratically moody
Overreactive to situations
Anxious seeking of reassurance from others
Anxiety
Self-sabotaging of relationships
Difficulty regulating moods
Difficulties with sustained, deep relationships
Expects disappointments
Highly self-critical
Pessimistic
Pursues praise manipulatively
Socially savvy
Feels misunderstood
Ambivalence: dependence and desire to withdraw/isolate
Self-pity
Depressive dependency
Stimulus-seeking
Allows others to mistreat/exploit her
Hypervigilance
Generally compliant
Vacillates between being pleasant/agreeable and passive aggressive/accusatory
Exhibitionistic and expressive
Intolerant of frustration
Possible: Generalized Anxiety Disorder
Possible: Masochistic Personality Disorder with Dependent, Histrionic, and OCPD features

TABLE 8.1   *(CONTINUED)*

PAI

Demanding behavior

Elevated and inconsistent mood

During stressful times: self-critical

Some bizarreness in thinking

Some identity difficulties

Current anxiety and stress

Some negative relationships

Fluctuating sense of self/self-esteem

Some paranoia

Irritability

Possible: Generalized Anxiety Disorder

Possible: Personality Disorder NOS with Borderline and Paranoid Features

Rorschach

Significant affective distress: depression

Acts more on how she feels/gut instinct than what she thinks

Avoids self-focusing

Feelings of loss

Emotional difficulties

Susceptible to anxiety and depression

Tends not to process emotions

Intellectualizes

Socially—initially favorable impression

Demonstrates maladaptive interpersonal behavior

Chronic and substantial stimulus overload

Markedly insecure/lacks confidence

Overvalues her personal worth

Preoccupied with her own needs at the expense of others'

Current situationally related stress

Lots of dependency

Confused about how she feels

Oppositional tendencies

Capable of attaching to people

Takes in more information from her environment than she can effectively handle

(Continued)

TABLE 8.1   *(CONTINUED)*

Reality testing impairment: especially in emotionally arousing situations
Underlying anger and resentment toward people
Interpersonally comfortable
Lack of adequate coping resources
Opts for superficial/transient relationships
When she does self-focus, is critical of her attitudes and motivations
Backs away from deep relationships out of fear they'll demand
more than she can handle
Can be socially withdrawn
Denial: attributes positive qualities to situations that are not positive
Excessive openness to experience/overly broad focus of attention
Good insight
Some impairment in logical thinking

Projective Drawings
Intellectualization
Resentment
Wants attention and approval
Self-critical
Searching for her identity
Good social understanding
Feelings of emptiness
Constricts emotion
Presents a façade to the world
Misses her mother
Confusion
The idea of family is not clearly defined to her

TAT
Resentment
Feels misunderstood
Emotionally distances from others
Black-and-White thinking
Weak identity
Consequences to behavior not well thought out
Dependency

TABLE 8.1	*(CONTINUED)*

Hiding/not feeling emotions
Interpersonally manipulative
Feels unwanted
Ambivalence about dependency and withdrawing
Denial of anything scary
Self-critical
Shallow emotion
Fear of loss/abandonment

IDENTIFYING THEMES

When labeling themes, many are vague at this stage (e.g., mood, social). Additionally, some may have a "flavor" to them at this stage that may change during the next. For example, the theme of dependence, when all of the data are viewed together, may feel more like feelings of loss, or something slightly different than dependence. This categorization process, again, may take several iterations in order to effectively link evidence in a thematically consistent way. At this stage, it is even necessary to have a miscellaneous (misc.) category for evidence that does not immediately fit any defined category. However, during the next stage, when all the data are viewed together for each theme, many of the vague themes and the miscellaneous theme will hopefully become clearer and easier to understand. The preliminary themes for Tati are listed in Table 8.2.

ORGANIZING THE DATA

It becomes apparent, when the data within themes are examined, that much of the evidence converges to offer much more specific themes than the titles previously given. Additionally, the misc. theme actually turns out to be meaningful. Tati's reorganized data are presented in Table 8.3.

The *mood* category from the last stage transformed into moodiness. There are multiple themes within this category, from restriction of emotion to signs of depression to emotional lability, all of which will be spelled out more clearly in the final report. For now, however, the heading *moodiness* can cover all of those subthemes. The social category, when all

TABLE 8.2   **LABELING OF TATI'S THEMES**

Themes

	MCMI-III
Mood	Erratically moody
Mood	Overreactive to situations
Dependence	Anxious seeking of reassurance from others
Anxiety	Anxiety
Mistrust	Self-sabotaging of relationships
Mood	Difficulty regulating moods
Mistrust	Difficulties with sustained, deep relationships
Mistrust	Expects disappointments
Self-esteem	Highly self-critical
Mood	Pessimistic
Social	Pursues praise manipulatively
Social	Socially savvy
Mistrust	Feels misunderstood
Dependence/Mistrust	Ambivalence: dependence and desire to withdraw/isolate
Social	Self-pity
Dependence	Depressive dependency
Misc.	Stimulus-seeking
Social	Allows others to mistreat/exploit her
Mistrust	Hypervigilance
Social	Generally compliant
Social	Vacillates between being pleasant/agreeable and passive aggressive/accusatory
Misc.	Exhibitionistic and expressive
Misc.	Intolerant of frustration
Anxiety	Possible: Generalized Anxiety Disorder
	Possible: Masochistic Personality Disorder with Dependent, Histrionic, and OCPD features
	PAI
Social	Demanding behavior
Mood	Elevated and inconsistent mood
Self-esteem	During stressful times: self-critical
Thinking	Some bizarreness in thinking
Self-esteem	Some identity difficulties
Anxiety	Current anxiety and stress
Mistrust	Some negative relationships

TABLE 8.2   (CONTINUED)

Themes

Self-esteem	Fluctuating sense of self/self-esteem
Mistrust	Some paranoia
Misc.	Irritability
Anxiety	Possible: Generalized Anxiety Disorder
	Possible: Personality Disorder NOS with Borderline and Paranoid Features

Rorschach

Mood	Significant affective distress: depression
Misc.	Acts more on how she feels/gut instinct than what she thinks
Self-esteem	Avoids self-focusing
Dependence	Feelings of loss
Mood	Emotional difficulties
Mood/Anxiety	Susceptible to anxiety and depression
Mood	Tends not to process emotions
Mood	Intellectualizes
Social	Socially—initially favorable impression
Social	Demonstrates maladaptive interpersonal behavior
Anxiety	Chronic and substantial stimulus overload
Self-esteem	Markedly insecure/lacks confidence
Self-esteem	Overvalues her personal worth
Social	Preoccupied with her own needs at the expense of others'
Anxiety	Current situationally related stress
Dependence	Lots of dependency
Mood	Confused about how she feels
Social	Oppositional tendencies
Dependence	Capable of attaching to people
Mistrust	Takes in more information from her environment than she can effectively handle
Thinking	Reality testing impairment: especially in emotionally arousing situations
Mistrust	Underlying anger and resentment toward people
Social	Interpersonally comfortable
Anxiety	Lack of adequate coping resources
Mistrust	Opts for superficial/transient relationships
Self-esteem	When she does self-focus, is critical of her attitudes and motivations
Mistrust	Backs away from deep relationships out of fear they'll demand more than she can handle

(Continued)

TABLE 8.2   *(CONTINUED)*

Themes

Mistrust	Can be socially withdrawn
Thinking	Denial: attributes positive qualities to situations that are not positive
Thinking	Excessive openness to experience/overly broad focus of attention
Thinking	Good insight
Thinking	Some impairment in logical thinking
	Projective Drawings
Mood	Intellectualization
Mistrust	Resentment
Self-esteem	Wants attention and approval
Self-esteem	Self-critical
Self-esteem	Searching for her identity
Social	Good social understanding
Self-esteem	Feelings of emptiness
Mood	Constricts emotion
Social	Presents a façade to the world
Dependence	Misses her mother
Thinking	Confusion
Mistrust	The idea of family is not clearly defined to her
	TAT
Mistrust	Resentment
Mistrust/Self-esteem	Feels misunderstood
Mistrust	Emotionally distances from others
Thinking	Black-and-White thinking
Self-esteem	Weak identity
Misc.	Consequences to behavior not well thought out
Dependence	Dependency
Mood	Hiding/not feeling emotions
Social	Interpersonally manipulative
Self-esteem	Feels unwanted
Dependence/Mistrust	Ambivalence about dependency and withdrawing
Thinking	Denial of anything scary
Self-esteem	Self-critical
Mood	Shallow emotion
Dependence	Fear of loss/abandonment

TABLE 8.3   TATI'S ORGANIZED DATA

Test: Concept/Theme	MCMI-III	PAI	Rorschach	Projective Drawings	TAT	Interview/Behavioral Observations
Low Self-Esteem/Weak Identity	Highly self-critical	During stressful times: self-critical	Avoids self-focusing	Wants attention and approval	Feels misunderstood	Always saw herself somewhere else by this point in her life
		Some identity difficulties	Markedly insecure/lacks confidence	Self-critical	Weak identity	Long search for spiritual identity
		Fluctuating sense of self/self-esteem	Overvalues her personal worth	Searching for her identity	Feels unwanted	Repeated noting of her "alcoholic" identity and clinging to AA
			When she does self-focus, is critical of her attitudes and motivations			
Moodiness	Erratically moody	Elevated and inconsistent mood	Significant affective distress: depression	Intellectualization	Hiding/not feeling emotions	Extremely reactive history
	Overreactive to situations		Emotional difficulties	Constricts emotion	Shallow emotion	
	Difficulty regulating moods		Susceptible to anxiety and depression			
	Pessimistic		Tends not to process emotions			

(Continued)

TABLE 8.3   (CONTINUED)

Test: Concept/Theme	MCMI-III	PAI	Rorschach	Projective Drawings	TAT	Interview / Behavioral Observations
			Intellectualizes Confused about how she feels			
Anxiety	Anxiety	Current anxiety and stress	Susceptible to anxiety and depression			Rapid speech without pauses
	Possible: Generalized Anxiety Disorder	Possible: Generalized Anxiety Disorder	Chronic and substantial stimulus overload			Smiling, fidgeting, and red complexion during interview
			Current situationally related stress			
			Lack of adequate coping resources			
Dependent Needs	Anxious seeking of reassurance from others		Feelings of loss	Misses her mother	Dependency	Loss of mother at an early age
	Depressive dependency		Lots of dependency		Ambivalence about dependency and withdrawing	Emotionally abusive stepmother

	Ambivalence: dependence and desire to withdraw/isolate		Capable of attaching to people		Fear of loss/abandonment	Strong feelings of abandonment
Interpersonal Mistrust	Self-sabotaging of relationships	Some negative relationships	Takes in more information from her environment than she can effectively handle	Resentment	Resentment	Reported creating "blockage" in relationships
	Difficulties with sustained, deep relationships	Some paranoia	Underlying anger and resentment toward people	The idea of family is not clearly defined to her	Feels misunderstood	Only one reported close friendship in her life
	Expects disappointments		Opts for superficial/transient relationships		Emotionally distances from others	
	Feels misunderstood		Backs away from deep relationships out of fear they'll demand more than she can handle		Resentment	
	Ambivalence: dependence and desire to withdraw/isolate		Can be socially withdrawn		Ambivalence about dependency and withdrawing	
	Hypervigilance					
Social → Interpersonally Manipulative Behavior	Pursues praise manipulatively	Demanding behavior	Socially—initially favorable impression	Good social understanding	Interpersonally manipulative	Reported acting out of resentment in childhood

(Continued)

TABLE 8.3 (CONTINUED)

Test: Concept/Theme	MCMI-III	PAI	Rorschach	Projective Drawings	TAT	Interview / Behavioral Observations
	Socially savvy		Demonstrates maladaptive interpersonal behavior	Presents a façade to the world		Passive aggressive toward roommate
	Self-pity		Preoccupied with her own needs at the expense of others'			
	Allows others to mistreat/ exploit her		Oppositional tendencies			
	Generally compliant		Interpersonally comfortable			
	Vacillates between being pleasant/ agreeable and passive aggressive/ accusatory					

Problems With Thinking	Some bizarreness in thinking	Reality testing impairment: especially in emotionally arousing situations	Confusion	Denial of anything scary	Circumstantial thinking in interview
		Denial: attributes positive qualities to situations that are not positive		Black-and-White thinking	
		Excessive openness to experience/overly broad focus of attention			
		Good insight			
		Some impairment in logical thinking			
Misc. → Impulsivity	Irritability	Acts more on how she feels/gut instinct than what she thinks		Consequences to behavior not well thought out	History of impulsive behavior
	Stimulus-seeking				College over-drinking
	Exhibitionistic and expressive				
	Intolerant of frustration				

the data are presented together, is more specifically a theme about inter-personal manipulativeness. It is important to note that even though the title of this theme sounds entirely negative, there are some positive pieces of data that contribute to this theme, including much evidence that Tati is socially savvy and adept. Still, with all the evidence viewed together, she seems to use this adeptness to meet her own needs, rather than to build genuine relationships. Finally, the miscellaneous category seems to be con-verging on problems with impulse control.

CONCEPTUALIZING

Remembering that the task at this point is to try to create a logical narra-tive amongst the themes so that it presents a coherent story, we have to connect the following themes:

- Low self-esteem and weak identity
- Moodiness
- Anxiety
- Dependent needs
- Interpersonal mistrust
- Interpersonally manipulative behavior
- Problems with thinking
- Impulsivity

Before deciding on the most logical way to fit all these themes together, we will first consider the model templates presented in Chapter 4: the diathesis-stress model, the developmental model, and the common func-tion model for conceptualization.

Diathesis-Stress Model

In applying the diathesis-stress model of conceptualization, we must try to divide the themes into (1) *traits* that are inherent within Tati that she likely developed at an early age, and that she "brings to the picture" (diatheses), (2) *external issues* that affect her functioning (stressors), and (3) *states* that are more situational or transient (outcomes). It is important to categorize each of our eight themes into these three types. Some may be arguable, but as long as the model is logical, it is not as important to be "correct" as to be convincing. Remember that the point of creating our narrative is not to change our conclusions or diagnoses, but rather to frame them in a palatable, understandable way for those receiving feedback. The way I categorize these themes here may differ from how others would, but I will give justification for each. Also, the order I am presenting them in is entirely arbitrary.

Sometimes it is easiest to begin with the outcomes, as many themes logically seem more transient (such as behavior) and not core to who the patient is. One way of thinking of outcomes and states is how responsive they are likely to be to psychotherapeutic (or psychopharmacological) intervention. Most symptoms that are highly responsive to treatment are more likely to be outcomes, inasmuch as core traits (diatheses) are likely to be harder to treat. Her manipulative interpersonal behavior, for example, seems to stem from other, more core, issues in her life. This is how she currently is dealing with her life and all the difficulties in it, coping by trying to maintain as much control over her interpersonal environment as possible. Therefore, her manipulative interpersonal behavior will be one of the outcomes.

As with behavior, certain symptoms are likely to be outcomes. Anxiety, for example, is not core to who Tati is, but rather it is how whatever is going on within her is manifesting itself symptomatically. Whatever is interacting at a more core level for her is spilling out as anxiety. Thus, anxiety is also an outcome.

Some symptoms and behaviors could be representative of either outcomes or diatheses. Some examples of this idea for Tati include (a) low self-esteem, which could be a developmental outcome of other problems or could be core to who she is currently; (b) impulsivity, which could be seen as a behavioral outcome or a trait central to who she is; (c) thinking problems, which very often both act as outcomes and cause further problems as diatheses; and (d) moodiness, which could be a behavior or a core trait. While it is less important where each of these themes ends up in our model, what is important is that the story we tell makes sense. So instead of deciding immediately where each of these will fall, it may be easier to move to the stresses before making these judgments.

When any of these eight themes is viewed as a stress, only one seems to lend itself to external factors. Her interpersonal mistrust, even though it seems like an internal concept, can be seen as a result of being let down in her life by others. Whoever she is at her core, her reaction to being let down by others and thus adopting a mistrustful stance toward relationships in general has created some unhealthy outcomes. Thus, her mistrust will be used as her stress.

Regarding her diathesis—who she is at her core and what she "brings to the table"—again it could be argued that several of these themes logically apply. In some ways, it is dependent on the person doing the interpretation how he or she chooses to conceptualize. As long as the argument can be made, and the argument is a *logical* one to most who would read it, the model will be effective. For diathesis, we have chosen two attributes that, given her history, seem likely to have developed earlier than some of the other themes. Developmentally, as her mother passed away when she was a pre-adolescent, we look for traits that are appropriate for a child of that age, traits whose development may have been arrested at that point.

For a child that age, the two traits that seem appropriate, even though they no longer are, are her dependent needs and her moodiness. Her dependent needs were appropriate for a child of 9 years old, but when her mother passed away and her father remarried, these needs went unmet. Additionally, moodiness is a trait that is healthy and normative for pre-adolescents and adolescents, though she seems not to have outgrown it. Further, even though we paired her low self-esteem and weak identity development initially, in the current model, thinking developmentally, we can add her weak identity (which would again be appropriate for a girl of 9) to the diathesis, while separating out low self-esteem as an outcome. Thus, her diathesis will consist of her dependent needs, her weak identity, and her moodiness.

This model leaves her impulsivity and her problems in thinking as outcomes. These are logical outcomes of our model. A woman who has high needs for dependency, has a poorly defined and understood sense of her own identity, and is emotionally moody and reactive, in combination with the fact that she has been let down by others in her past and thus mistrusts them, will be extremely conflicted about interpersonal relationships. She, on the one hand, wants and needs others. On the other hand, though, she does not believe that she can trust others to meet her needs. This would likely be extremely confusing, both cognitively and emotionally. Problems with logical thinking, anxiety, and attempting to manipulate social situations are logical results of this confusion. In addition, she is likely not to feel good about herself, so low self-esteem is another logical outcome. Her emotional confusion would likely lead to impulsive behavior, as well. The diathesis–stress model for Tati is shown in Figure 8.1.

This model is not too complex, and it seems as though it could be arguable. The key would be writing it up in a way that makes this model make absolute sense. The challenge would be to explain how each of the outcomes is a logical result of the interaction between her core internal functioning and the fact that she has been let down by others and has adopted a mistrustful attitude toward interpersonal relationships. Before deciding on using this model, however, consider other models as well.

Developmental Model

The developmental model for conceptualizing Tati may prove to be one of the more useful models, as she had a significant tragedy during her early development that seems to have impacted her significantly. Looking at her needs, wishes, and identity, we need to figure out at what developmental level she is generally functioning. Again, does she display feelings, needs,

FIGURE 8.1   DIATHESIS-STRESS MODEL FOR TATI

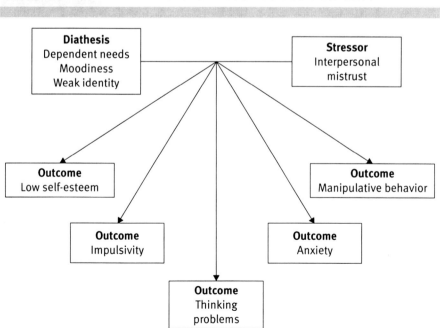

and attitudes normal for a pre-adolescent or adolescent (e.g., emotional lability, high need for peer approval, and a hazy identity)? Or does she more resemble a child (with high dependency need, difficulty telling fantasy from reality, and an inability to care for herself)? Or does she resemble an adult (with healthy independence, emotional maturity, and good decision-making skills)?

Remember that the developmental model will work only if there is a discrepancy between the level at which she is functioning and the actual age-related demands being placed on her. It is not interesting to say that she is functioning at the level of an adult and has adult demands being placed on her; this scenario should not lead to any problems. This model is interesting only when her level of functioning falls below what is being expected of her, such as being an adult with adult demands but functioning as a child. This mismatch between functioning and demands would likely lead to problems. And it seems as though Tati is struggling functionally, arguably because she is functioning at an earlier developmental level than required by adult demands that are being placed on her in life.

For Tati, there is evidence that she is functioning at varying levels of development among her different domains of functioning. Cognitively, she is functioning adequately as an adult (i.e., there is no evidence of mental retardation). Her emotional and personality functioning, however, seem to be at a much earlier developmental stage than her chronological age. Specifically, her high dependency needs, her weak identity, and her problems differentiating fantasy from reality (thinking problems) suggest childlike emotional functioning. Her moodiness, impulsivity, and manipulative interpersonal behavior (representing high needs for acceptance from peers) signify pre-adolescent emotional functioning. It is clear that her emotional and personality development, in some ways, stopped when she was around 9 years old, when her mother passed away and her life changed dramatically. Functioning at this level, yet facing the everyday demands of being an adult (needing to make autonomous decisions, navigating complex relationships, etc.), Tati has become anxious and mistrustful of others—not surprising when others likely do not fulfill all of her strong needs as she would like. The developmental model for Tati is shown in Figure 8.2.

Again, this model is not overly complex, but the emphasis of the argument in the report would be slightly different. In terms that are not too

FIGURE 8.2   DEVELOPMENTAL MODEL FOR TATI

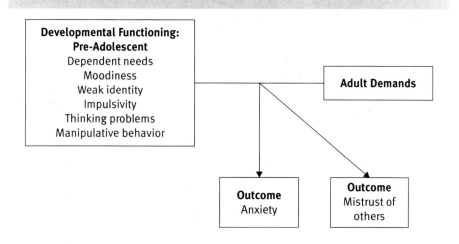

psychological, it would be necessary to explain how the themes that represent more pre-adolescent developmental functioning in fact do so. This would make a part of the assessment report psychoeducational, such that it informs the reader about human development. It is not difficult, though, to understand how an individual functioning at this level, in interaction with the adult demands, leads specifically to the anxious and mistrustful outcomes. Thus, the model has an inherent logic that most readers would easily identify. A drawback of this model is that many of the themes together make up the pre-adolescent developmental functioning domain, such that they are not interacting dynamically or interestingly. Thus, many of the subsections on themes would seem parallel rather than related directly to each other.

Common Function Model

The common function model explains the themes together as all serving a common purpose (often this purpose is served by one or two of the themes). Generally, the first step is to evaluate each of the themes to identify the overall defensive or coping strategies of the individual. This is somewhat difficult for Tati, as the major efforts of her strategies to cope with the world seem somewhat paradoxical. She has strong dependent needs, but at the same time is mistrustful of others. The overall goal, therefore, seems to be making sense of her interpersonal world, which seems extremely confusing to her. When we conceptualize her general functioning as existing within a confusing interpersonal world, the themes of dependent needs, lack of a clear identity and feeling low self-esteem, mistrust of others, and problems with thinking clearly all seem to explain why her interpersonal world is confusing (as it would be for anyone with all these competing needs and dynamics). All of the other themes, it must be argued, serve the purpose of helping her make sense of her confusing interpersonal world, which is not necessarily the easiest argument to make. The common function model for Tati is shown in Figure 8.3.

This model is compelling in that it centers on Tati's interpersonal world, which is seemingly chaotic and confusing for her. However, while her manipulative interpersonal behavior logically helps her make sense of this confusing interpersonal world, the other three themes need much further explanation. Although impulsivity, anxiety, and moodiness do not intuitively seem to be strategies to sort out this social world, the argument could still be made, as long as it is spelled out clearly in the conceptualization in the report. For example, it could be argued that affective distress on her part (most notably her anxiety and moodiness) is a tactic for gaining support from others. Additionally, her impulsivity can be seen as helping her deal with relationships when they become frightening (which is likely when they become too close). Thus, although these ties are not obvious and intuitive, an argument for them can definitely be made. However,

FIGURE 8.3 **COMMON FUNCTION MODEL FOR TATI**

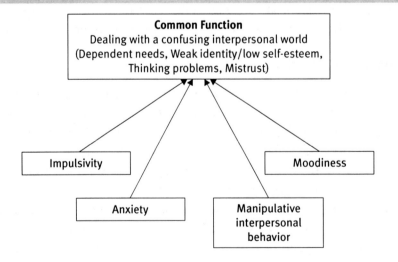

rather than stretch these logical connections, it is likely more useful to create a more complex model to explain Tati's emotional functioning.

Complex Model

Again, each of the three previous models may be adequate (especially one of the first two). However, a more complex model could be considered, if we thought there might be intermediate steps within the process of Tati's overall functioning. While each of the three previous models might be adequate, with so many themes and some problems with each of the models, it is useful to consider a more complex model. One way of coming up with a more complex model is to take the best features of several other models. For example, the developmental model seems to have some validity, inasmuch as much of her emotional world is functioning at the level of a pre-adolescent. However, she also at her core seems extremely conflicted about interpersonal relationships, as presented in the common functions model. The interaction between poor emotional development and deep interpersonal conflict is likely to have severe consequences—it is no stretch to imagine this could lead to anxiety and manipulative behavior, and even to some problems in thinking clearly. The model is shown in Figure 8.4.

FIGURE 8.4   COMPLEX MODEL FOR TATI

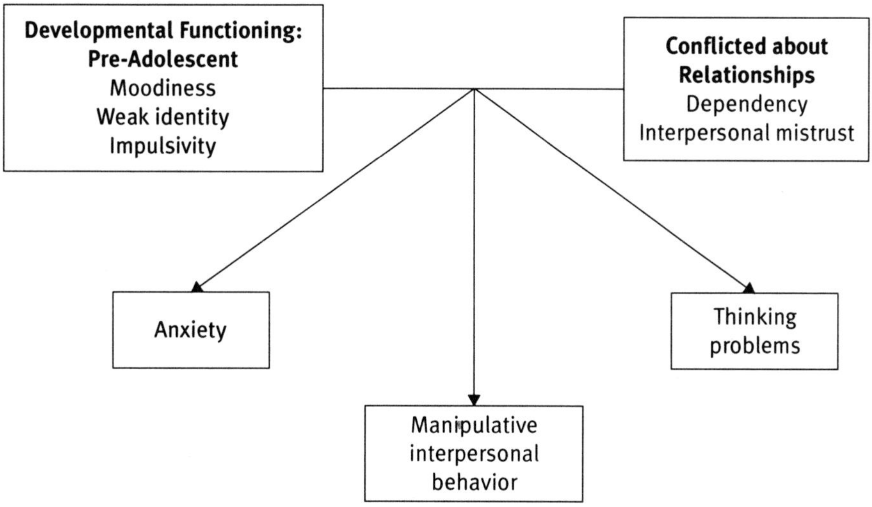

There are many more models that could be created to explain what is happening with Tati, but this last one will be used in the write-up of the report.

REPORT WRITING

Before the report is begun, one final step is necessary—the determination of diagnosis and recommendations. Our original hypotheses included a mood disorder, an anxiety disorder, a substance-related disorder, ADHD, and a personality disorder. Given the evidence that emerged on the tests, a few of these hypotheses can be ruled out relatively easily. While Tati reports poor attention and impulsivity, no evidence of ADHD emerged from the testing (her Working Memory Index on the WAIS-IV was adequate, which is a major indicator that her ability to attend is unimpaired). Similarly, although "moodiness" or lability in her mood emerged from the test data, no evidence of prolonged periods of depression or any other mood disorder was present. Although anxiety did emerge from the testing, when thinking about what exactly is impairing Tati's functioning, the assessor will have to make a judgment about whether anxiety is so great that it impairs her functioning. In Tati's case, the anxiety seems to be an outgrowth of deeper conflict within herself about interpersonal relationships, and the anxiety itself does not seem to be causing her much difficulty. ADHD, mood, and anxiety disorders can thus be ruled out and not applied to her. That leaves us with a substance-related disorder and a personality disorder as possible conclusions.

What seems to be truly affecting Tati's functioning is her interpersonal world, as well as its impact on her personally. Thus, we will look toward Axis II to see if she fits any of the personality disorder frameworks. As it happens, with her (a) unstable identity, (b) impulsivity, (c) moodiness, (d) occasional problems with thinking, and interpersonal conflict related to her, (e) manipulative interpersonal behavior, and (f) ambivalence about close relationships and history of strained relationships, Tati clearly meets criteria for borderline personality disorder. This diagnosis truly accounts for most of the themes and most of what is impairing her functioning currently. However, the question remains about a substance-related disorder.

Based on the testing and a close look at her history, Tati does not seem to have a dependence on alcohol. She presented initially with a strong emphasis on her alcohol use and her involvement in AA. Currently, she highly identifies with the label of being "an alcoholic," a trait that binds her to her family history and seems to give her some sense of identity. Rather than being dependent on alcohol, though, it seems to be just that—helping her with her identity, giving her a social and support network, and helping with some of her strong feelings about her family. As such, rather than give her an alcohol dependence diagnosis, we will give her an alcohol abuse diagnosis, in sustained full remission (as she does not use alcohol currently).

Recommendations, as will be presented in the assessment report that follows, will stem directly from the diagnoses and the themes. Because of the personality disorder, a recommendation either to enter dialectical behavior therapy (DBT) or the use of DBT techniques within her current psychotherapy will be recommended. Alternatively, techniques of expressive psychotherapy (another widely used treatment for borderline personality disorder) will be recommended. Additionally, her continued participation in AA will be encouraged, as it seems to bring her comfort and social support.

PSYCHOLOGICAL ASSESSMENT REPORT
CONFIDENTIAL

Identifying Information

Name:	Tati Lai	**Date of Report:**	12/3/2008
Sex:	Female	**Assessor:**	A. Jordan Wright, PhD
Age:	25	**Dates of Testing:**	10/2/08; 10/23/08;
Date of Birth:	1/1/83		11/20/08
Ethnicity:	Mixed Race		

Source of Referral and Referral Questions

The patient was self-referred for a psychological assessment. She was urged by her Alcoholics Anonymous (AA) sponsor to seek therapy to help her "take a moral inventory of myself," related to her 12 steps to recovery from alcoholism. She reported wanting help "figuring out my defects of character," in order to help her function better in her social and work life.

(Continued)

Measures Administered

- Clinical Interview
- Bender Visual-Motor Gestalt Test-Second Edition (Bender-2)
- Wechsler Adult Intelligence Scale-Fourth Edition (WAIS-IV)
- Personality Assessment Inventory (PAI)
- Millon Clinical Multiaxial Inventory, Third Edition (MCMI-III)
- Rorschach Inkblot Test, Comprehensive System (Rorschach)
- Thematic Apperception Test (TAT)
- House-Tree-Person and Kinetic Family Drawings (Projective Drawings)

Description of Patient

The patient is a 25-year-old mixed-race female of half Chinese and half Italian descent. She is slim, of average height, and looks her stated age. She was friendly and cooperative, and she arrived early for most of her appointments. She was dressed casually and appropriately for the assessment sessions.

Presenting Problem

The patient reported that she is currently having several "blockages" in her life. She currently feels "closed off" to relationships with men, feeling she is emotionally unavailable when it comes to romantic relationships. Additionally, she feels that she chooses only either "emotionally unavailable men" or men who do not return her affections, "unrequited love."

In addition to relationships, the patient reported feeling that "I create blockages with work." She is currently an auditioning stand-up comedian who supports herself through temp jobs. She reported that she struggles with procrastination, "overthinking things," and "beating myself up" over small difficulties. She reported that she is a perfectionist, and that "I always saw myself being somewhere else" by the age of 25.

Background Information

History of Presenting Problem

The patient reported a long history of very little socialization and few romantic relationships. She reported only having one significant romantic relationship in her life so far, with a woman, which lasted only a few months. After meeting the woman three weeks before graduating from college, she became heavily involved romantically with her—"she became my world." When the woman moved to France after graduating, they dated long-distance for about six months. When she went to France to visit her after the six months, the woman informed her that she had reconciled with her ex-girlfriend. The patient reported feeling extremely abandoned, which triggered many strong feelings of abandonment from her mother's death when she was 9 years old. Since then she has not had a significant romantic relationship, and she identified herself as heterosexual, despite this one relationship with a woman.

The patient reported that she was always an "achievement-oriented" person, not wanting relationships with others to "get in the way" of her success. She reported having only one good friend growing up, who lived a block away from her and "was a very good influence" on her, as she was also very achievement-oriented. She reported being "afraid" of a serious relationship with a man and intimacy because she felt it would "hold me back" from achieving her goals.

The patient reported that she is "very extreme with reactions" to circumstances in her life. Upon graduating from college, she moved in with her aunt in Washington. However, after breaking up with her girlfriend after college, she impulsively moved to New York City and took a job at a television network. In addition to extreme reactions like this, she reported that she tends to "distract" herself rather than addressing negative emotions—"I don't take time to metabolize." For example, she reported that her mother passed away on a Friday when she was 9 years old, and she begged to go back to school by the next Tuesday. She reported feeling "cut off" from her emotions, able to cry at movies and other things that are not directly related to her, but not processing emotion related to herself.

The patient reported a significant history of alcohol abuse. She began drinking when she went to college, and she drank heavily for several years. She blacked out often, not remembering spans of as many as 8 hours at a time. Additionally, she ended up in the hospital with a dangerously high blood alcohol content and several times woke up with men she could not remember. She is currently in AA and has been sober for about two years.

Symptomatic Evaluation

The patient was in therapy once before, after she had been hospitalized for her extreme alcohol abuse in college. She reported that she went for a very short time, dropping out of treatment after her therapist suggested that she go to AA. She began therapy several weeks ago with a therapist

(Continued)

at the present clinic, which she requested at the same time as the psychological assessment. She has never seen a psychiatrist or been evaluated for psychotropic medication.

The patient reported a significant history of alcohol abuse, but she denied any history of other substance use, except for using marijuana one time in college. She began drinking seriously at 18 years old when she moved to another town in Florida for college. At that time, she would drink heavily each weekend, getting drunk and often blacking out (not remembering long periods of time while drunk). She stated that she would drink "anything with alcohol," from light beer to Everclear. At one point in college she woke up in the hospital, not remembering much of the previous night, with a blood alcohol level of nearly .40, a dangerously high level. She reported that during times of stress she would remain drunk for long periods of time. For example, when her girlfriend broke up with her in France, she got drunk for several weeks. It was in New York, at around age 23, that she became sober and joined AA.

The patient reported a long history of alcoholism on her mother's side of the family, with her great grandmother, grandmother, and aunt all in AA, in addition to her mother likely dying from substance abuse. Additionally, her uncle is reportedly a "longtime, chronic alcoholic."

The patient denied any significant medical history, except for the one time she was hospitalized for excessive alcohol consumption. Diabetes runs in her father's side of the family. No other major medical or psychiatric illnesses were reported in her family.

The patient reported that she was born by Caesarian section a few days after her due date. She had "extreme colic" as a baby, requiring multiple visits to the hospital. Additionally, she "vaguely" remembers needing a walker at an early age in order to help her with walking, which was delayed. However, she reported no more difficulties with developmental milestones. She denied any history of physical abuse or witnessing domestic violence.

Psychosocial Evaluation

The patient is the only child of her mother and father's marriage, born and raised in Florida. Her parents divorced when the patient was around 7 years old, which she stated she does not remember much about. Her mother was an Italian Catholic who was an alcoholic. She passed away at 30 years old, when the patient was 9; the patient reported that she overheard people saying it was an overdose on cocaine that killed her mother, though she is not entirely clear on the reason for the death.

The patient's father is a Chinese Muslim who remarried a woman from China after his divorce from the patient's mother. They had one more child, the patient's half-brother, who is currently 13 years old. The patient reported not feeling as close to her stepmother or half-brother as she would like to be.

The patient reported that she was an "okay student" in school, only focusing and putting effort into subjects that "inspired me," like history. She reportedly became bored easily in school and found math very challenging, requiring tutors throughout most of school. Additionally, she reported having test anxiety, which is one reason she chose to study English in college, which requires fewer tests than papers.

The patient reported a "difficult relationship" with her stepmother. She feels that her stepmother "took out all her frustrations" on her and was "mean" to her. When her stepmother came to the United States and married her father, she reportedly had a difficult time acculturating, and she did not know that the patient would be living with them. She would say things like, "If I knew you were gonna live here, I wouldn't have married your father." As a result, they did not interact much, and they did not even have family meals.

The patient reported a very positive relationship with her aunt, who lives in Washington. She would spend her vacations there, over Christmas and summer. Her aunt is also in AA, and the patient feels that she has been a good influence on her.

The patient attended a private college in Florida, studying English and drama. She graduated in three years, very motivated to finish and leave Florida. She held one long-term job for about two years with a television company, after which she decided to pursue stand-up comedy. She was successful in attaining a stand-up comedy gig in a festival in New York from her first audition, but since then she has been auditioning unsuccessfully and temping to pay her bills. She is currently taking a stand-up comedy class, which she feels is extremely useful.

The patient reported a very limited social history. She described only one close friend growing up, and she currently is no longer friends with her, reportedly because their political views differ. They were friends originally because they lived one block away from each other, and the patient considers

(Continued)

her "a good influence," because she was responsible and encouraged the patient to be as well. When she moved to New York, she began to socialize with her roommate, whom she previously had not known, as well as her circle of friends. She became extremely close to a classmate of her roommate, who quickly "became like a brother." He subsequently moved to a city in the South and is about to get married, and they are no longer close friends. Currently, the majority of the patient's friends are from AA.

The patient reported a limited psychosexual history, because "I was really closed off." She became sexually active with the girlfriend she had in college. Additionally, when she moved to New York, there were several men with whom she had sex while drunk, some during states of blackout which she did not remember the next day. She is currently not sexually active. She did not report any difficulties with her sexual identity or sexual development, except for the one relationship with the woman from college. She currently identifies as heterosexual.

The patient did not report any previous criminal history or legal involvement.

The patient is half Chinese and half Italian and was born and raised in Florida. Although she reported that she was often mistaken for Hispanic, she always felt that she "did not fit the mold in Florida." She reportedly struggled with both her cultural and spiritual identity throughout her life. She attempted to "fit in" with what was expected of women in Florida, even becoming a cheerleader for one year, but she "hated it," so she quit. She felt "very American" in her home, especially with her stepmother from China.

The patient's spiritual identity reportedly "helped me through" many times in her life, including her mother's death. At times she went to mosque with her father, but she "didn't *get* that religion." She became a Southern Baptist for two years in high school, though she reported that she did so mostly for social reasons, as her friends were Southern Baptist. She found comfort in an organization called Fellowship of Christian Students in school, however, and began to form her own identity as a Christian. In college, she was reportedly drawn to the "social justice aspects of Catholicism," enjoying doing community service work for the homeless community in Florida. She took part in a one-week "plunge," during which a group of students lived in a homeless shelter for a week to interact with homeless individuals, an experience she noted was very important to her. She stated that she is "still close" with the people with whom she did the plunge. Additionally, her aunt, with whom she is very close, is a "very spiritual person," and the patient feels that she herself is very spiritual.

Mental Status

The patient was casually and appropriately dressed and groomed, and she was cooperative and friendly throughout the testing process, maintaining appropriate eye contact, even when discussing difficult topics. Her motor activity was slightly agitated at times, tapping her fingers or tapping a pencil on the desk repeatedly. She was open and talkative, asking appropriate questions and disclosing information freely. When speaking, more during the testing than during the clinical interview, her voice would become pressured and she would stutter by attempting to speak too quickly. Both her receptive and expressive language use were within normal limits. Her mood was reportedly "okay," and her affect was inappropriately bright and mood-incongruent, smiling and laughing when discussing difficult topics, like the death of her mother. Her thought process was goal-directed, though at times somewhat circumstantial, and her thought content was free of hallucinations, delusions, and suicidal and homicidal ideation. She reported some guilt about her relationship with her family, but otherwise she reported no depressive or anxious ideation. Her memory seemed within normal limits, except for periods in her life that she has "blacked out," mostly related to being overly intoxicated, but also including the divorce of her parents. Her attention and concentration were within normal limits. Her insight is good, but her impulse control is poor, as evidenced by her history of impulsive decision making and her report of having "very extreme reactions" to situations. Her judgment and planning are adequate.

Behavioral Observations

The patient was friendly and cooperative throughout the testing process, making appropriate eye contact throughout and answering questions openly. She exhibited only a few overt signs of anxiety, including tapping her pencil and shaking her leg during moments when she felt uncomfortable, and no motor difficulties. She appeared to give effortful attempts on all tests administered, maintaining a positive attitude and joking with the assessor. During the final assessment session, at the end of testing, she produced a list of difficulties she had created with her therapist to make sure the assessor had all the information on her current struggles.

Overall Interpretation of Test Findings

Cognitive Functioning

On the WAIS-IV, the patient's Full Scale IQ fell within the Average range (37th percentile) compared to other adults her age. The Full Scale IQ is a

(Continued)

good estimation of her overall functioning, though there was some variation among her subdomains in functioning. Specifically, her Verbal Comprehension, which fell within the Average range (70th percentile), constituted a significant strength in her functioning. Her Processing Speed was also Average (42nd percentile), and her Perceptual Reasoning and Working Memory fell within the Low Average range compared to others her age (18th and 23rd percentiles, respectively), revealing no significant impairment in her cognitive functioning. The patient exhibited no soft signs of neurological damage as evidenced by her Average to High performance on the Bender-2.

Verbal Comprehension. On measures of general verbal skills, such as verbal fluency, ability to understand and use verbal reasoning, and verbal knowledge, the patient's performance fell within the Average range of functioning compared to others her age (Verbal Comprehension Index, 70th percentile), and all subtests within this domain fell within the Average range. Compared to her own overall performance, her verbal ability constituted a significant strength. Her unimpaired verbal comprehension reflects knowledge gained in both formal and informal educational opportunities and demonstrates intellectual ambition and good ability to retrieve information from long-term memory.

Processing Speed. The patient exhibited Average performance compared to same-age peers on tasks that measure the ability to focus attention and quickly scan, discriminate between, and respond to visual information within a time limit (Processing Speed Index, 42nd percentile). Again, all of the subtests that makes up this index fell within the Average range. The patient's processing speed—the rate at which she can carry out cognitive processes—appears to be unimpaired.

Perceptual Reasoning. On tests that measure nonverbal reasoning, visuospatial aptitude, and induction and planning skills on tasks involving nonverbal stimuli such as designs, pictures, and puzzles, the patient performed within the Low Average range of functioning compared to others her age (Perceptual Reasoning Index, 18th percentile). It should be noted that there was some sign of potential for higher functioning in this area, as some of the subtests that make up this index fell within the Average range. Tasks in this domain assess the patient's abilities to examine a problem, draw upon visual-motor and visuospatial skills, organize thoughts, and create and test possible solutions.

Working Memory. On tasks that assessed the ability to memorize new information, hold it in short-term memory, concentrate, and manipulate information to produce some result or reasoning outcome, the patient's performance fell within the Low Average range compared to others her age

(Working Memory Index, 23rd percentile). Again, there was potential for higher functioning in this domain as one of the subtests that makes up this index fell within the Average range. Overall, she did not seem to exhibit a significant deficit in concentration or attention when focusing on specific auditory tasks.

Cognitive Summary. Overall, the patient exhibited no specific impairment in any cognitive area of functioning. While her overall ability is Average, her verbal skill is her most highly developed ability. Her cognitive functioning does not seem to be currently affected by anxious, emotional, or other personality factors.

Emotional Functioning

The patient was administered several standardized objective and projective measures of personality and emotional functioning. The results of the assessment suggest that, at her core, she is deeply conflicted about having deep relationships with others. She longs for and needs others to connect with, but she is also deeply mistrustful of others and of the hope that others will fulfill her needs, which causes resentment within her. Additionally, at her core, there are aspects of her emotional development that slowed when she was a pre-adolescent girl, which is natural given the fact that her mother passed away when she was 9 years old. Specifically, she is emotionally labile and erratic, shifting rapidly in extremes; has a poor sense of her own identity; and acts impulsively. Her conflicted feelings about interpersonal relationships in combination with the aspects of her that are functioning at the level of a pre-adolescent girl have led to several problems in her current functioning. This interaction has caused some anxiety, as she is constantly unsure about the motives of others, and her emotions react erratically to even minor slights from others. Additionally, to address her internal conflict about connecting with others and her pre-adolescent need for attention and identity definition, she attempts to maintain strict control over interpersonal relationships, so much that she behaves in manipulative ways. Finally, as a result of her rapidly shifting feelings about interpersonal relationships and situations that are not clear, there are times when she does not think clearly and rationally.

Interpersonal Ambivalence
The patient presents with deep internal conflict between needing and being dependent on others to boost her low self-esteem and help define who she

(Continued)

is and a deep mistrust that others will meet her needs fully. Her MCMI-III, Rorschach, and TAT suggested that she has very strong dependency needs, such that she longs for others to connect to. More specifically, her Projective Drawings suggested that her dependency is related to strong feelings of loss and longing for her mother, who passed away when she was young. Her MCMI-III revealed that, at times of great need, she seeks reassurance from others in an anxious way, such that not getting reassurance causes great distress. Also revealed in the testing, however, was a pattern of sabotaging relationships, withdrawing, and deep mistrust of others. Specifically, her Rorschach revealed that she prefers superficial, short-term relationships with others, and her MCMI-III revealed that she has difficulty tolerating sustained, deep relationships. Moreover, her MCMI-III and TAT revealed that she expects disappointment and feels misunderstood by others, and that consequently she self-sabotages any relationship that may be longer-lasting or deep. Further, her PAI, MCMI-III, TAT, and Projective Drawings all revealed a deep mistrust for others, almost to the point of paranoia. Her MCMI-III, Rorschach, and Projective Drawings revealed that she is constantly alert to the possibility of others using her, betraying her, or manipulating her, always staying aware of the possibility of being harmed by others. Her PAI revealed that the reason for this mistrust may stem from a history of negative, emotionally abusive, and disappointing relationships in her life.

Pre-Adolescent Emotional Development

Labile Mood. The assessment revealed that the patient struggles with dramatic mood swings, the kind that would be normal and expected in a pre-adolescent. Her MCMI-III, PAI, and Rorschach revealed that she has difficulty regulating her moods. As such, she can both appear and feel erratically moody. Her Rorschach and Projective Drawings suggested that she gets easily confused by emotions, and so she tries to constrict them and not process them. In order not to feel her emotions, her Rorschach revealed that she employs intellectualization as a defense. When this strategy fails, however, she becomes overreactive, as revealed in her MCMI-III and TAT. She is susceptible to significant emotional distress, including periods of depression, periods of elevated mood, and general irritability, which was revealed in her PAI. This moodiness contributes to some anxiety, problems at times with logical thinking, and acting impulsively.

Weak Identity. Likely a result of her childhood, especially losing her mother at the beginning of the process of learning who she really is, the patient has a weak sense of who she is, and consequently suffers from low self-esteem. Her PAI, Rorschach, TAT, and Projective Drawings revealed that she does not have a clear, focused identity and sense of who she is, which has led her both to be self-critical and to seek out self-definition in others. She tends to fluctuate between short periods of feeling good about herself, especially when she feels unique and distinct in her own personality, and longer periods of self-doubt and insecurity, as revealed by her Rorschach and TAT. Specifically, her MCMI-III and Rorschach revealed that she is extremely self-critical, comparing herself unfavorably to others. Her PAI suggested that she becomes more self-critical in times of stress and conflict.

Impulsivity. Again normal for a pre-adolescent, the patient's behavior is characterized by her becoming overly impulsive. Her MCMI-III revealed that she does not tolerate frustration well, and thus she does not tend to delay gratification or control her impulses. Her TAT, PAI, and MCMI-III revealed that she can become exhibitionistic and expressive during these periods, lacking inhibition. It is likely that this trait explains her history of making impulsive, life-changing decisions, including moving to different cities with very little planning or notice.

Anxiety

The patient's assessment revealed that, likely as a result of her deep conflict about interpersonal relationships and the fact that she is reacting to others at the level of a pre-adolescent, she is coping with some anxious feelings. Her MCMI-III, PAI, and TAT suggested that she struggles with broad feelings of discomfort and nervousness. Her Rorschach revealed that she does not have adequate resources to deal well with the demands of her life, especially right now. She seems to be going through a situation that is more stressful, and thus causing more anxiety, than normal, which is likely related to her ambivalent feelings and a current interpersonal relationship. Her TAT suggested that she does not process, or even like to allow herself to feel, this anxiety, which, when stored up inside her with no outlet, can cause problems with rational thinking and contribute to her moodiness.

Manipulative Behavior

Because she relies on others to boost her self-esteem, and because she is so ambivalent and mistrustful of these relationships, the patient has become somewhat manipulative interpersonally. Her Rorschach, TAT, and Projective Drawings suggested that she is comfortable socially for the most part, understanding behaviorally what is appropriate and being very

(Continued)

attuned to others and their needs and behaviors. In fact, her Rorschach revealed that she tends to make a very favorable social impression initially, when first meeting people. However, her MCMI-III revealed that she tends to vacillate between being pleasant and agreeable (allowing others to use her and seeking out praise from them) and feeling self-pity and becoming passive-aggressive and accusatory. Further, her PAI and TAT revealed that she can be extremely demanding of others, even very early in the relationship, and that she can be preoccupied with her own needs, at the expense of caring for others. Her MCMI-III and Projective Drawings revealed that she is extremely socially savvy, often understanding exactly how to manipulate others to get her needs met, especially at the beginning of relationships. However, because of her interpersonal ambivalence, she tends to sabotage relationships before they get deep and meaningful.

Problems With Thinking

The assessment revealed that, at times, the patient struggles with difficulty thinking logically and rationally, especially related to interpersonal relationships and understanding consequences of her own behavior. Her PAI and Projective Drawings suggested that at times she has some bizarreness in thinking, such that her logic does not match the logic of other people. Her Rorschach suggested that her ability to thinking logically and make decisions based on reality is compromised in emotionally arousing situations. Specifically, because she does not like to feel her emotions or her anxiety, when forced to do so she can become somewhat confused and illogical. Her Rorschach and TAT revealed that she tends to deny the negative qualities of situations and people, focusing only on the positive, until she cannot deny the negative aspects anymore, at which point she flips to a mostly negative view of the situations and people. Her PAI revealed that her problems in thinking are often related to her expectations of others, and her Rorschach revealed that at times she has difficulty understanding the consequences of her actions, especially when they are impulsive.

Summary and Recommendations

Tati Lai is a friendly and cooperative 25-year-old, mixed-race female of half Chinese and half Italian descent. She presented for an assessment due to having several "blockages" in her life, including feeling emotionally unavailable toward men, struggling with procrastination when it comes to work, "overthinking things," and "beating myself up" over small difficulties.

She also has a history of drinking alcohol heavily, causing a need to go to the hospital, and she is currently in Alcoholics Anonymous.

Cognitively, she exhibited no difficulties or deficits in any domain of functioning, exhibiting Average overall ability compared to others her age. The only variation in her functioning was a slight strength in her verbal ability compared to her other domains of functioning.

Emotionally, at her core, she is deeply conflicted about having deep relationships with others. Additionally, her development in some areas of her emotional functioning was arrested when her mother passed away when she was 9 years old, such that emotionally, the patient is functioning at the level of a pre-adolescent. As a result of these two core characteristics, she has developed some anxiety, has become socially manipulative, and has developed some difficulty thinking clearly and logically in certain situations, especially ambiguous situations relating to relationships with others.

Currently, her abuse of alcohol is in full remission, as she reported she does not drink alcohol. There was no evidence of tolerance or withdrawal, so it seems likely that she was not dependent on alcohol. Thus, she meets criteria for Alcohol Abuse.

Additionally, because of her unstable interpersonal relationships, labile mood, difficulty with her own self-image, impulsivity (including her alcohol overuse in college), resentment, and fear of abandonment, she meets criteria for Borderline Personality Disorder.

Diagnostic Impression

Axis I	305.00	Alcohol Abuse, Sustained Full Remission
Axis II	301.83	Borderline Personality Disorder
Axis III		None reported
Axis IV		Family difficulties, limited primary support group
Axis V	GAF =	58

Recommendations

Given the patient's current functioning, the following recommendations are being made:

- As her current primary support group is composed primarily of individuals she has met at Alcoholics Anonymous (AA), she should be encouraged to continue to attend AA as long as she feels it is helpful for her.

(Continued)

- Continued work in ongoing, long-term psychotherapy can focus on:
  - Helping her build realistic expectations about interpersonal relationships, and to behave within relationships accordingly,
  - Helping her understand her interpersonal needs and how they can best be met,
  - Helping her build a self-identity that is generally both realistic and positive,
  - Managing and tolerating both her mood swings/reactions and her anxiety, and
  - Monitoring her impulsive tendencies, helping her to be realistic about the consequences of her behaviors and choices.
- Skills like those taught in Dialectical Behavior Therapy (DBT), including mindfulness, social and interpersonal skills, and frustration tolerance may be beneficial to her treatment as well.
- Additionally, Expressive Psychotherapy techniques may be useful to manage her interpersonal conflicts and resentments, as well as her impulsivity and manipulative behavior.

A. Jordan Wright, PhD   Date
New York State Licensed Psychologist

Feedback

Preparation for Feedback

Giving the feedback that someone has borderline personality disorder is not easy. Especially within the mental health field, but also in many other contexts, there is a strong negative stigma about this diagnosis. Therefore, it is important in the feedback to Tati to break down the diagnosis into its component parts, into the different aspects of herself that she will likely not disagree with. In addition, because she was receiving psychotherapy in the same clinic as the one in which the assessment was conducted, it was possible and easy to give feedback to both Tati and her therapist at the same time. This proved valuable, as both Tati and her therapist reported an extremely positive relationship, so having her therapist there may soften any negative reaction Tati may experience.

Again, the major considerations when deciding exactly how to give feedback to Tati were (a) her level of cognitive and intellectual functioning, (b) her level of insight, and (c) the specific type and amount of information that needed to be relayed to her. Regarding her intellectual capacity, she exhibited no deficit in any area, and she showed strength in her verbal ability. Thus, Tati could be given the entire report as is, without the need to create a summary sheet. Regarding her level of insight, she herself reported several areas of concern, so these areas (her poor interpersonal history, her impulsivity, her moodiness) could serve as anchors to report and describe all of the different dynamics going on. The themes that emerged from the testing, taken together, can help explain what underlies some of the concerns she has. Some of the themes would likely not surprise her, though some would be tougher to explain (the assessor anticipated some resistance to the idea that she is interpersonally manipulative, for example).

As always, ultimately, the flow of the feedback session will take its pace both from the assessor and from Tati, as the assessor will constantly check in with her reactions and feelings about the feedback presented.

Feedback Session

Interestingly, Tati was about 25 minutes late for her 45-minute feedback session (after having confirmed the time the day before). The more psychoanalytically oriented reader may interpret this as some anxiety or ambivalence about receiving her feedback, but this is ultimately the job of her therapist, not her assessor, to process. It meant both that there was much less time to give feedback and also that the assessor needed to gauge Tati's readiness to receive feedback during the session. She apologized to both the assessor and her therapist, who was joining for the feedback session, and cited confusion about the appointment time as the reason for her lateness.

As always, the first task of the session was to orient her to the structure of the report. She, her therapist, and the assessor each had a copy of the report. Using the report as a guideline for the flow of the session, the assessor quickly took her through the major sections of the report, explaining which would be of interest and why. Pausing at the background information section, the assessor explained that they would not be going into detail with that section, as it is based on what she reported in the clinical interview. If upon reading it she found inaccuracies or missing information, she was encouraged to share this with her therapist, who would, if necessary, share it with the assessor. (Because of some of the dynamics of individuals with borderline personality disorder, including the potential for splitting the two providers into good and bad, and the fact that she had a therapist in the same clinic, it was extremely important to maintain a clear boundary for the end of the relationship between the assessor and Tati; therefore, she was discouraged from contacting the assessor directly after this session.) Then the rest of the report was gone through very briefly to explain that it all built up to the recommendations at the end.

Beginning with the cognitive functioning section, it was explained to Tati that there were no areas of deficit and that her verbal functioning is her greatest strength. She seemed unsurprised by this feedback, though she made a comment about how she had not been in school for awhile and would probably do better on some of the math sections if she had studied a bit. Both her therapist and the assessor validated the fact that some skills seem to diminish the further one gets from formal schooling, both confirming that they would likely not do too well on tests of basic mathematics at this point.

The bulk of the session, as it generally does when a personality disorder emerges from the assessment, focused on the personality and emotional functioning section. The assessor first explained that he would tell her all the results (i.e., the narrative from the first paragraph), then he would go through each of the parts of the results individually to explain and discuss them further. During the presentation of the overall narrative, Tati seemed calm and thoughtful, taking the information in seemingly openly. Then the session moved to the individual themes.

Beginning with the interpersonal ambivalence theme, Tati interrupted the explanation and reported that she agreed completely with this part of the assessment. She asserted that no more explanation was necessary, as she knows she is conflicted about getting close to others. She reported that it is probably because of her conflicted relationship with her father and stepmother, which was validated by the assessor and her therapist.

Similarly, she had little difficulty taking in, understanding, and almost immediately agreeing with any of the themes that constituted the pre-adolescent emotional development section. In fact, during this part of the feedback, the assessor stopped to check in with her several times, as it seemed almost that she was agreeing blindly with the results of the assessment. Although she denied any disagreement at this point, the assessor encouraged her to continue to think about the results and discuss her thoughts and feelings with her therapist, if at any point she feels that she does not agree with or is surprised by some of them. She smiled and laughed when discussing some of the themes, such as her impulsivity and moodiness, as it was clear that she not only had no disagreement with them but recognized a very real part of herself written on the page in front of her. Additionally, she really seemed to connect with the fact that she does not entirely know who she is as a person.

Interestingly, when discussing the outcomes (anxiety, manipulative behavior, and problems with clear thinking), she again had very little disagreement with any of them. Although the assessor anticipated some difficulty giving feedback that Tati is manipulative at times and irrational in her thinking at times, she was quick to give examples of when this was actually the case with her. She cited her behavior with her roommate as somewhat manipulative, as well as several behaviors in her history with her stepmother. She also identified being in a confused state when her girlfriend broke up with her in France, as well as when thinking about some of her feelings and behavior related to her roommate's friend from school who moved to the South.

Most notably, during the discussion of the emotional functioning section, Tati asked where her alcoholism fit in, and why it was not listed in the sections. The assessor acknowledged the very good question, but asked her to hold off until they discussed the diagnosis section of the report, which was coming soon.

After the emotional functioning was discussed, which was significantly easier and less conflicted than the assessor and the therapist had expected, the assessor went through the summary section quickly, restating what had already been discussed before coming to the diagnosis. Before discussing the diagnoses by name, the lists of DSM-IV-TR symptoms were discussed. That is, instead of saying that Tati had borderline personality disorder and explaining what that was, the assessor explained that diagnoses are simply clusters of symptoms, and made sure Tati understood and agreed with the list of symptoms that made up the diagnosis before naming it out loud.

Although the Axis I Alcohol Abuse diagnosis came first in the report, the assessor presented the Borderline Personality Disorder diagnosis first. Tati had no difficulty with the list of symptoms, as they had all been either discussed in the themes of the emotional functioning section or presented directly by her in the clinical interview. When it was labeled as Borderline Personality Disorder, she seemed less worried about this label than the fact that her self-proclaimed alcoholism seemed to be missing. It was explained that excessive use of alcohol (or other substances) was one of the criteria for Borderline Personality Disorder, but because her use had been extreme enough in college to require hospitalization, she was receiving a diagnosis of alcohol abuse, in sustained full remission.

The assessor explained that there was no evidence that she was actually dependent on alcohol, which the assessor and therapist tried to reinforce was good news. She visibly seemed to have a reaction of disappointment to this conclusion, however, and the assessor stated that it is clear that AA is useful to her and that she should continue to participate in the program (the assessor pointed out that this was a specific recommendation listed at the end of the report). Although there was not much time left in the session, the assessor and therapist both spent some time checking in with her reactions of this finding about her alcoholism. Her therapist also assured her that they could continue this conversation in their own session, which was scheduled later in the week.

Finally, the assessor took Tati through the recommendations, which stemmed directly from the themes and diagnoses. Tati seemed to understand and accept the recommendations, many of which were actually for her therapist. To conclude, the assessor asked Tati about her experience of the assessment overall and the feedback session specifically. She reported that it was useful, though hard, which she had expected. She quickly thanked the assessor, as if to end the session and leave, but both the assessor and therapist asked Tati to process her feelings about the feedback for just a few moments before she left, knowing that she and her therapist could continue to process in their regular therapy sessions. She smiled brightly and said she needed time to "digest" the information, but that nothing seemed blatantly "wrong" to her.

Interestingly, as her therapist walked her to the elevator to leave, Tati asked her somewhat hesitantly if this meant that the way their therapy was going had to change, because she did not want it to. Her therapist said they could discuss this further in their next session, but she assured Tati that any changes in the treatment would be discussed openly so that they could agree on them together.

Summary

Tati Lai is a good example of how at times psychological assessment can improve upon the accuracy of clinical judgment. Specifically, any mental health provider that had met Tati at that point in her life would have likely accepted the fact that she is indeed "an alcoholic"—that is, carrying the diagnosis of alcohol dependence. The assessment revealed that her alcohol overuse served several purposes for her emotionally (tying her to her family, dulling her erratic emotions, etc.), as does her participation in AA, which provides her with both a clear identity and a social network. Tati is reportedly doing well in treatment, more able now to integrate splits in her perceptions of others, which helps a great deal in organizing her thought process.

A major aspect of Tati's assessment that was extremely useful was the fact that her assessor and her therapist knew each other well, could collaborate closely about the course of her treatment, and could even have the feedback session jointly. Especially given her diagnosis of borderline personality disorder, which often comes with splitting (it would have been easy for Tati to idealize her therapist and devalue her assessor, for example, if they had not been clearly and explicitly "on the same page"), as well as knowing her theme of interpersonal manipulativeness, the more explicitly collaborative the relationship could be between the therapist and assessor, the more beneficial for her treatment. There was no way, for example, for Tati to manipulate the information she received in the feedback session to use in her therapy sessions to devalue the process or the assessor. Her therapist was there, and she can serve as a basis for reality when discussing the feedback—that is, the therapist can know exactly which of Tati's perceptions of the feedback session were based on reality and which were possibly distorted in Tati's mind, which would likely happen given her problems with logical and clear thinking when it comes to interpersonal situations. Tati's ongoing treatment can continually be reinformed by her and her therapist's recollections and reactions to the assessment.

CHAPTER 9

A Young Man Who Steals

Jeremy Chambers, a 21-year-old man, was referred to the clinic for a psychological assessment by his mother, who found the clinic online. Jeremy and his mother actually lived in Chicago (the clinic is in New York), but they decided that the clinic was the right place for the assessment, so they planned to travel to New York for a few days. On the application, which was clearly filled out by his mother, she reported that Jeremy was having several "difficulties with impulse control," including "a compulsion to steal," smoking, and being "obsessed with porn." When the assessor contacted Jeremy to schedule the appointments, they agreed to have two full days of assessment (with an optional third day, if needed), as he would be traveling to New York just for the assessment and only for a short time. The assessor already knew this would pose an interesting challenge, as he would not have much time to decide on a battery of tests after the clinical interview. Thus, he prepared to include many different tests in the battery, if needed.

THE CLINICAL INTERVIEW

Jeremy came slightly early for the first day of testing. He arrived with his mother, a kind-looking, Caucasian woman about 50 years old, who met the assessor and then left Jeremy to do the assessment alone. Jeremy was quite tall and looked Caucasian, and he had no defining accent. He looked slightly older than 21 years old, though this was partially because of his height. He made excellent eye contact right from the beginning of the assessment, and he was extremely cooperative and friendly. There was nothing remarkable about his appearance at the beginning of the assessment.

Before beginning the open-ended clinical interview, the assessor asked Jeremy a few factual identifying information questions. He confirmed that he was 21 years old, giving his date of birth. When asked his ethnicity, he reported that he is "half Black, even though I don't look it." His native language is English, having been born and raised in Chicago. He is currently single and is living with a roommate in Chicago.

As a note on the presentation of this clinical interview, the sections that follow are not categorized into symptomatic evaluation and psychosocial evaluation, as the flow of the clinical interview did not follow this structure. The subsections presented in the text reflect as closely as possible the clinical interview as it actually unfolded, as opposed to artificially grouping sections of information that did not present themselves sequentially. That is, the presentation that follows presents how the clinical interview happened chronologically, along with the overarching questions the assessor asked Jeremy. Clarifications were occasionally necessary throughout the interview, but those questions and comments are not presented here.

Presenting Problem: So Why Are You Here for an Assessment?

Once basic identifying information was gathered, the assessor began the clinical interview with an assessment of the presenting problem. Jeremy immediately echoed, almost verbatim, what his mother had reported on the application form, stating that he has "difficulties with impulse control." Interestingly, after this statement, he simply looked at the assessor and grinned silently. After a moment, the assessor asked him to clarify what he meant by difficulties with impulse control, asking specifically "what it looks like" in his life. He looked down for a moment, then openly disclosed that there is "behavior I'm not proud of," behavior that reportedly causes family problems and that he does not want to engage in anymore. He generally works in retail stores, and he reported that he occasionally steals money from these stores. He reported that "I've gotten caught a few times, I've gotten out a few times."

Additionally, he reported that he currently smokes cigarettes. Interestingly, when he reported this, he stated that he currently smokes, then he paused while looking at the assessor intently, then completed the sentence by clarifying cigarettes. The assessor made a note of this behavior, so that he made sure to revisit the topic of substance use later in the interview, when rapport had more solidly been built. The assessor also noted that Jeremy did not mention anything about pornography, which was listed on the application form. The assessor decided not to address it at this point in the interview, again because he wanted to assure more solid rapport before addressing a topic as potentially sensitive as this one.

When asked his mood, he reported that "I am optimistic and happy." He stated that he occasionally gets into "a bad mood," but he "keep[s] an eye on the positive to get through it."

History of Presenting Problem: Can You Tell Me a Little Bit About When These Impulse Control Problems All Started?

For Jeremy, in this clinical interview, this single open-ended question was enough to get him to begin disclosing much of his history and current situation. Rather than addressing the impulse control problems per se, he began by discussing his educational and social history, as well as providing information about his family.

Jeremy reported that he graduated from high school in 1999 and went to college for a year, but he left school after a year because he became frustrated that he was not "actually learning anything or building my résumé," but rather just going to classes. As if he had researched exactly what the assessor would need to know, he began to describe his social history in high school, stating that he had one or two close friends growing up, but that he never had a large group of friends. Now, he has a best friend, the youth director at his church. He reported that he also lives with a roommate, who is also "alright, I guess." He also reported that he was "lazy" in high school, rarely doing his homework but always going to class and doing well because "I picked up stuff easily in class."

Jeremy then began to describe his family, reporting that his mother is a retired teacher who lives near him in Chicago, and his father works for a hotel in Antigua (in the Caribbean), where his father is originally from. They divorced when Jeremy was 3 years old. He lived with his mother for about 10 years, who never remarried "or even dated another man." He then moved in with his father (in Antigua) when he was 12 years old.

He stated that he had "a happy childhood," which he stated as if to end the conversation about his family.

As the assessor was writing notes, Jeremy smiled and reported that he had been previously diagnosed with "ADD," apologizing for being "all over the place." He reported going to a psychiatrist when he was younger because he was "angry at what turned out to be the divorce." His father was currently on his seventh marriage—Jeremy's mother was his father's first marriage—and he was angry when his father left. He was prescribed Ritalin, which he took until seventh grade, when he moved in with his father, who took him off the medication. This psychiatrist also provided individual therapy from ages 6 to 10 years old.

History of Presenting Problem (Revisited): So, About Your Impulse Control Problems

The assessor felt the need to refocus the discussion on the presenting problem, as Jeremy had not yet responded to the history of his difficulties with impulse control. He began to talk about his first job, which was at a small clothing store when he was 17 years old. He worked there for about one and a half years, and during the final six months of working there, he began to steal money. He reported that he took money to buy Christmas presents and intended to pay the money back, but he never did. There was apparently a lot of money coming into the store, and nobody noticed. He reported that this is when his stealing "got out of hand." However, he got caught by his manager. The first time he got caught, he apologized "profusely" and promised to pay the money back. The second time he got caught, he lied about how much he had taken, and he agreed to work to pay off what he owed. The third (and final) time he got caught at this job, his manager threatened to call the police, at which time he sold his car to pay the money back and left the clothing store.

He reported that his next job was washing dishes, so there was no money around for him to steal. But his following job was at a store that sold audio and visual equipment; he reported that he is "very good at" retail jobs, which is why he returned to this industry. Because he was reportedly making "good money," he did not steal, though he reported that he gave a few free accessories to friends "here and there." However, a customer complained that he was drunk at work one day, which he claimed he was not.

He was fired from this job, after which he moved back to Chicago, where he reported that he had an entire year without stealing, working in a jewelry store. He left the jewelry store and worked at a clothing store, where he went three months without stealing. He planned to steal $100 from the store, but his boss found out his plan to steal and fired him. He then went back to the jewelry store.

Although he spent about two months back at the jewelry store without stealing, he then began not ringing up sales, changing figures, and taking money from the register. "It started small, but then it snowballed," so much that he was stealing about $200 a week. He was caught and fired. He then went to work at another electronics store, which he stated he loved and at which he was making good money, even though he did not like the owner. He began not ringing up certain items he sold, which gave him about $300 a week of extra money. "I didn't want to do it, but I kept doing it." He left this job a week before the current clinical interview, knowing he was "screwing up an awesome job." He lied and told his friend (the youth director) he was leaving the job because he was going bankrupt, and he called his mother and father, who "all came together to help me," finding the referral for this clinic, "which I've heard is just the best."

Criminal/Legal History: So Did You Ever have Legal Problems with All of This?

Jeremy reported that he had never been arrested or had any legal difficulties as a result of his stealing—"I just got fired." He did report that when he moved to Chicago, he was driving with a suspended license, of which he was unaware. He got into an accident, after which he spent one and a half hours in jail, paid a fine, and was released. He denied any other legal involvement.

Psychosocial History: Can I Ask You About Significant Relationships?

Jeremy reported that he has never "really" had a significant relationship, his longest being about five months in duration. He stated that he dated this girl in high school, but he has not had any significant relationships since then. He quickly pointed out that he would eventually like to be married and have children, but he needs to find "the right one" for this to happen.

Jeremy then reported that he is a volunteer leader at his church, and he is very close with a male youth director at the church, who is "quite a bit older" (17 years older) than Jeremy and leads the youth ministry. He reported that this man is really his only friend. Jeremy and this youth director spend much time together and with the children in the church, with whom he has established deep relationships. They take them on retreats, sometimes spending entire weekends with the children. He paused at this point, while the assessor continued writing notes. He took a deep breath and reported feeling "hypocritical," though, as a church volunteer who commits crimes such as stealing. As he said this, he looked away from the assessor for the first time in almost the entire interview so far. At this point, the assessor tried to empathize with Jeremy, stating that it must be hard for him to feel that way. Jeremy paused for a moment, but then he seemingly pulled himself together and stated that, in the future, he would be happy working entirely in the youth ministry. He felt he needed to "sort myself out" before he could commit himself to youth ministry, though.

Alcohol/Substance Use History: You Mentioned That You Currently Smoke; Any Other Use of Substances, Like Alcohol or Drugs?

Because Jeremy had now disclosed some negative feelings and shameful behaviors to the assessor, the assessor felt he could revisit the issue of substance abuse. Jeremy vigorously denied drinking, stating that he rarely drank any alcohol and had never been drunk. He then repeated that he smokes cigarettes. When prompted again about other drugs, he did disclose that his roommate smokes marijuana often, and that he had tried it occasionally, but he actually did not like "the feeling of not being in control," so he very rarely smoked it with his roommate.

Developmental and Medical History: Okay, Have You Ever Had Any Medical Problems?

Jeremy reported having had his last general physical exam about two years ago, with no problems emerging. He repeated that he had been diagnosed with attention-deficit disorder as a child, and he also reported that he was healthy all through birth and childhood, except for having spinal meningitis at around 15 months of age. He also reported that one of the reasons he wants to quit smoking was medical, as his grandfather had emphysema from smoking. When prompted for other family medical problems, he reported that his grandmother had diabetes, his great-grandfather was an alcoholic, and his family had several members with heart disease and high blood pressure.

Multicultural Evaluation: Okay, and You Mentioned That You're Half Black, Even Though You Don't Look Like It

Jeremy laughed and stated that "it's never been an issue" because he looks Caucasian. When he was in Antigua with his father, he had many Black classmates, but where he lived in Chicago he was one of very few. But because he did not look Black (or of mixed race), most people at school did not even notice, he reported. He spoke only English at home, and he reported no difficulties with his cultural identity.

When probed a bit further on his cultural identity, he explained that his father, born and raised in Antigua, was "very proper" and not very affectionate. His mother, on the other hand, was born and raised in a middle-class White family in the South, and Jeremy described her as "an amazing woman, so warm." He said that he had not been exposed to his father's culture much as a child, as he mainly lived with his mother until he was a teenager. He further reported that "I just don't think about it that much." Although a bit wary to push the subject with him, the assessor decided to continue asking about his cultural identity, but from another perspective. The assessor asked if Jeremy had difficulty adjusting to the culture of Antigua when he moved there at 12, or with the culture of Chicago when he moved back. Jeremy simply replied, "Nope," and after a few moments of silence, he continued, saying that he is "very adaptable," able to fit into almost any situation pretty easily.

Family History: Do You Have Any Brothers or Sisters?

It should be noted that the clinical interview on the first day of testing ended after the multicultural evaluation. After reviewing his notes that night, the assessor felt there were a few more things he wanted to know, so at the beginning of the second session, he asked Jeremy if he could "fill a few holes" from the original interview. The first was his family make-up. Relatively straightforward when asked if he minded, Jeremy answered simply, "Nope." He reported that he was an only child.

The assessor then asked for some clarification about why he moved to live with his father when he was 12 years old. Jeremy reported that during the summer before seventh grade, he simply decided he wanted to go live with his father. "It was my own decision." Although prompted further, he denied any other reason that he may have wanted to leave his mother or be with his father at that time. He reported that his mother was the most important person in his life, and even when he was living with his father, he "answered more to her than him."

Psychosexual History: Okay, I Want to Ask You About Your Sexual History

Jeremy reported, "Well, I've had sex, but I'm not sexually active now," and then looked at the assessor in silence. The assessor prompted him for further information, and he reported that he had been sexually active with the girl he dated in high school, but he had not engaged in sex since then. It was at this point when the assessor referred to the original application and informed Jeremy that it said he was addicted to pornography. Jeremy, without hesitation, said, "I'm not" in a cool and somewhat detached manner. The assessor worked hard to normalize the experience of watching pornography, stating that many people are curious about, watch, and enjoy pornography, but Jeremy simply denied it, continuing to look coolly into the assessor's eyes. The assessor decided not to push the matter any further, and they began the second round of testing at this point.

MENTAL STATUS EVALUATION

Appearance and Behavior

Jeremy's appearance was actually impeccable. He was dressed extremely well, wearing a casual suit to both sessions. He was friendly, cooperative, and exceedingly well-mannered. However, at times he seemed to be trying very hard to engage the assessor, sometimes in overly familiar ways. For example, he laughed and joked with the assessor excessively, and at times he mirrored the assessor's behavior, including his posture (crossing and uncrossing his legs whenever the assessor did), his tone of voice, and at one point taking his own watch off when the examiner took his watch off to time a subtest of the WAIS-III.

Speech and Language

Jeremy was extremely articulate, clearly understanding all questions and comments by the assessor and expressing himself clearly and succinctly. His speech was appropriate in rate and volume throughout the assessment.

Mood and Affect

Jeremy reported mostly euthymic mood currently, characterized by optimism. His affect was mood-congruent and appropriate to the situation, with no overt signs of anxiety or depression. Of note, when discussing his problems, Jeremy did not display any notable change in affect, laughing and joking throughout.

Thought Process and Content

Jeremy's thought content was free of hallucinations and delusions, though he exhibited some shame related to his youth ministry and stealing. He denied any suicidal or homicidal/aggressive ideation. His thought process was goal-directed and appropriate.

Cognition

Jeremy was alert throughout the clinical interview, and his attention and concentration seemed unimpaired. His memory seemed generally intact.

Prefrontal Functioning

Jeremy exhibited appropriate judgment during the sessions, though his history is characterized by impulsivity and poor judgment.

Hypothesis Building

Now that the clinical assessment (the clinical interview and the mental status evaluation) has been completed, the information gathered can be used to create hypotheses for what is going on for Jeremy.

Identify Impairments

Jeremy's major impairment in functioning seems to be centered on his compulsion to steal, which has affected his occupational functioning, his family, and his subjective well-being. However, there also seems to be another issue that may (or may not) be influencing his current functioning. There is something related to his interpersonal and social functioning that may be impaired—it was difficult to tell from the initial clinical interview, and it did not help that the assessor had to begin testing during the same session as the clinical interview and complete it the following day, without much time to reflect on or review the interview data. With his history of having few friends, not dating, and having only one person (other than his mother) he is close to (a man 17 years older than he), along with the bizarre feeling the assessor experienced when interacting with him, Jeremy seems to have some sort of relational difficulty.

Enumerate Possible Causes

Due to his denial of subjectively low mood and other symptoms of depression (he reported no change in sleep, appetite, or interest in usual activities), it is unlikely that he is suffering from a mood disorder. However, there could be several other causes of his stealing. First, his behavior could be a response to anxiety, such that it would be a compulsion. If this were the case, he would likely qualify for *obsessive-compulsive disorder*, as his stealing could be seen as a compulsion. If this behavior is not compulsive, and is simply a problem with impulse control related to stealing, the next hypothesis would be *kleptomania*. Further, though, if there is evidence that the stealing is only one of several impulse control problems (e.g., if there is evidence that he is impulsively utilizing pornography in a way that impairs his functioning), then he might meet criteria for a general *impulse control disorder*. Finally, although unlikely, his behavior could be a residual effect of the *attention-deficit/hyperactivity disorder* (ADHD) that was diagnosed in his childhood.

Remembering that these are only *hypotheses* about what *could be* going on with Jeremy, given the potential impairment in interpersonal functioning, some type of *personality disorder* will also be posited as a hypothesis. At this point, however, it is unclear which Axis II disorder would be the most appropriate candidate, so this hypothesis will have to remain somewhat vague as we begin to select tests.

You should *always* consider (a) that the presenting problems have an etiology in substance use and (b) that the presenting problems have an etiology in a medical condition. For Jeremy, there seems to be little possibility that either of these is the case. First of all, he denied any significant use of substances (though his marijuana use may be more significant than he reported). Additionally, because of the nature of his problems, they do not fit the pattern commonly associated with medical conditions. Stealing behavior on its own is unlikely due to any medical condition, especially at his young age (there is a chance that the personality changes caused by dementias could lead to stealing behavior). Moreover, his interpersonal problems (if there are truly any) do not seem to have changed significantly at any point in his life, so again a medical etiology is unlikely. Finally, he received a full physical exam two years ago (though a more recent one would be better) that revealed no significant medical problems. As such, it will be assumed that the symptoms are primarily psychological in nature.

SELECTING TESTS

Selecting tests for the current assessment was slightly tricky, as most of the decision had to be made before the hypotheses were formed. However, a battery of tests was selected from the application form, and it was then evaluated, given the clinical interview and subsequent hypotheses to make sure testing would be adequate. Cognitively, a screening for gross neurological impairment and a test of general intellectual functioning were chosen: the Bender Visual-Motor Gestalt Test, 2nd Edition (Bender-2) and the Wechsler Adult Intelligence Scale, 3rd Edition (WAIS-III), respectively. When evaluating these tests against the hypotheses generated, as none of the hypotheses are necessarily cognitive, except for ADHD, these tests should be adequate to address the hypotheses. The WAIS-III has an index (Working Memory Index, WMI) that requires sustained attention, among other cognitive skills, and if Jeremy performs poorly on that index, then additional measures for ADHD may be warranted. The WAIS-III was given on the first day and coded and scored while Jeremy was completing a self-report survey.

The other hypotheses include anxiety, impulse control, and personality disorders. Before the assessor even knew this, though, he chose a general battery that would assess Jeremy's emotional functioning. To balance the methods utilized, the assessor made sure to employ self-report, symptom-focused measures, a self-report inventory, and projective techniques. For self-report, symptom-focused measures, he had chosen to use a Beck Anxiety

Inventory (BAI), a Yale-Brown Obsessive Compulsive Scale (Y-BOCS), and a Beck Depression Inventory (BDI). After the interview, during which he had already denied symptoms of depression, the assessor chose not to use the BDI in the final battery.

For the self-report inventory, as he did not know what the presenting problem would be specifically, he chose to use what is most often considered the broadest and most comprehensive objective inventory, the Minnesota Multiphasic Personality Inventory, 2nd Edition (MMPI-2). For projective techniques, the Rorschach Inkblot Test, the Thematic Apperception Test (TAT), and Projective Drawings were chosen. Given the hypotheses posited from the clinical interview, these emotional measures should be adequate to determine whether or not Jeremy is struggling with an anxiety or impulse control disorder. However, because a hypothesis of a personality disorder emerged from the clinical interview, the assessor decided that on the second day he would add the Millon Clinical Multiaxial Inventory, 3rd Edition (MCMI-III). This measure's strength is its sensitivity to personality and character styles; together with the other measures it should reveal any personality pathology.

Thus, our assessment's battery of tests consists of

- Bender-2
- WAIS-III
- BAI
- Y-BOCS
- MMPI-2
- MCMI-III
- Rorschach
- TAT
- Projective Drawings

ACCUMULATING THE DATA

Table 9.1 shows the results from each individual measure administered. On the WAIS-III, Jeremy performed within the superior range as compared with others his age overall, with his verbal IQ falling within the very superior range. His WMI was a 119, so ADHD Inattentive Type does not seem to be likely at this point in his life. He also performed well on the Bender-2, revealing no signs of gross neurological impairment.

TABLE 9.1   ACCUMULATION OF JEREMY'S DATA

BAI

No evidence of significant amounts of self-reported anxiety

Y-BOCS

Subclinical range on severity of obsessions and compulsions

MMPI-2

Passive-aggressive tendencies

Low self-esteem

Pessimism

Insincere in relationships

Persisting and intense anger, with difficulties expressing it appropriately

Anger toward family members

Narcissism

Dependency

Immaturity

Impulsivity

Hedonism

Impatience

Possible gender role confusion

Low boredom tolerance

Strong need to be around people

Feels misunderstood

Low obsessiveness

MCMI-III

Manipulative

Relationships with others are a means to an end

Weak identity

Some grandiosity

Low self-esteem

Oppositionalism

Extreme sociability

TABLE 9.1   (CONTINUED)

Feels inferior to others

Dependent

Highly controlled in social situations

Rorschach

Difficulty experiencing and expressing emotion

Guardedness and reluctance to be forthcoming

Strong achievement orientation

Dependency

Anger and resentment

Low frustration tolerance

Resistance to change

Decisions based on careful thinking

Low self-esteem

Little energy toward understanding complex events—oversimplifies

Gratifies needs as they arise

Intellectualizes

Inflexible

Projective Drawings

Struggles with gender identity

Strong women, weak men

Low self-esteem

Very keen observation of others

Feelings about the past are impacting him currently

TAT

Negatively affected by how he feels others see him

Impulse control difficulties

Most vulnerable when out of control

No strong men—saviors always women

Dependence on family

Desire for independence

(Continued)

TABLE 9.1   *(CONTINUED)*

Manipulative behavior

Family seen as very controlling

Behavioral Observations/Other Data

No strong male figure in life

Strong female figures salient throughout life

Stealing behaviors

Self-deprecating remarks

Some shame around stealing vs. church volunteering

Accompanied to appointments by mother

Mother responsible for application for assessment

High social comprehension on WAIS-IV

Matching behaviors of examiner

Looking at examiner during drawing tasks as if to gauge reactions

Laughing/joking with examiner excessively

Few friends

IDENTIFYING THEMES

As always at this stage, when labeling themes, some are vague (e.g., social) and some are clearer (e.g., self-esteem). Typically, this categorization process may take several iterations in order to effectively link evidence in a thematically consistent way. With this assessment, there is definitely a need to have a miscellaneous (misc.) category for evidence that does not immediately fit any defined category. Additionally, some of the evidence may not fit cleanly into categories but will be placed in them to see whether, together with the rest of the data, they make sense. For example, the MCMI-III revealed a theme of oppositional behavior, which will be placed in the family issues theme to see whether it makes sense in the context of the rest of the family issues data (if it does not, it can be recategorized later). Moreover, there are a few data that apparently could fit both into family issues and identity problems. Specifically, issues related to the weakness of men and the uncertainty of masculinity, as well as the strength of women and femininity, could fit in either category. Later we can decide which of the categories they seem to fit best. The preliminary themes for Jeremy are presented in Table 9.2.

TABLE 9.2   **LABELING OF JEREMY'S THEMES**

Themes	
	BAI
	No evidence of significant amounts of self-reported anxiety
	Y-BOCS
	Subclinical range on severity of obsessions and compulsions
	MMPI-2
Social	Passive-aggressive tendencies
Self-esteem	Low self-esteem
Misc.	Pessimism
Social	Insincere in relationships
Family	Persisting and intense anger, with difficulties expressing it appropriately
Family	Anger toward family members
Self-esteem	Narcissism
Family	Dependency
Identity	Immaturity
Impulsivity	Impulsivity
Impulsivity	Hedonism
Impulsivity	Impatience
Identity	Possible gender role confusion
Impulsivity	Low boredom tolerance
Social	Strong need to be around people
Self-esteem	Feels misunderstood
Misc.	Low obsessiveness

(Continued)

TABLE 9.2   *(CONTINUED)*

Themes	
	MCMI-III
Social	Manipulative
Social	Relationships with others are a means to an end
Identity	Weak identity
Self-esteem	Some grandiosity
Self-esteem	Low self-esteem
Family	Oppositionalism
Social	Extreme sociability
Self-esteem	Feels inferior to others
Family	Dependent
Social	Highly controlled in social situations
	Rorschach
Misc.	Difficulty experiencing and expressing emotion
Social	Guardedness and reluctance to be forthcoming
Misc.	Strong achievement orientation
Family	Dependency
Family	Anger and resentment
Impulsivity	Low frustration tolerance
Identity	Resistance to change
Misc.	Decisions based on careful thinking
Self-esteem	Low self-esteem
Social	Little energy toward understanding complex events—oversimplifies
Impulsivity	Gratifies needs as they arise
Misc.	Intellectualizes
Identity	Inflexible
	Projective Drawings
Identity	Struggles with gender identity
Family/Identity	Strong women, weak men
Self-esteem	Low self-esteem
Social	Very keen observation of others
Family	Feelings about the past are impacting him currently

TABLE 9.2	*(CONTINUED)*

Themes

	TAT
Self-esteem	Negatively affected by how he feels others see him
Impulsivity	Impulse control difficulties
Misc.	Most vulnerable when out of control
Misc.	No strong men—saviors always women
Family	Dependence on family
Family	Desire for independence
Social	Manipulative behavior
Family	Family seen as very controlling
	Behavioral Observations/Other Data
Family/Identity	No strong male figure in life
Family/Identity	Strong female figures salient throughout life
Impulse	Stealing behaviors
Self-esteem	Self-deprecating remarks
Self-esteem	Some shame around stealing vs. church volunteering
Family	Accompanied to appointments by mother
Family	Mother responsible for application for assessment
Social	High social comprehension on WAIS-IV
Social	Matching behaviors of examiner
Social	Looking at examiner during drawing tasks as if to gauge reactions
Social	Laughing/joking with examiner excessively
Social	Few friends

ORGANIZING THE DATA

It becomes apparent, when the data within themes are examined, that much of the evidence converges to offer much more specific themes than the titles previously given. For example, the social theme clearly becomes a theme about Jeremy's wanting to maintain strict control over social situations. In this case, the misc. theme did not turn out to be significantly meaningful, so some of the data were reorganized into other categories that were arguably connected or similar. Jeremy's reorganized data are presented in Table 9.3.

TABLE 9.3   J E R E M Y ' S   O R G A N I Z E D   D A T A

Test: Concept/ Theme	MMPI-2	MCMI-III	Rorschach	Projective Drawings	TAT	Interview/Behavioral Observations
Low Self-Esteem	Low self-esteem	Some grandiosity	Low self-esteem	Low self-esteem	Negatively affected by how he feels others see him	Some shame around stealing vs. church volunteering
	Narcissism	Low self-esteem				Self-deprecating remarks
	Feels misunderstood	Feels inferior to others				
Impulsivity	Impulsivity		Low frustration tolerance		Impulse control difficulties	Stealing behaviors
	Hedonism		Gratifies needs as they arise			
	Impatience					
	Low boredom tolerance					
Identity Problems	Possible gender role confusion	Weak identity	Inflexible	Struggles with gender identity		No strong male figure in life
	Immaturity		Resistance to change	Strong women, weak men		Strong female figures salient throughout life

Family Issues	Persisting and intense anger, with difficulties expressing it appropriately	Oppositionalism	Dependency	Feelings about the past are impacting him currently	Dependence on family	Accompanied to appointments by mother
	Anger toward family members	Dependent	Anger and resentment		Desire for independence	Mother responsible for application for assessment
	Dependency				Family seen as very controlling	
Control Over Social Situations	Passive-aggressive tendencies	Extreme sociability	Guardedness and reluctance to be forthcoming	Very keen observation of others	Manipulative behavior	High social comprehension on WAIS-IV
	Insincere in relationships	Highly controlled in social situations	Little energy toward understanding complex events—oversimplifies			Matching behaviors of examiner
	Strong need to be around people	Manipulative				Looking at examiner during drawing tasks as if to gauge reactions
		Relationships with others are a means to an end				Laughing/joking with examiner excessively
						Few friends

(Continued)

TABLE 9.3 (CONTINUED)

Test: Concept/Theme	MMPI-2	MCMI-III	Rorschach	Projective Drawings	TAT	Interview/Behavioral Observations
Misc.	Pessimism → impulsivity		Difficulty experiencing and expressing emotion → impulsivity		Most vulnerable when out of control → social	
	Low obsessiveness		Strong achievement orientation → social		No strong men—saviors always women → identity	
			Decisions based on careful thinking → social			
			Intellectualizes → social			

Several of the themes emerged clearly and cleanly, such as low self-esteem and impulsivity. There is more than enough evidence to support the fact that Jeremy has low self-confidence, and there is no need to adjust this theme at all. Especially interesting is the fact that the identity problems theme seems mostly to have to with gender identity issues, which may ultimately be related to his family issues.

CONCEPTUALIZING

Remembering that the task at this point is to try to create a logical narrative among the themes so that it presents a coherent story, we have to connect the following themes:

- Low self-esteem
- Impulsivity
- Identity problems
- Family issues
- Control over social situations

Before deciding on the most logical way to fit all these themes together, we will first consider the model templates presented in Chapter 4: the diathesis-stress model, the developmental model, and the common function model for conceptualization.

Diathesis-Stress Model

In applying the diathesis-stress model of conceptualization, we must try to divide the themes into (1) *traits* that are inherent within Jeremy that he likely developed at an early age and that he "brings to the picture" (diatheses), (2) *external issues* that affect his functioning (stressors), and (3) *states* that are more situational or transient (outcomes). It is important to categorize each of our five themes into these three types. Remember that as long as you can make a convincing argument for how each theme relates to the others, Jeremy will be more likely to receive feedback and take recommendations.

For Jeremy, several of the themes could be *either* part of the diathesis or outcomes. Thus, there are several different "stories" that could be constructed that would adequately describe what is currently affecting Jeremy's functioning. When thinking about stressors, however, it seems that only one of the themes that emerged from the testing makes sense as an external force on him—family issues. That is, given whatever type of person he is (whatever we decide is the diathesis in this case), because he had significant issues with his family environment growing up and currently, it has led to some problems (whatever we decide the outcomes are). More specifically, he seems to have had a difficult time negotiating the task of balancing dependency on his family with fostering his own independence, which seems to lead, at least in part, to the possibility that his mother is or was over-functioning. This struggle has left him with anger and resentment toward his family, which is in itself at odds with his dependency. Because his family environment did not support the healthy negotiation of this individuation process, given the early divorce and significant change of environment right at the moment when he should be developing his individual identity (around 12 years old), this external stressor has led to some problems in his life.

More difficult is the decision about what is more core to who Jeremy is as a person and what is more of an outcome of his personality and early family difficulties. An argument could be made for several of our themes to be diatheses, but for the sake of (somewhat arbitrarily) choosing one, we will choose his need for control over how others see him and how situations play out in general as the diathesis. It can easily be argued that he is simply the type of person whose temperament leans toward a more controlling nature, rather than this being an outcome of something else (though this alternate explanation could also easily be argued).

Because his need for control is at odds with his dependency, he has developed feelings of inadequacy and ineffectiveness, generally feelings of low self-worth. This low self-esteem is an outcome. Low self-esteem can be easily understood as an outcome in most cases, as it is general practice to try to understand the root cause of low self-esteem, rather than viewing it as core to the individual himself or herself. Also due to his controlling nature interacting with his struggle with dependency on his family, especially his mother, Jeremy had difficulty developing a clear identity of his own, especially related to understanding his role as a man and his own gender identity. Finally, his impulse control problems seem also to be an outcome, as underlying resentment about his struggle between wanting to be in control and independent and his dependency on his mother at times "spills" out, causing him to act impulsively. The diathesis-stress model for Jeremy is shown in Figure 9.1.

FIGURE 9.1   DIATHESIS-STRESS MODEL FOR JEREMY

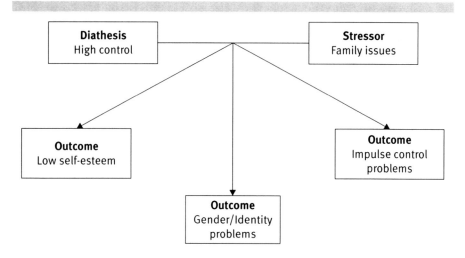

This model is not overly complex, and it appears to be arguable. The key to this model is explaining it in a way that makes intuitive sense. For example, the idea that impulse control problems would stem from the interaction between family problems and being controlling in nature may not make sense without clearer explanation that the underlying resentment that is caused by the interaction at times "leaks" out as impulsive behavior. This explanation makes clearer what may not be obvious. However, before deciding on using this model, let us consider other models as well.

Developmental Model

When considering the developmental model for conceptualizing Jeremy, it is interesting to note that he had some significant disruptions in what might be considered a normative and adaptive developmental environment—the divorce of his parents and his significant change of environment when he was 12 years old. As such, thinking developmentally may be useful for understanding what may be impacting his current functioning. Looking at his needs, wishes, and identity, we need to figure out at what developmental level he is generally functioning. Again, does he most closely resemble the feelings, needs, and attitudes normal for a child, a pre-adolescent or adolescent, or an adult? Remember that the developmental model will work only if there is a discrepancy between the level at which he is functioning and the actual age-related demands being placed on him. It is not interesting to say that he is functioning at the level of an adult and has adult demands being placed on him; this scenario should not lead to any problems. This model is interesting only when his level of functioning falls below what is being expected of him, such as being an adult with adult demands but functioning as a child. This mismatch between functioning and demands would likely lead to problems. It seems as though Jeremy is currently struggling functionally, arguably because he is functioning at an earlier developmental level than required by the adult demands that are being placed on him in life.

Jeremy is first and foremost functioning extremely well cognitively. His emotional and personality functioning, however, seem to be at a much earlier developmental stage than his chronological age. Specifically, he is struggling between the need to be dependent on a parent and feeling resentful about this dependency, an early stage of the separation-individuation process (Mahler, Pine, & Bergman, 2000). It should be noted that this process of separating and individuating from parents is necessary and normative for individuals during their pre-adolescence and adolescence in Western cultures. Additionally, he is beginning the process of identity moratorium (Marcia, 1966; 1991), the process of being curious about and trying different identities, especially around his gender identity. Finally, he is displaying poor impulse control, associated normatively with pre-adolescent or adolescent functioning.

Because he is functioning at this less-developed level that is inadequate to the demands being placed on him, there are two primary outcomes. First and foremost, he is experiencing low self-esteem, resulting from not feeling successful or adequate. Second, to cope with these felt inadequacies, he attempts to exert control over his environment and other people as much as possible. This helps him decrease the amount of unpredictability in his environment, increasing his ability to cope with the world. The developmental model for Jeremy is shown in Figure 9.2.

Again, this model is not overly complex, but the emphasis of the argument in the report would be slightly different. In terms that are not too psychological, it would be necessary to explain how the themes that represent more pre-adolescent developmental functioning in fact do so. This would make a part of the assessment report psychoeducational, such that it informs the reader about human development. It is not difficult, though,

FIGURE 9.2   DEVELOPMENTAL MODEL FOR JEREMY

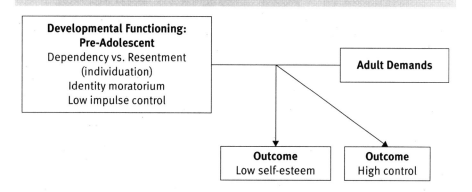

to understand how an individual functioning at this level, in interaction with the adult demands, leads specifically to the outcomes such as low self-esteem and wanting to keep tight control over situations. Thus, the model has an inherent logic that most readers would easily identify. Again, the drawback of this model is that many of the themes together make up the pre-adolescent developmental functioning domain, such that they are not interacting dynamically or interestingly. Thus, many of the subsections on themes would seem parallel rather than related directly to each other.

Common Function Model

The common function model explains the themes together as all serving a common purpose (often this purpose is served by one or two of the themes). Generally, the first step is to evaluate each of the themes to identify the overall defensive or coping strategies of the individual. This model is difficult for Jeremy, because the themes that emerged from the testing seem not to be clearly related to coping strategies. Therefore, it may be difficult to conceptualize each of the themes as serving a common purpose. However, if forced to create a model focusing on a common function, there may be a way to argue that each of the themes serves the common purpose of trying to control the world around him. That is, each of the themes represents an effort to maintain control over how others view him (for the purpose of bolstering his self-esteem, which is highly dependent on how he imagines others view him).

His family issues, which combine dependent needs with a strong longing for independence from a family he sees as controlling, along with subsequent resentment, could represent an attempt to be an individual with independent functioning while still having his mother meet some of his needs. His identity difficulties could represent an attempt to overly control how others see him in any given situation, at the expense of creating a true core personality. Finally, his impulse control problems could represent an attempt to gain attention, as the results of his poor impulse control do not place him in any significant danger (such as using alcohol excessively might), but rather seem selectively minor enough to "act out" his independence. This model is not the easiest argument to make in Jeremy's case, but if written appropriately, it could make sense. The common function model for Jeremy is shown in Figure 9.3.

This model focuses on a major dynamic that seems to be affecting Jeremy's functioning currently—the fact that he works hard to manipulate and control situations so as to maintain control over how others view him, which is how he evaluates his own self-esteem. The model does not spend time explaining this dynamic or where it came from, but it clearly describes a pattern that could easily be addressed in psychotherapy. Obviously, describing his family issues, weak identity, and impulse control problems as ultimately efforts to control his environment is not the easiest argument to make, but if it is written effectively, this narrative becomes both compelling and useful in terms of informing recommendations. However, rather than stretching these logical connections, it is

FIGURE 9.3   **COMMON FUNCTION MODEL FOR JEREMY**

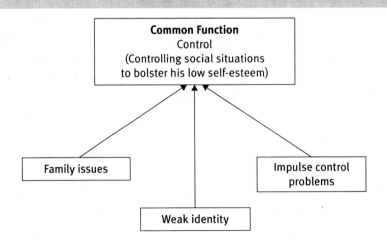

probably more useful to create a more complex model to explain Jeremy's emotional functioning.

Complex Model

While each of the models presented would be adequate, there may be other narratives that could explain the themes more intuitively and more clearly. Rather than building from one of the three existing models, however, in this case it seems to make more sense to think about which of the themes would likely lead to the other themes (such that some of the themes are both outcomes and dynamics that lead to other outcomes). If the family problems are considered the most core theme (i.e., the earliest chronologically), then it makes sense that the struggle between dependence and autonomy, along with the resultant resentment, would cause difficulty in developing a clear identity. Having a weak sense of who he is can easily lead to low self-esteem and feelings of inadequacy, which Jeremy may attempt to compensate for by trying to control social situations and how others view him, to garner as much positive feedback from others as he can, thus bolstering his self-esteem. This linear model makes sense, but in view of the impulse control problems, these may actually come from an interaction between his resentment toward his family and his low self-esteem, such that feeling badly about himself and his family occasionally spills out as oppositional behavior. The resulting model is shown in Figure 9.4.

FIGURE 9.4   **COMPLEX MODEL FOR JEREMY**

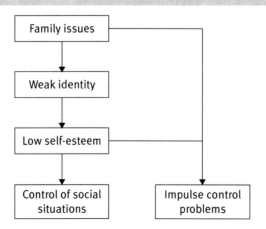

There are always multiple ways to describe how the themes work together to explain an individual's current functioning, and this is simply one more that seems to make intuitive sense. One strength of this model is that it situates Jeremy's impulse control problems (the major presenting problem) as an outcome of other internal dynamics, which can serve to decrease some of the shame about the possibility of Jeremy's being a "bad person" because he steals. Based on this model, he steals because of strong feelings he has about himself and his family, which he cannot process or express appropriately.

REPORT WRITING

Before the report can be written, one final step is necessary—the determination of diagnosis and recommendations. Our original hypotheses included obsessive-compulsive disorder (OCD), kleptomania, another impulse control disorder, ADHD, and a personality disorder. When looking at the evidence that emerged on the tests, a few of these hypotheses can be ruled out relatively easily. While Jeremy reported a previous diagnosis of attention deficit and clearly presents with impulsivity, no evidence of ADHD emerged from the testing (his Working Memory Index on the WAIS-III was adequate, which is a major indicator that his ability to attend is unimpaired). Additionally, he was able to tolerate two full days of testing with very little difficulty and exhibited no hyperactive or impulsive behaviors during the assessment. Additionally, no anxiety (in general form) actually emerged from the testing, and in actuality the BAI, Y-BOCS, and MMPI-2 revealed *low* levels of obsessiveness, so there is no evidence of OCD. Thus, ADHD and OCD can be ruled out and not ascribed to him. That leaves us with kleptomania, another impulse control disorder (potentially not otherwise specified), and a personality disorder as possible conclusions.

The major questions for Jeremy's diagnosis are (a) whether there is evidence of any impulse control problems other than the stealing and (b) whether the stealing relieved tension above and beyond monetary need. That is, kleptomania generally relates to stealing objects of insignificant value (often objects that could be afforded otherwise) in order to relieve some sort of tension. If there is no evidence of impulsivity other than stealing and the stealing represents something beyond needing money, then he would meet criteria for kleptomania. If there are other impulse control problems in addition to the stealing, or if the stealing is truly for the money, then he would meet criteria for impulse control disorder, not otherwise specified. In this case, it seems that his impulsive behavior is centered almost completely on stealing. In fact, much of his other behavior actually seems *overly* controlled. Additionally, he reported not wanting to steal any longer, but not being able to control himself, rather than doing it because he needed the money. Consequently, he seems to meet criteria for kleptomania.

The next major consideration is the question of a possible personality (Axis II) disorder. It is clear that Jeremy has some features of narcissistic personality disorder, including some grandiosity related to his low self-esteem. Moreover, he has some features of dependent personality disorder as well, which was clear from the testing data. The primary question at this point is whether or not these personality characteristics significantly impair his functioning. Although this is debatable, it seems that his social functioning *is* significantly impaired by his style of relating to others. He has an extremely limited social support system, especially outside of his immediate family. Therefore, because he does not meet full criteria for any one Axis II disorder, Jeremy is given the diagnosis of personality disorder not otherwise specified, with dependent and narcissistic features.

Recommendations, as will be presented in the assessment report that follows, will stem directly from the diagnoses and the themes. His kleptomania should be treated with a combination of cognitive-behavioral therapy and consideration of medication therapy, which together have been shown to be effective at treating the disorder. Because of the personality disorder, which is related to his interaction with others, a recommendation to enter individual psychotherapy is made. This therapy can address multiple aspects of his functioning, including each of the themes: low self-esteem, building his identity, processing resentment toward his family, and his style of interacting with others. Additionally, he will be referred to a smoking cessation program in Chicago.

Identifying Information

Name:	Jeremy Chambers	**Date of Report:**	6/28/2007
Sex:	Male	**Assessor:**	A. Jordan Wright, PhD
Age:	21	**Dates of Testing:**	6/16/07; 6/17/07
Date of Birth:	1/1/1986		
Ethnicity:	Mixed-race		

Source of Referral and Referral Questions

Jeremy Chambers was referred by his mother to the clinic to assess him for "impulse control problems," including a compulsion to steal and smoking cigarettes.

Measures Administered

- Clinical Interview
- Bender Visual-Motor Gestalt Test-Second Edition (Bender-2)
- Wechsler Adult Intelligence Scale-Third Edition (WAIS-III)
- Beck Anxiety Inventory (BAI)
- Yale-Brown Obsessive-Compulsive Scale (Y-BOCS)
- Minnesota Multiphasic Personality Inventory-Second Edition (MMPI-2)
- Millon Clinical Multiaxial Inventory, Third Edition (MCMI-III)
- Rorschach Inkblot Test, Comprehensive System (Rorschach)
- Thematic Apperception Test (TAT)
- House-Tree-Person and Kinetic Family Drawings (Projective Drawings)

Description of Client

The client is a mixed-race (half Black, half Caucasian) male who was 21 years 7 months at the time of testing. He is a tall, affable man who looks Caucasian and has no defining accent. He is courteous, personable, and smiles and laughs often.

Presenting Problem

The client reported that he has "difficulties with impulse control." When asked to clarify what he meant by this, he stated that there is some "behavior I'm not proud of," which causes difficulties within his family. He reported that he no longer wants to behave in this way, but he is having difficulty stopping. Specifically, he has been fired from several retail jobs for stealing money and merchandise. Additionally, he reported that he currently smokes cigarettes and would like to quit.

Background Information

History of Presenting Problem

The client reported that his first episode of stealing money occurred during his first job in high school, when he stole money initially to buy Christmas gifts, intending to pay it back. After that episode, he said it "got out of hand." He was caught three times by this employer, the third time having to sell his car to repay what he had taken. After that, he had several other jobs. At each of the retail jobs he held, he continued to steal either merchandise or money from his employers, each time getting caught and being fired. He left his most recent retail job because he wanted help with his problem of stealing. Although he has been fired from many jobs, he has never had any formal legal problems as a result of his stealing.

Symptomatic Evaluation

The client was diagnosed with Attention-Deficit Disorder (ADD) as a child, and he saw a psychiatrist who both monitored his medication and provided therapy from 6 to 10 years old. He was prescribed and taking Ritalin for several years, until his father took him off the medication. His previous therapy revealed that he was "angry at what turned out to be the divorce" of his parents. His father is currently married to his seventh wife—the client is the son of his father's first wife.

The client denied use of any substances, except for cigarettes and "occasionally" trying marijuana.

The client reported that he was diagnosed with spinal meningitis at around 15 months of age. Other than this, he denied any significant medical problems. Additionally, he denied significant medical and psychiatric problems in his family, except for a great-grandfather with alcoholism and other family members with heart disease, diabetes, emphysema, and high blood pressure.

Psychosocial Evaluation

The client lives with a roommate in Chicago. Aspiring to work full time in his church's youth ministry, he has been living in Chicago since he dropped

(Continued)

out after a year of college. He has had and lost many jobs, mostly in retail (which he says he is "very good at").

The client's parents divorced when he was 3 years old. He lived with his mother, who is currently single, for 10 years in Chicago. His mother is a retired middle school teacher who currently lives near him in Chicago. He then moved to Antigua to live with his father for his high school years. The move was his own decision, wanting to spend more time with his father. His father works for a hotel in Antigua. He reported that his mother is the most important person in his life.

The client reported that he has very few friends, and this has always been the case. He has one real friend, a youth director at his church, who is "quite a bit older" than he is (17 years older). The client has reportedly never had a serious romantic relationship with a woman, his longest lasting about five months while he was in high school. He reported that he is not sexually active.

The client reported that he does not "think about" his cultural identity much, except for feeling hypocritical for devoting time and energy to his church but committing crimes like stealing. Although his father is a Black Caribbean man with a very "proper" demeanor and his mother is a "warm" and caring White woman from the South, the client reported that because he looks Caucasian, he never had difficulty with his racial identity. He further reported that he had no difficulties transitioning back and forth between Chicago and Antigua growing up.

Mental Status

The client was somewhat formally and impeccably dressed, well-groomed, and extremely cooperative and friendly throughout the testing process, maintaining appropriate eye contact, even when discussing difficult topics. At times he seemed overly familiar with the examiner, joking and laughing excessively and mirroring his behaviors. His motor activity was within normal limits. He was open and talkative, asking appropriate questions and disclosing information freely. Both his receptive and expressive language use were extremely good. His mood was reportedly euthymic and characterized by optimism, and his affect was mood-congruent and appropriate to the situation, except for his continued smiling and joking while discussing difficult topics. His thought process was goal-directed, and his thought content was free of hallucinations, delusions, and suicidal and homicidal ideation. His memory seemed within normal limits, and his attention and concentration were very good. His insight is fair, but his history is characterized by poor impulse control and judgment.

Behavioral Observations

The client exhibited no problem adjusting to the testing situation, very cooperative and amiable to both the examiner and the assessment itself. Often smiling, he maintained a personable, friendly demeanor throughout the testing sessions. He seemed to concentrate relatively well on the tasks for someone his age.

The client joked often about the length of the tests and testing session, specific items (especially on the MMPI-2), and the nature of the projective tests (the Rorschach and the TAT, specifically). At several points he apologized for his performance on the projective tests: On the Projective Drawings he apologized for the time it took him to draw his large family, and on the Rorschach he apologized for not being "good at it," claiming all he really saw were inkblots on cards. Additionally, when completing drawing tasks, he constantly glanced at the examiner as if to gauge the examiner's reaction to his performance on the tasks.

Often trying to engage the examiner, including the joking and laughing, the client noticeably never exhibited any behaviors that would make the examiner view him negatively. During the WAIS-III, when the examiner took off his watch to time one of the subtests, the client mirrored him by taking his watch off simultaneously. He employed many other such mirroring behaviors, including crossing and uncrossing his legs simultaneously with the examiner, throughout testing. When discussing his problems, the client did not display any notable affect.

Overall Interpretation of Test Findings

Cognitive Functioning

On the WAIS-III, the client exhibited significant variation between his verbal and nonverbal functioning. Specifically, his Verbal IQ fell within the Very Superior range of functioning compared to others his age (98th percentile), while his Performance (nonverbal) IQ fell within the Average range compared to his same-age peers (68th percentile). Specifically, all domains of his functioning were Above Average, except for his speed of processing information, which was Average (Processing Speed Index, 27th percentile). The client exhibited no signs of neurological damage as evidenced by his Average performance on the Bender-2 (68th percentile).

(Continued)

Verbal Comprehension. On measures of general verbal skills, such as verbal fluency, ability to understand and use verbal reasoning, and verbal knowledge, the client's performance fell within the Very Superior range of functioning compared to others his age (Verbal Comprehension Index, 99th percentile). He exhibited a specific significant strength compared both to his peers and his own overall performance on a subtest requiring him to define words presented to him, which assesses word knowledge, ability to express himself clearly, and long-term memory (Vocabulary, 99th percentile). Additionally, he exhibited a strength on a subtest that required him to propose answers to everyday social problems and explain general social principles, which assesses his understanding of social situations and expressive ability (Comprehension, 95th percentile). Compared to his own overall performance, his verbal ability constituted a significant strength. His extremely strong verbal comprehension reflects knowledge gained in both formal and informal educational opportunities and demonstrates intellectual ambition and good ability to retrieve information from long-term memory.

Perceptual Organization. On tests that measure nonverbal reasoning, visuospatial aptitude, and induction and planning skills on tasks involving nonverbal stimuli such as designs, pictures, and puzzles, the client performed within the High Average range of functioning compared to others his age (Perceptual Organization Index, 86th percentile). Tasks in this domain assess the client's abilities to examine a problem, draw upon visual-motor and visuospatial skills, organize thoughts, and create and test possible solutions. While most of the subtests that make up this index were Above Average, he exhibited a strength on a task requiring him to solve visual puzzles by selecting the missing piece from choices presented, which assesses visual processing, mental flexibility, and visual logic (Matrix Reasoning, 82nd percentile).

Working Memory. On tasks that assessed the ability to memorize new information, hold it in short-term memory, concentrate, and manipulate information to produce some result or reasoning outcome, the client's performance fell within the High Average range compared to others his age (Working Memory Index, 90th percentile). Tasks in this domain require sustained attention and concentration, and well as fluidity of mental processing. All of the subtests in this domain fell within the Average or Above Average range of functioning.

Processing Speed. The client's only slight cognitive weakness, compared to his own very high functioning, was on tasks that measure the ability to focus attention and quickly scan, discriminate between, and respond to visual information within a time limit, which fell within the Average range of functioning compared to others his age (Processing Speed Index, 27th percentile). All of the subtests that make up this index fell within the Average range. The client's processing speed—the rate at which he can carry out cognitive processes—would not be considered impaired, though it is slightly lower than would be expected given his otherwise excellent cognitive functioning.

Cognitive Summary. The client's performance revealed that he is functioning generally Above Average cognitively. His greatest strength is his verbal ability, and he exhibited a slight weakness in his speed of processing information. This minor psychomotor slowing seems to be his only cognitive difficulty.

Emotional Functioning

The client was administered several standardized objective and projective measures of personality and emotional functioning. The results of these measures suggest that the client has in the past and is currently struggling with his role within his family, both wanting to depend on them and resenting their overinvolvement in his life. As a result of this struggle, he has had difficulty creating a clear identity or sense of who he is. This weak identity has led to low self-esteem, for which he tries to compensate by being overcontrolling of himself and situations he is in, in order to get as much positive feedback from others as possible. However, his resentment toward his family and his low self-esteem have led to problems with his impulse control, which manifest as sporadic acting-out behaviors.

Family Issues. The testing revealed that the client struggles with very conflicting feelings about his family, actively depending on them on the one hand, but harboring anger and resentment toward them because he does not feel independent from them. His MMPI-2, MCMI-III, and Rorschach all revealed that he is a highly dependent person, deeply needing others to help him function in everyday life. His TAT revealed that this dependence is focused heavily on his family, and in particular on his mother, who is extremely important in his life. This dependency may explain the fact that the client's mother submitted the application for the assessment and accompanied him to sessions. His TAT, however, also revealed that he views his family as overly controlling and wants to assert his own independence from them. This was supported in his MCMI-III, which revealed that he actively tries to assert his independence by being oppositional at times.

(Continued)

The tension between his dependency and longing for independence from his family has led him to feel angry and resentful toward them, which was revealed on his MMPI-2 and Rorschach. Furthermore, his Projective Drawings revealed that lingering feelings about his family from the past, which include his reported anger about his parents' divorce, are affecting him currently. This internal tension about his family has made it difficult for him to develop a clear, independent identity and sense of who he is as an adult.

Weak Identity. The client has not yet developed a clear sense of who he is in the world. His MCMI-III revealed that he has a very weak identity, unclear of what kind of person he is and can be. His MMPI-2 revealed a general immaturity in terms of his thoughts and feelings, which the Rorschach revealed can manifest as him being inflexible and resistant to change. This immaturity seems to be related to the fact that he has not yet developed a clear adult identity. Additionally, the client seems to be struggling with his gender identity, as revealed on his MMPI-2 and Projective Drawings. His MMPI-2 revealed that he may have general confusion about gender roles and where he fits, and his TAT and Projective Drawings included pervasive themes of strength in women and weakness in men. This gender role confusion may be related to anger toward his father, who left him early in his life, as well as to his over-involvement with and dependency on his mother, who is a strong female figure in his life. The result of his difficulty creating a clear adult identity is that he suffers with low self-esteem.

Low Self-Esteem. The client does not feel good about himself, suffering from low self-esteem. His MMPI-2, MCMI-III, Rorschach, and Projective Drawings all revealed his low self-confidence. His self-esteem is highly dependent on others and how others view him. Specifically, his TAT revealed that he is significantly and negatively affected by how he feels others view him. His MMPI-2 revealed that he feels misunderstood by others, and his MCMI-III revealed that he feels generally inferior to other people around him. Interestingly, to compensate for this low self-esteem, at times he can portray an overly confident or grandiose demeanor, as revealed by his MMPI-2 and MCMI-III. Even with this compensation, though, he made self-deprecating remarks throughout the assessment and reported some shame about his stealing behavior and involvement in his church. In order to bolster his self-esteem, which is highly social in nature, he has adopted a style of being overly controlling of himself and social situations.

Control of Social Situations. The client is highly adept at controlling social situations and how others view him, a tactic he employs in order to elicit favorable feedback from those around him to bolster his low self-esteem. His MMPI-2 and MCMI-III revealed that he is extremely sociable and comfortable in social situations. His Projective Drawings suggested that he carefully observes others and their behavior in order to understand them, and his WAIS-III revealed very good understanding of social norms and behavior. However, his MCMI-III revealed that relationships with others are means to an end; that is, he builds and maintains relationships primarily for what he can get out of them. As such, he is highly controlled and guarded in social situations, as revealed by his MCMI-III and Rorschach. His Rorschach revealed that he tends not to act or make decisions until he has thought through them carefully and weighed different options. Additionally, his MMPI-2, MCMI-III, and TAT suggested that he can actually be insincere and manipulative in his relationships with others. His MMPI-2 also suggested that he can be passive-aggressive in relationships, and his TAT revealed that he feels extremely vulnerable when he is not in control of situations. This high control of social situations was exhibited in the assessment by his matching behaviors of the examiner, his over-familiarity and excessive joking, and his constant glances toward the examiner during drawing tasks as if to gauge the examiner's reaction to his performance. The shallowness of interpersonal relationships may explain why he reported having so few friends.

Impulse Control Problems. As a result of his underlying resentment toward his family and his low self-esteem, the client has developed problems with controlling his impulses, which spill out occasionally. His Rorschach revealed that he had difficulty experiencing and expressing his emotions, and his MMPI-2 revealed a general pessimism, both which lead to impulsive behavior. Additionally, his Rorschach revealed difficulty coping with frustration, and his MMPI-2 revealed difficulty tolerating boredom and general impatience. Additionally, his MMPI-2 and Rorschach revealed that he tends to try to gratify all of his needs as they arise, unable to delay this gratification, which is an ability necessary for functioning well socially. His TAT revealed that the result of all of this is that he has trouble managing his impulses, and he acts out accordingly. His Y-BOCS and BAI revealed that these problems with impulse control do not seem to be due to anxiety.

Summary and Recommendations

Jeremy Chambers is a personable, friendly 21-year-old mixed-race male who was referred for assessment for "impulse control problems," specifically a compulsion to steal. Cognitively, he exhibited extremely well-developed verbal abilities and no difficulties or deficits in any domain of functioning. The only slight weakness compared to his own excellent cognitive ability

(Continued)

was his speed of processing information, which was slightly slower than would be expected for his excellent cognitive aptitude. This slightly slower speed of processing information is likely related to his style of maintaining strict control over situations.

Emotionally, the client is struggling with mixed feelings about his role within his family, both wanting to depend on them and resenting their over-involvement in his life. As a result of this struggle, he has had difficulty developing a clear sense of his own identity. This weak identity has led to low self-esteem, for which he tries to compensate by overcontrolling himself and situations he is in, in order to get as much positive feedback from others as possible. His resentment toward his family and his low self-esteem have led to problems with his impulse control, which manifest as sporadic acting-out behaviors.

Currently, because he exhibits stealing behaviors and a subsequent inability to stop them from happening, he meets criteria for Kleptomania. Currently, his diagnosis of Attention-Deficit/Hyperactivity Disorder (ADHD), for which he was previously medicated as a child, does not seem to be impairing his functioning, so it will be considered in remission. Because of his own concern with smoking, he will be given a diagnosis of Nicotine Dependence.

Diagnosis

Axis I	312.32	Kleptomania
	314.9	Attention-Deficit/Hyperactivity Disorder Not Otherwise Specified (In Remission)
	305.10	Nicotine Dependence
Axis II	301.9	Personality Disorder Not Otherwise Specified, With Narcissistic and Dependent Features
Axis III		None known
Axis IV		Problems with primary support group Occupational problems
Axis V	GAF =	61

Recommendations

Given the client's current functioning, the following recommendations are being made:

It is recommended that he enter dynamic talk-therapy to address his self-esteem, family, identity, and impulse control issues. Cognitive-behavioral techniques may also be useful in tempering his impulse control problems more immediately.

A suggested referral, which will be discussed in feedback to the client, is Jane Frost, PhD, at 800-555-2475 ext. 1. Additional referrals can be obtained from the Illinois Psychological Association at www.illinoispsychology.org or at 312-372-7610.

His therapist can connect him with a local smoking cessation program.

_____   _____

A. Jordan Wright, PhD   Date
New York State Licensed Psychologist

FEEDBACK

Preparation for Feedback

The feedback for Jeremy posed a specific problem, as it would necessarily have to occur well before the assessment report was completed. This was agreed on before the testing began, so that feedback could be given before he returned to Chicago. During the feedback session the assessor and Jeremy could collaborate about the best way to proceed with recommendations, such that he can be connected with a therapist in Chicago as quickly as possible and the assessor can get a copy of the report to the therapist as well as to Jeremy. For the feedback session, however, a summary sheet of results needed to be created.

This summary sheet serves the purpose of having something more concrete and permanent that he could follow along with during the session and keep afterward. It included a brief summary of cognitive functioning, emotional functioning, diagnosis, and recommendations. Including the diagnosis was a judgment call on the assessor's part, and it was decided that it would not harm Jeremy significantly for him to see it written and that he would likely not have a strong negative reaction to it. It certainly could be argued that it would be better not to include the diagnosis, but the assessor made the judgment call to include it for the feedback session.

Again, the major considerations when deciding exactly how to give feedback to Jeremy were (a) his level of cognitive and intellectual functioning, (b) his level of insight, and (c) the specific type and amount of information that needed to be relayed to him. Regarding his intellectual capacity, he exhibited no deficit in any area and even displayed a strength in verbal ability. Regarding his level of insight, it is unclear how much insight he has. He seems willing to address the stealing behaviors pretty readily, but he did not report much concern with his interpersonal functioning. It will be extremely important to gauge how the session is going as these themes are discussed. As always, ultimately, the flow of the feedback session will take its pace both from the assessor and from Jeremy, as the assessor will constantly check in with his reactions and feelings about the feedback presented. Taken altogether, there are no compelling reasons that he could not eventually see the report in its entirety. For the feedback session, though, only a summary sheet was possible.

PSYCHOLOGICAL ASSESSMENT REPORT SUMMARY
CONFIDENTIAL

Name: Jeremy Chambers   **Date of Feedback:** 6/18/2007
Age: 21   **Assessor:**   A. Jordan Wright, PhD

Cognitive Functioning

Verbal Comprehension:	Very Superior
Perceptual Organization:	High Average
Working Memory:	High Average
Processing Speed:	Average

Cognitive Summary. The client's performance revealed that he is functioning generally Above Average range cognitively. His greatest strength is his verbal ability, and he exhibited a slight weakness in his speed of processing information. This minor psychomotor slowing seems to be his only cognitive difficulty.

Emotional Functioning

Family Issues. The client has conflicting feelings about his family, depending on them but also harboring some anger and resentment because of their over-involvement in his life and not feeling independent from them.

Weak Identity. Because of his internal struggle between dependence on and independence from his family, the client has not yet developed a clear sense of who he is.

Low Self-Esteem. His unclear identity has led to low self-esteem, though he at times seems to overvalue his own worth outwardly, to protect himself internally, as his feelings about himself are largely dependent on how he feels others view him.

Control of Social Situations. In order to compensate for his weak identity and low self-esteem, he overly controls himself and situations he is in, in order to get positive feedback from others.

Impulse Control Problems. Because of his resentment toward others and his low self-esteem, at times he acts out impulsively and oppositionally.

Diagnosis and Recommendations

Diagnostic Impression

Axis I	312.32	Kleptomania
	314.9	Attention-Deficit/Hyperactivity Disorder NOS (In Remission)
	305.10	Nicotine Dependence
Axis II	301.9	Personality Disorder Not Otherwise Specified, With Narcissistic and Dependent Features
Axis III		None known
Axis IV		Problems with primary support group Occupational problems
Axis V	GAF =	61

Recommendations

Given the client's current functioning, the following recommendations are being made:

It is recommended that he enter dynamic talk-therapy to address his self-esteem, family, identity, and impulse control issues. Cognitive-behavioral techniques may also be useful in tempering his impulse control problems more immediately.

A suggested referral is Jane Frost, PhD, at 800-555-2475 ext. 1. Additional referrals can be obtained from the Illinois Psychological Association at: www.illinoispsychology.org or at: 312-372-7610.

His therapist can connect him with a local smoking cessation program.

_____   _____
A. Jordan Wright, PhD   Date
New York State Licensed Psychologist

Feedback Session

Jeremy arrived on time for his feedback session, which occurred the day after his final testing session. He again arrived with his mother, and as he came into the session alone, he asked if he "should" bring his mother into the feedback session. The assessor, as they both sat down in the office, decided to process for a moment why Jeremy would or would not want his mother present for the feedback. Before any feedback was given about ambivalence about his role in his family, this theme was played out in the room. Jeremy reported that his mother had "come all this way for me" and that she "deserves" to receive the feedback from the assessment. However, when asked if there were any "cons" to having his mother present during the feedback session, he stated, "Well, I'm an adult, so I guess I don't really need her." After speaking for a few minutes about whether or not to include his mother, the assessor suggested that he give Jeremy the feedback alone first; then Jeremy could decide whether or not he wants to bring his mother into the session to receive the feedback from both himself and the assessor. So the feedback session continued with Jeremy alone.

Before giving Jeremy the summary sheet, the assessor restated why Jeremy had originally presented for an assessment (mostly the impulse control problems) and explained how the summary sheet and session would be organized. Specifically, the assessor told Jeremy that the feedback would be separated into cognitive functioning, emotional functioning, and the diagnosis and recommendations. Once it was clear that Jeremy was oriented to the session, the assessor gave him the summary sheet, with the caveat that some of the terms on it may need a bit of explanation.

The beginning of the feedback was extremely easy to give, as Jeremy is functioning extremely well cognitively. His slightly lower processing speed was contextualized by the possible reasons for psychomotor slowing, including anxiety, emotional "stuff," and personality characteristics. However, the assessor emphasized the fact that his processing speed was not weak as compared with others, so there was no evidence of any cognitive difficulty whatsoever.

By far the bulk of the session focused on the first emotional theme— his ambivalence about dependence on and independence from his family. The assessor presented this theme as a developmental task that *everybody* goes through at some point in his or her life, turning from dependence on family to independence and "individuation" from them. He clearly had a reaction when reading this theme, and the assessor decided to stop the feedback and check in with Jeremy about what he was thinking and feeling. This was the first time he showed any real difficulty in looking the assessor in the eye, as he stated that his mother had "been through so much" and was "so important" to him. When pressed on why he was then having a strong reaction, he hesitantly reported that there were times when he felt "smothered." The assessor empathized with these mixed feelings and also again normalized them as natural developmentally. Almost suddenly, Jeremy laughed, looked at the assessor, and said, "Good thing I didn't bring her in here for this!" Making a joke at this point when he was confronted with deep emotions would be used later in the session to illustrate his control over social situations and over himself and his emotions.

The next two themes were presented almost simultaneously as outcomes of his ambivalent feelings about dependency. He reported that although he does not like people to know how bad he feels about himself, at times he actually does want them to know. Not in a joking way, he commented how amazing it was that the tests could pick that up, because he works hard not to let people know that he does not feel good about himself. When discussing his weak identity, he looked at the assessor and asked whether the assessor thought that was why he wanted to be a youth minister. Rather than answering this question, the assessor simply remarked that this was an interesting observation on Jeremy's part.

The final two themes did not cause much reaction. Clearly the final theme of impulse control problems was his reason for wanting the assessment originally. Control over social situations and over himself, though he had not "conceptualized it that way," also resonated with him—and the example of his joking earlier when faced with difficult emotions was employed to illustrate the point. He did state that it was "interesting" to think about where his impulse control problems are coming from (as they were presented as outcomes of the other themes). All in all, at this point, nothing had surprised Jeremy about the results.

When discussing the diagnoses, the assessor first explained what diagnoses really are—descriptions of clusters of symptoms that get in the way of a person's functioning. When he immediately looked down and saw "kleptomania," he clearly had a reaction to it, seemingly not because he did not agree with it or understand why he qualified, but he reported it was the first time anyone had used that term. Having the term applied to him was then processed a bit, such that he was encouraged to discuss what it meant to him to be diagnosed with kleptomania. He had already admitted that his stealing behaviors were a problem, but having it diagnosed as "an illness" brought up feelings in him that he was not sure about. In fact, when probed, he could not even identify whether the feelings were generally positive or negative. He said "they just feel weird." At this point, the assessor decided to stay with this rather than move on, to see whether Jeremy could identify what he might be feeling and encouraging Jeremy to consider that he may even be feeling different and conflicting emotions. Eventually, Jeremy was able to identify slightly ambivalent feelings about his behavior being marked as an illness, though overriding his ambivalence was some hope that he could get help for the behavior.

Once the assessor was satisfied that Jeremy had processed this first diagnosis adequately (at least for the limited amount of time allowed in a feedback session), he presented the ADHD and nicotine dependence diagnoses, which were much easier for Jeremy to hear. In fact, he latched onto the phrase "in remission" and began using it throughout the rest of the session. For example, when receiving the recommendations, he asked how long it would take for his kleptomania to go "in remission." He used the phrase somewhat jokingly, and the assessor pointed out that his joking manner may be one of those socially controlling behaviors.

The final, and perhaps most difficult, diagnosis to present to Jeremy was the personality disorder. The assessor first explained what Axis II means, emphasizing that diagnoses on Axis II are generally concerned with an individual's style of interacting with others and the world around him or her that may be getting in the way of succeeding in life entirely. This point was restated several times in several different ways, such that the personality disorder was presented as a maladaptive style of dealing with other people. "Oh, I've got one of those!" was his response, relating to his overcontrolling nature in interpersonal interactions. This exclamation seemed less of an "aha moment" and more of a somewhat joking but somewhat protective stance, seeing clearly on the page that he was indeed diagnosed with a personality disorder. The terminology of the "not otherwise specified" was explained to him as clearly as possible. Before he and the assessor were able to process his reaction to this diagnosis in depth, he quietly said, "I guess I need some help, then." This comment steered the session toward the recommendations, rather than staying with the discussion about diagnosis.

The discussion of recommendations focused more on the prognosis when it comes to treating what he is dealing with. The assessor assured Jeremy that now that he has accepted that he wants help, especially for his stealing behaviors, psychotherapy can be extremely effective at helping with issues of dealing with emotions, controlling his behaviors, helping him develop his identity more clearly, and dealing with others better. He asked whether Dr. Frost was "good," and as the assessor had worked with her previously, he assured Jeremy that she was extremely good; he asked if she was "as good as" the assessor, somewhat jokingly. At this point, the session switched to a discussion about giving feedback to Jeremy's mother, who was still in the waiting room.

Again, Jeremy presented his ambivalence about sharing the feedback with his mother, listing both pros and cons to doing so. In the end, he asked if he could be the one to give the feedback to his mother, "in my own words," while the assessor observed and answered any questions that arose. This process seemed like an excellent way not only to give his mother the feedback but also to solidify Jeremy's understanding of the feedback and ensure that there was no miscommunication about it. Jeremy's feedback to his mother was almost identical to the feedback he had received from the assessor, and the assessor rarely even needed to speak in the rest of the session. The assessor asked whether either had any questions at the end, which they did not, and they thanked the assessor and left, asking him to send the report to them as soon as it was ready. At this point, Jeremy scheduled a phone call with the assessor for two weeks from that day to discuss the report and the referral. That phone call confirmed that Jeremy had begun working with Dr. Frost and had given her a copy of the report.

SUMMARY

Jeremy Chambers's assessment, while a bit unusual in its time constraint, is a good example of how psychological assessment can add to clinical impressions. It would have been obvious to most mental health professionals that he suffered from kleptomania. If this were the primary presenting problem in a clinical intake, a behavioral therapy may have been recommended to stop the compulsive behavior. However, what underlies his compulsion to steal, and especially all of the interpersonal difficulties and ambivalence about his family, were not as apparent from simply interviewing. Jeremy struggles in many areas of his life. His occupational functioning is clearly compromised by his stealing, but his social functioning is also impaired, which may have been overshadowed by the more salient problem of stealing and getting fired from jobs. At a six-month check-in, Jeremy's therapist told the assessor that he was "making progress" in therapy on two core issues: his individuation and his identity development. He had not stolen since the assessment, though this likely was in part because he had not taken a retail job where it would have been easier for him to do so.

CHAPTER 10

A Boy in Foster Care

Dashawn Terry, a 12-year-old Black boy who had been in foster care for about nine years, was referred for an assessment within his foster care agency for two purposes. First, as he was in a pre-adoptive foster home and going through the adoption process, the court required an assessment to allow the adoption to go through. Second, the referral stated that he "persistently lies and exaggerates and has pervasive behavior problems." From the referral form, Dashawn had reportedly been in many foster placements during the past nine years, manifesting extremely difficult behavior, but his behavior had "improved remarkably" under his current foster family's care. Dashawn's biological parents had not had contact with him since he was removed from their home, and unfortunately nobody from his foster family was able to come in for the clinical interview. It was decided that the clinical interview would take place with both Dashawn and his case worker, Katie, who had been with him during his entire involvement with the foster care agency.

THE CLINICAL INTERVIEW

Dashawn and his case worker came for the initial clinical interview together, and they showed up about 20 minutes late. Dashawn was very thin and slightly short for his age. He looked slightly younger than 12, and he was dressed in a basketball jersey, long shorts, and somewhat new-looking sneakers. He did not look at the assessor much, beyond a glance here and there, and he was very difficult to engage. He did not seem to be acting oppositionally, but he would not answer questions or engage the assessor in conversation, even about basketball. Because he was so unresponsive, the assessor asked if it would be okay to ask Katie, his case worker, questions about him, including about his past. He nodded slightly, and the assessor assured him that he could "jump in" at any time if he wanted to.

As previously, the sections that follow are not categorized into symptomatic evaluation and psychosocial evaluation, because the flow of the clinical interview did not follow this structure. The subsections present the clinical interview as closely as possible to the way it actually unfolded, rather than artificially grouping sections of information that did not present themselves sequentially. That is, the presentation reflects the clinical interview as it happened chronologically, along with the overarching questions the assessor asked Katie and Dashawn. Clarifications were occasionally necessary throughout the interview, but those questions and comments are not presented here.

Presenting Problem: So Tell Me a Little Bit About How Dashawn's Doing?

Katie began to report on how Dashawn is currently doing, though she quickly transitioned into his history in foster care. She reported that he is currently having some behavioral problems at home and at school, though "much less than he used to." Whenever she made positive comments like this, she somewhat emphasized them with her voice and glanced over at Dashawn, before looking back at the assessor and continuing in her normal tone. He told lies often, especially about food, which he steals in the home and at school and "hoards" in his room. When asked further about this hoarding, Katie reported that he does not hoard more than a snack or two in his room at any time, but that he often takes an extra snack or two to keep for later. Additionally, he reportedly begs often, in a manner "more like a younger child." Knowing she would get back to his current behavioral problems, the assessor chose to ask about this seemingly younger behavior than would be appropriate for his age.

History of Presenting Problem: Has He Always Acted Young Like This?

Katie made a point of saying out loud that all of the information she was about to share with the assessor had been discussed openly with Dashawn many times. She reported that he had been severely delayed in his developmental milestones. He had entered foster care when he was about 3 years old, and he was not toilet trained and could not use language well enough to ask for what he wanted or needed. Although he had "caught up" for the most part, he was "still catching up socially." She reported that he currently had no friends, did not initiate conversations with anyone, including his current foster family, and seemed "afraid" of other people such as his teachers.

Presenting Problem (Revisited): Okay, So the Referral Said He Also Has Pervasive Behavior Problems?

Katie reported that Dashawn tends to be oppositional at home and at school, throwing "tantrums" when he gets frustrated. She reported that he does not deal with frustration or his emotions very well. At this point she turned to Dashawn and said, "That's right, isn't it, D?" He did not respond, continuing to look down at his lap. Katie continued, reporting that Dashawn has significant academic difficulties, and that he was placed in special education many years ago. She stated that he generally acts out when he is frustrated, either with his schoolwork or with his family at home. At times he hits other students in his class and his foster mother, though he responds relatively well to "time out" punishment. She reemphasized that he acts out much of the time, "but it's not surprising, given what he's been through—but we'll get back to that."

Family History: Well, Why Don't We Talk About His Family History Now? Would That Be Okay, Dashawn?

Again, Dashawn was mostly unresponsive, though he nodded slightly again, which Katie said was about as strong an "okay" as he was bound to give. She reiterated that she and he had talked about his family history often, that there were no secrets. So she began to talk about his history, beginning with being abandoned by his biological mother around the time he was 2 years old. She said that they were not sure whether he had been physically abused by her (or someone else) before that time, but they suspected he had been. He was reportedly living alone in an apartment for several months at that age until he was taken into foster care. How he survived is unclear, but he was extremely emaciated when he came to the foster care agency and went into his first foster home. He did not speak, did not walk well, and was not toilet trained.

Katie then recounted his experiences with foster families. His first foster mother, with whom he reportedly connected well, died after only a few months of caring for him. Her daughter then became his foster mother, but she physically and mentally abused him, including punishing him by making him eat sour and spoiled food. Despite this, Dashawn had a strong attachment to this home and this foster mother, the original foster mother's daughter. After about a year, the foster care agency closed this foster home, and he moved to about 15 other homes within the next few years. During these years, Dashawn was "uncontrollable" and "unruly," and he did not connect well with any of the foster parents.

When he was about 7 years old, he moved to a pre-adoptive foster home with a foster mother, foster father, and foster brother (who had also been fostered by the family for about a year before Dashawn arrived). Dashawn reportedly behaved much better when he moved in with this family. Shortly after he moved to this home, the foster brother was moved to a therapeutic foster home, as he was seemingly "emotionally disturbed." Dashawn began acting out again, and his foster parents "called him stupid" and used adoption as a threat, telling him that if he did not behave, they would not adopt him and nobody else ever would either. This foster home was closed by the agency as well, and Dashawn was extremely upset, especially at losing his foster father.

At this point, several years ago, Dashawn moved into his current pre-adoptive foster home. His current home, according to Katie, is very good and highly nurturing. His behavior, reportedly, has improved dramatically at home. His current foster mother wants to adopt him, "which is fantastic, isn't it, D?" Again, she elicited only a slight nod from Dashawn. She went on to state that he still has some problems, but he is doing "much better" than he ever has.

Psychosocial History: Can You Tell Me About Significant Friends He's Had?

Katie reported that he had never really had any friends that she knows about. There had been some peers he had "gotten along with" at different times, but he never engaged them or went up to them at school. She turned and asked Dashawn if she was wrong, but she got no response from him. She reported that his foster mother reported the same to her. Katie added that it was "a shame 'cause he's a really nice kid, really." The assessor told Katie that he was going to ask her several very specific questions at this point.

Criminal/Legal History: Any Legal Involvement, Other Than Foster Care?

Katie denied any history of legal involvement for Dashawn.

Alcohol/Substance Use History: Do You Know If He Uses Any Drugs or Drinks Alcohol?

Katie reported that she was "fairly sure" he did not use any substances.

Psychosexual History: Do You Know If He Is Sexually Active?

Katie, who clearly had a comfortable relationship with Dashawn, laughed, looked at him, and said, "He better not be!" It was at this point that Dashawn first showed any sort of reaction, glancing at her and smiling slightly.

Medical History: Has He Ever Had Any Significant Medical Problems?

Other than his delays in developmental milestones, Katie reported that he had not had any significant medical issues.

Psychiatric History: Has He Been in Therapy or Any Other Psychiatric Treatment?

Katie reported that he had consistently been in play therapy at the foster care agency since he first came to the agency. She reported that different therapists had diagnosed him with "depression, anxiety, and delinquent disorders," but that in his consultations with psychiatrists he had never been put on psychotropic medication. She reported that she was not sure if the play therapy had been helpful, but because of his behavior the agency required it. He had not been in therapy for the past nine months because of turnover at the agency, however.

Multicultural Evaluation: Can You Tell Me a Bit About Dashawn's Cultural Background?

Katie looked at the assessor a little puzzled when asked this. Admittedly, the assessor was not sure how salient this issue was for Dashawn, but he asked anyway, just in case it turned out to be interesting. Upon clarification, Katie reported that all his foster home placements had been Black, and that his school was predominantly Black, so she doubted that played a large role in his adjustment. At this point, the assessor asked Katie to leave so that he could speak with Dashawn alone for a bit.

Follow-Up: So, Do You Agree With Everything Katie Said, or Did She Miss Anything?

Although he did not look at the assessor, Dashawn did speak, stating, "I guess that's it." Upon probing, he did not reveal any more about himself, but he did confirm that he agreed with everything Katie had reported.

MENTAL STATUS EVALUATION

Appearance and Behavior

Dashawn was well groomed and casually dressed in a basketball jersey. He was very small and thin, though he did not look unhealthy. During the clinical interview, he was extremely disengaged and made very little eye contact with the assessor or his case worker. During the testing sessions, he at times became oppositional, not wanting to finish tasks and throwing some of the testing materials around the room.

Speech and Language

Dashawn did not speak much, but when he did he was coherent. He made points simply and clearly, and there was no evidence of receptive language difficulty.

Mood and Affect

Dashawn did not report his current mood, even when asked, and his affect was flat and disengaged throughout, except for the times when he was noticeably angry. He did report some sadness toward the end of the assessment.

Thought Process and Content

Dashawn's thought process seemed clear and logical, free of hallucinations and delusions. His thought content was difficult to assess, though late in the assessment, during casual conversation, he did report some sadness.

Cognition

Despite being quiet and disengaged, Dashawn seemed alert throughout the clinical interview, and his attention and concentration seemed unimpaired. His memory seemed generally intact.

Prefrontal Functioning

Dashawn exhibited, and his case worker reported, difficulties with impulse control. His decision-making and planning abilities seemed delayed for his age.

HYPOTHESIS BUILDING

Now that the clinical assessment (the clinical and collateral interviews and the mental status evaluation) has been completed, the information gathered can be used to create hypotheses for what is going on for Dashawn.

Identify Impairments

Dashawn's two major impairments in functioning seem to be his interpersonal difficulties and his behavior problems, both at home and at school. His interpersonal impairment was exhibited both in his extremely limited socialization at school and his guarded, closed-off interactions within the clinical interview and testing sessions. Additionally, he is clearly having academic difficulties, and it will be important to try to determine how much of this is due to his behavior problems in school and how much is due to his cognitive functioning or learning ability. Clearly, his environmental instability, especially with regard to his shifting from family to family so much, has had a great impact on his current functioning.

Enumerate Possible Causes

Beginning with his interpersonal difficulties, there could be several reasons for Dashawn's guarded and inhibited social behavior. Knowing that he had been severely abused and neglected early in his life, it is possible that he would meet criteria for *reactive attachment disorder, inhibited type*. However, there are other possibilities for this behavior as well. Specifically, he could meet criteria for a *pervasive developmental disorder (PDD)*, as each PDD includes disturbance in interpersonal connectedness and behavior. Additionally, it could be part of a less pervasive problem, such as *depression* or *anxiety*. However, because there does not seem to have been a change in this inhibited interpersonal behavior during the past nine years, it is likely that one of the first two diagnoses is more appropriate.

When considering his behavior problems, we must consider both *oppositional-defiant disorder* and *conduct disorder*, though the behavior does not seem nearly severe enough to fall under the latter category. Oppositional-defiant disorder, however, should be the last choice to explain the behavior, diagnosed only if every other possible cause has been ruled out. The other possible causes for his behavior disturbance include an *adjustment disorder*, as he has clearly had chronic stressors and transitions in his life; a *mood disorder*, such as one of the depressive disorders; or an *anxiety disorder*, such as post-traumatic stress disorder or a more generalized anxiety disorder. His acting out could also be related to the possibility of the *pervasive developmental disorder*, though given his circumstances and traumatic history, his behavior may be beyond what would be explainable by the PDD.

Turning to his academic problems, while his behavior at school seems to be playing a large role in his academic difficulties, there is a chance that there is something additional going on cognitively. While, again, this impairment could be caused by the possible *pervasive developmental disorder*, it could also be caused by a *learning disorder*. Alternatively, his academic difficulties may stem from poor intellectual functioning, so we must consider *mental retardation* and *borderline intellectual functioning*.

You should always consider (a) that the presenting problems have an etiology in substance use and (b) that the presenting problems have an etiology in a medical condition. For Dashawn, neither of these seems to be the case. The foster care agency conducts drug screenings on all foster children (and foster parents) over the age of 10, and drug tests had shown no evidence that Dashawn was using any substances. Further, as part of the adoption process, Dashawn was required to have a full physical examination and blood workup, which revealed no evidence of medical problems. It will be assumed that the symptoms are primarily psychological in nature, which is not surprising given his severely traumatic history.

SELECTING TESTS

Selecting tests for the current assessment should seem relatively straightforward. However, because of the constraints of the setting, there was a limited amount of time available to complete the assessment. Some measures, even though ideally they would be part of the battery, were impossible to give. It was decided that the cognitive testing would be slightly truncated, not because it is less important, but because his academic functioning was not the central question of the adoption assessment. Moreover, whereas a measure of IQ is *extremely* important for several of our hypotheses (including the pervasive developmental disorders, mental retardation, and borderline intellectual functioning), once an IQ score emerged, the importance of achievement testing for the possible learning disorder could be reevaluated. That is, if it turned out that Dashawn had extremely low intellectual functioning, he would not be expected to do well academically, nor would he likely meet criteria for a learning disorder. So it was decided that, for the cognitive testing, the battery would include the Bender Visual-Motor Gestalt Test, 2nd Edition (Bender-2) and the Wechsler Intelligence Scale for Children, 4th Edition (WISC-IV). The Bender-2 would help rule out gross neurological impairment, and the WISC-IV would provide the general level of intellectual functioning. If needed (i.e., if his IQ alone would not explain his academic difficulties), then several subtests of the Woodcock-Johnson Tests of Achievement, 3rd Edition (WJ-III) would be added to the battery.

The other hypotheses include anxiety, mood, adjustment, reactive attachment, and oppositional-defiant disorders. Because of his age and the lack of reliable people in his life to report collateral information on him, the types of measures able to be used were limited. Ideally, measures such as the Behavioral Assessment for Children, 2nd Edition (BASC-2), the Personality Inventory for Children, 2nd Edition (PIC-2), and the Vineland Adaptive Behavior Scales, 2nd Edition (Vineland-II) would be chosen for an assessment such as Dashawn's to obtain collateral measures of his functioning, but they were not feasible in this case. The objective measure chosen for this assessment was the Millon Pre-Adolescent Clinical Inventory (M-PACI), to obtain a self-report perspective on how Dashawn is functioning in general. To supplement the assessment, several projective tests were chosen, to reveal Dashawn's underlying dynamics as accurately as possible. For these projective techniques, the Rorschach Inkblot Test, the Thematic Apperception Test (TAT), the Sentence Completion Test—Child, and Projective Drawings were chosen. Given the hypotheses posited from the clinical interview, these emotional measures should be adequate to determine what is underlying Dashawn's problem behaviors.

Thus, our assessment's battery of tests will consist of

- Bender-2
- WISC-IV
- WJ-III (if needed)
- M-PACI
- Rorschach
- TAT
- Sentence Completion Test—Child
- Projective Drawings

ACCUMULATING THE DATA

Table 10.1 shows the results from each individual measure administered. On the WISC-IV, Dashawn performed within the borderline range as compared with others his age overall (Full Scale IQ of 74, 4th percentile). His verbal comprehension and perceptual reasoning indices both fell within the borderline range (8th and 5th percentiles, respectively); his processing speed was low average (9th percentile); and his working memory was average (32nd percentile). He performed within the low average range on the Bender-2, with adequate motor and perceptual performance. Because of the limited time available and his low performance on the WISC-IV

TABLE 10.1   ACCUMULATION OF DASHAWN'S DATA

M-PACI
Fears and anxiety
Some depressive moods
Disruptive behaviors
Extremely high inhibited score
Very low confident score
Very low outgoing score

Rorschach
Susceptible to periods of affective disturbance, including depression
Unable to process complex emotions
Oppositional tendencies
Resentment toward environment
Fear of others
Very limited capacity to form close attachments
Less interest in others than others his age
Difficulty understanding complex situations
Simplistic in his view of the world
Anger
Loneliness
Low self-esteem

TAT
Anger toward others
Aggressive tendencies
Isolation
Fear of others in his environment
Concrete thinking
Feelings of vulnerability
Lack of support
Inability to create positive connections to other people

Sentence Completion Test—Child
Loneliness
Aggression
Very little positive interpersonal capacity
Frustration
Anger toward adults

(Continued)

TABLE 10.1 *(CONTINUED)*

Projective Drawings
  Unwillingness to form attachments to others
  Loneliness
  Low self-esteem
  Resentment toward others in his life
  Lack of strong support in his life
  Simplistic view of the world and other people

Behavioral Observations/Other Data
  Reportedly lies often
  "Pervasive behavior problems"
  Neglect and abuse from mother
  Abuse within foster homes
  Academic difficulty/special education
  Begs a lot
  Severe delays of developmental milestones
  No friends
  All drawing tasks—extremely aggressive with pencil
  Detached from assessor
  Inhibited
  Oppositional behavior in sessions
  Became fidgety when emotional content emerged in the testing

overall, it was decided not to administer the WJ-III to evaluate for a learning disorder.

IDENTIFYING THEMES

At this stage, some of the themes are clearer than others. For example, there seems to be a great deal of evidence that Dashawn is struggling with depressed mood as shown by all of the testing instruments. However, some themes are less clear, such as something that is emerging about his environment. Additionally, as usual, there is a need for a miscellaneous category in order to examine some of the evidence together to try to make sense of it. The preliminary themes for Dashawn are presented in Table 10.2.

TABLE 10.2   **LABELING OF DASHAWN'S THEMES**

Themes

	M-PACI
Fear	Fears and anxiety
Depression	Some depressive moods
Behavior	Disruptive behaviors
Interpersonal	Extremely high inhibited score
Depression	Very low confident score
Interpersonal	Very low outgoing score
	Rorschach
Depression	Susceptible to periods of affective disturbance, including depression
Miscellaneous	Unable to process complex emotions
Behavior	Oppositional tendencies
Environment	Resentment toward environment
Fear	Fear of others
Interpersonal	Very limited capacity to form close attachments
Interpersonal	Less interest in others than others his age
Cognitive	Difficulty understanding complex situations
Cognitive	Simplistic in his view of the world
Anger	Anger
Depression	Loneliness
Depression	Low self-esteem
	TAT
Anger	Anger toward others
Behavior	Aggressive tendencies
Interpersonal	Isolation
Fear	Fear of others in his environment
Cognitive	Concrete thinking
Fear	Feelings of vulnerability
Environment	Lack of support
Interpersonal	Inability to create positive connections to other people
	Sentence Completion Test—Child
Depression	Loneliness
Behavior	Aggression

(Continued)

TABLE 10.2   (CONTINUED)

Themes

Interpersonal	Very little positive interpersonal capacity
Miscellaneous	Frustration
Anger	Anger toward adults
	Projective Drawings
Interpersonal	Unwillingness to form attachments to others
Depression	Loneliness
Depression	Low self-esteem
Environment	Resentment toward others in his life
Environment	Lack of strong support in his life
Cognitive	Simplistic view of the world and other people
	Behavioral Observations/Other Data
Behavior	Reportedly lies often
Behavior	"Pervasive behavior problems"
Environment	Neglect and abuse from mother
Environment	Abuse within foster homes
Cognitive	Academic difficulty/special education
Miscellaneous	Begs a lot
Cognitive	Severe delays of developmental milestones
Interpersonal	No friends
Anger	All drawing tasks—extremely aggressive with pencil
Interpersonal	Detached from assessor
Interpersonal	Inhibited
Behavior	Oppositional behavior in sessions
Miscellaneous	Became fidgety when emotional content emerged in the testing

Organizing the Data

When the data are examined within themes, some of the themes become clearer and more specific. For example, the behavior theme clearly converges as acting-out behavior. Some of the themes do not seem to come together just yet, but laying it out this way can help us to think about the data in a more thematic way and to reconsider some of the themes. Dashawn's reorganized data are presented in Table 10.3.

When the data are laid out this way, it seems that several themes can be combined to create more coherent, better supported alternative

TABLE 10.3 DASHAWN'S ORGANIZED DATA

Test: Concept/Theme	M-PACI	Rorschach	TAT	Sentence Completion-Child	Projective Drawings	Interview/ Behavioral Observations
Fear	Fears and anxiety	Fear of others	Fear of others in his environment			
Depression	Some depressive moods	Susceptible to periods of affective disturbance, including depression		Loneliness	Loneliness	
		Loneliness				
		Low self-esteem			Low self-esteem	
Acting-Out Behavior	Disruptive behaviors	Oppositional tendencies	Aggressive tendencies	Aggression		Reportedly lies often
						Oppositional behavior in sessions
						"Pervasive behavior problems"
Interpersonal Inhibition	Extremely high inhibited score	Very limited capacity to form close attachments	Isolation	Very little positive interpersonal capacity	Unwillingness to form attachments to others	No friends
	Very low outgoing score	Less interest in others than others his age				Detached from assessor
						Inhibited

(Continued)

TABLE 10.3 (CONTINUED)

Test: Concept/Theme	M-PACI	Rorschach	TAT	Sentence Completion-Child	Projective Drawings	Interview/ Behavioral Observations
Environment	Resentment toward environment		Lack of support		Resentment toward others in his life	Neglect and abuse from mother
					Lack of strong support in his life	Abuse within foster homes
Concrete and Limited Cognitive Ability		Difficulty understanding complex situations	Concrete thinking		Simplistic view of the world and other people	Academic difficulty/ special education
		Simplistic in his view of the world				Severe delays of developmental milestones
Anger		Anger	Anger toward others	Anger toward adults		All drawing tasks— extremely aggressive with pencil
Miscellaneous		Unable to process complex emotions		Frustration		Begs a lot
						Became fidgety when emotional content emerged in the testing

themes. Specifically, in figuring out which theme is truly emerging about Dashawn's environment, it seems that some of the other themes center on his environment as well. Consequently, a combined theme of fear and resentment toward his environment can emerge. Much of the miscellaneous data can fit into the concrete cognitive theme. The final themes are shown in Table 10.4.

CONCEPTUALIZING

Remembering that the task at this point is to try to create a logical narrative among the themes so that it presents a coherent story, we have to connect the following themes:

- Fear and resentment toward his environment
- Depression
- Acting-out behavior
- Interpersonal inhibition
- Concrete and limited cognitive ability

Before deciding on the most logical way to fit all these themes together, we will first consider the model templates presented in Chapter 4: the diathesis-stress model, the developmental model, and the common function model.

Diathesis-Stress Model

In applying the diathesis-stress model of conceptualization, we must try to divide the themes into (1) *traits* that are inherent within Dashawn that he likely developed at an early age and that he "brings to the picture" (diatheses), (2) *external issues* that affect his functioning (stressors), and (3) *states* that are more situational or transient (outcomes). It is important to categorize each of our five themes into these three types. Remember that as long as you can make a convincing argument for how each theme relates to the others, Dashawn, the foster care agency, and even the court will be more likely to receive feedback and take recommendations.

For Dashawn, this model seems pretty straightforward and easy to construct. That is, there is one theme that is very clearly a stressor, and one of two themes could arguably be the diathesis. Specifically, especially given what we know about Dashawn's background and family life, his chaotic

TABLE 10.4   DASHAWN'S REORGANIZED DATA

Test: Concept/Theme	M-PACI	Rorschach	TAT	Sentence Completion-Child	Projective Drawings	Interview/ Behavioral Observations
Fear and Resentment Toward His Environment	Fears and anxiety	Fear of others	Fear of others in his environment		Resentment toward others in his life	Neglect and abuse from mother
	Resentment toward environment	Anger	Lack of support		Lack of strong support in his life	Abuse within foster homes
			Anger toward others	Anger toward adults		All drawing tasks— extremely aggressive with pencil
Depression	Some depressive moods	Susceptible to periods of affective disturbance, including depression		Loneliness	Loneliness	
		Loneliness				
		Low self-esteem		Low self-esteem	Low self-esteem	
Acting-Out Behavior	Disruptive behaviors	Oppositional tendencies	Aggressive tendencies	Aggression		Reportedly lies often

Category						
						Oppositional behavior in sessions
						"Pervasive behavior problems"
						Begs a lot
Interpersonal Inhibition	Extremely high inhibited score	Very limited capacity to form close attachments	Isolation	Very little positive interpersonal capacity	Unwillingness to form attachments to others	No friends
	Very low outgoing score	Less interest in others than others his age				Detached from assessor
						Inhibited
Concrete and Limited Cognitive Ability		Difficulty understanding complex situations	Concrete thinking	Frustration	Simplistic view of the world and other people	Academic difficulty/ special education
		Simplistic in his view of the world				Severe delays of developmental milestones
		Unable to process complex emotions				Became fidgety when emotional content emerged in the testing

environment, and his reactive feelings toward it, the combination of these is very likely what triggered any predisposition for difficulty he may have had. In terms of diathesis, both his inability to form relationships and his limited cognitive ability could arguably fit in the model.

However, it is probably more logical to consider his limited cognitive ability the factor that he contributes more basically. A child with limited ability to understand everything that goes on around him as well as his own emotions, combined with an abusive and chaotic environment, could be easily expected to have some problematic outcomes. In this case, his inability to form attachments to others, his depression, and his acting-out behaviors emerge as a result of his limited cognitive ability and his abusive environment. This is likely not a difficult model to "sell" in a report—it makes intuitive sense. The diathesis-stress model for Dashawn is shown in Figure 10.1.

This model is straightforward, intuitive, and easily arguable. A child who has difficulty understanding his own emotions and interpersonal and environmental nuances when faced with a chaotic and abusive environment is very likely to become inhibited in social interactions, to be depressed, and to act out. This may be the easiest and most easily received model, but before deciding on using this model, other models should be considered as well.

FIGURE 10.1   **DIATHESIS-STRESS MODEL FOR DASHAWN**

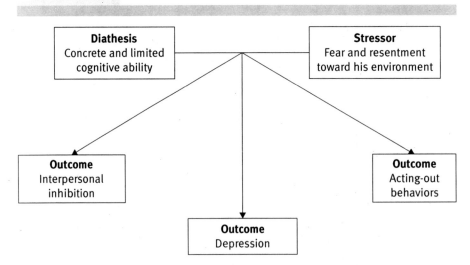

Developmental Model

The developmental model for Dashawn requires knowledge of normative development for a pre-adolescent male. What would be expected is the beginning of his own identity development, including balancing a healthy dependence on his family with an increasing focus on peer relationships. It is important to keep in mind that the majority of pre-adolescents and adolescents navigate this period of life well, so even though some moodiness and erratic or boundary-testing behavior is associated with this age, extremes of any of these would still be considered atypical. Given the themes that emerged from Dashawn's testing, a few provide evidence of his level of developmental functioning. First of all, combined with his level of cognitive functioning as measured by the WISC-IV, his concrete and limited cognitive ability is more normative for a much younger child. Similarly, his interpersonal inhibition indicates normative functioning for a much younger child who is still highly dependent on his or her caregivers, before he or she has begun wandering out and testing the world. Dashawn's developmental functioning seems to be that of a much younger child, which is not surprising in view of his upbringing. However, he is still faced with the real-world challenges of a pre-adolescent boy.

Because he is functioning at this less-developed level, which is inadequate to meet the demands being placed on him, there are three primary outcomes. First and foremost, it is no surprise that he would fear and resent his environment, because anyone at the age at which he is functioning has many dependent needs, which in his case have not been consistently met (if at all). In addition, his low developmental functioning and pre-adolescent life demands are causing his depression and acting-out behaviors. The developmental model for Dashawn is shown in Figure 10.2.

This model, like the diathesis-stress model, is relatively straightforward and intuitive. The benefit of this model is its emphasis on the developmentally delayed aspect of Dashawn's presentation. While he may not meet criteria for some sort of developmental delay diagnosis, the developmental model nonetheless offers a useful way of conceptualizing Dashawn's functioning. Additionally, it can help predict his behavior (he is likely to respond, at least somewhat, as a much younger child would respond in similar situations), as well as drive a developmental treatment. The major drawback to this model would be clearly explaining the link between the

FIGURE 10.2   DEVELOPMENTAL MODEL FOR DASHAWN

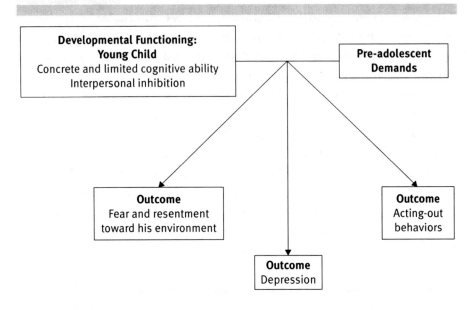

developmental level, the age-related demands, and some of the nuances of the outcomes, such as resentment toward his environment. Had only fear toward his environment emerged, this model might have fit his presentation in a "cleaner" way. However, in a write-up, this model would still not be too difficult to argue.

Common Function Model

The common function model explains the themes taken together as all serving a common purpose (often this purpose is indicated by one or two of the themes). Generally, the first step is to evaluate each theme to identify the overall defensive or coping strategies of the individual. For Dashawn, it makes the most sense to begin with what the common function would likely be. Given his themes, it is most likely that he would be working hard to deal with his fear and resentment toward his environment, especially given his difficulty dealing with complex situations and understanding his own emotions.

The remaining themes must be conceptualized as ways of dealing with his scary and maddening environment. His interpersonal inhibition certainly seems to make sense within this perspective: He has been so hurt by others that he simply keeps himself isolated as much as possible from people, who all have the capacity to hurt him. Further, his acting-out behaviors could also serve the purpose of distancing himself from others (they certainly distance him from his foster mother and his teachers, but likely also him from peers).

The only theme that is difficult to conceptualize in this way is his depression and loneliness. While these seem more like outcomes of his (somewhat failing) common function, depression can still be conceptualized as a distancing mechanism. Those who feel depressed often isolate themselves, and their affect is often off-putting to those around them. While the aptness of this model is not the easiest argument to make in Dashawn's case, if written appropriately, it could make sense. The common function model for Dashawn is shown in Figure 10.3.

The major benefit of this model is that it works effectively to de-pathologize what is happening with Dashawn. While he is manifesting symptoms such as depression and behavior problems, the overarching cause of these problems is firmly rooted in his chaotic and abusive environment. The model emphasizes the impact his extremely difficult upbringing has had on his current functioning. Its only real drawback is the non-intuitiveness of positing that his depression acts as a coping mechanism of

FIGURE 10.3   **COMMON FUNCTION MODEL FOR DASHAWN**

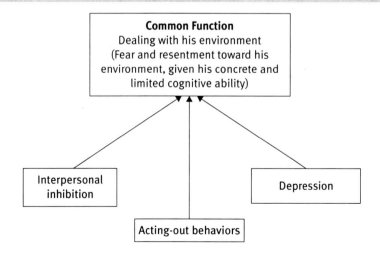

some sort for his chaotic environment. Before committing to this or one of the other models, let us consider a more complex model, incorporating some of the strengths of the other models.

Complex Model

Although all the models presented explain Dashawn's functioning pretty well, there are other narratives that could explain the themes somewhat differently. Regarding the major strengths of these models, the diathesis-stress model offers a good argument for what is underlying most of his difficulties. That is, the combination of his limited cognitive ability and the chaotic, difficult environment he has grown up in seem to explain why he would have any difficulties at all. However, the common function model offers a compelling argument that his interpersonal inhibition is a way of coping with the difficult environment, rather than simply just a result of it.

Rather than linking his depression to his cognitive ability, as the diathesis-stress model does, it may be more logical to relate it to a combination of his difficult environment and his interpersonal isolation, which intuitively could easily cause an individual to become depressed (regardless of his or her level of cognitive functioning). Acting-out behaviors are often seen as a result of childhood depression and thus could easily just be linked to the depression, because part of the limited cognitive ability results from his difficulty in understanding his own emotions. Furthermore, his limited cognitive functioning would likely exacerbate the acting-out behaviors as a way his depression is manifested. The complex model for Dashawn is shown in Figure 10.4.

Although this model *looks* slightly complicated and difficult to explain when presented graphically, each of the relationships between the themes in this model makes intuitive sense and can be easily argued. More importantly, the acting-out behaviors are situated in this model as a manifestation of his depression. This link both incorporates what is known about childhood depression and informs the diagnosis (acting-out behaviors can be a symptom of depression, rather than calling for a diagnosis such as oppositional-defiant disorder alone). As always, there are definitely other ways of combining the themes that would make sense for Dashawn's situation, but this one provides a clear way to organize the data.

FIGURE 10.4   **COMPLEX MODEL FOR DASHAWN**

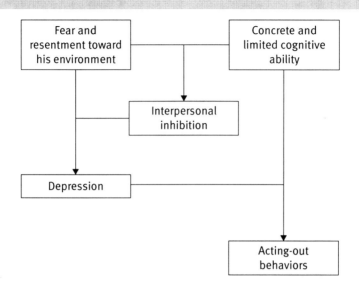

REPORT WRITING

Before the report can be written, one final step is necessary—the determination of diagnosis and recommendations. Our original hypotheses included a pervasive developmental disorder (PDD), reactive attachment disorder, learning disorder, cognitive deficit (mental retardation or border-line intellectual functioning), mood disorder, anxiety, oppositional-defiant disorder (ODD), and adjustment disorder. While a diagnosis such as ODD should be a last resort, to be chosen after all other diagnoses that might explain Dashawn's behavior problems have been ruled out, the first major hypothesis that should be addressed—as it would, if chosen, encompass many of his functional impairments—is pervasive developmental disorder.

Dashawn does exhibit some delay in his functioning, especially in his cognitive development. However, he does not exhibit the symptoms of any of the specific PDDs, such as autistic disorder or Asperger's disorder. The only possibility would be a pervasive developmental disorder, not otherwise specified (PDD NOS), which includes developmental delays along the autistic spectrum of disorders that do not meet the full criteria for any specific PDD. However, Dashawn is lacking one of the hallmark symptoms of a PDD—the repetitive or stereotyped behavior or narrowly focused attention on a single topic or area of interest. In fact, he does not exhibit any symptoms of the PDDs except for his low cognitive functioning. Therefore, a pervasive developmental disorder does not seem to be the best way of describing his cluster of symptoms.

Having ruled out a PDD, we still need to explain his major functional impairments: his disturbed interpersonal functioning, his academic difficulties, and his behavior problems. Taking his interpersonal functioning and his behavior together with the themes that emerged from the testing of fear and resentment toward his environment and his inability to form relationships—as well as his abusive history—Dashawn seems best to fit the criteria of reactive attachment disorder, inhibited type. As the anxiety that emerged from the testing is being attributed to this diagnosis, we can rule out the possibility of an anxiety disorder.

Regarding his academic difficulties, his WISC-IV revealed that he is functioning overall within the borderline range as compared with others his age, though there was some indication of the possibility for higher functioning (i.e., average working memory). Because of these markers of higher potential, Dashawn's cognitive functioning is not consistent with mental retardation. However, it is consistent with a diagnosis of borderline intellectual functioning, especially with the theme that emerged from the emotional testing about his concrete thinking and difficulty understanding complex situations. It was decided not to administer a test of academic achievement because his intellectual functioning was low.

Although we cannot be 100% certain, we can be confident that his borderline intellectual functioning is contributing heavily to his academic difficulties, and it is unlikely that he has a learning disorder as well. For that to be the case, he would have to be performing academically at a level significantly lower than even his borderline IQ would predict. If that were the case, he would likely not even have been promoted to his current level in school at this point. Accordingly, we will not diagnose a learning disorder.

Finally, none of these diagnoses has yet accounted for Dashawn's acting-out behaviors. The final diagnoses to consider include mood disorder, adjustment disorder, and oppositional-defiant disorder. As his acting-out behaviors were present well before his recent life transition (i.e., moving into his most recent foster home), it is unlikely that the behaviors are related only to adjusting, so an adjustment disorder is unlikely. In view

PSYCHOLOGICAL ASSESSMENT REPORT
CONFIDENTIAL

Identifying Information

Name: Dashawn Terry   **Date of Report:**   10/27/08
Sex: Male   **Assessor:**   A. Jordan Wright, Ph.D.
Age: 12   **Dates of Testing:**   10/2/08; 10/6/08
Date of Birth: 1/1/1996
Ethnicity: Black

Source of Referral and Referral Questions

Dashawn Terry was referred for a psychological assessment by his foster care agency, in order to assess for purposes of adoption.

Measures Administered

- Clinical Interview
- Collateral Interview with Foster Care Case Worker
- Bender Visual-Motor Gestalt Test-Second Edition (Bender-2)
- Wechsler Intelligence Scale for Children-Fourth Edition (WISC-IV)
- Millon Pre-Adolescent Clinical Inventory (M-PACI)
- Rorschach Inkblot Test, Comprehensive System (Rorschach)
- Thematic Apperception Test (TAT)
- Sentence Completion Test-Child (Sentence Completion)
- House-Tree-Person and Kinetic Family Drawings (Projective Drawings)

Note on Testing

The majority of background information on the client came from the collateral interview with his Case Worker. Although the assessor tried to contact the client's current foster mother, she was unable to come in for the assessment. Additionally, the client, although he confirmed the information given by his Case Worker, did not add much information himself. Because he confirmed the information, it is assumed that all the information given is valid.

Description of Client

The client is an African American male who was 12 years 9 months at the time of testing. He is of slightly short and thin for his age, and he rarely smiled and was difficult to engage during sessions. He has a long history

(Continued)

in the foster care system, and he seemed to engage the assessor with apprehension.

Presenting Problem

The client is reportedly exhibiting behavioral problems at home and at school, including oppositional and aggressive behavior toward peers, teachers, and his foster mother. Additionally, he reportedly both lies and begs often, and he has no friends and difficulty with interpersonal relationships.

Background Information

History of Presenting Problem

The client has been in foster care since he was about 3 years old, having moved to and from multiple foster homes since that time. He has a long history of oppositional and aggressive behavior, reported in most of his foster care placements. Additionally, he has always had difficulty with interpersonal interactions, which has led to very few significant peer or friend relationships and difficulty connecting to foster parents. Having been neglected by his biological mother before the age of 2 and subsequently abused by at least one foster parent, he has exhibited difficulty attaching to others, though he has attached at least somewhat to several foster parents in the past.

Symptomatic Evaluation

The client reportedly had significantly delayed developmental milestones. Although no information was available about him before the age of 3, he had difficulty walking on his own at that point, could not use language effectively to communicate, and was not toilet trained. Early in his foster care placements, he "caught up" in these domains, but he still has difficulty with reciprocal interpersonal communication.

The client was reportedly diagnosed previously with depressive, anxiety, and "delinquent" disorders by previous therapists. He was in play therapy treatment from the time he entered the foster care agency until about nine months ago, because of staff turnover at the agency. He has never been on psychotropic medication, though he has been evaluated several times by psychiatrists at the agency.

The client's Case Worker denied any substance abuse or significant medical problems, and no information was available about his family of origin's history of medical or psychiatric illness.

Psychosocial Evaluation

The client was abandoned by his biological mother at about 2 years old. There is no information about the client before this time. He was reportedly living alone in an apartment for several months at that age, until he was taken into foster care. How he survived is unclear, but he was extremely emaciated when he came to the foster care agency and went into his first foster home.

The client then went through a series of multiple foster homes from 3 years old until his most recent pre-adoptive placement, which happened about two years ago. He moved from foster home to foster home, either because he was abused and the home was closed by the agency or because his behavior problems were too difficult for the families to handle. His current foster home is reportedly highly nurturing, and his behavior has reportedly improved significantly.

The client is currently in special education at a public school, where he continues to have academic difficulties. His Case Worker denied any legal involvement or sexual activity, which he confirmed.

Mental Status

The client was well groomed and appropriately and casually dressed throughout the assessment. He was disengaged and made very little eye contact throughout, except when he became oppositional during some of the tests, throwing some of the testing materials around the room. His motor activity was within normal limits. Both his receptive and sparse expressive language use were within normal limits. His mood was difficult to assess, though he reported some sadness, and his affect was flat and disengaged throughout. His thought process was goal-directed, and his thought content was free of hallucinations, delusions, and suicidal and homicidal ideation. His memory seemed within normal limits, and his attention and concentration were adequate. His history is characterized by poor impulse control and judgment, and his decision-making and planning abilities were significantly delayed for his age.

Behavioral Observations

The client was disengaged and made poor eye contact throughout the assessment process, especially during the clinical interview. However, during the testing itself he seemed to give effortful attempts on all tests. At certain points during the testing, he became oppositional and somewhat angry and frustrated, complaining that he did not want to continue and throwing some of the testing materials around the room. When the

(Continued)

assessor tried to engage him in casual conversation between tests, he seemed inhibited and closed off, sharing very little about himself and not responding very openly to questions.

During the drawing tasks, he seemed to handle the pencil aggressively, pressing very hard and making quick, sharp lines on the paper. He broke several pencil leads throughout the process. Additionally, when emotional content came up in any of the tests, he became noticeably fidgety and uncomfortable.

Overall Interpretation of Test Findings

Cognitive Functioning

On the WISC-IV, the client exhibited some variation among his different domains of cognitive functioning. Specifically, his Verbal Comprehension and Perceptual Reasoning Indices both fell within the Borderline range compared to others his age (8th and 5th percentiles, respectively). His Processing Speed Index fell within the Low Average range (9th percentile), and his Working Memory Index fell within the Average range compared to others his age (32nd percentile). The client exhibited no signs of gross neurological damage as evidenced by his Low Average performance on the Bender-2 (9th percentile).

Verbal Comprehension. On measures of general verbal skills, such as verbal fluency, ability to understand and use verbal reasoning, and verbal knowledge, the client's performance fell within the Borderline range of functioning compared to others his age (Verbal Comprehension Index, 8th percentile). While all subtests in the domain constituted weaknesses compared to others his age, he showed a specific deficit in his knowledge of factual information, which assesses his long-term memory and fund of knowledge (Information, 1st percentile). His difficulty in understanding and using language will likely cause difficulty in most academic domains.

Perceptual Reasoning. On tests that measure nonverbal reasoning, visuospatial aptitude, and induction and planning skills on tasks involving nonverbal stimuli such as designs, pictures, and puzzles, the client performed within the Borderline range of functioning compared to others his age (Perceptual Reasoning Index, 5th percentile). Tasks in this domain assess the client's abilities to examine a problem, draw upon visual-motor and visuospatial skills, organize thoughts, and create and test possible solutions. Again, most subtests constituted weaknesses compared to others his age. However, compared to his own functioning, he exhibited a slight strength in a task requiring him to manipulate blocks to copy a design presented to him, which assesses visual-motor coordination and nonverbal reasoning ability (Block Design, 50th percentile).

Processing Speed. On tasks that measure the ability to focus attention and quickly scan, discriminate between, and respond to visual information within a time limit, the client's performance fell within the Low Average range of functioning compared to others his age (Processing Speed Index, 9th percentile). The subtests that make up this domain fell consistently in the Low Average range compared to others his age.

Working Memory. On tasks that assessed the ability to memorize new information, hold it in short-term memory, concentrate, and manipulate information to produce some result or reasoning outcome, the client's performance fell within the Average range compared to others his age (Working Memory Index, 32nd percentile), which constituted a significant strength compared to the rest of his functioning. Tasks in this domain require sustained attention and concentration, and well as fluidity of mental processing. All of the subtests in this domain fell within the Average range.

Cognitive Summary. The client's performance revealed that he is cognitively functioning generally in the Borderline range compared to others his age, especially in his verbal and nonverbal ability. However, there was some indication of possible higher functioning, as he exhibited a strength compared to his own performance in his ability to hold information in short-term memory and manipulate it. Overall, especially given his poor verbal ability, it is expected that he will likely struggle in school somewhat.

Emotional Functioning

The client was administered several standardized objective and projective measures of personality and emotional functioning. The results of these measures suggest that the client is experiencing both fear and resentment toward his environment, which has been chaotic and not supportive enough. Additionally, his thinking is concrete and limited in ability. Together, his limited cognitive ability and his fear and resentment toward his environment have led him to avoid interpersonal contact and closeness. His interpersonal inhibition and negative feelings about his environment have led him to become depressed, which, partially because of his limited cognitive ability and partially because of his age, manifests as acting-out behaviors.

Fear and Resentment Toward His Environment. The client's assessment revealed that he has a great deal of fear and resentment toward his environment, especially adults. While his M-PACI revealed general fears and

(Continued)

anxiety, his Rorschach and TAT revealed that this fear is focused on other people within his environment. This fear is not surprising, given his history of being abused within his home and foster homes. Beyond fearing others, however, his Rorschach, TAT, and Sentence Completion revealed that he harbors a great deal of anger toward others, especially adults. His M-PACI and Projective Drawings characterized this anger as resentment toward others in his life, likely related to his feelings that he has never had enough support from others, which was revealed in his TAT and Projective Drawings. This lack of support seems to stem from his history in foster care, as far back as his being neglected by his biological mother.

Concrete and Limited Cognitive Ability. Likely related to his somewhat limited verbal ability as measured in the Cognitive Functioning section above, the client's assessment revealed that his thinking ability is both limited and extremely concrete. Specifically, his Rorschach, TAT, and Projective Drawings suggested that he has an overly simplistic and concrete way of viewing the world and other people. He likely has difficulty understanding and processing complex information; this was revealed on the Rorschach, which includes both complex situations and complex emotions within himself. His Sentence Completion revealed that these complex situations lead to frustration within him, as they do not fit his more simplistic view of the world. For example, when emotional content emerged from the testing, he became noticeably fidgety and uncomfortable, likely frustrated by the complex content. His limited cognitive ability has led to academic difficulties throughout his life, and it may be related to the severe delays in his developmental milestones.

Interpersonal Inhibition. Because of his limited ability to process complex information and his general fear and resentment toward others, the client has developed an inhibited and isolated stance toward other people. His Rorschach and Projective Drawings revealed that he simply does not want to form attachments to other people, including others his own age. Beyond this unwillingness, however, his Rorschach and Sentence Completion revealed that he does not actually have the capacity to form close relationships with others, likely because he has not developed this ability, given his history. As a result, his M-PACI and TAT revealed that he acts in an inhibited and isolated way, not making efforts to be outgoing and pursue relationships. This explains why he seemed so detached from the assessor and inhibited during the assessment, as well as why he currently has no friends.

Depression. Because of his strong negative feelings about his environment and his tendency to isolate himself, the client has become depressed. While his M-PACI and Rorschach revealed evidence of depression, his Rorschach, Sentence Completion, and Projective Drawings characterized his depression as mostly related to feeling extremely lonely. This loneliness makes sense, given both the lack of stable and consistent people in his life and his unwillingness and inability to form close attachments to others. Additionally, his Rorschach and Projective Drawings revealed that he has low self-esteem, likely feeling bad about himself due to his traumatic history.

Acting-Out Behaviors. The client's depression is manifesting itself as acting-out behaviors, which is common in children, especially younger children functioning at the same developmental level as the client's limited cognitive ability. His TAT and Sentence Completion revealed that he has aggressive tendencies, turning his angry feelings into aggressive behaviors. His M-PACI revealed that when frustrated he can become disruptive and unruly. His Rorschach revealed that these behaviors are likely to have a quality that is oppositional, resisting being told what to do and going against authority. These oppositional and disruptive behaviors are common for children who are younger than the client, but who are functioning cognitively around the same level. These acting-out behaviors, related to his feelings of depression, constitute what are reportedly his "pervasive behavior problems," as well as his lying, his begging, and his oppositional behavior during the testing sessions.

Summary and Recommendations

Dashawn Terry is a small, thin 12-year-old African American male who was referred for testing to determine whether he should proceed with adoption by his current foster mother. He has a long history of neglect and abuse, having been in many foster homes between the ages of 3 and 10, when he entered his current foster home placement. He has a history of oppositional, difficult, and aggressive behavior, which has reportedly gotten better but is still present. He is in special education and is struggling academically.

Cognitively, he is generally functioning in the Borderline range compared to others his age. There was some indication of possible higher functioning, as he exhibited a strength compared to his own functioning

(Continued)

in his ability to hold information in short-term memory and manipulate it. However, currently his cognitive functioning is a relative weakness for someone his age.

Emotionally, the client is experiencing both fear and resentment toward his environment, which has been chaotic and not supportive enough. Additionally, his thinking is concrete and limited in ability. Together, his limited cognitive ability and his fear and resentment toward his environment have led him to avoid interpersonal contact and closeness. His interpersonal inhibition and negative feelings about his environment have led him to become depressed, which, partially because of his limited cognitive ability and partially because of his age, is manifested as acting-out behaviors.

Currently, because of his limited cognitive ability, which is impairing his educational functioning, he meets criteria for Borderline Intellectual Functioning.

Additionally, his style of relating to others is impairing his functioning. Specifically, he does not initiate social interaction and has fear and difficulty responding when others initiate it. He is significantly inhibited, and he has a history of maltreatment by caregivers. As such, he meets criteria for Reactive Attachment Disorder, Inhibited Type.

Additionally, he seems to be struggling with significant levels of depression, though he does not meet criteria for Major Depressive Disorder. As such, he meets criteria for Depressive Disorder, Not Otherwise Specified.

Diagnosis

Axis I	313.89	Reactive Attachment Disorder, Inhibited Type
	311	Depressive Disorder, Not Otherwise Specified
Axis II	V62.89	Borderline Intellectual Functioning
Axis III		None known
Axis IV		History of abuse and neglect
		Long history in foster care
		Academic problems
		Social problems
Axis V	GAF =	41

Recommendations

Given the client's current functioning, the following recommendations are being made:

It is recommended that, as he seems to be doing well within his current foster family placement, he should go ahead with the adoption into his current family. Any signs of positive attachment with his adoptive mother should be taken as a very positive sign.

Additionally, he should reenter individual therapy at the foster care agency, which should include cognitive remediation, to provide him support during the adoption transition, as well as address his social skills and depression.

A. Jordan Wright, PhD   Date
New York State Licensed Psychologist

of the themes that emerged from the assessment, the two that are unaccounted for so far are depression and acting out, which we know are often related in childhood. Therefore, it seems most likely that Dashawn is depressed, and this (in combination with his limited cognitive ability) is why he is acting out. Thus, it seems his behavior problems are related to a mood disorder, so we can rule out ODD. He does not seem to meet the criteria for Major Depressive Disorder, so the diagnosis of Depressive Disorder, Not Otherwise Specified is given.

In terms of recommendations, the first one must be related to whether there are indications that he should or should not go ahead with the adoption as planned. For Dashawn, as he seems to be doing well in his current pre-adoptive foster home, there are no indications that he should not go ahead with adoption. In terms of addressing his problems, recommendations for cognitive remediation (to make sure he will be able to keep up in school) and individual therapy (to address his depression and interpersonal difficulties) will be made. Because his depression is not severe enough even to warrant a diagnosis of Major Depressive Disorder, there will not be a firm recommendation for a psychiatric consultation. However, should his depressive or behavioral symptoms worsen, the family should consider consulting with a psychiatrist to see whether medication may be helpful.

FEEDBACK

Preparation for Feedback

Feedback to clients at the foster care agency was difficult, as it was policy not to provide pre-adoptive assessment feedback to the clients or to their biological or foster families. However, it was agreed that Dashawn could be given some feedback about the other findings of the assessment. The only feedback that was authorized, however, was the information about his environment, his socialization, and his current emotional state. The report was not to be given, and no specific diagnosis was to be made. Thus, the decisions of what feedback to give and how it should be given had been decided for the assessor.

Feedback Session

Dashawn and Katie came for the feedback session. The assessor had met with Katie beforehand to give her the report and verbal feedback and explanation, but the focus of this session was to give feedback directly to Dashawn, using language that he and Katie could then use later to talk about these concepts. The assessor began by restating the referral question and presenting problems, reiterating that the purpose of the assessment was (a) to make sure that being adopted by his current family was a good idea and (b) to see why he engages in some difficult behavior at school and at home. Dashawn, now somewhat better related to the assessor than in the initial clinical interview session, made little eye contact but nodded slightly, acknowledging that he understood and agreed.

The scope of feedback to Dashawn was limited and not ambitious. However, the assessor decided to embed the feedback in the context of what Dashawn had been through. The first major goal for the assessor was to convey how difficult it must be to have had the past Dashawn had, noting his strength for surviving such difficult circumstances in his life. During this feedback, Dashawn managed to look the assessor in the eyes several times (much more than he had previously), and he even betrayed a slight smile. The purpose of emphasizing the context of his difficult life was to normalize (to as much an extent as possible) the two other major pieces of feedback.

The first piece of psychological feedback was the fact that he did not "trust" other people very easily, and for that reason he did not want to socialize or build relationships with them readily. Again, this was framed within the context of how many people had let him down in his life, from the very beginning. The assessor used self-referencing language throughout, conceding that he would likely not want to trust people or be in relationships either had he gone through what Dashawn had gone through. The second piece of feedback was about how all of this has caused him to be somewhat lonely and sad. Again, this feedback was framed in a "who wouldn't be" kind of way, given his difficult life so far.

The assessor explained to him that sometimes when people feel sad, they get irritable or stubborn, and that they may misbehave. Throughout these two major psychological pieces of feedback, Dashawn remained looking down toward the floor, except for several moments when he glanced at the assessor, usually when the assessor was either self-referencing or normalizing the difficulties. As the assessor continually checked in with him about whether or not he understood the feedback being given, he simply continued to nod his head slightly to acknowledge and answer the question affirmatively. When asked if he felt like all of this was true for him, he actually spoke, though quietly, affirming, "Yeah, I think so."

Finally, the assessor gave feedback about the recommendations that came from the assessment. These were framed in a way that was as hopeful as possible, linking them to the previous feedback given. Given his problems with building relationships and connecting with people, the assessor told him that the primary recommendation was that he should go through with being adopted by his current foster family. It was restated that he seems to be doing better recently and that being adopted by them means that he should not have to move to a different home or a different family again, so that his current family will not be taken from him. Upon hearing this, Dashawn actually looked at the assessor and smiled widely (differently than his usual slight smile). He nodded, more vigorously than usual, when asked how he felt about the recommendation.

The final recommendation was to reenter individual therapy, which was framed as "extra support" for him. He quickly and easily agreed to this, looking toward Katie. Katie immediately affirmed that she would organize it so that he could restart therapy as soon as possible. Again, he had very little response when asked how he felt about this recommendation, but he nodded in agreement. At the end of the session, the assessor thanked him and held out his hand to shake Dashawn's, which Dashawn took and shook firmly. Katie then took Dashawn to her office, presumably to follow up and confirm that he understood all of the feedback.

SUMMARY

Dashawn Terry's assessment is a good example of some of the real-world constraints that can be put on an assessment (i.e., the fact that the clinical interview information was so incomplete, due to the setting). Additionally, it shows how an assessment can help clarify the choice between possible diagnoses. Dashawn's presentation is very similar to that of a child with a pervasive developmental disorder (PDD). A PDD could usually explain someone like Dashawn's limited cognitive functioning, interpersonal inhibition, and even emotional difficulty, three issues that in the end took three different diagnoses to explain. However, the assessment revealed two things. First, there were some cognitive domains that were in fact *not* limited, especially his working memory, which signifies the potential for slightly higher functioning. Second, the assessment revealed no evidence of the stereotyped or repetitive behavior usually found within PDD presentations. While he did have some developmental delays, some of his other symptoms, especially his loneliness and depression, can be addressed in more traditional psychotherapeutic ways, rather than with treatment specific to PDDs.

CHAPTER 11

An Anxious Girl

Heather Daltry was a 15-year-old White girl who was referred for an assessment by her parents, who were worried about her anxiety. Both of her parents suffer from anxiety, and for the past few years, Heather's anxiety has seemingly gotten worse. Additionally, her parents were worried that she may be depressed, though they were not sure. They wanted to know exactly what was going on with Heather and how best to help her.

THE CLINICAL INTERVIEW

Although an appointment was made for Heather, her mother, and her father all to come in to do the clinical interview, only her mother and father turned up for the appointment. Consequently, the first clinical interview session was conducted with Heather's parents alone. The second clinical interview happened with Heather alone, on the first day of actual testing.

Heather's parents were an average-looking, middle-aged White couple, dressed conservatively and extremely polite. They arrived early for the first session, stating that because they were driving into the city for the assessment, they came early to make sure they could find parking, which they did relatively easily. They made polite, easy conversation at the beginning of the session, explaining that they "felt it was better" for them to come to the first session without Heather so that the assessor would "understand all that's going on" before meeting her.

As previously, the sections that follow are not categorized into symptomatic evaluation and psychosocial evaluation, as the flow of the clinical interview did not follow this structure. The subsections present the clinical interview as closely as possible to the way it actually unfolded, rather than artificially grouping sections of information that did not present themselves sequentially. That is, the presentation that follows reflects the way the clinical interview happened chronologically, along with the overarching questions the assessor asked Heather's parents and, later, Heather. Clarifications were occasionally necessary throughout the interview, but those questions and comments are not presented here.

Presenting Problem: So What's Going On With Heather?

Heather's mother did most of the talking during the first clinical interview session, though her father jumped in occasionally when he felt clarification was necessary. Heather's mother reported that Heather had been "having problems" for the past few years. Specifically, she had a great deal of anxiety and had been very upset and depressed recently. When asked for clarification, her mother reported that Heather became extremely anxious when she had to socialize, including when she was encouraged to go out with acquaintances from school or other family members. She reportedly got so anxious socially that she became sick to her stomach, at times to the point of vomiting. Her mother reported that, perhaps as a result of her anxiety, she had difficulty sustaining relationships with any peers.

When asked about her being "upset and depressed," her mother reported that she was irritable and "demanding" at home. She seemed to alternate between being loving and affectionate and having "an attitude." Her father reported that "she has a good head on her shoulders, but when I try to speak to her, she doesn't listen." Both her mother and father laughed this trait off as normal for a 15-year-old, which the assessor validated cautiously. Her parents became quiet for a moment, then her mother stated that Heather "takes things too hard." She reportedly became extremely upset about very small things, including her parents asking about school or not having the dessert she wanted. The assessor asked specifically about suicidal ideation, and her mother reported that Heather had told her that she thought about death before, but she had never considered actually killing herself.

History of Presenting Problem: Has She Always Had These Problems?

Heather's mother reported that these problems had "always been going on," though she stated that Heather thought the social problems had been present only during the past three years. Her mother took this opportunity to state that she and her daughter were "best friends," that Heather told her everything, and the assessor would likely get confirmation on all of this from Heather during the next session. She went on to report that Heather's social anxiety "got a little better" between the ages of 10 and 12, but that the past few years had been extremely difficult for them. She also reported that Heather had some academic difficulties when she was younger, but she currently had a math tutor and was on the honor roll in her academically rigorous private school.

Family History and Family Psychiatric History: Does Anyone Else in the Family Have Difficulties Like These?

Heather's mother reported that she had two other daughters, both of whom were older than Heather. The oldest, who was 21 years old, also had anxiety problems, but the middle daughter, who was 18, did not. She reported that she herself also suffered from anxiety, stating half jokingly that she had struggled with it all her life and had "become a neurotic mother." Heather's father, who worked as a contractor, reported that he also suffered from "extreme, sometimes debilitating anxiety." All five family members lived at home together at the time of the assessment.

Together, Heather's mother and father reported that Heather's maternal grandfather had suffered from depression and anxiety and that her paternal grandfather had been diagnosed with bipolar disorder.

Developmental History and Medical History: Can You Tell Me About Heather as a Baby, Including Your Pregnancy With Her?

Her mother reported that Heather was the "easiest" of her pregnancies, with very few difficulties at all, except that she (her mother) had developed asthma during pregnancy. She reported that Heather met all developmental milestones early—"she was very advanced." She reported that Heather had never had any serious illnesses or hospitalizations, stating that she was an extremely healthy child, adding "physically" to the end of the sentence and looking slightly sad. At this point, the assessor spent the rest of this session exploring how Heather's parents were feeling about what was going on with her and offering support. He assured them that the assessment would help come up with concrete, specific recommendations to help Heather with her difficulties. At the end of the session, the assessor asked a few quick, concrete questions, and Heather's mother confirmed that she had no history or criminal activity or legal involvement, did not use alcohol or any other drugs, was not sexually active, and had never been in any form of psychiatric or psychotherapeutic treatment before. Additionally, they stated that she had recently had a full physical exam, and there was nothing medically wrong with her currently. She does not have difficulties sleeping and has no problem with her appetite.

Session 2

Heather came with her parents to the second session, though after a few minutes her parents left the room so that the assessor could meet with Heather alone. She looked like a typical American teenage girl, of average height and weight for her age, dressed nicely in age-appropriate clothing, and her hair styled with a trendy haircut. There was nothing clinically remarkable about her appearance. She was extremely polite and friendly, making good eye contact and speaking openly with the assessor, with very little apparent anxiety.

Presenting Problem and History of Presenting Problem: So Tell Me About Your Anxiety With Friends

Heather reported that her mother had probably told the assessor everything, because she shared everything with her mother and "really never" hid anything from her. She reported that interacting with other people was her biggest problem, and that this had been a problem for about the past three years. Before then, she had made a group of friends at school, but the friends ended up fighting among themselves, being friends one day and talking about each other the next. After a short period of this, Heather stopped socializing with this group of girls, as well as anyone else, and she began to get extremely nervous when she had to interact with other people, including having severe stomach pains. When asked about friends now, she reported that she had a few people she saw "occasionally on weekends," and that she went out socially "every once in awhile," but that she had no close friends and no best friend. She reported that she had had a best friend, but that she "stabbed me in the back."

Presenting Problem and History of Presenting Problem: And Your Parents Mentioned That You've Been Kind of Down Lately

Heather looked down at her lap, where she was fidgeting with her fingers, and was silent for a moment. She reported that she had been "moody" recently, and that she had begun to get lonely and unhappy. She reported that when she gets "down," she does not feel good about herself, feeling unworthy of being friends with others and not liking the way she looks. She restated that her mother was her best friend, but that at times she wishes she had other people she could trust and who would not judge her. Specifically, she said, "I just want to fit in with people at school." She stated that her moodiness had only begun over the past few years, that she remembered being a happy child for the most part, until recently.

Information Verification: Can I Just Confirm With You Some Information That Your Parents Shared With Me?

The assessor and Heather went through most of the information that her parents had reported in the previous session, and Heather confirmed every single detail. She confirmed her passive suicidal ideation and reiterated that she had no actual intent to harm herself. Notably, when asked how she felt about herself, she stated that it depended on her mood. She stated that at times she did not like the way she looked, but most of the time she knew that "I am a good person." She agreed with all the other information her parents reported.

Multicultural Evaluation: Tell Me About Your Culture and Religion?

Heather reported with a slight laugh that she was "a WASP," stating that she was "just like" most of the other teens with whom she went to school. "Pretty much all of us are White and nonpracticing Christians." She reported that she had never had difficulties because of her culture, race, ethnicity, or religion.

MENTAL STATUS EVALUATION

Appearance and Behavior

Heather was always dressed appropriately and groomed extremely well, with her hair carefully done. She was of average height and weight, had a

bright smile, and dressed in a manner that was somewhat preppy and appropriate for her age. She was extremely friendly and cooperative throughout
the assessment.

Speech and Language

Heather was articulate and precise when she spoke. She did not exhibit
any difficulties understanding directions or questions from the assessor.

Mood and Affect

Though she reported her mood as "somewhat down," her affect was bright
and even throughout the assessment. Had she not reported her depressed
mood, the assessor would have been unable to tell that she was having
any affective difficulties. She also did not appear anxious during sessions,
except for occasional slight shaking of her hand and obvious unhappiness
about some of her drawings.

Thought Process and Content

Heather's thought process seemed clear and logical, free of hallucinations
and delusions. Her thought content was characterized by some anxiety and
depressive ideation, but was free of suicidal and homicidal ideation.

Cognition

Heather was alert and engaged throughout the assessment. Her attention,
concentration, and memory seemed intact.

Prefrontal Functioning

Heather exhibited good impulse control, planning, and judgment.

HYPOTHESIS BUILDING

Now that the clinical assessment (the clinical and collateral interviews and
the mental status evaluation) has been completed, the information gathered
can be used to create hypotheses for what is going on for Heather.

Identify Impairments

Heather has two major impairments in functioning. First, and most saliently, she has difficulty socially, related to her extreme anxiety, to the point that it causes physical symptoms. Second, she is having subjectively felt distress, related to her being upset, depressed, and anxious, and seemingly resulting in some irritability with her parents and at school. Academically, she is not exhibiting any difficulties, so the current evaluation will focus on her social and emotional functioning.

Enumerate Possible Causes

Beginning with her subjectively felt distress, it seems clear that Heather is struggling with mood disorder symptoms, such as depression. However, there could be several diagnostic possibilities for these feelings, along with the resultant irritability. Specifically, while she could be suffering from *major depressive disorder*, her mood symptoms could be better explained by *dysthymic disorder* or an *adjustment disorder, with depressed mood.*

When considering her interpersonal difficulties, along with her clear anxiety, there could be several diagnostic possibilities. While some developmental disorder diagnoses are associated with difficulty socializing, she did not exhibit symptoms consistent with autism or Asperger's disorder. Her interpersonal difficulty seems to be related much more directly to her anxiety. Given that, the best explanation will likely be an anxiety disorder. Differential diagnosis for Heather will likely be between *generalized anxiety disorder* and *social phobia*, though other diagnoses must be considered as well. The physical symptoms related to her emotional functioning suggest the possibility of a *somatoform disorder*, and the pervasiveness of her interpersonal avoidance may be related to an *avoidant personality disorder*, or even a *schizoid personality disorder*, though these are less likely given her age and the patterns of her social difficulty.

You should *always* consider (a) that the presenting problems may have an etiology in substance use and (b) that the presenting problems may have an etiology in a medical condition. For Heather, there seems to be little possibility that either of these is the case. Both she and her parents denied any use of alcohol or drugs, and she recently had a full physical exam that revealed no evidence of any medical problems. Therefore, it will be assumed that the symptoms are primarily psychological in nature.

SELECTING TESTS

Selecting tests for the current assessment is relatively straightforward, as we have very few differential diagnoses to make, and they are all psychological (rather than cognitive, academic, etc.) in nature. Even though Heather's cognitive functioning is not necessarily in question, it is important to confirm that she does not have cognitive limitations. Understanding her functioning overall, including feeling confident in the emotional data that emerge from testing, requires the understanding of her cognitive functioning. So it was decided that, for the cognitive testing, the battery would include the Bender Visual-Motor Gestalt Test, 2nd Edition (Bender-2) and the Wechsler Intelligence Scale for Children, 4th Edition (WISC-IV). As always, the Bender-2 will help rule out gross neurological impairment, while the WISC-IV will provide the general level of intellectual functioning. Assuming that nothing remarkable will emerge from these tests, no other cognitive testing is necessary. Of course, if something unexpected does emerge, additional cognitive testing can be reconsidered.

The other hypotheses include anxiety, mood, adjustment, somatoform, and personality disorders. Because of Heather's age, candid nature, and seeming maturity, the objective measure chosen for her was self-report, rather than parent-report. Both could be used, but it was decided that for this case her self-report would likely be reliable as an objective measure of her subjectively felt distress. Accordingly, the objective measure chosen for this assessment was the Millon Adolescent Clinical Inventory (MACI). Multiple projective measures were chosen for the current assessment, simply to build evidence for her emotional functioning. For these projective techniques, the Rorschach Inkblot Test, Roberts Apperception Test for Children (RAT-C), the Animal Identification and Devaluation Task (AID), Projective Wishes, and Projective Drawings were chosen. Given the hypotheses posited from the clinical interview, these emotional measures should be adequate to determine what is underlying Heather's interpersonal and emotional difficulties.

Thus, our assessment's battery of tests will consist of

- Bender-2
- WISC-IV
- MACI

- Rorschach
- RAT-C
- AID
- Projective Wishes
- Projective Drawings

ACCUMULATING THE DATA

Table 11.1 shows the results from each individual measure administered. On the WISC-IV, Heather performed within the average range as compared with others her age overall (full scale IQ of 95, 37th percentile). Her verbal comprehension, perceptual reasoning, and working memory were all average,

TABLE 11.1   ACCUMULATION OF HEATHER'S DATA

MACI

Anxious feelings

Mild self-devaluation

Mild peer insecurity

Introversive personality style—socially "out of touch"

Introversive personality style—detached

Inhibited personality style—hypersensitivity to anticipated pain

Inhibited personality style—social self-consciousness

Submissive personality style—passive and submissive to others

Submissive personality style—lack of self-confidence

Rorschach

Coping deficit

Internalized feelings of sadness and depression

Highly focused on herself

Feelings of her needs not being met

Unmet needs for closeness

Limited ability to manage interpersonal relationships

Behaviorally passive and acquiescent

(Continued)

TABLE 11.1   *(CONTINUED)*

Something getting in the way of forming close attachments to others

Superficial, transient relationships

Ineffective interpersonal behavior

Avoidant style

Bases judgments on incomplete information

Not motivated to understand complex information

RAT-C

Passivity and compliance

Resentment toward those with whom she acts passively

Sadness and feelings of worthlessness

Self-image and self-esteem are dependent on how others see her

Strong need for acceptance from peers

Pleasing others is in competition with getting her own needs met

Many needs not being met by others

Genuine niceness, hope, optimism

Wants positive interactions with others

AID

Avoidance of others to cope

Need for affiliation

Mistrust of interpersonal relationships

Longing to be more assertive

Projective Wishes

Hope and optimism

Views herself as a genuinely good person

Wanting to be more assertive

Mistrust of others

Projective Drawings

Low self-esteem

Some emptiness

Some resentment toward family

TABLE 11.1   *(CONTINUED)*

Misjudges others

Anxiety about others

Easily hurt

Easily let down

Eager to please others

Behavioral Observations/Other Data

Extreme anxiety, especially about socializing

Interpersonal isolation

Vomiting from extreme anxiety

Irritability

"Takes things too hard"

Unhappiness

Loneliness

Feels like a good person

Wants to "fit in" at school

Cooperative and friendly

and her processing speed was low average (composite score of 85, 16th percentile). Her performance on the Bender-2 was varied, with perfect scores on the motor and perception subtests, high performance on the copy phase (standard score of 124, 94.52nd percentile), and low average performance on the recall phase (standard score of 89, 23.17th percentile), indicating that there may have been some interference with her short-term memory.

IDENTIFYING THEMES

Heather's themes are somewhat more difficult to discern than those of some of the other assessments. One of the major problems is that there seem to be many data related to interpersonal relationships, all of which seem to describe Heather well but do not necessarily fit cleanly together in an obvious way at first. It will be helpful to see the data placed side by side in a chart so that more specific themes can emerge. Additionally, there are some data that do not seem to fit in with the rest of the data, such as the anxiety from the MACI and the cognitive data from the Rorschach, which may need to be considered more broadly to see whether they can work within one of the larger themes. Heather's preliminary themes are presented in Table 11.2.

TABLE 11.2   **LABELING OF HEATHER'S THEMES**

Themes

	MACI
Anxiety	Anxious feelings
Self-esteem	Mild self-devaluation
Interpersonal	Mild peer insecurity
Interpersonal	Introversive personality style—socially "out of touch"
Interpersonal	Introversive personality style—detached
Sensitivity	Inhibited personality style—hypersensitivity to anticipated pain
Interpersonal	Inhibited personality style—social self-consciousness
Interpersonal	Submissive personality style—passive and submissive to others
Self-esteem	Submissive personality style—lack of self-confidence
	Rorschach
Sensitivity	Coping deficit
Depression	Internalized feelings of sadness and depression
Sensitivity	Highly focused on herself
Sensitivity	Feelings of her needs not being met
Dependency	Unmet needs for closeness
Interpersonal	Limited ability to manage interpersonal relationships
Interpersonal	Behaviorally passive and acquiescent
Interpersonal	Something getting in the way of forming close attachments to others
Interpersonal	Superficial, transient relationships
Interpersonal	Ineffective interpersonal behavior

TABLE 11.2   (*CONTINUED*)

Themes

Interpersonal	Avoidant style
Cognitive	Bases judgments on incomplete information
Cognitive	Not motivated to understand complex information
	RAT-C
Interpersonal	Passivity and compliance
Interpersonal	Resentment toward those with whom she acts passively
Depression	Sadness and feelings of worthlessness
Self-esteem	Self-image and self-esteem are dependent on how others see her
Interpersonal	Strong need for acceptance from peers
Interpersonal/ Sensitivity	Pleasing others is in competition with getting her own needs met
Dependency	Many needs not being met by others
Positive self	Genuine niceness, hope, optimism
Interpersonal	Wants positive interactions with others
	AID
Interpersonal	Avoidance of others to cope
Dependency	Need for affiliation
Interpersonal	Mistrust of interpersonal relationships
Dependency	Longing to be more assertive
	Projective Wishes
Positive self	Hope and optimism
Positive self	Views herself as a genuinely good person
Dependency	Wanting to be more assertive
Interpersonal	Mistrust of others
	Projective Drawings
Self-esteem	Low self-esteem
Depression	Some emptiness
Family	Some resentment toward family

(Continued)

TABLE 11.2	(CONTINUED)

Themes	
Interpersonal	Misjudges others
Interpersonal	Anxiety about others
Sensitivity	Easily hurt
Sensitivity	Easily let down
Interpersonal	Eager to please others
	Behavioral Observations/Other Data
Interpersonal	Extreme anxiety, especially about socializing
Interpersonal	Interpersonal isolation
Miscellaneous	Vomiting from extreme anxiety
Depression	Irritability
Sensitivity	"Takes things too hard"
Depression	Unhappiness
Depression	Loneliness
Self-esteem	Feels like a good person
Dependency	Wants to "fit in" at school
Miscellaneous	Cooperative and friendly

ORGANIZING THE DATA

When the data are examined within themes, some of the themes become clearer and more specific. For example, the behavior theme clearly converges as acting-out behavior. Some of the themes do not seem to come together just yet, but laying it out like this can help us think about the data in a more thematic way and reconsider some of the themes. Heather's reorganized data are presented in Table 11.3.

Laid out this way, the themes that emerged initially do not seem "clean" enough to be useful for the conceptualization. Some reorganization seems necessary. First of all, the self-esteem category seems somewhat contradictory. However, if we reconceptualize the negative self-esteem data that emerged as part of the depression category, Heather's generally

TABLE 11.3 **HEATHER'S ORGANIZED DATA**

Test: Concept/Theme	MACI	Rorschach	RAT-C	AID and Projective Wishes	Projective Drawings	Interview/Behavioral Observations
Self-Esteem and Positive Self	Mild self-devaluation		Self-image and self-esteem are dependent on how others see her	Views herself as a genuinely good person	Low self-esteem	Feels like a good person
	Submissive personality style—lack of self-confidence		Genuine niceness, hope, optimism			
Interpersonal	Mild peer insecurity	Limited ability to manage interpersonal relationships	Passivity and compliance	Avoidance of others to cope	Misjudges others	Extreme anxiety, especially about socializing
	Introversive personality style—socially "out of touch"	Behaviorally passive and acquiescent	Resentment toward those with whom she acts passively	Mistrust of interpersonal relationships	Anxiety about others	Interpersonal isolation
	Introversive personality style—detached	Something getting in the way of forming close attachments to others	Strong need for acceptance from peers	Mistrust of others	Eager to please others	

(Continued)

TABLE 11.3   (CONTINUED)

Test: Concept/Theme	MACI	Rorschach	RAT-C	AID and Projective Wishes	Projective Drawings	Interview/Behavioral Observations
	Inhibited personality style—social self-consciousness	Superficial, transient relationships	Pleasing others is in competition with getting her own needs met			
	Submissive personality style—passive and submissive to others	Ineffective interpersonal behavior	Wants positive interactions with others			
		Avoidant style				
Sensitivity	Inhibited personality style—hypersensitivity to anticipated pain	Coping deficit	Pleasing others is in competition with getting her own needs met		Easily hurt	"Takes things too hard"
		Highly focused on herself			Easily let down	
		Feelings of her needs not being met				

Depression	Internalized feelings of sadness and depression	Sadness and feelings of worthlessness		Some emptiness	Irritability	Unhappiness Loneliness
Dependency	Unmet needs for closeness	Many needs not being met by others	Need for affiliation			Wants to "fit in" at school
			Longing to be more assertive			
			Wanting to be more assertive			
Miscellaneous	Anxious feelings	Bases judgments on incomplete information		Some resentment toward family		Vomiting from extreme anxiety
		Not motivated to understand complex information				Cooperative and friendly

positive view of herself can be related to her generally sensitive disposition. Most importantly, however, the interpersonal theme must be cleaned up. When the data are examined in this fashion, two overarching interpersonal themes seem to emerge: (1) a general trait of being submissive and dependent (this can be combined with her dependency theme, which actually shows evidence of her wanting more independence as well) and (2) her adopting a style of being detached from and avoidant of others. This latter theme can be broken down even further, if needed, to the interpersonal anxiety she feels and the resultant inhibition and avoidance of others. When the miscellaneous data are considered, the anxiety seems to fit well with this detachment and social avoidance, whereas the cognitive data could fit either in this social inhibition category or in her sensitivity, as she reacts hastily to stimuli, rather than considering the complex information. The final themes are shown in Table 11.4.

CONCEPTUALIZING

Remembering that the task at this point is to try to create a logical narrative among the themes so that it presents a coherent story, we have to connect the following themes:

- Interpersonal anxiety
- Interpersonal avoidance
- Sensitivity
- Depression
- Dependency and submissiveness

Before deciding on the most logical way to fit these themes together, we will first consider the model templates presented in Chapter 4: the diathesis–stress model, the developmental model, and the common function model for conceptualization.

Diathesis-Stress Model

In applying the diathesis-stress model of conceptualization, we must try to divide the themes into (1) *traits* that are inherent within Heather that she likely developed at an early age, and that she "brings to the picture"

TABLE 11.4

HEATHER'S REORGANIZED DATA

Test: Concept/Theme	MACI	Rorschach	RAT-C	AID and Projective Wishes	Projective Drawings	Interview/Behavioral Observations
Interpersonal Anxiety	Mild peer insecurity	Limited ability to manage interpersonal relationships	Resentment toward those with whom she acts passively	Mistrust of interpersonal relationships	Misjudges others	Extreme anxiety, especially about socializing
	Anxious feelings			Mistrust of others	Anxiety about others	Vomiting from extreme anxiety
	Inhibited personality style—social self-consciousness				Some resentment toward family	
Interpersonal Avoidance	Introversive personality style—socially "out of touch"	Something getting in the way of forming close attachments to others		Avoidance of others to cope		Interpersonal isolation
	Introversive personality style—detached	Superficial, transient relationships				
		Ineffective interpersonal behavior				

(Continued)

TABLE 11.4   (CONTINUED)

Test: Concept/Theme	MACI	Rorschach	RAT-C	AID and Projective Wishes	Projective Drawings	Interview/Behavioral Observations
	Avoidant style	Not motivated to understand complex information				
Sensitivity	Inhibited personality style—hypersensitivity to anticipated pain	Highly focused on herself	Pleasing others is in competition with getting her own needs met	Views herself as a genuinely good person	Easily hurt	"Takes things too hard"
		Feelings of her needs not being met	Self-image and self-esteem are dependent on how others see her		Easily let down	
		Bases judgments on incomplete information	Genuine niceness, hope, optimism			
Depression	Mild self-devaluation	Internalized feelings of sadness and depression	Sadness and feelings of worthlessness		Some emptiness	Irritability

Dependency/ Submissiveness					Low self-esteem	Unhappiness
						Loneliness
	Submissive personality style—lack of self-confidence	Unmet needs for closeness	Many needs not being met by others	Need for affiliation	Eager to please others	Wants to "fit in" at school
	Submissive personality style—passive and submissive to others	Behaviorally passive and acquiescent	Passivity and compliance	Longing to be more assertive		Cooperative and friendly
			Strong need for acceptance from peers	Wanting to be more assertive		
			Pleasing others is in competition with getting her own needs met			
			Wants positive interactions with others			

(diatheses), (2) *external issues* that affect her functioning (stressors), and (3) *states* that are more situational and/or transient (outcomes). It is important to categorize each of our five themes into these three types. As always, the more convincing these categorizations are, the more likely Heather and her parents are to accept the recommendations given.

For Heather, this model is somewhat difficult, as none of the themes that emerged from the testing seem inherently to be external stressors— each of the five themes is more internal or descriptive of the type of individual Heather is. Therefore, a justification must be made for at least one of the themes to be somewhat related to external stressors. In this case, the only one that would make any sense would be her interpersonal anxiety, which is based on mistrust and misunderstanding of other people, many of whom have let her down in the past. That is, given her history of being let down, disappointed, and "stabbed in the back" by others, she has developed an anxiety about engaging other people or building relationships. This may be a stretch, but for the diathesis-stress model, an external stressor of some sort is necessary.

With the stressor decided, the next task is to decide which theme or themes constitute the diathesis and which make up the outcomes. This task proves to be relatively straightforward for Heather. Depression is generally seen as an outcome of other dynamics, and given that the stressor is related to being let down by others, a logical outcome of this (and one that does not seem to have been present from an early age) is her avoidance and interpersonal inhibition. Her sensitivity seems to be core to who she is, which makes it a logical part of the diathesis.

The theme remaining is her dependency and submissiveness. This trait could be seen as an outcome. Because Heather is so sensitive as a person and has been let down by others in the past and now has anxiety about relationships, she simply acquiesces and acts dependently in order to avoid the stress of confrontation and complexities of deep relationships. The trait could also be seen as part of her diathesis, however. She is a somewhat needy, sensitive individual who has been let down by others in the past and has developed anxiety about relationships, and consequently became depressed and began avoiding others. Either of these explanations could work. At the moment, the former will be presented. The diathesis-stress model for Heather is shown in Figure 11.1.

FIGURE 11.1   DIATHESIS-STRESS MODEL FOR HEATHER

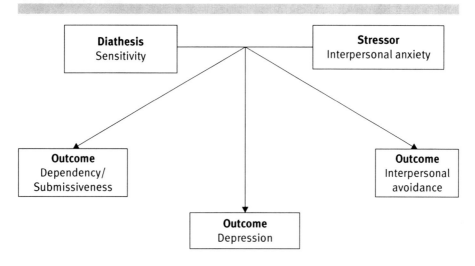

This model is straightforward, intuitive, and easily arguable. A girl who is extremely sensitive, has been let down by others, and has developed anxiety about socialization and relationships would easily do what she could to manage this anxiety, including avoiding others and avoiding conflict by being submissive and passive. Additionally, a girl such as this could easily become depressed, including having low self-esteem. One benefit of this model is that it does not have to be explained straightforwardly as a diathesis–stress model in the report—that is, the reader does not necessarily need to know that the interpersonal anxiety theme is being stretched and justified as an external stressor. The model simply needs to be explained in terms of the themes, and this one makes good intuitive sense.

Developmental Model

The developmental model for Heather is again somewhat complicated. Along a developmental spectrum, she is chronologically in the middle of adolescence, so it would be expected that she is struggling with issues of identity development and individuation. Developmentally, however, what is salient is her normatively high dependency needs and behaviors and her sensitivity and lack of ability to cope emotionally with the demands of her life. These features are much more normative for a very young child, who is still highly dependent on her caregiver.

Thinking of Heather developmentally (in some aspects) as a young child, facing the normal demands of an adolescent, the developmental model would then posit that the rest of the themes are outcomes of this mismatch of her ability and what she faces. If a very young child were faced with the actual demands of an adolescent, it would not be surprising for her to become interpersonally anxious, as interpersonal relationships for adolescents are much more complex than those of a young child, which could be frightening. Additionally, a child in this context could easily become both depressed and avoidant, withdrawing from the scary adolescent world. This model is highly arguable and understandable. The developmental model for Heather is shown in Figure 11.2.

This model makes intuitive sense, in general. One of its major drawbacks, however, is that Heather, in many areas of her life, is not functioning as a young child. She is actually functioning quite well (for example, academically) as an adolescent. When meeting with her, the assessor found her polite and mature. Thus, it may be difficult for her or her parents to relate to a model that is based on the supposition that she is somehow

FIGURE 11.2   **DEVELOPMENTAL MODEL FOR HEATHER**

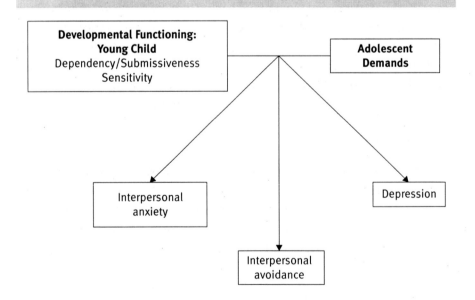

delayed developmentally, even if it is only in her emotional functioning. The assessor chose not to use this model, because he did not want to stigmatize or offend Heather and her parents.

Common Function Model

The common function model requires the themes to align such that all of the themes are serving a common purpose, which is generally embodied in one or two of the themes. The first step is to understand the common function Heather would organize her defenses around addressing—that is, what are her basic underlying needs, which the other themes serve to address? One way of organizing this model to apply to Heather is around her need to cope with her own sensitivity, which at the moment is causing depression. Given this as the common function, the other three themes must arguably help her achieve this goal—they must logically help her cope with her own sensitivity and depression. As she does not have the resources to cope with the world around her herself, her dependency and submissiveness allow her to rely on others (especially her parents) to help her cope.

Additionally, because her depression—and more specifically her own self-esteem—is largely based on how others see her, her acquiescent behavior can help minimize any conflict with others. The fact that her self-worth is reliant on how she feels others view her, however, is a double-edged sword. She can behave passively to stay in others' good favor, but that can also lead to great anxiety when she is faced with interpersonal interactions. Thus, her interpersonal anxiety serves as a warning mechanism that she must be careful how she behaves in front of others, ultimately serving the common function of coping with her sensitivity and depression. Similarly, because her self-worth is so tied to how others view her, she avoids others so as not to tempt their negative evaluations of her, again serving the ultimate common function of coping with her sensitivity. The common function model for Heather is shown in Figure 11.3.

If argued appropriately in the report and feedback, this model can make intuitive sense. It does not have the drawback of the developmental model, which could possibly offend Heather and her parents. Instead, it contextualizes her interpersonal feelings and behavior firmly within her internal world; she feels and acts the way she does with others because she is a sensitive,

FIGURE 11.3   COMMON FUNCTION MODEL FOR HEATHER

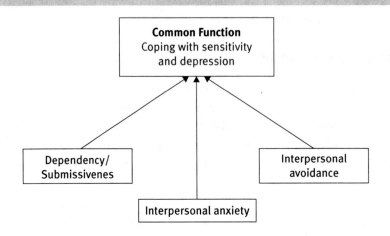

emotional person. This statement is likely to "ring true" with both Heather and her parents, as they already view her as sensitive and intuitive.

Complex Model

Each of these models makes some intuitive sense, and each is wholly applicable to describe what is going on for Heather. Each requires some explanation, which is not unusual. If a slightly more complex model is considered, many different models could emerge and have validity. One way of building a complex model is by beginning with one of the basic models and seeing whether some alterations help it make even more intuitive sense. This would be possible for each of the former models in this case; however, another way is to think about what each of the models has in common.

Each of the three previous models starts with Heather's sensitive personality. If this trait is considered core to who she is, the other themes could flow directly from it alone. That is, an individual who is so sensitive (including lacking coping resources and relying heavily on how others view her for her own self-worth) would need to behave in a passive, acquiescent manner in order to gain the support of those around her. Still, she may also develop anxiety about dealing with other people, who

FIGURE 11.4 **COMPLEX MODEL FOR HEATHER**

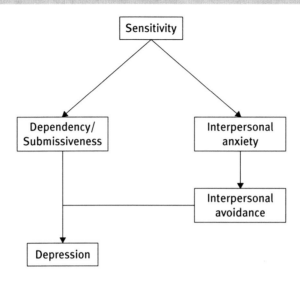

may often disappoint and even hurt someone so sensitive. This interpersonal anxiety has led Heather to become socially avoidant, so that she does not have to cope with the anxiety that interacting with others causes. However, this brings about a very core conflict for Heather—she both needs other people deeply and fears interacting with them. This conflict between longing for approval by others and avoiding others has led to depression, which makes sense; the confusing nature of the conflict within her could be turned inward, making her feel that she is worthless. The complex model for Heather is shown in Figure 11.4.

This model fits Heather well—she has conflicted feelings about being with others. On one hand, she longs for relationships and to be accepted by peers. On the other hand, she does experience a great deal of anxiety in interacting socially and building relationships, which has led her to avoiding others. This model highlights that struggle within her, as well as explaining that her interpersonal functioning is directly related to how sensitive a person she is. Of course, this model is no more "valid" than any of the others, but it may simply be easier to write up and argue than some of the previous models.

REPORT WRITING

Before the report can be written, one final step is necessary—the determination of diagnosis and recommendations. Our original hypotheses included a mood disorder, an anxiety disorder, an adjustment disorder, a somatoform disorder, and a personality disorder. In terms of ruling any of these out rather easily, the duration of the symptoms and the lack of a clear predisposing event rules out the likelihood that her symptoms are related to an adjustment disorder. Additionally, while her vomiting may constitute a gastrointestinal complaint to meet criteria for undifferentiated somatoform disorder, it seems clear from our model that this symptom is much better explained by some type of anxiety disorder. Thus, an anxiety disorder, a mood disorder, and the possibility of a personality disorder are left.

In terms of her depressive symptoms, which emerged pretty clearly from the assessment, the principal task is to determine which of the disorders the cluster of symptoms most closely resembles and which disorder she meets the criteria for. The hypotheses included major depressive disorder and dysthymic disorder. Her symptoms seem more consistent with a dysthymic disorder than a major depressive disorder, because of the persistent, long-term, low-grade depressive sadness and irritability. Specifically, her depressive symptoms include sadness and irritability, but do not include changes in sleep, appetite, energy, or concentration. Because of the lack of other symptoms, she does not meet the full criteria of dysthymic disorder. Given her subjectively felt distress and her parents' concern, her depressive symptoms are causing impairment in her functioning. The only option left is to diagnose her with depressive disorder not otherwise specified, which will account for the significant level of sadness and irritability that emerged from the assessment.

The more difficult differential diagnosis for Heather is that of her anxiety and social avoidance symptoms. The major considerations are (a) whether the anxiety is generalized or more specific to social situations (i.e., generalized anxiety disorder vs. social phobia); (b) if it is specific to social situations, whether it is more of an anxiety-driven disorder or is ingrained into her character (i.e., social phobia vs. a personality disorder); and (c) if it is more ingrained in her personality, whether she is upset about the lack of socialization or is emotionally detached from and indifferent to it (i.e., avoidant vs. schizoid personality disorder).

In terms of the first differential diagnosis distinction, Heather's anxiety certainly does seem limited to social and interpersonal situations—the themes that emerged (as well as clinical data reported by her and her parents) support this. Consequently, generalized anxiety disorder can be ruled out. More difficult is deciding whether the symptoms are primarily anxiety driven or more a deeply ingrained part of her personality. Given her young age, the salience of the anxiety symptoms (especially the vomiting), and the fact that she did at one point socialize at least somewhat more freely and openly, her difficulties seem to fit the criteria of social phobia better. The third distinction is now moot, since a personality disorder has been ruled out (though her presentation would certainly be closer to avoidant than schizoid personality disorder).

In terms of recommendations, considering her diagnoses, some sort of psychotherapeutic treatment is warranted. Her major difficulty at this point seems to be the social phobia, and the treatment of choice for this disorder is cognitive-behavioral therapy (CBT), perhaps in conjunction with medication. Additionally, she could consider joining an adolescent socialization therapy group to improve her social skills. Because her depression is not severe enough to warrant a diagnosis of major depressive disorder, there will not be a recommendation for a psychiatric consultation for her depressive symptoms. With effective CBT therapy, both her anxious and depressive symptoms should be effectively addressed to enable her to function much better in general.

An interesting note with this assessment report is the fact that her cognitive functioning testing revealed very little interesting material, other than low processing speed. The subtests that make up each of the indices (VCI, PRI, WMI, and PSI) all fell within the average range for the former three indices and the low average range for the latter. Because of these results, and because the cognitive functioning is not central to the referral questions, presenting problems, or her current functional impairment, an abbreviated cognitive functioning section is used in the current report.

Identifying Information

Name:	Heather Daltry	**Date of Report:**	6/15/08
Sex:	Female	**Assessor:**	A. Jordan Wright, PhD
Age:	15	**Dates of Testing:**	5/25/08; 5/29/08;
Date of Birth:	1/1/1993		6/8/08
Ethnicity:	Caucasian		

Source of Referral and Referral Questions

The patient was referred by her parents to assess for diagnostic and treatment purposes. Specifically, she and her parents reported wanting help with her anxious and depressive symptoms.

Measures Administered

- Clinical Interview
- Collateral Interview with Mother and Father
- Bender Visual-Motor Gestalt Test, 2nd Edition (Bender-2)
- Wechsler Intelligence Scale for Children, 4th Edition (WISC-IV)
- Millon Adolescent Clinical Inventory (MACI)
- Rorschach Inkblot Test, Comprehensive System (Rorschach)
- Roberts Apperception Test for Children (RAT-C)
- Animal Identification and Devaluation Task (AID)
- Projective Wishes Task (Projective Wishes)
- House-Tree-Person and Kinetic Family Drawings (Projective Drawings)

Description of Patient

Heather Daltry is a 15-year-old, Caucasian female of average height and weight for her age. She was dressed nicely and appropriately, and she was extremely polite and friendly with the assessor throughout the assessment process.

Presenting Problem

The patient and her parents reported that she suffers from anxiety, especially related to social and interpersonal relationships. Specifically, she is reportedly extremely sensitive, "taking things too hard," at times becoming sick to her stomach when she is supposed to socialize. She reported that she gets extremely nervous when she is in situations where she has to interact with others. As a result, she has difficulty sustaining relationships, and she becomes upset and "depressed."

The patient's parents reported that she is loving and affectionate, with "a good head on her shoulders." However, her father reported that she has begun to "get an attitude," not listening when he tries to speak to her. Other than that, her parents reported no difficulties with her at home, and the patient reported that she has a very close relationship with her mother, to whom she tells "everything."

Currently, the patient reported her mood as fluctuating, occasionally feeling depressed. When depressed, she does not feel good about herself, at times feeling unworthy of being friends with others and not liking the way she looks. She reported passive suicidal ideation, but she denied any intent to harm herself. In general, she reports feeling she is "a good person."

Background Information

History of Presenting Problem

The patient's parents reported that she has always had some social anxiety, though it was reportedly "better" between the ages of 10 and 13. However, the patient reported that her social problems have only become apparent during the past three years, not recalling any social difficulty or anxiety before then.

About three years ago, she joined a group of friends, but over the years those friends began fighting among themselves. She recently began high school, where she is more often forced to interact with larger groups of peers. She reported that she has "people I see occasionally on weekends" and that she goes out occasionally. However, she currently does not have a close friend; her previous best friend "stabbed me in the back."

Symptomatic Evaluation

The patient's parents reported no difficulties during her mother's pregnancy with her, except for her mother developing asthma during pregnancy. She reached all developmental milestones early, and although she had some academic difficulty early on, she is currently on the honor roll at a "difficult school"; she currently sees a mathematics tutor. Her father, mother, and one sister all suffer from anxiety, one grandfather had bipolar disorder, and her other grandfather suffered from depression and anxiety. No known current or past significant medical issues were reported, she

(Continued)

denied any current or past drug or alcohol use, and she has not been in any form of psychological or psychiatric treatment in the past.

Psychosocial Evaluation

The patient is the youngest of three daughters, all of whom live with their mother and father. Her sisters are 18 and 21 years old. The family seems extremely loving and supportive, and the patient is extremely close with her mother. The patient does not currently have any close friends, but she does socialize occasionally with peers on weekends and outside of school, though this causes her much anxiety. She does have a history of friendships, however.

The patient denied any criminal or legal involvement and is not dating or sexually active. She reported that she is culturally part of the majority within her school and community, which is predominantly White, and that she has never had any difficulties because of her culture, race, ethnicity, or religion as a nonpracticing Christian.

Mental Status

The patient was nicely and appropriately dressed, well-groomed, and extremely cooperative and friendly throughout the testing process, maintaining appropriate eye contact, except when discussing her own depression. Her motor activity was within normal limits. She was extremely candid, open, and talkative, disclosing information freely. Both her receptive and expressive language ability were extremely good. Her mood was reportedly "somewhat down," though her affect was bright and mood-incongruent. Her thought process was goal-directed, and her thought content was free of hallucinations, delusions, and homicidal ideation. She reported passive suicidal ideation, but she denied any intent to harm herself. Her memory seemed within normal limits, and her attention and concentration were adequate. Her insight, impulse control, and judgment were all good.

Behavioral Observations

The patient was extremely friendly and cooperative throughout testing. She gave effortful attempts on all tests administered. During tasks requiring drawing and copying, she often paid attention to minute details, clearly unhappy with her efforts, erasing often and sighing. At times, she exhibited slightly anxious behaviors, including her hand shaking slightly; however, it is believed that the current testing is an accurate representation of her current functioning, given her effort.

Overall Interpretation of Test Findings

Cognitive Functioning

The patient's Full Scale IQ score on the WISC-IV fell within the 37th percentile, within the Average range when compared to others her own age. Her Verbal Comprehension, Perceptual Reasoning, and Working Memory Indices all fell within the Average range compared to her same-age peers (61st, 39th, and2 34th percentiles, respectively), while her Processing Speed Index fell within the Low Average range (16th percentile). The patient exhibited no soft signs of gross neurological damage as evidenced by her Average to High Average performance on the Bender-2; however, she did exhibit possible slight interference in her short-term memory with her Low Average performance on the Recall subtest of the Bender-2 (16th percentile).

Weakness in processing speed, which measures the speed at which she processes novel information, as well as memory of visual information, can be attributable to several factors, including emotional interference, personality characteristics such as perfectionism, and structural cognitive impairment. Given the rest of her functioning, it is likely that her speed of processing information is being impaired by her current emotional state, and that in general she is exhibiting Average, adequate cognitive functioning compared to others her age.

Emotional Functioning

The results of the patient's assessment suggest that, at her core, she is an extremely sensitive, intuitive, and caring person. Because of this extreme sensitivity, she relies heavily on others to reassure her, evaluate her positively, and help her feel as though she fits in, which has led to some dependency on others and passive and submissive behavior. However, also due to her sensitivity, she is extremely anxious and hesitant when it comes to interacting with and trusting others, as she has been severely hurt in the past. Because of this interpersonal anxiety, a big part of her simply wants to avoid other people and not risk being hurt by them. However, because of the struggle between the part of her that avoids others and the part of her that needs others to bolster how she feels about herself, she has become depressed.

(Continued)

Sensitive Style. The patient relates to the world in a specific way marked by introversion, sensitivity, and general optimism, which places her at risk for being both easily manipulated by others and hurt by unfavorable interactions. While her Projective Wishes revealed that she views herself as a genuinely good person, and her RAT-C revealed genuine niceness, hope, and optimism, her RAT-C also revealed that how she views herself is highly dependent on how she feels others see her. Her Rorschach revealed that she is highly focused on herself and the fact that others do not generally meet her needs, a theme also revealed in her RAT-C. As such, her Projective Drawings revealed that she is easily hurt by others and easily disappointed. In fact, her MACI revealed that she has come to anticipate pain in interactions with others, and she is highly sensitive to even minor letdowns. She is so attuned to minor slights by others that she tends to make conclusions about how others feel about her hastily and based on incomplete information, likely only hearing negativity, as revealed in her Rorschach. This sensitive style is likely why her parents feel she "takes things too hard," even minor inconveniences. This sensitive style has led both to her interpersonal dependency and passivity and to her interpersonal anxiety.

Interpersonal Dependency and Passivity. Because she is such a sensitive person, the patient has a strong need for others to accept her, reassure her that she is worthwhile, and have positive interactions with her. Her Rorschach, RAT-C, and AID revealed that she longs for closeness, acceptance, and positive peer interactions. Her RAT-C revealed that she genuinely wants positive interactions with others, but that her needs for closeness are not being fulfilled in her life currently. Her MACI suggested that her self-esteem is likely heavily influenced by being accepted by others. These needs explain why she reported that she wants to "fit in" at school. Because of these needs, her MACI, Rorschach, RAT-C, Projective Wishes, and AID revealed that she has become passive in interpersonal relationships, not asserting herself or her needs, likely to avoid negative interaction, which she takes extremely personally. Her Projective Drawings further revealed that she is extremely eager to please others, again likely in order to receive positive feedback from them, even though her RAT-C suggested that this eagerness to please likely interferes with her getting her own needs met. This passivity and eagerness to please is likely responsible for her being so pleasant and cooperative during the assessment process. However, it is also in competition with her extreme interpersonal anxiety.

Interpersonal Anxiety. Because she is such a sensitive person and highly attuned to being disappointed or abused by others, the patient has also become extremely anxious about interacting with others, especially peers. While her Projective Drawings revealed some tendency to misjudge others and her Rorschach revealed some difficulty in her ability to manage interpersonal relationships, her RAT-C, AID, Projective Wishes, and Projective Drawings highlighted that her feelings toward others are largely characterized by mistrust and resentment. Her MACI revealed that this mistrust has led to anxiety, and both her MACI and Projective Drawings specified that this anxiety is targeted toward self-consciousness about interacting with others, especially with peers. This anxiety is being felt clearly by the patient, who self-reported her anxiety and has felt it to the point of vomiting when anticipating having to be in a social situation. This anxiety has become so overwhelming that it has led her to isolate and become interpersonally avoidant.

Interpersonal Avoidance. Because her interpersonal anxiety has made it so uncomfortable for her to socialize, the patient has become isolated and interpersonally avoidant. Her MACI and Rorschach revealed that she has become socially detached from others, and her Projective Wishes revealed that this is a mechanism she uses to cope with the extreme anxiety she has about interacting with others. While she has some ineffective interpersonal behavior, according to her Rorschach, she prefers superficial and shallow relationships and has little motivation to understand the complex dynamics of interpersonal interactions. This avoidance is consistent with her and her parents' report that she has no close friends and avoids socializing with peers in general. This avoidance, however, is in direct conflict with her need for support from and approval by others, which has led to depression.

Depression. Because of the conflict between the part of her that needs approval and support from others and the part of her that avoids others due to the anxiety of interacting and potentially being disappointed or abused, the patient has become depressed. Her Rorschach and RAT-C revealed feelings of sadness, and her Projective Drawings revealed feelings of emptiness, which were confirmed by her self-reported occasional unhappiness. Additionally, her MACI, RAT-C, and Projective Drawings revealed feelings of inadequacy, worthlessness, and low self-esteem, again which were self-reported by the patient as feeling unworthy to be friends with others. Her self-reported loneliness is likely contributing to her feeling depressed, and her recent irritability represents a common manifestation of depression in adolescents.

(Continued)

Summary and Recommendations

Heather Daltry is a 15-year-old, Caucasian female who currently lives with her parents. She was referred for psychological assessment to assess the reason for her difficulties with social relationships. Cognitively, she is currently functioning within the Average range compared to others her age, with no evidence of deficit in any domain. The only exception is slightly slowed processing speed, which is likely a result of emotional distress.

Emotionally, at her core, she is a highly sensitive and kind person. This sensitivity has led both to a need for support and reassurance from others, as she is easily hurt, and to mistrust and anxiety about interacting with others, as she is so sensitive to rejection and disappointment. This anxiety has led her to become socially isolated and interpersonally avoidant, which is in direct conflict with her need for support and reassurance from others. Because of this conflict, she has become depressed, which includes feeling unhappy, low self-esteem, and irritability.

Because of her significant anxiety about, and resulting avoidance of, interacting with others, she currently meets criteria for Social Phobia. Additionally, because her depression and irritability is causing her distress, but because she does not have any symptoms related to her energy level, her interest in activities, her sleep, or her appetite, she meets criteria for depressive disorder not otherwise specified.

Diagnostic Impression

Axis I	300.23	Social Phobia
	311	Depressive Disorder Not Otherwise Specified
Axis II	V71.09	No diagnosis on Axis II
Axis III		None known
Axis IV		Interpersonal difficulties
Axis V	GAF =	60

Recommendations

Given the patient's current functioning, she should consider individual psychotherapy in order to address her depression and social phobia. Specifically, cognitive-behavioral therapy (CBT), in conjunction with collateral meetings with parents and/or family therapy sessions, will be useful in targeting her anxiety and depression. One possible referral would be Dr. Jada Fink, at 212-555-5104.

A social skills group for adolescents may be considered as well, in order to practice both appropriate social skills and tolerating the ambiguities of relationships. In collaboration with the therapist chosen, one resource for adolescent groups to consider is the New York Institute for Group Therapy, at 212-555-0124.

A. Jordan Wright, PhD	Date
New York State Licensed Psychologist	

Feedback

Preparation for Feedback

When considering exactly what feedback to give and how to give it to Heather and her parents, one major point of interest is that the conclusions drawn from the assessment were not necessarily going to be new information for them; in fact, the conclusions from the assessment are exactly what Heather and her parents suspected was going on for her. This fact is both a good thing and a bad thing. While it would likely be extremely validating for this family that they are highly aware of what was going on with Heather, the fact that nothing striking emerged from the assessment could potentially be a bit disheartening, given that there is no new or "magical" angle that treatment can focus on to help her. The recommendations that emerged from the testing are likely more specific than the family was considering previously (i.e., CBT individual therapy, rather than just any individual therapy), though this is based on the assessor's knowledge of treatments of choice for various disorders. Even though nothing groundbreaking emerged from the assessment, the prognosis for Heather is relatively good, inasmuch as both social phobia and depression are generally highly responsive to treatment.

The major considerations when deciding exactly how to give feedback to Heather and her parents were (a) the level of cognitive and intellectual functioning of both Heather and her parents, (b) their level of insight, and (c) the specific type and amount of information that needed to be relayed to them. The additional complication with an adolescent assessment is deciding how to structure the feedback. Generally, the assessor would first give feedback to the adolescent alone and then invite the parents in to receive feedback in front of the adolescent, in order to balance the issues of the adolescent's autonomy and trust in the assessor. For this case, however, the assessor decided to give feedback to Heather and her parents together, given the dynamics of Heather's relationship with her parents and the nature of the feedback. Regarding their intellectual capacity, Heather exhibited no major deficit in any area, so she and her parents could be given the entire report as is, without needing to create a summary sheet. Regarding their level of insight, as discussed previously, all three were extremely aware of Heather's problems. The amount of feedback to give them was driven only by the report itself, as no other concerns emerged that Heather or her parents might have a negative reaction or a major problem with the results or recommendations.

The assessor also decided to give the feedback before giving the family the actual report. Because the feedback was relatively straightforward and because the family struggles with anxiety, the assessor did not want to overwhelm the family from the beginning with the report. So the plan was to go through the feedback for the first half of the session and to go through the report (which would reiterate the feedback) for the second half. Ultimately, the flow of the feedback session will take its pace both from the assessor and from Heather and her parents, because the assessor will constantly check in with their reactions and feelings about the feedback being presented.

Feedback Session

When Heather and her parents came in for the feedback session, the first thing the assessor did was ask Heather what she had thought of the entire process. She glanced at her mother and then said she was eager to find out the results. As usual, the assessor oriented her to how the feedback session would flow, letting all three of them know that they could stop the assessor at any point if they had questions or reactions to anything being said. He let them know that there would be some information that would already be apparent to them, that the assessment simply put a label on it, and that there might be some information that they were not yet aware of, which may or may not align with what they think or feel. They were encouraged to let the assessor know whenever anything did not align with their own thoughts or feelings. They had no questions at this point, so the assessor moved on to the cognitive feedback.

When giving the (very brief) feedback on Heather's cognitive functioning, the focus was on how there were no major impairments or deficits. Rather than emphasize words like "average," the assessor chose to emphasize that there were no major weaknesses in cognitive ability as compared with others her age. Obviously, the major piece of data that emerged from the cognitive testing was the slightly slowed speed of processing information. When presenting this evidence, the assessor contextualized it as common when there is some "emotional stuff going on." Up to this point, there was very little reaction from Heather or her family, because there was not much to react to yet. The assessor paused to confirm that everything was clear and to ask whether they had any reactions, but the session quickly moved to the emotional functioning section.

Rather than beginning by telling the entire story, the assessor decided to start by focusing on the fact that, at her core, Heather is a very sensitive person. As soon as the assessor said this, all three of the family members shared glances and slight smiles. Before even explaining what he meant by "sensitive," the assessor noted aloud that they seemed to have a reaction to this. Heather's mother said that Heather had always been extremely emotional and sensitive and that this trait is what made her "such a good and caring person." Heather added that it also made her "really upset" sometimes. The assessor validated that this trait could be "a double-edged sword," with both extremely positive aspects but also some painful ones for Heather. Traits such as empathy and kindness were discussed, as was taking disappointments and negative interactions too hard. All of this clearly resonated with Heather and her family, as they all obviously recognized these traits in Heather. The focus of the session then shifted to the two things that this sensitivity led to, which were presented together to highlight their inherently battling goals.

The assessor explained that there were two major outcomes from her sensitive nature. The first was an overreliance on how she feels others view her and a strong need for reassurance and support from others, which had led to passive and acquiescent behaviors. Before checking in about this theme, the assessor presented the second outcome of her sensitivity, which was her anxiety about interacting with others, because she was always prepared to be let down, disappointed, or taken advantage of. At

this point, the assessor went back to the first of the two themes to clarify
and get the family's reactions.

He explained that her wanting support and approval from others is not
unusual, but that the level of her passivity was slightly greater than most
other girls her age, which, again, has both positive and negative aspects.
Her acquiescence makes her a cooperative, pleasant person—"unlike most
teens her age," her mother added, half-jokingly. The negative side of the
passivity was not necessarily getting her needs met or her perspective heard
with her peers. Heather looked down at her lap, seeming almost ashamed
of what was being discussed, and the assessor reemphasized that "everyone
wants to fit in," so the trait itself is not unusual, but that it can become a
bit too much. Her mother began to rub her daughter's back and said that
Heather does not tend to assert herself in school. Heather addressed this by
saying, "I'd like to be more assertive, though." The assessor validated that
this was a good goal, and an achievable one at that, assuring the family that
the topic of recommendations would be discussed soon and that this is one
goal that could be achieved.

When revisiting the second outcome theme, interpersonal anxiety,
there seemed to be an easy consensus in the room, given that this was the
major problem Heather came in to assess. Explaining this theme further,
the assessor introduced the outcome of the anxiety as being her isolation
and avoidance of social and interpersonal situations. The focus was how
this avoidance was competing with her need for reassurance and support
from others. When this conflict was presented, Heather's mother turned
to her and said, "No wonder you've been upset." It was at this point that
the assessor discussed the outcome of the conflict as depression, which can
come out as sadness, not feeling good enough, or irritability. When checking in with Heather and her parents, they did not have much to say, other
than agreeing that it "sounds like her."

Rather than continue to focus on the emotional functioning section, the
assessor presented his recommendations, including the specific modalities
and the fact that in the report there were specific referrals with contact
information. Again, the family had very little to say about this feedback,
other than to agree that it "sounds like a good idea." The assessor decided
to check in specifically with Heather, as her mother had been serving as
the spokesperson for the family for most of the feedback session. Heather

said she wanted to do "whatever it takes" to feel better and deal with her anxiety. She asked the assessor if he was taking on patients; at that point he was not taking on any therapy patients, but he assured her and her parents that he knew the referrals he was making personally and felt that they would be an excellent match for her.

The assessor then gave them a copy of the report to look over and oriented them to it, running through each of the sections and reiterating the feedback he had just given earlier in the session. He spent extra time on the diagnosis and recommendation sections, the former because he had not gone over the diagnosis earlier, and the latter because he wanted to emphasize that the prognosis for Heather's problems was very good. He explained the diagnosis and what it meant—they were "relieved" when the diagnosis of depressive disorder not otherwise specified was explained to them. The feeling that "it could be worse" helped them understand why the assessor was so hopeful about the prospect of therapy being helpful. They had no questions about social phobia, which was also explained to them.

Finally, the assessor discussed a plan for follow-up after the feedback session. Heather's father agreed to call the assessor in a week to confirm that the referral had been successful (given the many things that can go wrong with referrals). The family thanked the assessor, each member shaking his hand as they left. The following week, Heather's father called to inform the assessor that they had scheduled an appointment with the new therapist for that week.

SUMMARY

While the case of Heather is not one of those psychological assessments that uncovered surprising and previously unknown dynamics (as is the case in many other assessments), it is a good illustration of putting together a narrative that makes clear, intuitive sense to the person being assessed (as well as her parents). Putting together the dynamics of what was going on for Heather into a narrative was ultimately more important than the diagnosis, for example. The same diagnosis likely could have been made with a little more probing in the clinical interview. However, using the testing to rule out the possibilities that her problems were stemming from something other than what was apparent to herself and her parents is ultimately just as important as uncovering some previously unknown dynamic. Additionally, the assessment report was given to Heather's new therapist, and it informed and drove the treatment, so that her depression was not addressed as early or as aggressively as her sensitivity and her interpersonal problems. Even though not every assessment turns out to be groundbreaking in its conclusions, the process is no less valuable in cases such as Heather's.

CHAPTER 12

An Aggressive Boy

Christopher Santiago was a 6-year-old Latino boy who was referred by his school for an assessment for several reasons. He was in a bilingual (English-Spanish) first-grade class in a public elementary school, but he was struggling with reading. Additionally, he was acting out in class, inappropriately disrupting the class at least two times per school day. The purpose of the assessment was to evaluate why he might be having difficulties reading and why he was acting out in school.

THE CLINICAL INTERVIEW

The first appointment for the clinical interview was made for Christopher's parents alone. Given the boy's age, the assessor felt that it would be most beneficial to hear about his difficulties without his being present. The second clinical interview occurred on another day of assessment, and it included meeting with Christopher alone to discuss any difficulties at school or at home and meeting with Christopher and his parents together to observe their family interaction. A third interview was conducted over the telephone with Christopher's teacher.

Christopher's mother came on time for the first session, though his father was about 20 minutes late. His mother was dressed casually in a dress, appropriate for the session. She was an attractive Latina woman in her early 30s who smiled freely and was extremely polite, and she apologized profusely for her husband's tardiness. When his father arrived, they

439

exchanged a very noticeable nonverbal exchange: She glared at him angrily and breathed loudly and deeply, he raised his eyebrows somewhat apologetically, and she rolled her eyes. He was dressed in work attire, wearing a button-down shirt and slacks. He was also attractive and in his early 30s, and he apologized for being late.

As usual, the sections that follow are not categorized into symptomatic evaluation and psychosocial evaluation, because the flow of the clinical interview did not follow that structure. The subsections present the clinical interview as closely as possible to the way it actually unfolded, rather than artificially grouping sections of information that did not present themselves sequentially. That is, the presentation mirrors the way the clinical interview happened chronologically, along with the overarching questions the assessor asked Christopher's parents, Christopher, and his teacher. Clarifications were occasionally necessary throughout the interview, but those questions and comments are not presented here.

Presenting Problem: So Can You Tell Me What's Going On With Christopher?

Christopher's mother began speaking, answering the question as though defending Christopher. She stated that he had always been "a good kid," that he had never had difficulties in school or with his behavior before this school year. In his kindergarten class, he had been attentive and cooperative, and he had never had academic difficulties. At home, he had always behaved—she said they had a loving family and had never had any difficulties. After some time of this kind of reporting, the assessor interjected, "So some of that has changed?"

"Well," she responded, "his teacher is concerned." She went on to report that his teacher had discussed with them a noticeable problem with Christopher's reading ability, which was reportedly lagging behind others in his class. She also said that in the past several months Christopher had been misbehaving at school and at home. As she said this, she glanced at her husband. The assessor asked both of them to describe what she meant by "misbehaving." His mother began by stating that Christopher does not listen to his father, throwing tantrums whenever he asks him to do anything, even if it is very minor and inconsequential. At this point, the assessor chose to stop his mother from going on in order to ask his father about this behavior. "Just what she said—anything I ask him to do sets him off." He went on to report that they have a "relatively good relationship," that as long as he is not requesting anything, Christopher is very loving and warm with him. His father reportedly reads him bedtime stories every night, a ritual that Christopher loves and cannot get to sleep without. "But when I ask him to do anything, he gets aggressive, hitting me, screaming, and crying."

His mother reported that this misbehavior happens occasionally with her as well and has begun happening at school. She reported that he apparently disrupts the classroom with outbursts several times during the day, though he is able to be calmed down by his teacher—"she's very good." Again glancing at her husband, his mother stated that they do not understand why there has been such a change in Christopher's behavior.

History of Presenting Problem, Developmental History, and Educational History: So You Said That This Is a Pretty Big Change in His Behavior, Huh?

Both Christopher's mother and father adamantly stated that he had been "a model child" before about four months ago, when these behavioral problems began. He had reportedly been "a good sleeper" as a baby, generally crying only when hungry or in need of a diaper change. He had met all of his developmental milestones on time; he was a curious child who crawled and walked easily, and toilet training had gone smoothly. He was a verbal child, and his parents had read to him every night since he was a baby.

Christopher's mother reported some difficulty with his first day of kindergarten, when he did not want his mother to leave the classroom. "But after the first day, he loved it and had no problem going from then on." In kindergarten, he had excelled academically, with no reported difficulties from his teacher in his reading (or other academic areas) or in his behavior for the entire year. When he went into the first grade, he changed teachers (as all the children in his school do), but both parents felt that his first-grade teacher was excellent and warm.

Family History: Okay, I Want to Ask Some More General Information So I Can Learn About Christopher; Can You Tell Me More About Your Family?

Again, Christopher's mother answered the question. She reported that Christopher is the only child in the family, and he had been born about six years after she and her husband married. She was "a stay-at-home mom," after having worked for the first six years of their marriage as a teacher's assistant in a school, but she had been taking night classes for the past three years to get a nursing degree. Her husband reported that he worked as a customer service representative in a bank. He added that their schedule "works well," because he comes home and can be with Christopher while she goes to school, which is why he reads Christopher his bedtime stories each night. Both agreed that it was good that Christopher was never without one of them when he was at home each day.

Suspecting from their interaction that something may be going on between the couple, the assessor asked more specific details about their relationship, beginning with how they met. They reported that they had met in high school; they were both part of a very small group of students who had been born in Puerto Rico but had moved to New York as younger children. They dated "on and off" for several years before getting married around the time they were 21 years old. Having Christopher was planned and expected, and they had agreed that his mother would stay at home and raise him during his childhood. There was a long, somewhat awkward pause, during which they glanced at each other knowingly. The assessor noted aloud that he felt there was something more they were not yet telling him.

Christopher's mother stated that they both loved Christopher very much, and that they felt they were very good parents. She reported, though, that they were having difficulties in their own relationship, but that they were "working hard to keep it from Christopher." They were fighting often, sometimes about money and sometimes about "petty, inconsequential things," but they were careful never to fight when Christopher was home. Generally, they fought in the morning after Christopher had left for school, and occasionally they fought "quietly" after he had gone to bed and his mother had come home from school. Both parents were looking down toward their laps, not making eye contact with the assessor, and his father reported that they were starting to think about whether or not their marriage "works." Their greatest fear was, if they decided to divorce, how to handle telling Christopher. They both quickly reassured the assessor, both looking at him for the first time during this section of the interview, that the other was a good parent and that they would share custody and be friendly with each other while raising Christopher. The assessor empathized with the difficulty of their situation and validated their commitment to their son.

Medical and Psychiatric History and Family Medical and Psychiatric History: Now, I Want to Switch Gears a Bit and Ask You Some Specific Questions About Christopher, If That's Okay

Christopher's parents looked somewhat relieved not to have to talk about their own marital difficulties, and they said they were happy to answer questions about Christopher. The assessor asked about medical and psychiatric history, and both parents denied any history of serious medical problems and any history of any form of psychiatric or psychotherapeutic treatment. They stated that they had "had it easy" with Christopher from the beginning.

The assessor asked, "Okay, what about the two of you and the rest of your family? Any medical or psychiatric problems?" Both denied any major medical problems or psychiatric history. His mother reported that her grandfather had died of heart disease, but that nobody else had had any major medical problems in her family. His father reported that he thought his own mother may have been depressed when she moved from Puerto Rico, but that she had not been diagnosed or received treatment. About four years ago, she and his father (Christopher's paternal grandfather) had moved back to Puerto Rico, and he said that she seemed "much happier there."

Alcohol and Substance Abuse History: Any History of Alcohol or Drug Abuse in Your Family?

Both parents denied using any substances, except for his father having "an occasional beer" with friends. They said they did not want Christopher exposed to such things in the home, so they did not even keep alcohol in their house or refrigerator. Christopher's father reported that he had had a great uncle in Puerto Rico who had "drunk himself to death," so they "just want[ed] to be safe" and not expose Christopher to alcohol or any other drugs.

Social History: Tell Me About Christopher's Social Life

Both parents seemed to brighten in their demeanor at this question. His mother reported that he had many friends, some from the neighborhood and children of their own friends, and some from school. "He's very popular—even his teacher says so." Christopher both attended and hosted sleepovers with friends, and he had a best friend, Jonathon. They had been best friends since about the second week of kindergarten, and even though they had been placed in different first-grade classrooms, they had remained best friends, always sitting together at lunch and playing together at recess. Christopher's parents said they liked Jonathon, "a good kid," and his parents, and they were happy that Christopher had so many friends in school.

Psychosexual History and Criminal/Legal History: Here Are Some Questions I Ask Everybody; Does Christopher Have Any History of Physical or Sexual Abuse, or Any Other Involvement With the Law?

Both parents denied any history of abuse and legal involvement, both for Christopher and themselves. His father asked, almost incredulously, whether any 6-year-old the assessor had assessed had been in trouble with the law. The assessor explained that if any child had, it would be important for him to know in order to understand the child or family entirely.

Multicultural Evaluation: So You're Both From Puerto Rico— Was It Difficult Adjusting to New York

Both parents looked at the assessor a bit confused, perhaps wondering why he was asking about their acculturation (as opposed to something about Christopher), but they answered anyway. Both reported that what really helped them acculturate was the small community of Puerto Ricans they lived near in New York, as well as the small group of Puerto Rican children in school. Although they spoke only Spanish at home growing up, both had chosen to speak only English in school and with each other—their home now was a monolingual English-speaking home—in order to help them "fit in" better in mainland America. They both reported that Christopher's school was very diverse and "open" to different races. His mother noted that Jonathon, Christopher's best friend, was Black, and that his other friends were "all different colors."

Session 2

Christopher came in with his parents for the second session, and the session began with all three of them in the room together with the assessor. Christopher was a small, athletic child with a very bright smile and had very little difficulty engaging the assessor, a complete stranger. He was dressed casually in jeans and a T-shirt and played with the foam basketball and hoop in the room almost immediately after being introduced to the assessor. Both of his parents played with him, lovingly, as they chatted casually with the assessor. After some play time, the family sat with the assessor and explained to Christopher why he was there, and the assessor explained what the sessions would entail. The assessor then asked Christopher if it would be okay to meet with him alone, without his parents, and he shrugged and said, "Sure."

Presenting Problem: So Tell Me About School

The assessor decided to do the clinical interview while playing foam basketball with Christopher in the office. They maintained a good, casual conversation while shooting baskets, dribbling the ball ineffectively (foam balls do not dribble well), and running around the office. Christopher said that school was "good" and that he liked his teacher. He said that some of it was "hard," though, saying that sometimes he did not understand what was going on in class. When asked for details, Christopher was not able to explain, and he became more energetic in his basketball playing. "I hear you have a lot of friends." To this Christopher smiled widely and started talking about his best friend, Jonathon, who was "awesome." He talked about several "pretend games" they played, usually being wizards who can turn any bad thing that happens into a good thing.

"And how's everything going at home?" Christopher stopped running around for a moment, as if thinking about the question, then said, "Okay, I guess." When the assessor asked, "You guess?" Christopher said that he wished his parents would see him more. When asked what he meant by this, Christopher shrugged and went back to playing basketball. The assessor asked how he feels when his parents do not see him enough, and he reported that he gets "sad like them." Again, he was unable (or unwilling) to elaborate what he meant by this. He did deny that he ever considered hurting himself. They continued to play basketball for a bit, then they began doing some testing.

Collateral Interview With Teacher

Christopher's parents signed a release form for the assessor to speak with Christopher's teacher. When they were able to speak on the phone for a good amount of time, the assessor asked her to discuss Christopher's functioning at school.

Presenting Problem: Tell Me About Christopher at School

Christopher's first-grade teacher spoke openly about Christopher. She reported that, overall, he was an extremely well-behaved child. She was very good friends and close colleagues with his kindergarten teacher, and she had expected him to be a model student on entering the first grade. Only a few weeks after beginning, however, he began to have some difficulties in class. He had been an average student in kindergarten, and moving him into a bilingual English–Spanish classroom in the first grade was meant to improve his academic performance. At this point, the assessor clarified with the teacher that half of the day was taught in English and half was taught in Spanish, which she confirmed as correct. She reported that many of the Hispanic children in the school were placed on a bilingual track, and almost all of them performed better in these bilingual classes than in their previous monolingual English classes.[1]

She continued to report almost identically what Christopher's parents had reported, that when he became frustrated in class he tended to misbehave, not listening to her instructions, occasionally throwing a book or

---

[1]After this collateral interview, even though no testing had been done yet, the assessor called Christopher's parents to confirm that they were aware that he was in a bilingual classroom. They reported that it may have been mentioned, but that they had not realized it. The assessor again confirmed that they spoke only English at home, and he recommended, even before the testing, that they have him transferred to a monolingual English-speaking classroom.

pushing a chair over in a tantrum. She also confirmed that she was able to calm him down relatively easily and get him "back on track." She also reported that his reading ability did not seem to be improving in class as much as his peers'. She was not sure whether that was because of a learning disability or "something else," but there was something interfering with his reading skill. She then offered to speak again if the assessor felt he needed any more information, and they hung up.

MENTAL STATUS EVALUATION

Appearance and Behavior

Christopher was well groomed and casually and appropriately dressed for all sessions. He was a small, athletic 6-year-old boy with a bright smile and a friendly demeanor. He had no difficulty engaging the assessor or adapting to the testing situation.

Speech and Language

Christopher was open and articulate, and his speech was generally goal-directed and logical, except for a few times when he would speak rapidly and tangentially about his friends. He spoke fluent, grammatically correct English with no defining accent. He had no difficulties with receptive language, understanding all the directions on all of the tests administered.

Mood and Affect

Christopher was reportedly and observed to be happy throughout most of the assessment. There were several times he reported that he would become "sad," and his facial expression and demeanor were congruent with this feeling. Generally, this would occur when discussing his parents and their "unhappiness."

Thought Process and Content

Christopher's thought process seemed clear and logical, free of hallucinations and delusions. He became slightly tangential when discussing his friends, telling the assessor long stories about games that he would play with them. His thought content was free of suicidal and homicidal ideation, and he did not report any anxiety.

Cognition

Christopher was alert and engaged throughout the assessment. His attention, concentration, and memory seemed intact.

Prefrontal Functioning

Christopher exhibited good planning and judgment. His impulse control was adequate, except when he at times got carried away with the energetic games played in session, when he would become overly excited and impulsive.

HYPOTHESIS BUILDING

Now that the clinical assessment (the clinical and collateral interviews and the mental status evaluation) has been completed, the information gathered can be used to create hypotheses for what is going on for Christopher.

Identify Impairments

Christopher has two major impairments in functioning, which seem separate but may be related. First, he is struggling academically. Although it seems obvious that a child who does not speak Spanish should not be in a bilingual, English-Spanish classroom, he is having significant trouble reading, even in English, his primary language. Thus, his academic difficulty seems as though it might be related to a cognitive difficulty. Second, he is acting out behaviorally, both in school and at home. This behavior has come on only recently and is markedly different from the way his parents report he "usually is."

Enumerate Possible Causes

Thinking first about Christopher's academic difficulties, there are a few major reasons he might be struggling with reading. The obvious first major hypothesis is a *reading disorder*. If he is reading at a level below what would be expected given his general aptitude (IQ) and educational opportunity (which at the moment includes being in an inappropriate classroom), he would qualify for this specific learning disorder. The criteria for the reading disorder, however, reveal two other hypotheses. The null hypothesis, the fact that in actuality nothing is inherently wrong with Christopher academically, is a much more realistic option in this case than in many others, given the fact that he is in a clearly inappropriate learning environment (his bilingual classroom). However, there still may be reading difficulties above and beyond this classroom problem.

The second additional hypothesis revealed by the criteria of the learning disorder is the possibility that he simply has low cognitive functioning and would not actually be expected to read at a higher level. This hypothesis creates two possible diagnoses—*borderline intellectual functioning* and *mental retardation*. He does not seem to have any of the markers of a more general cognitive disorder that would impair his reading ability, such as a communication disorder, so these seem like the most likely diagnoses. However, as is the case with all academic problems, a final hypothesis could be that his emotional and behavioral functioning is interfering with his learning. That is, if his acting out during school is impeding his attending to lessons and taking in the information taught, then he simply would not grow academically at the same rate that his peers who pay attention would. Based on his teacher's report, however, his acting out in class does not seem to be to such a severe degree that he is missing most of his lessons.

His acting-out behavior, both at home and in school, which is a marked change from previous behavior, may have several explanations diagnostically. While they may be signs of an *oppositional-defiant disorder (ODD)*, this diagnosis would be the choice of last resort, to be chosen only if it is determined that the acting-out behavior is not secondary to any other problems. These "other problems" that the acting-out behavior could be secondary to are emotional difficulties. That is, it is widely accepted that emotional problems in children are often exhibited as behavioral problems. Therefore, both *anxiety* and *depressive disorders* should be included as possibilities. Included in these anxiety and depressive disorders would be an *adjustment disorder*. At his present age he is really adjusting to many different identifiable stressors, though the symptoms would have to be clearly linked to one of these transitions or changes to qualify for an adjustment disorder diagnosis.

You should *always* consider (a) that the presenting problems have an etiology in substance use and (b) that the presenting problems have an etiology in a medical condition. For Christopher, there seems to be little possibility that either of these is the case. At 6 years old, it is extremely unlikely that he is using any substances without his parents' knowledge, and they denied any use, so it is unlikely that his symptoms are attributable to substance use. Additionally, he recently had a full physical exam that revealed no evidence of any medical problems. Accordingly, it will be assumed that the symptoms are primarily psychological in nature.

SELECTING TESTS

Because there are several cognitive hypotheses in question, test selection should include a larger battery of cognitive tests than some of the other assessments presented previously that were primarily emotional. To understand Christopher's academic difficulties, the first step is to understand his overall intellectual ability, which is measured with the Wechsler Intelligence Scale for Children, 4th Edition (WISC-IV). As part of this overall understanding, as always, the Bender Visual-Motor Gestalt Test, 2nd Edition (Bender-2) will provide a screening measure of gross neurological impairment. Importantly, though, we must also understand his academic achievement functioning in general, as well as his reading ability more specifically. To assess his general academic functioning, a broad achievement test will be used—the Wechsler Individual Achievement Test, 2nd Edition (WIAT-II). For a more specific assessment of his reading functioning, including exactly how it may be impaired, the Gray Diagnostic Reading Tests, 2nd Edition (GDRT-2) will be used. This test provides measures of decoding separate from measures of comprehension, which will help identify where in the process of reading he is having difficulty (if he has, in fact, a reading disorder). Additional reading tests (such as tests for reading fluency, etc.) could be added if the results from these tests are inconclusive.

For the emotional, personality, and behavioral assessment, because of his age, a broad-based objective collateral-report measure will be used, which his parents fill out—the Behavior Assessment System for Children, 2nd Edition (BASC-2). This measure includes both clinical and adaptive scales on both behavioral and emotional constructs. It should give an excellent overview of any specific difficulties, from inattention, to somatization, to the anxiety and depressive information that will be important for the hypotheses generated previously. Additionally, the BASC-2 will offer a quantified report of Christopher's aggression and conduct problems. Several projective measures will be used, both to establish more evidence of his emotional functioning and because they provide less threatening and more fun activities than many other psychological tests. For Christopher's age, a Rorschach Inkblot Test can be used, and for the projective storytelling technique (e.g., a Thematic Apperception Test) for his age, the Children's Apperception Test (CAT) will be used. Additional brief (and somewhat fun) projective measures will include the Animal Identification and Devaluation Task (AID), the Sentence Completion Task, Projective Wishes, and Projective Drawings. Together, the BASC-2 and the multiple projective tests should reveal what, if any, emotional disturbance is present.

Thus, our assessment's battery of tests will consist of

- Bender-2
- WISC-IV
- WIAT-II
- GDRT-2
- BASC-2
- Rorschach
- CAT
- AID
- Sentence Completion Task
- Projective Wishes
- Projective Drawings

ACCUMULATING THE DATA

Table 12.1 shows the results from each individual measure administered. On the WISC-IV, Christopher performed within the average range as compared with others his age overall (full scale IQ of 100, 50th percentile). All of his indices were average, including his verbal comprehension index, which was a 99 and fell within the 47th percentile. His performance on the Bender-2 was average across all of the subtests.

| TABLE 12.1 | ACCUMULATION OF CHRISTOPHER'S DATA |

BASC-2

Nervousness and anxiety

Sadness

Poor adaptability

High aggression

Conduct problems

Rorschach

Coping deficit

Hypervigilance

Takes in too much information

Some anxiety

Sadness and internalized negative affect

Feelings of vulnerability

Dependency needs not being met

Highly aware of not being taken care of

Acting out behavior

Anger

Good interpersonal skills

Adequate self-esteem

CAT

Resentment at not being attended to

Focus on parental discord

Attuned to others

Feeling neglected

Anxiety about not being able to take care of himself

Acting out when confused about emotions

Sadness and loneliness

AID

Wants more power and security

Wants to be taken care of

Sentence Completion

Aware of his parents' unhappiness

Anxious in general

TABLE 12.1   (CONTINUED)

Feels vulnerable

Angry

Projective Wishes

Wants parents' attention

Feels uncared for and unsupported

Feels needs are not met

Projective Drawings

Sadness

Fear of the world and its instability

Extremely attentive to detail

Highly attuned to others

Parents focused on each other more than
on him

Behavioral Observations/Other Data

Tantrums at home

Misbehaving in school

Wants to be able to turn bad things into
good (wizard games)

Wanting his parents to see him more

Gets sad at times

Aware that his parents are unhappy

His performance on the WIAT-II and the GDRT-2 was varied. On the WIAT-II, his reading and writing indices were in the low average range (both in the 12th percentile), with his greatest weaknesses appearing on the word-reading and pseudoword decoding subtests (both in the 6th percentile). His mathematics and oral language indices were both average. On the GDRT-2, his general reading composite fell within the low average range as compared with others his age. Interestingly, his comprehension composite was average (27th percentile), while his decoding composite fell within the borderline range (6th percentile). It became clear that he was reading words by recognition rather than by decoding them phonetically. Thus, he was reading at a significantly lower level than would be expected given his average IQ (and especially his average verbal comprehension ability). His comprehension of what was read (revealing that his word recognition while reading was somewhat effective) was adequate for his age. His writing, while weak, was at the expected level given his difficulties in reading.

IDENTIFYING THEMES

As with many assessments at this stage, the most straightforward way to begin identifying themes with Christopher's data is to begin somewhat broadly and narrow down afterwards. Starting with the objective measure (the BASC-2) is a good way to do this, as it generally gives more broad information than some of the projectives, which will help qualify and illuminate some nuances to the general themes. Looking for all of the data that describe his ability to cope, for example, is a broad way to begin, but looking at them all together, side by side in a chart, will help characterize exactly what the data are saying about his ability to cope. Thus, a coping theme may end up being labeled differently in the end, but it is a good place to begin to pull together themed data. The preliminary themes for Christopher's data are presented in Table 12.2.

TABLE 12.2   **LABELING OF CHRISTOPHER'S THEMES**

Themes

	BASC-2
Anxiety	Nervousness and anxiety
Sadness	Sadness
Coping	Poor adaptability
Anger	High aggression
Anger	Conduct problems
	Rorschach
Coping	Coping deficit
Aware	Hypervigilance
Aware	Takes in too much information
Anxiety	Some anxiety
Sadness	Sadness and internalized negative affect
Coping	Feelings of vulnerability
Needs	Dependency needs not being met

TABLE 12.2   *(CONTINUED)*

Themes

Needs	Highly aware of not being taken care of
Anger	Acting out behavior
Anger	Anger
Interpersonal	Good interpersonal skills
Self	Adequate self-esteem
	CAT
Needs	Resentment at not being attended to
Aware	Focus on parental discord
Aware	Attuned to others
Needs	Feeling neglected
Anxiety/coping	Anxiety about not being able to take care of himself
Anger	Acting out when confused about emotions
Sadness	Sadness and loneliness
	AID
Coping	Wants more power and security
Needs	Wants to be taken care of
	Sentence Completion
Aware	Aware of his parents' unhappiness
Anxiety	Anxious in general
Coping	Feels vulnerable
Anger	Angry
	Projective Wishes
Needs	Wants parents' attention
Needs	Feels uncared for and unsupported
Needs	Feels needs are not met
	Projective Drawings
Sadness	Sadness
Anxiety	Fear of the world and its instability
Aware	Extremely attentive to detail
Aware	Highly attuned to others
Needs	Parents focused on each other more than on him

(Continued)

TABLE 12.2 *(CONTINUED)*

Themes

	Behavioral Observations/Other Data
Anger	Tantrums at home
Anger	Misbehaving in school
Coping	Wants to be able to turn bad things into good (wizard games)
Needs	Wanting his parents to see him more
Sadness	Gets sad at times
Aware	Aware that his parents are unhappy

ORGANIZING THE DATA

When the data are examined within themes, some of the themes become clearer and more specific. As discussed previously, the coping theme seems to be describing Christopher's inability to cope with the demands of life, as well as his own feelings of vulnerability. Thus, the theme can be renamed *vulnerability*. Other themes seem to hang together extremely well just as they are, such as the anxiety and sadness themes. At this point, the assessor chose to label the theme sadness, rather than depression, partly because the data that emerged focused specifically on subjectively felt sadness, and also because many people understand the term "depression" differently, including mental health professionals, who associate it with more than just subjective sadness. Christopher's reorganized data are presented in Table 12.3.

These themes seem to be relatively "clean" as they are. While some positive aspects are still categorized as miscellaneous, when the results are written up, a logical place to include them may emerge. Otherwise, they can be incorporated into the overall story, as they reflect general strengths in Christopher's personality and emotional functioning.

CONCEPTUALIZING

Remembering that the task at this point is to try to create a logical narrative among the themes so that it presents a coherent story, we have to connect the following themes:

- Anxiety
- Sadness

TABLE 12.3   CHRISTOPHER'S ORGANIZED DATA

Test: Concept/Theme	BASC-2	Rorschach	CAT	AID and Sentence Completion	Projective Wishes and Drawings	Interview/Behavioral Observations
Anxiety	Nervousness and anxiety	Some anxiety	Anxiety about not being able to take care of himself	Anxious in general	Fear of the world and its instability	
Sadness	Sadness	Sadness and internalized negative affect	Sadness and loneliness		Sadness	Gets sad at times
Coping→Vulnerability	Poor adaptability	Coping deficit	Anxiety about not being able to take care of himself	Wants more power and security		Wants to be able to turn bad things into good (wizard games)
		Feelings of vulnerability		Feels vulnerable		
Anger→Acting Out	High aggression	Anger	Acting out when confused about emotions	Angry		Tantrums at home
	Conduct problems					Misbehaving in school
Aware→High Awareness		Hypervigilance	Focus on parental discord	Aware of his parents' unhappiness	Extremely attentive to detail	Aware that his parents are unhappy

(Continued)

TABLE 12.3 (CONTINUED)

Test: Concept/Theme	BASC-2	Rorschach	CAT	AID and Sentence Completion	Projective Wishes and Drawings	Interview/Behavioral Observations
		Takes in too much information	Attuned to others		Highly attuned to others	
Needs→Unmet Needs		Dependency needs not being met	Resentment at not being attended to	Wants to be taken care of	Wants parents' attention	Wanting his parents to see him more
		Highly aware of not being taken care of	Feeling neglected		Feels uncared for and unsupported	
					Feels needs are not met	
					Parents focused on each other more than on him	
Miscellaneous		Good interpersonal skills				
		Adequate self-esteem				

- Vulnerability
- Acting out
- High awareness
- Unmet needs

Before deciding on the most logical way to fit all these themes together, we will first consider the model templates presented in Chapter 4: the diathesis-stress model, the developmental model, and the common function model for conceptualization.

Diathesis-Stress Model

In applying the diathesis-stress model of conceptualization, we must try to divide the themes into (1) *traits* inherent within Christopher that he likely developed at an even earlier age and that he "brings to the picture" (diatheses), (2) *external issues* that affect his functioning (stressors), and (3) *states* that are more situational and/or transient (outcomes). It is important to categorize each of our six themes into these three types. As always, the more convincing these categorizations are, the more likely Christopher's parents are to accept the recommendations given.

For Christopher, this model is relatively straightforward and intuitive. There are several themes that are easily outcomes, as they are generally not seen as inherent to an individual and his or her personality. There are two that seem more like personality characteristics. And there is one theme that seems clearly related to the impact of external forces on him. Beginning with this external theme, it seems clear that the fact that he has unmet needs is related to his external environment. At his age, these needs likely stem from his parents and secondarily from his teachers, school, and peers. The fact that he has environmental needs that are not being met can easily be argued as an external stressor.

The three themes that are generally not thought of as core to who an individual is in his or her personality or character are anxiety, sadness, and acting out. The assessor could easily argue that these are outcomes of other, more underlying, dynamics occurring within an individual. While an individual may be born with some kind of (perhaps genetic) predisposition for depression, very few people believe that a child can be born inherently sad. Other factors must play a part in creating this sadness. Especially with Christopher, the changes in his emotional and behavioral functioning (i.e., the fact that several years before he did not seem to be anxious, sad, or acting out) are also good clues that these themes may not be inherent to who he is as a person and that they are not likely diatheses.

However, the remaining two themes—his high awareness of what goes on around him and his vulnerability and lack of ability to cope with difficult things on his own—*do* seem to be more characteristic of who Christopher is as a person. These seem to be more related to his overall personality and defensive structure than to his current emotional or situational functioning. The diathesis-stress model for Christopher is shown in Figure 12.1.

When considering the viability of this model, we have to decide whether the model makes intuitive sense with the three categorized parts. That is, would the diathesis posed, combined with the external stressor, likely cause the outcomes? A boy who is highly vulnerable to becoming overwhelmed and who is acutely aware of what is happening around him, when he feels (perhaps rightly so) that his needs are not being met, could develop emotional symptoms such as anxiety and depression, and he could begin acting out behaviorally. This model seems to be arguable and relatively intuitive. The fact that this model is so straightforward and yet so comprehensive serves as a strength, as Christopher's parents would likely understand it relatively easily.

FIGURE 12.1   **DIATHESIS-STRESS MODEL FOR CHRISTOPHER**

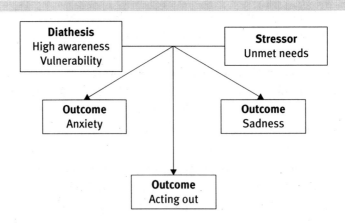

Developmental Model

The developmental model for Christopher is extremely interesting to think about, as he is only 6 years old. Along a developmental spectrum, he should be beginning to struggle with the task of taking initiative and leadership, according to Erikson's model of psychosocial development, as well as separation and individuation from his parents. According to Margaret Mahler and her colleagues (Mahler, Pine, & Bergman, 2000), he should feel that his parents offer a safe "home base," but he should also feel comfortable exploring his new social world at school, separate from them. What characterizes his current developmental functioning, however, are his lack of independent coping resources (his vulnerability) and his acute awareness of the world around him. These characteristics seem more like those of a toddler, who still needs his parents to help him cope with the world around him and is learning everything for the first time, taking in as much information as possible from the world around him, than a school-aged child. Accordingly, his developmental functioning and his real-world demands are not on the same developmental level, and this would likely cause problems.

Interestingly, although this is conceptualized differently, the model is almost identical to the diathesis-stress model for Christopher. Christopher's developmental model is shown in Figure 12.2.

This model (still) makes intuitive sense, in general. There are two major benefits to conceptualizing Christopher in this way. First, rather than characterizing his vulnerability (and to a lesser extent his high awareness) as

FIGURE 12.2   **DEVELOPMENTAL MODEL FOR CHRISTOPHER**

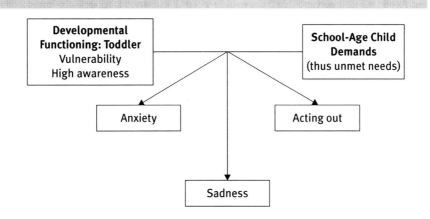

some sort of weakness or problem, this model situates these traits along a developmental continuum, representing very normal behavior that is lagging slightly behind where he should be at this point. Second, this developmental model of his emotional and personality functioning could end up tying in well with any academic or cognitive delays he may have. Knowing that he is having difficulties in reading, but not in his cognitive or verbal ability overall, this reading difficulty could similarly be conceptualized as a normal but delayed developmental/academic process. The major drawback of this model, however, is that it would require a great deal of explanation of normal development for it to make sense to Christopher's parents. It may, in the end, just be too complex to be useful to the family.

Common Function Model

The common function model, as always, requires all of the themes to align such that they are serving a common purpose, which is generally embodied in one or two of the themes. The first step is to understand what common function Christopher would organize his defenses around addressing. That is, what are his basic underlying needs, which the other themes serve to address? In Christopher's case, it seems that what he really needs to cope with are his general vulnerability and his unmet needs. If coping with these themes is the common function, our model will need to argue that all the other themes are serving the purpose of coping with them.

His high awareness of his environment could certainly be argued to be a coping mechanism for his vulnerability and unmet needs, as he is hypervigilant to any potential threats around him. His acting-out behavior, as well, may serve the purpose of putting attention on the fact that he needs extra support. His anxiety and sadness, however, seem less like defensive or coping mechanisms to deal with his vulnerability; they seem more like outcomes of his vulnerability and unmet needs. In fact, a more logical model, rather than this common function model, might be a common cause model, in which the arrows come down from the common cause of the unmet needs and vulnerability to lead to the outcomes of high awareness, acting out, anxiety, and sadness. This model may be easier to argue than one in which each of the themes serves the common purpose of coping with vulnerability and unmet needs. Although it would not make intuitive sense, the common function model for Christopher is shown in Figure 12.3.

FIGURE 12.3   **COMMON FUNCTION MODEL FOR CHRISTOPHER**

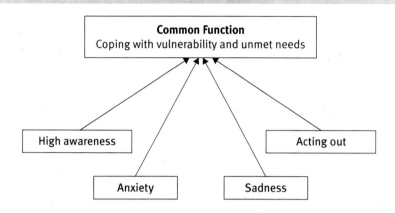

This model could be argued, but it would be difficult to explain how anxiety and sadness are helping Christopher cope with his vulnerability and unmet needs. Consequently, the assessor would likely abandon this option pretty quickly.

Complex Model

Both the diathesis–stress model and the developmental model seem to fit Christopher well. Either could be used for the final report. However, thinking about the themes in a slightly more complex way may lead to a more logical way to link several of them. While there would likely be no difficulty explaining how his diathesis (high awareness and vulnerability) and stressor (unmet needs) together lead to anxiety and sadness, their direct link to Christopher's acting-out behavior may make slightly less sense. Additionally, knowing that in childhood and adolescence acting-out behavior is often secondary to emotional difficulties, it may make more sense to explain the acting-out behaviors as a result of his anxiety and sadness, as the way he expresses these emotional problems.

This formulation represents only a slight modification of the diathesis-stress model, but conceptually it may be an important one, especially when

FIGURE 12.4   **COMPLEX MODEL FOR CHRISTOPHER**

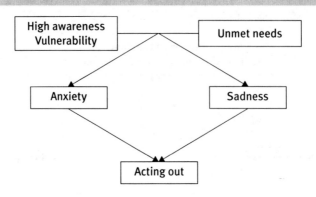

it comes to diagnosis. Explaining to Christopher's parents that acting-out behaviors are often the result of anxiety or depression means that a diagnosis of anxiety or depression would encompass that theme. If the theme were on the same level as the anxiety and depression, it would make more sense that it is a third, equal outcome, and it may warrant its own diagnosis (something like oppositional-defiant disorder). However, with this slight shift in the model, the assessor is including some psychoeducation to the parents about how anxiety and depression present in childhood. The complex model for Christopher is shown in Figure 12.4.

This model explains Christopher's difficulties well. Because he is somewhat vulnerable and lacks adequate coping mechanisms to deal with the world at the level he should, and because he is highly aware of his surroundings, especially his parents' marital difficulties, combined with not having all of his emotional needs met by his parents (perhaps also as a result of their own marital difficulties), he has developed some anxiety and sadness. These are resulting in some acting-out behaviors, as that is often how emotional difficulties are expressed in children. Although this model is not necessarily more "valid" than any of the others, it is certainly easier to write up and argue than some of the previous models.

REPORT WRITING

Before the report can be written, the final step of determining diagnosis and recommendations must be addressed. Beginning with Christopher's academic difficulties, the determination must be made whether he has

(a) a reading disorder, (b) borderline intellectual functioning, (c) mental retardation, or (d) no cognitive/academic diagnosis (because he is in an inappropriate bilingual classroom or his behavior problems have interfered with his attending to classroom lessons). Based on his average WISC-IV results, both borderline intellectual functioning and mental retardation are easily ruled out.

The determination of whether he has a reading disorder is slightly more difficult. The test results certainly suggest that his reading ability is lagging behind what would be expected, given his average IQ. However, whether the reason for this lag is some sort of reading disorder or is related to his inappropriate schooling is less clear. The major evidence that helps make this determination is the fact that his reading comprehension in English is average. The actual difficulty Christopher is having in reading is in his capability to decode words and read phonetically. He is reading primarily via word recognition, which is working for him somewhat but will ultimately not work, as vocabulary becomes more difficult with higher-level reading. However, because of his inappropriate classroom placement and the fact that his reading is not far below expected, no reading disorder will be given. He would benefit from work with a reading specialist to help his phonetic reading skills, though.

As for his acting-out behaviors at school and at home, the testing data suggest that oppositional-defiant disorder, which should be diagnosed only when the acting-out behaviors cannot be attributed to any other reason or disorder, is not an appropriate diagnosis for Christopher, inasmuch as his behavior seems to stem from anxious and depressed feelings. It is clear that these symptoms are impairing his functioning and that they warrant a diagnosis. Thus, the major decision is how to diagnose these anxious and depressed feelings (which should encompass the acting-out behaviors as well)—an adjustment disorder, some type of anxiety disorder, or a depressive disorder.

Currently, because there does not seem to be a concrete, identifiable stressor that triggered these symptoms (although the onset of his parents' marital difficulties likely contributed significantly), an adjustment disorder can be ruled out. When only the symptoms reported by his parents and his teacher are considered, Christopher does not meet full criteria for any anxiety disorder or for major depressive disorder; he has no sleep or appetite difficulties and no reported concentration problems, fatigue, or thoughts of death. However, his depressive and anxious feelings are impacting him significantly, so a final diagnosis to encompass his sadness, his anxious feelings, and his acting-out behaviors will be depressive disorder not otherwise specified.

PSYCHOLOGICAL ASSESSMENT REPORT
CONFIDENTIAL

Identifying Information

Name:	Christopher Santiago	**Date of Report:**	2/28/09
Sex:	Male	**Assessor:**	A. Jordan Wright, PhD
Age:	6	**Dates of Testing:**	1/21/09; 1/25/09;
Date of Birth:	1/1/03		2/11/09;
Ethnicity:	Latino		2/13/09

Source of Referral and Referral Questions

The patient was referred by his school to assess both his academic and behavioral functioning. Specifically, he is having difficulty with reading and is acting out behaviorally in school and at home.

Measures Administered

- Clinical Interview
- Collateral Interview with Mother and Father
- Collateral Interview with Teacher
- Bender Visual-Motor Gestalt Test, 2nd Edition (Bender-2)
- Wechsler Intelligence Scale for Children, 4th Edition (WISC-IV)
- Wechsler Individual Achievement Test, 2nd Edition (WIAT-II)
- Gray Diagnostic Reading Tests, 2nd Edition (GDRT-2)
- Behavior Assessment System for Children, 2nd Edition (BASC-2)
- Rorschach Inkblot Test, Comprehensive System (Rorschach)
- Children's Apperception Test (CAT)
- Animal Identification and Devaluation Task (AID)
- Sentence Completion Task
- Projective Wishes Task (Projective Wishes)
- House-Tree-Person and Kinetic Family Drawings (Projective Drawings)

Description of Patient

Christopher Santiago is a 6-year-old, Latino boy of somewhat small stature and athletic build for his age. He was well-groomed and dressed casually and appropriately. He has a bright smile and a friendly demeanor, and he was extremely cooperative with the assessor throughout the assessment process.

Presenting Problem

The patient's parents and teacher all reported two primary presenting problems: The patient is having some difficulty with reading, and he is acting out in school and at home. Reportedly, he has "tantrums" whenever his father asks him to do anything, as well as sometimes with his mother and when he is frustrated at school. These tantrums include screaming, crying, and occasional aggressive behavior like hitting and throwing things. Both at school and at home, he is able to be calmed down from these tantrums and refocused.

The patient reported that at times he becomes sad, especially when he feels his parents do not see him enough, but he denied any thoughts of harming himself.

Background Information

History of Presenting Problem

The patient was an average student a year ago in his kindergarten class, and this year he moved to a bilingual English-Spanish first grade class, despite the fact that he does not speak Spanish (his home is monolingual English speaking). His reading ability was Average last year, but this year he has not learned at the same rate as his peers. He has difficulty getting through the words and passages in class.

Behaviorally, the patient has no history of acting-out behaviors prior to this school year. His tantrums began about a month after beginning the first grade. They had been consistent since that time (about four months before this evaluation), occurring about two times per day in school and almost daily at home, especially with his father. Other than beginning the first grade, there were no other clear changes or transitions in his life prior to the beginning of the acting-out behaviors.

Symptomatic Evaluation

The patient's parents reported no difficulties during her mother's pregnancy with him. He reportedly had an easy temperament as a baby, crying only when hungry or in need of a diaper change, and easily consoled. He slept well throughout his infancy. He met all developmental milestones on time and easily, including relatively easy toilet training. His parents reported no major medical or psychiatric problems in their own or the patient's history, and none of the family members had ever received psychiatric treatment. The patient's paternal grandmother had reportedly been

(Continued)

depressed, but she had never been diagnosed or treated. No other family psychiatric history was reported. The patient's parents denied any use of alcohol or drugs by the patient or themselves.

Psychosocial Evaluation

The patient is the only child in his family, and his parents have been married for about 12 years. His mother is attending nursing school at night, and his father works as a customer service representative at a bank. They reported an open and loving relationship with their son, including reading to him nightly as he goes to bed. They also reported, however, that they are having marital difficulty, to the point of considering divorce. They reported working hard to hide their marital problems from the patient, confining their fights to times when he is at school or asleep. At the time of this report, they had not yet made a decision whether or not to divorce.

Other than with reading, the patient performs academically adequately in school, and he has many friends, including a best friend he has had for about a year and a half. He is reportedly popular among his peers, and he socializes often, both in and out of school. He has no history of abuse and no legal problems. He is one of several Latino children in his very diverse school, and he socializes freely with most of the other children.

Mental Status

The patient was casually and appropriately dressed, well groomed, and extremely cooperative and friendly throughout the testing process, maintaining appropriate eye contact throughout. His motor activity was within normal limits. He disclosed information freely, except when asked to elaborate on anything negative he had reported, when he generally shrugged his shoulders and said, "I don't know." Both his receptive and expressive language ability were extremely good. His mood and affect were both happy, though he reported and exhibited some sadness at times. His thought process was generally goal-directed, and his thought content was free of hallucinations, delusions, and suicidal and homicidal ideation. His memory seemed within normal limits, and his attention and concentration were adequate. His judgment and planning were good, and his impulse control was adequate, except when he got overly excited while playing an energetic game in sessions.

Behavioral Observations

The patient was extremely friendly and cooperative throughout testing. He gave effortful attempts on all tests administered. At times he became "bored" with some of the tests, so games were used as incentives to continue with the tasks at hand. He seemed to enjoy competitive games, but his mood was not highly affected by his winning or losing. He seemed just to enjoy playing the games with the assessor, regardless of who won.

Overall Interpretation of Test Findings

Cognitive Functioning

Cognitive Ability. The patient's Full Scale IQ score on the WISC-IV fell within the 50th percentile, within the Average range compared to others his own age. His functioning across all of the domains that make up his Full Scale IQ, including his verbal comprehension, which is especially important to his ability to function in school and learn reading and writing, was consistently Average compared to his same-age peers. There were no indications of significant strengths or weaknesses within his Average overall functioning; there were no areas of deficit or weakness. Additionally, he exhibited no soft signs of gross neurological damage as evidenced by his Average performance on the Bender-2.

Academic Achievement. The patient's functioning across different academic disciplines, as measured by the WIAT-II, was varied. Specifically, he performed in the Average range compared to others his age in mathematics (50th percentile) and oral language abilities (75th percentile). However, his reading and writing both fell within the Low Average range of functioning (both 6th percentile). The GDRT-2 revealed that his ability to understand what he reads is Average compared to others his age (Comprehension Composite, 27th percentile), but his ability to break down words into their component parts and read them phonetically is a significant weakness (Decoding Composite, 6th percentile), somewhat poorer than would be expected in view of his Average verbal ability. Given this difficulty with reading phonetically, his performance in writing on the WIAT-II fell at the expected level.

Cognitive Summary. The patient's cognitive ability is generally Average. On tests of academic performance, he performed as expected, in the Average range, on measures of mathematics and oral language ability. However, he showed minor weakness in both reading and writing ability, slightly below what would be expected given his Average overall ability, suggesting the possibility of a learning disorder. However, it is likely that he is lagging slightly because he is an inappropriate (bilingual) classroom placement.

(Continued)

Emotional Functioning

The results of the patient's assessment suggest that he is a child who is both highly vulnerable to becoming overwhelmed, as he does not have the adequate resources to cope with his environment on his own, and highly aware of what is happening in his environment. Specifically, he is currently highly aware of his parents' marital difficulties, which have led to the patient having many unmet needs for attention and care from them. Together, his vulnerability, high awareness, and unmet needs have led to both feelings of anxiety, fearing the world around him, and feelings of sadness, including some loneliness. As is often the case with children experiencing emotional difficulties, his sadness and anxiety are exhibiting themselves as acting-out behaviors both in school and at home. Countering his feelings of sadness and anxiety are good interpersonal skills and adequate feelings of self-esteem.

Vulnerability. The patient is extremely vulnerable to becoming overwhelmed by changes in his life, because he does not have the coping skills necessary to adapt appropriately to transition. His Rorschach and Sentence Completion Task revealed that he feels extremely vulnerable, lacking both his own resources and adequate supports to deal with the world around him. This vulnerable feeling is likely related to the fact that he has fewer coping resources than others his age to deal with the world, which was revealed in his Rorschach. Additionally, his BASC-2 revealed that he does not adapt well to change in his life, likely again because of a lack of coping resources. His AID and CAT revealed that he feels he needs more security in his life, and more control, as he feels unable to care for himself well enough. This vulnerability is likely why he plays pretend games about being a wizard and having more control over turning bad things into good ones. This concern over caring for himself, as it is an unusual concern for a 6-year-old, is likely related to the fact that his needs are not being met by his parents.

High Awareness. The patient is highly attuned to what goes on around him, maintaining a great awareness of those around him. His CAT and Projective Drawings revealed that he is highly attuned to other people, much more so than most children his age, and that he is extremely attentive to details of situations. His Rorschach revealed that this awareness of his surroundings is excessive and anxious, to the point that he takes in much more information from the world than he can effectively handle. His CAT and Sentence Completion Task, along with his own report, revealed that he is especially aware of his parents' unhappiness with each other, despite the fact that they are trying to hide their marital problems from him. This awareness likely relates to his feeling that his needs are not being attended to enough by his parents.

Unmet Needs. Although his parents are caring and loving toward him, the patient feels that his needs for security, attention, and support are not being met by them. His Rorschach, AID, and Projective Wishes all revealed that he does not feel his parents are taking care of him enough, which means his general emotional needs are not being taken care of by them, as revealed in his Rorschach and Projective Wishes. He feels under-supported and somewhat resentful that he is not being attended to enough, as revealed by his Projective Wishes and CAT. His CAT and Projective Wishes also revealed that he feels somewhat neglected by his parents and feels they are not paying enough attention to him. He stated that he wishes his parents would see him more, likely a reflection of wanting more of his parents' attention. His Projective Drawings suggested that he feels his parents are more highly focused on each other, given their marital difficulties, than on him, likely a result of his being acutely aware of their problems, even though they try to hide them from him. Together with his vulnerability, his awareness and unmet needs are leading to anxious and sad feelings.

Anxiety. As a result of being extremely vulnerable and highly aware of his needs not being met, the patient has developed anxiety about the world. General feelings of anxiety were revealed on the patient's BASC-2, Rorschach, and Sentence Completion. His CAT revealed that the anxiety is focused on being able to care for himself, and his Projective Drawings revealed that he fears the instability of the world and his environment, likely because of feeling unsupported by his parents and potentially confused by their marital problems, which he is aware of even though they are trying to hide them from him. This anxiety is contributing to his acting-out behaviors in school and at home.

Sadness. Also as a result of his poor coping resources and his lack of support from his parents, the patient has become sad. This sadness was revealed on his BASC-2, Rorschach, CAT, and Projective Drawings, as well as his own self-report. His Rorschach suggested that the sad feelings are related to negative feelings that he has turned inward onto himself, and his CAT revealed that part of his sadness is related to feeling lonely. Along with his anxiety, this sadness is being expressed by his acting out in school and at home.

(Continued)

Acting-Out Behaviors. The patient's sadness and anxiety are being transformed into anger and expressed in acting-out behaviors at home and at school. His Rorschach, CAT, and Sentence Completion revealed underlying anger and resentment about not being supported enough by his parents. His CAT revealed that when he is overwhelmed or confused by his emotions, he tends to respond by lashing out behaviorally. These behavioral problems were also revealed on his BASC-2, as well as by his parents' and teacher's reports.

Summary

Christopher Santiago is a 6-year-old, Latino male who currently lives with his parents. He was referred for psychological assessment to assess his reading difficulties and his recent behavioral acting out at school and at home. He is currently in a bilingual Spanish-English classroom, though he does not speak any Spanish. Additionally, his parents are having marital difficulties, which they are trying to keep hidden from the patient.

Cognitively, he is currently functioning within the Average range compared to others his age in his overall ability. His reading, however, falls below what would be expected given this Average ability. Specifically, he is having difficulty with decoding individual words and reading them phonetically, generally reading words by recognition. His comprehension, however, is not impaired. It is likely that being in an inappropriate (bilingual) classroom is getting in the way of his reading growth at this point.

Emotionally, he is highly vulnerable to becoming overwhelmed, as he does not have enough coping resources to deal with his environment. Additionally, he is acutely aware of what is happening in his environment, especially with his parents. Because of their marital difficulties, they are not currently meeting his needs for attention and care. Together, his vulnerability and high awareness of his unmet needs and parents' marital problems have led him both to become anxious about the instability of the world around him and to become sad. These anxious and sad feelings are exhibiting themselves as acting-out behaviors in school and at home.

Because his sad and anxious feelings are leading to behavioral problems and difficulties in school and at home, he currently meets criteria for Depressive Disorder Not Otherwise Specified. Additionally, because of his parents' marital difficulties, and how they are affecting him, he meets criteria for Relational Problem Not Otherwise Specified.

Diagnostic Impression

Axis I	311	Depressive Disorder Not Otherwise Specified
	V62.81	Relational Problem Not Otherwise Specified
Axis II	V71.09	No diagnosis on Axis II
Axis III		None
Axis IV		Parents' marital difficulties, inappropriate bilingual classroom placement
Axis V	GAF =	65

Recommendations

Given the patient's current functioning, he should be referred to a reading specialist to remediate his phonetic reading skill. More exposure and practice in decoding words and carefully sounding them out should help improve his reading ability relatively rapidly. One possible referral would be the Center for Psychoeducational Services, at 212-555-0124. Additionally, the patient should be placed in a monolingual English-speaking classroom as soon as possible.

The patient and his parents should be referred for family therapy, in order to address both his parents' marital difficulties and his feelings that he is not supported enough by them. Additionally, individual play therapy would be useful for helping him develop more and better coping skills, as well as realistic expectations from the world around him. Both of these referrals can be made to the New York Center for Psychotherapy, at 212-555-3262.

_____   _____

A. Jordan Wright, PhD   Date
New York State Licensed Psychologist

The major recommendation that emerges from this diagnosis is some sort of psychotherapeutic treatment, which will enable Christopher to gain coping skills and to become less vulnerable. Additionally, a major problem that is impacting him is his parents' marital difficulties. Because there is no specific diagnosis for the relational problems of family members and their impact on the individual, a diagnosis of relational problem not otherwise specified will be given, as will a recommendation of family therapy, which would be useful both to help his parents' marital difficulties and to help them make sure they are meeting the needs of their son.

FEEDBACK

Preparation for Feedback

When considering exactly what feedback to give and how to give it to Christopher's parents, perhaps the most important consideration is the fact that his parents are likely not expecting to hear that their marital problems are impacting Christopher significantly, especially given that they think he is unaware of them. Additionally, care must be taken not to shame his parents and make them feel that any problems are entirely their fault. This is extremely important, because by almost all accounts, they are very good parents. Their lack of transparency with their son, who happens to be overly perceptive of his surroundings and does not cope with uncertainty or change that well, must be addressed, however.

The major considerations when deciding exactly how to give feedback to Christopher's parents were (a) the level of cognitive and intellectual functioning of his parents, (b) their level of insight, and (c) the specific type and amount of information that had to be relayed to them. With a 6-year-old child, the assessor decided to give feedback to the parents alone and then to bring Christopher in to receive some very abridged feedback in front of his parents. Regarding their intellectual capacity, Christopher's parents were bright and articulate, so they could be given the entire report as is, without needing to create a summary sheet. Regarding their level of insight, as discussed previously, they seemed relatively unaware of Christopher's emotional state and their impact on it. The amount of feedback to give them must be driven both by the report itself and constant reevaluation of how they were responding to the feedback, as some of it would likely be difficult for them to hear. Ultimately, the assessor was confident that Christopher's parents would take the recommendations, because their primary concern was their son's well-being.

The assessor also decided to give the feedback verbally before giving Christopher's parents the actual report. He wanted to ensure that they understood every piece of the feedback and had an opportunity to ask questions or discuss reactions, without the distraction of needing to look at a lengthy report. The plan was to discuss the cognitive/academic feedback first, including the recommendations related to it, and then to discuss the emotional functioning, with plenty of time for reactions and questions.

Feedback Session

Christopher and his parents came in for their feedback session, and a colleague played with Christopher in another room while the assessor gave feedback to his parents. As always, the assessor oriented them to how the feedback session would flow, letting them know that they could stop the assessor at any point if they had questions or reactions to anything being said. He emphasized the point that there would be two parts to the feedback—one focusing on Christopher's academic functioning and the other focusing on his acting-out behavior. They were encouraged to let the assessor know whenever anything did not align with their own thoughts or feelings. They had no questions at this point, so the assessor moved on to the cognitive feedback.

The cognitive feedback, although a major focus of the assessment and the current feedback session, was relatively straightforward to give. The parents had already been encouraged to have Christopher transferred from his bilingual English-Spanish class to a monolingual English-speaking classroom, which had been successfully done the week before. The assessor explained that there were no deficits or weaknesses in his overall cognitive ability, that he was functioning adequately cognitively, which they seemed happy to hear.

He also reported that, as anticipated, Christopher's reading ability was somewhat lower than would be expected. He explained that at least part of this weakness is likely due to the fact that he was in an inappropriate classroom. He explained in detail how when Christopher read words correctly, his comprehension was unimpaired, but that Christopher was not decoding words into their component parts (i.e., reading them phonetically) in order to read them. He further explained that work with a reading specialist on phonetic decoding would be extremely helpful and would likely lead to marked improvement relatively quickly. They had no questions, other than asking where they could find a reading specialist. The assessor told them there was a specific referral on the report, including a phone number, if their school did not have one on staff.

The rest of the session focused on the emotional functioning section of the feedback. The assessor began by explaining that the first part of the feedback was about some of Christopher's personality characteristics, the "type of child" he is. He began by stating that Christopher has a great number of strengths, including extremely good social skills, good self-esteem, and a loving family. He then reported that, based on the assessment, Christopher has some difficulty coping with and adapting to changes in the world around him and in his life. This feedback elicited some reaction from his parents, who then reported that he had always had difficulty with change. They told a story about moving into a new apartment when he was 3 years old and how he had cried for about a week about it. His mother stated that she thought he had gotten better at adapting, because of his relatively smooth transition to school in kindergarten. They seemed a bit apologetic for not mentioning some of these things earlier in the process, and they understood that Christopher's gaining coping skills was a process, that he might be better than he was before, but he still has some growing to do.

The second aspect of his personality that emerged was his extremely acute awareness of what was going on around him, in his environment and with his parents. His parents looked at each other cautiously, and then his father said somewhat quietly, "He knows about us, doesn't he?" The conversation then turned to the next theme—the fact that he has needs that are unmet by his parents. Rather than simply reporting this theme, however, the assessor asked his parents how they imagined it might affect Christopher to know about their marital difficulties but not to be told about them, as though they might not actually exist. His mother said "confusing," and his father said "frightening and unsettling." The assessor validated their insights, as well as empathizing with the difficult position they were in. He assured them that no parents want their children to know about marital difficulties. He also repeated that Christopher's seeing it but the family's not discussing it could be confusing, frightening, and unsettling, using their words. He then specified that with Christopher, it was causing some sadness and anxiety.

The focus of the session then moved to the fact that, in childhood, sadness and anxiety are often manifested as behavior problems. The assessor explained that Christopher's acting out at home and at school was his way of expressing his emotional difficulties. Both of his parents listened quietly while nodding their heads slightly. When he asked if this feedback made sense, they both confirmed that it made sense and clearly explained what was going on with Christopher. His mother then asked what they should do about it, if and how they should talk to him about their marital problems. The assessor then made the recommendation of family therapy. He explained that family therapy could be helpful in several ways, and even if they decided to divorce, it could help them do so in the most beneficial way possible for Christopher.

The assessor noted that family therapy could also help them work through some of their difficulties as a couple, but he emphasized how it could refocus their attention on what is best for Christopher. He then added that individual therapy could be useful for Christopher as well, to improve his coping skills. Interestingly, Christopher's parents had a conversation, almost as if the assessor were not present, about beginning family therapy. They discussed how it could work logistically, with their schedules, and how it could benefit all three of them, and they decided to try it. The assessor then gave them a copy of the report and led them quickly through it, encouraging them to read it in its entirety when they got home and let him know whether they had any questions about it. They thanked the assessor and began to get up to leave, but the assessor reminded them that he wanted to give Christopher some feedback as well, so that he did not think he did all that testing for no reason. Christopher's father left to get Christopher and brought him back into the room.

When Christopher was in the room with his parents, he first gave the assessor a high five (a ritual at the beginning of each of his testing sessions). The assessor explained that he wanted to let Christopher know what had come out of all the "puzzles and things" they had been doing. The way he framed it, though, was organized around the recommendations rather than the problems. He began by telling Christopher that he thought he should get some extra help with reading, as he knew his current struggles could be "kind of frustrating for you." The assessor said that he was going to work with his parents to find "someone nice" to help him practice. He seemed happy about this. Next, the assessor said that he was going to find someone to help them have "family time" every week, so that they could make sure everything was "going right" in the family.

Christopher then looked at his parents, both of whom had an encouraging look on their faces. His mother added that they wanted to make sure they were doing everything they could so that he knew how much they loved him. He responded by jumping into her lap and letting her hug him.

His father scooted his chair so that it was touching his wife's chair, so that he could put his hand on Christopher as well. The assessor added that his parents were also going to find someone else that he could talk to "about stuff" and play with, just to get out any frustrations he was having.

Christopher seemed too involved in the family hug to respond to the assessor, but the assessor wanted to make sure that his parents heard the language he was using to explain family therapy and individual play therapy to Christopher, so that they could repeat it when they needed to. As they got up to leave, thanking the assessor, Christopher ran full-speed into the assessor's leg, throwing his arms around it in a tight hug. He looked up at the assessor with a wide smile, then he giggled and ran out of the room, as his parents shook the assessor's hand and left.

SUMMARY

Christopher's case uncovered two major areas that needed to be addressed in his life—his inappropriate placement in a bilingual classroom and the parental secret of their marital difficulties. From a family systems perspective, Christopher was charged with keeping this family secret, though the information was likely confusing, as he may not know whether to trust his own observation (that there was a problem) or his parents (who were hiding it). All of this converges to cause problems for Christopher. The way he was expressing his emotional difficulties was by acting out behaviorally, which in many ways is lucky. Had he not saliently had difficulties (e.g., had he just hidden any unhappiness or emotional difficulty inside), he might not have been referred for services. He could have stored up these negative feelings for much longer until they became dangerous. Luckily, his acting out was noticed and addressed relatively early, so that the negative feelings could be dealt with before they grew. Although his parents felt some guilt about contributing to their son's difficulties, ultimately their care and concern for him would lead them to find some extra support to make sure he was doing well.

References

Acklin, M. W., McDowell, C. J., Verschell, M. S., & Chan, D. (2000). Interobserver agreement, intraobserver reliability, and the Rorschach Comprehensive System. *Journal of Personality Assessment, 74*, 15–47.

Akhtar, S., & Thomson, J. A. (1982). Overview: Narcissistic personality disorder. *The American Journal of Psychiatry, 139*(1), 12–20.

Barlow, D. H. (2008). *Clinical handbook of psychological disorders: A step-by-step treatment manual* (4th ed.). New York, NY: Guilford Press.

Bellak, L., & Abrams, D. M. (1997). *The thematic apperception test, the children's apperception test, and the senior apperception technique in clinical use* (6th ed.). Needham Heights, MA: Allyn & Bacon.

Bornstein, R. F., & Masling, J. M. (2005). The Rorschach Oral Dependency scale. In R. F. Bornstein & J. M. Masling (Eds.), *Scoring the Rorschach: Seven validated systems* (pp.135–157). Mahwah, NJ: Lawrence Erlbaum.

Butcher, J.N., & Rouse, S.V. (1996). Personality: Individual differences and clinical assessment. *Annual Review of Psychology, 47*, 87–111.

Carr, A. (2009). *What works with children, adolescents, and adults?: A review of research on the effectiveness of psychotherapy*. New York, NY: Routledge.

Christophersen, E. R., & Mortweet, S. L. (2001). *Treatments that work with children: Empirically supported strategies for managing childhood problems*. Washington, DC: American Psychological Association.

Cohen, B. M., Hammer, J. S., & Singer, S. (1988). The Diagnostic Drawing Series: A systematic approach to art therapy evaluation and research. *The Arts in Psychotherapy, 15*(1), 11–21.

Craig, L. A., Browne, K. D., Hogue, T. E., & Stringer, I. (2004). New directions in assessing risk for sexual offenders. *Issues in Forensic Psychology, 5*, 81–99.

Downey, G., & Coyne, J. C. (1990). Children of depressed parents: An integrative review. *Psychological Bulletin, 108*, 50–76.

Exner, J. E. (2002). *The Rorschach: Basic foundations and principles of interpretation.* Hoboken, NJ: Wiley.

Exner, J. E., & Erdberg, P. (2005). *The Rorschach, advanced interpretation.* Hoboken, NJ: Wiley.

Feher, E., VandeCreek, L., & Teglasi, H. (1983). The problem of art quality in the use of the Human Figure Drawing Test. *Journal of Clinical Psychology, 39,* 268–275.

First, M. B., Frances, A. F., & Pincus, H. A. (2002). *DSM-IV-TR handbook of differential diagnosis.* Washington, DC: American Psychiatric Publishing.

Fuller, G. B., Parmelee, W. M., & Carroll, J. L. (1982). Performance of delinquent and nondelinquent high school boys on the Rotter Incomplete Sentence Blank. *Journal of Personality Assessment, 46,* 506–510.

Gardner, J. M. (1967). The adjustment of drug addicts as measured by the Sentence Completion Test. *Journal of Projective Techniques & Personality Assessment, 31,* 28–29.

Graham, J. R. (2006). *MMPI-2: Assessing personality and psychopathology* (4th ed.). New York, NY: Oxford University Press.

Grønnerød, C. (2003). Temporal stability in the Rorschach method: A meta-analytic review. *Journal of Personality Assessment, 80,* 272–293.

Grønnerød, C. (2004). Rorschach assessment of changes following psychotherapy: A meta-analytic review. *Journal of Personality Assessment, 83,* 256–276.

Groth-Marnat, G. (2009). *Handbook of psychological assessment* (5th ed.). Hoboken, NJ: Wiley.

Grove, W. R., Barden, C., Garb, H. N., & Lilienfeld, S. O. (2002). Failure of Rorschach-Comprehensive-System-based testimony to be admissible under the Daubert/Kumho Standard. *Psychology, Public Policy, and Law, 8*(2), 216–234.

Haak, R. A. (1990). Using the sentence completion to assess emotional disturbance. In C. F. Reynolds & R. W. Kamphaus (Eds.), *Handbook of psychological and educational assessment of children: Personality, behavior and context* (pp.147–167). New York: Guilford Press.

Hammen, C., Burge, D., Burney, E., & Adrian, C. (1990). Longitudinal study of diagnoses in children of women with unipolar and bipolar affective disorder. *Archives of General Psychiatry, 47,* 1112–1117.

Hammer, E. F. (1997). *Advances in projective drawing interpretation.* Springfield, IL: Charles C. Thomas.

Hiller, J. B., Rosenthal, R., Bornstein, R. F., Berry, D. T. R., & Brunell-Neuleib, S. (1999). A comparative meta-analysis of Rorschach and MMPI validity. *Psychological Assessment, 11*(3), 278–296.

Horowitz, M. (1989). Clinical phenomenology of narcissistic pathology. *Psychiatric Clinics of North America, 12,* 553–570.

Kapes, J. T., & Whitfield, E. A. (2001). *A counselor's guide to career assessment instruments* (4th ed.). Broken Arrow, OK: National Career Development Association.

Kernberg, O. (1975). *Borderline conditions and pathological narcissism.* New York, NY: Jason Aronson.

Killian, G. A., & Campbell, B. (1987). House-Tree-Person technique. In D. Keyser & R. Sweetland (Eds.), *Test critiques compendium* (pp. 206–221). Kansas City, MO: Test Corporation of America.

Lah, M. I. (1989). Sentence completion tests. In C. S. Newmark (Ed.), *Major psychological assessment instruments*, 2 (pp. 133–163). Boston, MA: Allyn & Bacon.

Lehman, E. B., & Levy, E. I. (1971). Discrepancies in estimates of children's intelligence: WISC and human figure drawings. *Journal of Clinical Psychology, 27*(1), 74–76.

Lezak, M. D., Howieson, D. B., Loring, D.W., Hannay, H. J., & Fischer, J. S. (2004). *Neuropsychological assessment* (4th ed.). New York, NY: Oxford University Press.

Lilienfeld, S. O., Wood, J. M., & Garb, H. N. (2000). The scientific status of projective techniques. *Psychological Science in the Public Interest, 1*(2), 27–66.

MacKinnon, R. A., Michels, R., & Buckley, P. J. (2006). *The psychiatric interview in clinical practice* (2nd ed.). Arlington, VA: American Psychiatric Publishing.

Mahler, M. S., Pine, F., & Bergman, A. (2000). *The psychological birth of the human infant: Symbiosis and individuation.* New York, NY: Basic Books.

Marcia, J. E. (1966). Development and validation of ego identity status. *Journal of Personality and Social Psychology, 3,* 551–558.

Marcia, J. E. (1991). Identity and self-development. In R. Lerner, A. Peterson, & J. Brooks-Gunn (Eds.), *Encyclopedia of adolescence* (Vol. 1). New York, NY: Garland.

McConaughy, S. H. (2005). *Clinical interviews for children and adolescents: Assessment to intervention.* New York, NY: The Guilford Press.

McGrath, R. E. (2008). The Rorschach in the context of performance-based personality assessment. *Journal of Personality Assessment, 90,* 465–475.

Meyer, G. J., Finn, S. E., Eyde, L. D., Kay, G. G., Moreland, K. L., Dies, R. R., . . . Reed, G. M. (2001). Psychological testing and psychological assessment: A review of evidence and issues. *American Psychologist, 56*(2), 128–165.

Meyer, G. J. (2004). The reliability and validity of the Rorschach and Thematic Apperception Test (TAT) compared to other psychological and medical procedures: An analysis of systematically gathered evidence. In M. J. Hilsenroth & D. L. Segal (Eds.), *Comprehensive handbook of psychological assessment*, 2: *Personality assessment* (pp. 315–342). Hoboken, NJ: Wiley.

Millon, T., & Bloom, C. (2008). *The Millon inventories: A practitioner's guide to personalized clinical assessment* (2nd ed.). New York, NY: The Guilford Press.

Morey, L. C. (1996). *An interpretive guide to the personality assessment inventory (PAI).* Odessa, FL: Psychological Assessment Resources, Inc.

Pattee, L. E. (1994). The Draw A Person questionnaire: A comparison of responses between inpatients and normal controls. Unpublished doctoral dissertation, George Washington University.

Piotrowski, C. (1984). The status of projective techniques: Or, "wishing won't make it go away." *Journal of Clinical Psychology, 40,* 1495–1502.

Raskin, R., Novacek, J., & Hogan, R. (1991). Narcissism, self-esteem, and defensive self-enhancement. *Journal of Personality 59*(1), 19–38.

Rhodewalt, F., & Morf, C. C. (1998). On self-aggrandizement and anger: A temporal analysis of narcissism and affective reactions to success and failure. *Journal of Personality and Social Psychology, 74,* 672–685.

Rosenthal, R., Hiller, J. B., Bornstein, R. F., Berry, D. T. R, & Brunell-Neuleib, S. (2001). Meta-analytic methods, the Rorschach, and the MMPI. *Psychological Assessment, 13*(4), 449–451.

Roth, A., & Fonagy, P. (2005). *What works for whom?: A critical review of psychotherapy research* (2nd ed.). New York, NY: Guilford Press.

Rotter, J. B., Lah, M. I., & Rafferty, J. E. (1992). *Rotter incomplete sentences blank* (2nd ed.). New York, NY: Psychological Corporation.

Sattler, J. M. (2008). *Assessment of children: Cognitive foundations* (5th ed.). La Mesa, CA: Jerome M. Sattler.

Seligman, L., & Reichenberg, L. W. (2007). *Selecting effective treatments: A comprehensive, systematic guide to treating mental disorders* (3rd ed.). San Francisco, CA: Jossey-Bass.

Shaffer, T. W., Erdberg, P., & Haroian, J. (1999). Current nonpatient data for the Rorschach, WAIS–R, and MMPI–2. *Journal of Personality Assessment, 73,* 305–316.

Sommers-Flanagan, J., & Sommers-Flanagan, R. (2002). *Clinical interviewing* (3rd ed.). Hoboken, NJ: Wiley.

Strauss, E., Sherman, E. M. S., & Spreen, O. (2006) *A compendium of neuropsychological tests: Administration, norms, and commentary* (3rd ed.). New York, NY: Oxford University Press.

Sullivan, H. S. (1970). *The psychiatric interview.* New York, NY: Norton.

Suzuki, L. A., Ponterotto, J. G., & Meller, P. J. (2008). *Handbook of multicultural assessment: Clinical, psychological, and educational applications* (3rd ed.). San Francisco, CA: Jossey-Bass.

Tuerlinckx, F., De Boeck, P., & Lens, W. (2002). Measuring needs with the Thematic Apperception Test: A psychometric study. *Journal of Personality and Social Psychology, 82*(3), 448–461.

Viglione, D. J. (1999). A review of recent research addressing the utility of the Rorschach. *Psychological Assessment, 11,* 251–265.

Viglione, D., & Hilsenroth, M. (2001). The Rorschach: Facts, fictions, and future. *Psychological Assessment, 13,* 452–471.

Walsh, W. B., & Savickas, M. L. (2005). *Handbook of vocational psychology* (3rd ed.). Mahwah, NJ: Lawrence Erlbaum.

Wanderer, Z. W. (1969). Validity of clinical judgments based on human figure drawings. *Journal of Consulting and Clinical Psychology, 33*(2), 143–150.

Weiner, I. B. (1966). *Psychodiagnosis in schizophrenia.* Hillsdale, NJ: Lawrence Erlbaum.

Weiner, I. B., & Greene, R. L. (2007). *Handbook of personality assessment.* Hoboken, NJ: Wiley.

Weissman, M. M., Wickramaratne, P., Nomura, Y., Warner, V., Pilowsky, D., & Verdeli, H. (2006). Offspring of depressed parents: 20 years later. *American Journal of Psychiatry, 163,* 1001–1008.

Winter, D. G., & Stewart, A. J. (1977). Power motive reliability as a function of retest instructions. *Journal of Consulting and Clinical Psychology, 45,* 436–440.

Wood, J. M., Nezworski, N. T., Garb, H. N., & Lilienfeld, S. O. (2001). The misperception of psychopathology: Problems with the norms of the Comprehensive System for the Rorschach. *Clinical Psychology: Science and Practice, 8,* 350–373.

Wood, J.M., Nezworski, M.T., Lilienfeld, S.O., & Garb, H. N. (2003). *What's wrong with the Rorschach? Science confronts the controversial inkblot test.* New York, NY: Jossey-Bass.

Yama, M. F. (1990). The usefulness of human figure drawings as an index of overall adjustment. *Journal of Personality Assessment, 54*(1–2), 78–86.

Zubin, J., & Spring, B. (1977). Vulnerability: A new view of schizophrenia. *Journal of Abnormal Psychology, 86,* 103–126.

Name Index

Subject Index

STUDY PACKAGE
CONTINUING EDUCATION
CREDIT INFORMATION

Conducting Psychological Assessment: A Guide for Practitioners

Our goal is to provide you with current, accurate and practical information from the most experienced and knowledgeable speakers and authors.

Listed below are the continuing education credit(s) currently available for this self-study package. *Please note: Your state licensing board dictates whether self study is an acceptable form of continuing education. Please refer to your state rules and regulations.*

COUNSELORS: PESI, LLC is recognized by the National Board for Certified Counselors to offer continuing education for National Certified Counselors. Provider #: 5896. We adhere to NBCC Continuing Education Guidelines. This self-study package qualifies for **4.5** contact hours.

SOCIAL WORKERS: PESI, LLC, 1030, is approved as a provider for continuing education by the Association of Social Work Boards, 400 South Ridge Parkway, Suite B, Culpeper, VA 22701. www.aswb. org. Social workers should contact their regulatory board to determine course approval. Course Level: All Levels. Social Workers will receive **4.5** (Clinical) continuing education clock hours for completing this self-study package.

PSYCHOLOGISTS: PESI, LLC is approved by the American Psychological Association to sponsor continuing education for psychologists. PESI, LLC maintains responsibility for these materials and their content. PESI is offering these self- study materials for **4.5** hours of continuing education credit.

ADDICTION COUNSELORS: PESI, LLC is a Provider approved by NAADAC Approved Education Provider Program. Provider #: 366. This self-study package qualifies for **5.5** contact hours.

Procedures:

1. Review the material and read the book.

2. If seeking credit, complete the posttest/evaluation form:

     -Complete posttest/evaluation in entirety; including your email address to receive your certificate much faster versus by mail.

     -Upon completion, mail to the address listed on the form along with the CE fee stated on the test. Tests will not be processed without the CE fee included.

     -Completed posttests must be received 6 months from the date printed on the packing slip.

Your completed posttest/evaluation will be graded. If you receive a passing score (70% and above), you will be emailed/faxed/mailed a certificate of successful completion with earned continuing education credits. (Please write your email address on the posttest/evaluation form for fastest response) If you do not pass the posttest, you will be sent a letter indicating areas of deficiency, and another posttest to complete. The posttest must be resubmitted and receive a passing grade before credit can be awarded. We will allow you to re-take as many times as necessary to receive a certificate.

If you have any questions, please feel free to contact our customer service department at 1.800.844.8260.

PESI LLC
PO BOX 1000
Eau Claire, WI 54702-1000

PESI

Conducting Psychological Assessment: A Guide for Practitioners

PO BOX 1000
Eau Claire, WI 54702
800-844-8260

Any persons interested in receiving credit may photocopy this form, complete and return with a payment of $20.00 per person CE fee. A certificate of successful completion will be sent to you. To receive your certificate sooner than two weeks, rush processing is available for a fee of $10. Please attach check or include credit card information below.

Mail to: PESI, PO Box 1000, Eau Claire, WI 54702 or fax to PESI (800) 554-9775 (both sides)

CE Fee: $20: (Rush processing fee: $10)   **Total to be charged** _____

Credit Card #: _____   **Exp Date:** _____ **V-Code*:** _____
(*MC/VISA/Discover: last 3-digit # on signature panel on back of card.) (*American Express: 4-digit # above account # on face of card.)

	LAST	FIRST	M.I.

Name (please print): _____   _____   _____

Address: _____ Daytime Phone: _____

City: _____ State: _____ Zip Code: _____

Signature: _____ Email: _____

Date Completed: _____ Actual time (# of hours) taken to complete this offering: _____ hours

Program Objectives After completing this publication, I have been able to achieve these objectives:

1. Understand the role of the clinical assessment (interview, review of collateral measures, MSE) in the hypothesis testing model.   1. Yes No
2. Create hypotheses about what may be impairing functioning from clinical assessment data.   2. Yes No
3. Logically and coherently choose tests to address different hypotheses generated from the clinical assessment.   3. Yes No
4. Understand the role and limits of psychological tests in the assessment process.   4. Yes No
5. Compile test data coherently into themes that emerge across tests.   5. Yes No
6. Consider several alternative conceptualizations for a group of themes that emerge from test data.   6. Yes No
7. Write a psychological assessment report that ultimately supports recommendations made.   7. Yes No
8. Write a cohesive cognitive functioning section in an assessment report from data that emerge from cognitive testing.   8. Yes No
9. Write an integrated emotional functioning section in an assessment report that reflects a narrative conceptualization of the data that emerged from tests.   9. Yes No
10. Create clear, specific, and logical recommendations based on the conclusions drawn from the testing report.   10. Yes No
11. Understand major considerations when deciding how to structure a feedback session.   11. Yes No

PESI LLC
PO BOX 1000
Eau Claire, WI 54702-1000

ZNT042825   CE Release Date: 9/27/2010

Participant Profile:

1. Job Title: _____ Employment setting: _____

1. The hypothesis testing model of psychological assessment aims to:
a. standardize the process of assessment
b. integrate clinical data collected by a mental health professional with data that emerge from tests
c. build evidence across tests to account for each test's inherent weaknesses and error
d. all of the above

2. When assessing the presenting problem during a clinical interview, you should always include all of the following except:
a. symptoms, as specifically as possible
b. suicidal ideation
c. how whatever symptoms are reported are affecting family members
d. how whatever symptoms are reported are actually affecting the client's life

3. The psychosocial evaluation part of the clinical interview is important to assess because:
a. humans are social creatures
b. it provides a context in which symptoms are arising
c. it fills out a good portion of the assessment report
d. it is actually not that important to assess

4. Which of the following is not a standard part of a Mental Status Evaluation?
a. ethnic identity
b. thought process
c. thought content
d. affect

5. When using a specific test in a battery, you should always consider its:
a. inter-rater reliability
b. face validity
c. construct validity
d. all of the above

6. An assessment provides data that fit into the themes: work stress, perfectionism, and anxiety. If conceptualizing this case with the diathesis-stress model, the diathesis would most likely be:
a. work stress
b. perfectionism
c. anxiety
d. none of the above

7. The developmental model for conceptualizing themes works best when:
a. the level of development represented by the themes is below what is expected given the life demands being placed on the client
b. the level of the life demands being placed on the client is lower than the level of development represented by the themes
c. the level of development represented by the themes is equal to what is expected given the life demands being placed on the client
d. the level of development represented by the themes is representative of adolescent functioning

8. The ultimate purpose of assessment and the assessment report is:
a. to describe the strengths and weaknesses of the client
b. to diagnose the client
c. to make useful recommendations to improve the client's functioning
d. to portray the client as accurately as possible

9. Feedback sessions are considered "hybrid sessions" because:
a. they are a mixture of the therapist talking and the client talking
b. they are a mixture of structure and flexibility
c. they are a mixture of boundaries and looseness
d. they are a mixture of assessment and therapy sessions

10. The decisions of whether or not to give a copy of the report to the client and whether or not to disclose his or her diagnosis should, first and foremost, be guided by:
a. the client's IQ
b. what will be most helpful
c. the potential that such information may be harmful
d. the age of the client

PESI LLC
PO BOX 1000
Eau Claire, WI 54702-1000